THE GOOD CAPTAIN

THE GOOD CAPTAIN

A Personal Memoir of America at War

R. D. HOOKER, JR.

CASEMATE

Philadelphia & Oxford

AN AUSA BOOK
Association of the United States Army
2425 Wilson Boulevard, Arlington, Virginia, 22201, USA

Published in the United States of America and Great Britain in 2022 by
CASEMATE PUBLISHERS
1950 Lawrence Road, Havertown, PA 19083, USA
and
The Old Music Hall, 106–108 Cowley Road, Oxford OX4 1JE, UK

Hardback Edition: ISBN 978-1-63624-148-7
Digital Edition: ISBN 978-1-63624-149-4

A CIP record for this book is available from the British Library

Printed and bound in the United Kingdom by TJ Books

Typeset in India by Lapiz Digital Services, Chennai.

For a complete list of Casemate titles, please contact:

CASEMATE PUBLISHERS (US)
Telephone (610) 853-9131
Fax (610) 853-9146
Email: casemate@casematepublishers.com
www.casematepublishers.com

CASEMATE PUBLISHERS (UK)
Telephone (01865) 241249
Email: casemate-uk@casematepublishers.co.uk
www.casematepublishers.co.uk

Dedication

To my soldiers, who remain ever young.

Understand this ... when we lay our heads down out here, we're all prisoners.
CAPTAIN JOSEPH J. BLOCKER, *HOSTILES*

Contents

Foreword

This book is memoir, not history, although I have tried to be as accurate and factual as memory and open sources will allow. In a long military career, I found myself at the center of great events occasioned by the breakup of the Soviet Union and by 9/11. Over 32 years of military service as a soldier and officer of parachute infantry, I served all over the world in peace and war: in the invasion of Grenada; in Somalia in humanitarian crisis and tribal strife; in Rwanda in the immediate aftermath of the genocide; with the first American unit to enter Bosnia and the first to enter Kosovo; as a peacekeeper in the Sinai desert; as a witness to the attack on the Pentagon on 9/11; at the height of the war in Iraq and, at the end of my career, with my son in Afghanistan.

My life has been shaped and defined by war—as a child, as a career soldier, and even into retirement through my sons, both paratroop officers and combat veterans. As a young man I sought adventure and to lead troops in combat. I had my fill, and more. Along the way I served four presidents in the White House, struggling with the weighty questions of strategy and policy. I have come to believe that we fight too much, and win too little, with the costs of war falling only on a narrow slice of our society. But as a soldier, I acknowledge the right of the people and their elected leaders to make those decisions, though at times I regretted them. An Army that picks and chooses its wars has no place in a democracy.

I feel profound gratitude for my West Point classmates and for the officers, sergeants, and troopers I was blessed to serve with. They made a difficult and dangerous life rich, full, and rewarding. Above all, I thank my beautiful and wise wife Beverly and my wonderful children. Their love and support made it possible for me to serve.

At the top and in the trenches, our wars taught me much, but above all about American combat soldiers. Profane, independent, stubborn, and aggressive, they are also warm-hearted, intelligent, selfless, and always, always brave. As Churchill famously said, "Courage is the first of all the virtues, because it enables all the rest." He was right. This, then, is my story, and theirs.

CHAPTER I

Duty, Honor, Country

I have made fellowships,
untold of happy lovers in old song.
For love is not the binding of fair lips ...
but wound with war's hard wire whose stakes are strong.

WILFRED OWEN, "APOLOGIA PRO POEMATE MEO"

In early February of 2017, I walked into the main dining room of the Army Navy Club on Farragut Square in Washington to have dinner with Lieutenant General H. R. McMaster, who had just been announced as President Trump's national security advisor. With me was Major General Rick Waddell, soon to be selected as deputy national security advisor. My own appointment as special assistant to the president and senior director for Europe and Russia at the National Security Council would follow soon after. The three of us were old friends, all graduates of West Point, and all veterans of years spent fighting in Iraq and Afghanistan. Our careers had intersected many times around an Army posted in far-flung places and almost constantly at war. The dinner was not festive, nor a joyous reunion. We had few illusions about what came next. Over our brandy, I admitted to Rick that despite my deep respect and admiration for him and for McMaster, I had serious misgivings about joining the Trump administration. I have never forgotten his response: "We are sworn officers of the Republic. When asked to serve, we serve."

My journey to Farragut Square and the White House began some 40 years before as an 18-year-old soldier, but its origins ran much deeper than that. People like to glorify their past, but so far as I can tell my family, on both sides, was of humble origins, coming to America long before the Revolution in search of a better life. My father's family descends from an English colonist, Thomas Hooker, who immigrated to the Jamestown colony in 1620. His descendent, Samuel B. Hooker, was born in 1778 and served in a Tennessee militia regiment during the War of 1812. Many Hookers from southern Tennessee and northern Mississippi later served, mostly as private soldiers, in the army of the Confederacy. (The famous northern general, "Fighting Joe" Hooker, was born in Massachusetts and was probably not related.)

My mother's family was better documented, and we know that Abraham Macklemore, a merchant and tradesman, emigrated to the New World from Ayrshire in Scotland in 1668. By the early 1700s, he owned more than 700 acres in North Carolina, and as younger sons moved westward the family continued to prosper. By 1860, Abraham's great-grandson John Dabney McLemore was established in Carroll County, Mississippi; the 1860 census valued his net worth at more than $700,000, a stupendous sum for the time. Both his sons, Price and Jefferson, enrolled at the University of Mississippi and, at the outbreak of war, joined the entire student body in enlisting in Company A, 11th Mississippi Volunteer Infantry, the famous "University Greys." Jefferson appears on the roll as "Third Lieutenant," but he transferred to the cavalry where he fought at First Manassas and was badly wounded, shot through the hip, outside Atlanta in 1864. Price, my great-great-grandfather, was called "The Prince" by his friends. He served throughout the war as company first sergeant and was captured at High Bridge, in Virginia, only two days before the surrender at Appomattox.

Price, it would seem, had a war that was both glorious and terrible. His regiment fought in most of the major engagements in Lee's Army of Northern Virginia, participating in Pickett's Charge at the battle of Gettysburg, where the 11th Mississippi suffered 100 percent casualties, penetrating more deeply into northern positions than any other. Price suffered a serious head wound that day (he would be wounded four times during the war), and the 11th would show only 13 original members at war's end. There is a pretty story, probably apocryphal, telling of his arrival at home on sick leave the same day that a telegram arrived announcing his death in action. Price cannot have enjoyed good health afterwards. Settling in Tennessee after the war he lived only 11 more years, dying at 37. Nor did his family's wealth survive the war. In a petition for amnesty filed in 1865, his father claimed debts of $300,000. He and the southern planter class he represented bore much of the responsibility for this, the most terrible of America's wars, and one fought for the worst of all causes, to preserve the institution of slavery. Sam Houston, still governor of Texas in 1860 and an experienced general, had warned the South that it would likely lose. "Let me tell you what is coming," he prophesied. "After the sacrifice of countless millions of treasure and hundreds of thousands of lives, you may win Southern independence, if God be not against you, *but I doubt it* … the North is determined to preserve this Union … they move with the steady momentum and perseverance of a mighty avalanche." Houston was right, and it was perhaps not unjust that John Dabney's portion was mutilated sons and financial ruin.

Like many southern families, the McLemores held fast to their memories of antebellum life in the south and especially their Civil War service (Price's widow lived until 1922). During visits to my grandmother in the 1960s I would often hear tales of veterans she had actually known; of the burning of Meridian, her home, by Union troops during the war; and of course, of the redoubtable Price. While the Hookers never rose to any social prominence, the McLemores seemed to have at least partially recovered after Reconstruction. Most of the men were educated and prosperous, and the family plantation in the Mississippi Delta was still a going concern in the 1920s.

That ended in the Great Depression, when Price's grandson Baskerville lost the "Arrowhead" plantation house, and all but 200 acres of the family land. Neither family appeared to play a significant role in the World Wars.[1] My grandfather Arco Hooker, like Baskerville too young for World War I and too old for World War II, served as a skilled aviation mechanic, while his younger brother John Thomas fought in the Pacific as a sailor. Baskerville died of heart failure in 1941 leaving only daughters.

Through World War II my family members had thus served, like so many Americans, only as volunteer soldiers in time of war. My father, Colonel "Dick" Hooker, was the first professional soldier to arise in either family. Graduating from the University of Mississippi in 1957, the year I was born, he was commissioned into the infantry. While in college he married my mother Bonnie, a Kappa Kappa Gamma sorority girl and Price's great-granddaughter. Posted to the 504th Parachute Infantry Regiment, he served in North Carolina and in Germany and commanded a paratroop company. In the early 60s, our family grew to three children, including my two sisters Dorothy and Mary Anne, in a life dominated by peacetime Army routine—field exercises, cocktail parties, genteel poverty and regular moves. Some of my earliest memories are of driving to the drop zone with Mom to watch the men jump, the skies filled with parachutes and the drone of big transport planes. Her life, and ours, changed forever with the outbreak of the Vietnam War.

Selected for advisor duty in 1963, my father endured a year of Vietnamese language training before deploying to South Vietnam in 1964. As a young captain he served with a Vietnamese infantry battalion, along with an American sergeant and two radio operators. 1964 was not a good year, for Dad, or for the South Vietnamese. Domestic coups, endemic corruption, a resurgent enemy (blooded and experienced after winning the First Indochina war against the French) and a shoestring American

---

1 Baskerville was named for Alice Baskerville, his grandmother, who was descended from Sir John Baskerville, who fought in the King's entourage at the battle of Agincourt in 1415. The Baskervilles originally came from the village of Bacqueville in Normandy and fought with William the Conqueror at the battle of Hastings.

effort had him eating dog, carrying an M1 carbine and dodging mortar rounds for six months. By then, his team had been killed or wounded and he was out of a job.

With rare language skills, he was next posted to Saigon as General William C. Westmoreland's junior aide de camp. As commander Military Assistance Command Vietnam (MACV), Westmoreland directed U.S. military forces and presided over the transition from an advisory war to a full-blown conflict that at its height included 500,000 American soldiers and Marines. Dad's job was to travel with Westmoreland, coordinate troop visits, translate for him, and arrange for his personal security. A rare opportunity for a junior officer, the experience gave him unique insights into the war effort and into the heady atmosphere of a four-star wartime headquarters.

In 1965, Dad came home with a Bronze Star and the coveted Combat Infantryman's Badge. Loading the family into his Dodge Rambler, he drove from the Mississippi gulf coast to Fort Knox, Kentucky, where he would serve for the next few years as an instructor, preparing young officers for their initiation to combat in Vietnam.

Those days at Fort Knox seemed endless and carefree, but eventually the call came again, and Dad left as a major for his second tour, this time serving as a staff officer and sharing an office with Gordon Sullivan, later the 32nd chief of staff of the U.S. Army. Vietnam was different now. By 1968, the big war was raging, with hundreds of casualties every week, non-stop coverage in the media, and an increasingly virulent and angry anti-war movement. My mother had moved us to Green Cove Springs, Florida, about 25 miles south of Jacksonville near St. Augustine and the St. John's River. Green Cove was supposed to be a nice place for officers' wives to congregate while the men served their tours. The naval base in Jacksonville provided convenient base shopping and medical care, the beach was nearby, the climate was balmy, and the cost of living was low. In fact, Green Cove was an island of lonely, scared young women. Every week, news of a death, wounding, firing or affair would send shock waves through an already traumatized pool of wives. Long before the days of "Family Support Groups," Skype, or email, these young women struggled to raise their children in a desperate atmosphere of fear and separation.

My childhood was a blur of Army posts: Bad Kreuznach, Fort Bragg, Fort Benning, Fort Ord, Fort Knox, Fort Leavenworth. Like most Army kids I have only hazy childhood memories of my father. He was gone long before my sisters and I began the day. For months each year he would be in the field, and beginning in 1964 he deployed for the first of three tours to Vietnam. I can remember the interludes between combat tours, and crew-cut young men in Bermuda shorts and white T-shirts, sitting in cheap lawn chairs in the front yards of post housing, smoking unfiltered Kent cigarettes, drinking cheap Falstaff beer, and grilling steaks. The wives were there too, in their 60s hairdos and frocks, always it seemed with a drink in their hands, smoking, chatting, and slightly wild-eyed. Their men were home, for a brief while, before returning to the fight, a fight which seemed to have no foreseeable end. The weeks and months passed in a frantic round of promotions, commands, reassignments, awards, reliefs, divorces, wounds, and death.

Even as a child I wondered at the curious convention which assumed that once children were put to bed, they could not hear the women's loud voices downstairs. As a 10-year-old I found myself reasonably up to date on the love affairs, scandals, future plans, finances, hopes and dreams of any number of young wives and mothers, but always there was their fear. Fear of loss, fear of abandonment, fear of the unknown, fear of the future, all gripped these women in a fearful embrace. They lived their lives not knowing whether their men would return or return whole. At the time, I thought they were all desperate, damaged women. Today I think maybe they were the true heroes.

If all this was hard for mothers, it was doubly hard for the kids, who understood dimly or not at all what the war was about, and when or if their fathers would return. Today it is hard to recall that, unlike Iraq or Afghanistan, Vietnam in the peak years of 1965–70 saw literally thousands killed and wounded each month. Hanging in our house were pictures of Major Bernie Dibbert, Dad's former company commander, gravely wounded in Korea and later killed in Vietnam, and Lieutenant Colonel Bob Carter, his close friend and recipient of two Silver Stars, also killed in action. As a seventh grader these fears were acute and magnified by the absence of familiar family and friends—there were no grandparents or cousins to soften or distract us from the images and impacts of an increasingly brutal war. For my sisters and me, the best time of day was the final few minutes before sleep. No harbinger had come that day, and morning was far off. For those few moments, we were free.

Dad's return in 1969 filled us with joy and relief, but he already knew his stay would be brief. Within a few weeks he was back in Vietnam to assume command of an infantry battalion, with an accelerated promotion to lieutenant colonel. Dad went through the motions of consulting with Mom, but it was clear what his answer would be. He was a professional soldier, there was a war on, and he was being asked to lead in combat. That is what infantry officers do.

His decision, and sudden departure, threw us all back into a welter of depression and unhappiness. None of us, even Mom, understood or accepted his decision. It didn't occur to us that to say no would be to renounce his calling, not to mention any hope of further advancement. It didn't seem fair, or right. By then, it was hard to see how the U.S. could emerge from Vietnam with anything that might look like victory. We felt anger and mistrust, at Dad, at the Army, and eventually even at each other. From then on, we were all a bit different. My mother became harder, more distant, and less joyful about the small things. At 12, I seemed to have stopped being a boy almost overnight. Until now, we had coped. By 1970, and Dad's third tour, the war had become our own private nightmare.

Dad took command of the 1st Battalion, 50th Infantry operating in the central highlands. On his flight out to the combat base to take command, his helo was hit by ground fire, crash landing at the airfield in front of the reception party. By 1970 the Army had begun to devour itself. Few draftees wanted to be among the last to die in Vietnam. Drugs, alcohol, race riots and "fragging"—the murder or attempted murder of officers and sergeants, often with a fragmentation grenade or "frag"—had become almost commonplace. After six years of "big" war, the country had largely turned its back on the war effort and on the soldiers who served in it. The challenge of command under these conditions must have been tough indeed. Years later, Dad shared two anecdotes that characterized his tour.

In the first, a soldier was arrested after attempting to "frag" a junior officer. Lacking any detention facilities, Dad ordered him confined in a metal CONEX or supply container until the military police arrived. They finally showed up about three days later. Apparently, there was more concern in higher headquarters about how the trooper was detained than about the attempted murder. I imagine it was hot in the CONEX. I imagine the word got around.

Another time, a lieutenant led a squad of soldiers on an ambush patrol which encountered a larger enemy force. Rather than attack the enemy the young officer let them pass. When Dad called him in for an explanation, he claimed "it was too dangerous ... and not worth it anyway." He was relieved of course, but as he had no ambitions to stay in the Army, he probably could have cared less.

But this was still an Army led by long-serving professionals. It could still fight. On one occasion during Dad's command a small scout element stumbled upon a large Viet Cong detachment of some 60 men. The battalion swung into action, launching a "Quick Reaction" platoon of 30 soldiers by helicopter to pursue. (An audio tape was made of the action which, four decades later, still fascinates.) Soon after landing, the platoon leader was wounded and evacuated, leaving the senior NCO in charge. As the Americans pursued, artillery units from all around the area began to fire "harassing and interdiction" fires at trail intersections, stream crossings and any other likely locations for the fleeing VC. Helicopter gunships from miles away joined the fight, which soon petered out as the VC split into smaller and smaller groups to avoid detection. The action was typical of the war at that stage. American commanders, by now deeply experienced in choreographing fire support and aviation, were able to marshal incredible resources and sequence them into battles almost effortlessly. But the enemy was wily and elusive and would not often stand and fight in the face of American might.

All wars end, and eventually Dad came home as Vietnam wound down and the U.S. handed over to the South Vietnamese. He would follow his combat service with five years in the Pentagon. We didn't see much of him, as he left for work early and came home late, but life in the northern Virginia suburbs and the chance to put down roots somewhere was a welcome change. I played football and tennis, swam on the swim team, worked as a lifeguard, chased girls, and downed the occasional illicit beer. I thought vaguely about college, rarely took school seriously, and managed to graduate with a B average, several varsity letters, and $500 in the bank.

A few months before graduation Dad casually asked, "What are your plans?" Just as casually I answered, "Well, I thought about going to college." He thoughtfully replied, "Great idea. Can you afford it?" That brought me up short. "Well, I thought you might be willing to support me." Looking at me intently he said, "Why would you think that?"

To be fair, he had a point. On his lieutenant colonel's salary, he was making a house payment, a car payment, supporting both his parents, and putting my older sister through the University of Southern Mississippi. And the cost of living in the DC area, even then, was not exactly low. But there was more to it. Dad had been the first of his family ever to go to college, and he had worked his way through, with a wife and child. As a teenager he had worked as first mate on my grandfather's charter boat and had run away to go to Ole Miss against his father's objections (annoyed, no doubt, at the loss of so much free labor). Throughout my childhood, Dad had forced me to be entirely self-sufficient. If I wanted to play Little League baseball, I'd mow lawns to earn money to buy a glove, and walk to practice, no matter how far. There was no allowance, no car, no dispensation of cash to finance Friday night dates. He wasn't being cruel. He had been born in the Depression to working-class parents, raised during World War II, struggled through college, and lived his entire adult life on a modest Army salary. Dad believed you should carry your own water. The conversation ended and I was left to consider my options.

There weren't many. I hadn't really thought about the military. In fact, I was pretty sure I didn't want to follow in the old man's footsteps. Vietnam had left me only with painful memories, and the military—at least as an enlisted man—was not where a middle-class officer's kid wanted to be in the mid-1970s. But the service academies were out of reach with my grades, and I was sure I couldn't handle the intensive math and engineering coursework there anyway. The more I thought about it, the more I came back to the idea of enlisting in the Army.

There were some good points. I could eventually finance a college education through the GI Bill. There was the promise of adventure, and travel. Maybe I'd pick up some focus and discipline and grow up a little. Without much deeper thought than that, I had Dad take me down to the recruiting station, and that day I signed an enlistment contract as an airborne infantryman, with a guaranteed assignment to the 82nd Airborne Division at Fort Bragg, North Carolina.

The night before I left for the Army, I took one last drive around the neighborhood past my old haunts, listening to Crosby, Stills, Nash & Young's "4 Way Street" on my 8-track. Like millions before me, I was filled with foreboding. I reminded myself that I should be okay. I was a good athlete, reasonably bright, with some understanding of military life from my father. We were at peace and seemed likely to remain so. I should have felt exhilarated about the adventure that lay ahead, but

I felt only apprehension. My father had given me no pep talk, only reminding me to keep my mouth shut and do as I was told.

The next morning at sunrise I felt better. My military career started on October 6, 1975, when I arrived at Fort Knox for basic training. We were housed in old wooden barracks, in a training area later made famous as the backdrop for the Bill Murray movie *Stripes*. I found I liked Basic, with its ordered routine, early morning runs in formation, road marches, and range firing. There was some serious shouting going on more or less continuously, but after August two-a-days during high school football, there wasn't much the Army could throw at me to shake me up.

Still, I had been thrown into a world I had never experienced before. On my first day my drill sergeant finished a tirade by announcing, "Now mens, when I tells you to fall out, I wants you to fall out. Fall out!" Clearly, the lowest common denominator among us was low indeed. But while most enlisted soldiers of that era were poorly educated, non-high school graduates, there were occasional outliers. For example, my bunkmate, Marshall Savage from Rifle, Colorado, boasted an IQ of 163. Enlisting on the spur of the moment after a failed romance, he would serve for three years as an infantryman, graduate from the University of Southern California, and embark on a successful career as an author, entrepreneur, business executive and energy innovator. For me, the chance to live and work with people from all walks of life, from every stratum of society and every corner of America, was intensely interesting and rewarding—if not always easy. After eight weeks, I finished as the honor graduate of my class and boarded a bus for Fort Polk, Louisiana, and Infantry School.

Here things were more serious. Most of the officers and sergeants who trained us had served in combat, the Cold War was still at its height, and we were now supposed to be learning much more than how to march and fire a rifle. There was less shouting, more teaching, and much more to master. We learned to lay mines, throw hand grenades, employ simple demolitions, call for artillery fire, apply combat first aid, navigate with map and compass, and fire all manner of grenade launchers, rocket launchers, recoilless rifles, and machine guns.

The Army of the 1970s was in trouble in many ways, but the lessons of World War II, Korea, and Vietnam still lingered. So did the threat of major theater war with the Soviet Union. Accordingly, our training included dangerous evolutions unknown today. In one, we were ordered into a narrow-slit trench while a 60-ton main battle tank drove over us. In another, we low crawled for a hundred meters through barbed wire while machine guns poured live rounds over our heads. Personal disputes were adjudicated by issuing boxing gloves, forming an impromptu ring with the rest of the platoon, and allowing the parties to whale away until exhausted. For our officers and drill sergeants, combat wasn't an academic or theoretical topic.

It was the whole point of our existence. The language and manners of that time would surely not pass muster today, but a different philosophy was at work. We were taught and trained by rough men to do rough work, and there was little hand holding or sentimentality about it.

On the last night, we occupied a night defensive position, and then on signal (a red star cluster) fired all our weapons in a demonstration of "final protective fires." The sights and sounds of massed machine guns, mortar and artillery fires, grenades, and claymore mines, all going off at once, gave us real confidence in the terrific power of the rifle company. Afterwards we marched the 25 miles back to the barracks, wolfed down steaks and cold Schlitz beer in the mess hall, and graduated. We were now full-fledged infantrymen, authorized to wear the coveted crossed rifles and light blue infantry cord.

Most of my buddies headed off for their units, but as a prospective paratrooper I had one more stop before reporting to Fort Bragg—jump school at Fort Benning, Georgia. Then as now, jump school consisted of three weeks: ground week, tower week and jump week. The day began with a grueling in-ranks inspection by the feared "black hats," the airborne cadre, followed by calisthenics and long formation runs in boots. Looming over the training area were the famous 250-foot jump towers, originally amusement rides at the 1939 World's Fair in New York and used to train paratroopers ever since. The training regimen was simplicity itself. In ground week, we did physical training or PT, and practiced parachute landing falls incessantly, punctuated by hundreds of pushups for real or imagined offenses. During tower week we did more PT, many more pushups, and dozens of practice exits from the 34-foot jump tower, leaping out of the door, tucking into a "good, tight body position," and sliding down horizontal steel cables. Once deemed ready, we were strapped into a parachute harness, hoisted 250 feet into the air, and released to float down to earth under a real, free-floating canopy. Only then were we cleared to progress to jump week.

The final week was different. There were no annoying, fastidious uniform inspections, no five-mile runs, no harassing pushups. Practice was over. We would now exit an aircraft "while in flight." Almost 40 years later, I can recall my first jump in detail, like all paratroopers. I was frightened, more scared than I expected to be. The flight was short, only long enough to get to a jump altitude of 1,250 feet and line up on the approach heading. Soon the red lights flashed on inside the C130 drop aircraft, signaling the start of the "actions in the aircraft" sequence. By now our responses were automatic: stand up, hook up, check static line, check equipment, sound off for equipment check! Three minutes out from the drop zone (DZ) the Air Force loadmasters opened the paratroop doors, flooding the aircraft with sound and wind. In each door the jumpmasters, masters of the universe it seemed to us, gripped the door frames, stamped down on the jump platform, and then, with only heels and fingertips left in contact with the plane, leaned far out in the slip stream to identify the DZ just ahead. The excitement was indescribable, as we pressed forward to close up the stick and prepare to jump.

After a final door check, the jumpmasters turned to face their sticks, gave each other a thumbs up, and hollered "Stand in the door!" The first jumpers took up a door position and waited, breathlessly, for the red light to flash green. For long seconds we stood, grasping our static lines hooked up to the anchor line cables overhead, in a whirlwind of screaming engines. I felt as though I couldn't breathe or move. Then the green light flashed on, the jumpmasters screamed "Go," the first jumper was seemingly whirled into space, and the stick began to move. We shuffled towards the door, our hearts in our throats, there was a flash of blinding light as I neared the door, I leaped, and felt tossed in the slipstream like a leaf in a hurricane. Barely remembering to count ("One thousand, two thousand, three thousand, four thousand!"), I had a momentary feeling of panic as I nosed over headfirst towards the earth, before my canopy deployed, righting me. Now the sound was gone. I reached up, grasped the risers, checked to make sure I had a full round canopy, and then looked around to see a sky which seemed full of fellow jumpers. There was no sensation of falling, only of floating. This was heaven! Then I heard bullhorns below, more black hats on the ground shouting: "Jumper with the malfunction, activate your reserve!"

With another jolt of adrenaline, I looked up again to make sure I was not the intended target of these frantic appeals, but all seemed well. Looking about again, I saw reserve chutes popping everywhere, as excited first-time jumpers, sure the warning was meant for them, pulled their ripcords. One jumper, below and ahead, had a strange, two-lobed parachute above him. This I recognized from our classes as a "Mae West," caused by a suspension line looped over the canopy during the chute's deployment, reducing the jumper's lift and resembling an old-fashioned brassiere. His reserve was out, so I turned my attention to my own problems.

Now it was time to get ready to hit the ground, or in airborne parlance, "prepare to land." Grasping the risers, I pulled a slip into the wind, tucked my chin into my chest, brought my hands in front of my face and tried to relax my legs. About 25 feet from the ground my sensations changed abruptly from floating to falling, as the ground rushed up at dizzying speed. I slammed into the ground, much harder than expected, and lay stunned for a good 10 seconds, trying to determine if I was seriously hurt or not. Soon a black hat ran by, shouted at me to get moving, and ran off. I gathered up my chute, stuffed it into the aviator's kit bag we all carried, and trotted off the drop zone. The feeling was other-worldly. I had done it!

We jumped four more times that week, with combat equipment and finally at night, before graduating on Friday on the drop zone. I was now not only an infantryman, but a qualified paratrooper, no longer a "leg" or non-jumper. Amazingly, in 1975, some of the Army's very first parachutists were still on active duty. Their exploits had long since become the stuff of legend, and I felt proud and honored to be one of them. I looked forward to getting to the 82nd, or to "Division," as its veterans always say, with eagerness and anticipation.

After a short leave I took a bus to Fort Bragg and reported in to the division replacement depot, or "repl depl," on a Monday morning. My reception was not at all what I expected. No one seemed impressed by my shiny boots or silver wings or "high and tight" haircut. In fact, no one seemed interested in me at all. The first few days were a blur of forms to be filled out, shots to be taken, gear to be issued, and classes to attend. Halfway through the week, I was summoned by a young, bored corporal who informed me that, due to my high test scores, I was being assigned to the division headquarters as a clerk. I protested that I had a signed contract guaranteeing me duty as an airborne infantryman, but to no avail.

On my lunch break, I managed to get to a pay phone and called Dad, who advised me to sit tight. The next morning, I was called in again, this time by the repl depl first sergeant, a truly august personage. Obviously annoyed, he informed me that, as I clearly had friends in high places, the headquarters assignment was off, and I was to be given my choice of infantry units. Taking me to a bulletin board festooned with "flashes"—the colored patches worn behind jump wings, indicating one's unit—he said, "Take your pick." Noticing a sharp red and white flash, I said, "I'll take that one."

Much can turn on such small things. I had picked, not an infantry battalion, but the 1st Squadron (Airborne), 17th Cavalry, the 82nd's divisional cavalry squadron. The unit consisted of a headquarters troop, a ground troop with gun jeeps, and three air cavalry troops, each with a helicopter gunship platoon of AH1H Cobras, a lift platoon of UH1H Huey helicopters, and a "blues" platoon of infantrymen, called the aero rifle platoon or ARPs. Unknown to me, the ARPs were full of castoffs from the infantry battalions, the refuse of the division. (The first sergeant's wry smile at my selection now came back to me, pregnant with meaning.)

Upon reporting to my platoon leader, I learned that I was the only high school graduate in the platoon and would therefore be assigned as his radiotelephone operator or RTO. This was a responsible job. I not only had to keep track of the radio codes, used to encode messages in an era before all radios were secure. I also had to carry the PRC77 FM radio, and a second unit cabled to it, called a KY38, which through a diabolical set of "keys" could theoretically be manipulated in certain ways to permit secure communications to headquarters. No one was ever able to make it work, but I carried it on every field problem. The PRC77 and KY38 together, with spare batteries, antenna base, and antenna, weighed 54lbs. My job was to "hump" that, along with the same gear everyone else carried. That explained the huge rucksack I was issued.

Next, I was shown to the barracks and given a room. The environment I now entered was surreal. The Army in 1976 was in desperate straits. Military service was unpopular and entrance standards had been lowered dramatically to meet enlistment quotas. Soldiers were allowed to reenlist regardless of their qualifications or misdeeds. Many soldiers, and some sergeants, were functionally illiterate. Criminal records were common, and drug and alcohol abuse rampant. My new roommate was a farm boy from Kentucky, who liked to inhale glue every night. On most nights, dope smoke cloaked the hallways of the barracks, undisturbed by any visiting duty officer. Fights were common. Most soldiers slept with a knife or bunk adapter (a short, heavy piece of metal pipe) close at hand. There seemed to be two cliques in the unit: farm boys, who liked to drink, and inner-city guys, who liked to smoke dope. All expressed contempt for "lifers," meaning career sergeants or officers. The junior NCOs who lived in the barracks exercised no real control. Instead, they acted as ring leaders, leading opposing factions divided along racial lines. Senior NCOs and officers rarely entered the barracks, and never after duty hours.

All new soldiers in airborne units are called "cherries" and must endure rites of passage that had become, over many years, hoary, time-honored rituals. In the 1970s these could be dangerous. Some of us were thrown down stairwells inside wall lockers. Others were hung, upside down, out of third-story windows in our sleeping bags. In my first week, I was approached by three veterans with a demand that I agree to drop off and pick up their laundry each week, on the grounds that "that's what all cherries do." I was intimidated but realized instinctively that giving in now would be far more painful later. I refused, and a shoving match ensued that quickly turned into a short but vicious beating. That night, a bunk adapter went under my pillow. I reflected grimly that prison life couldn't be much different than this.

My first jump in the unit represented another rite of passage. In later years, the 82nd would require all new jumpers to conduct a daylight, "Hollywood" jump (officially called an "admin, non-tactical" jump with no combat equipment) before progressing to more difficult and dangerous airborne operations. In 1976, there were no such considerations. Six of us were mixed into a full planeload of veteran jumpers, at night, wearing our full complement of web gear, a heavy rucksack rigged under the chest-mounted reserve, and a rifle strapped under the left arm in an M1950 weapons case. Like sardines, we were crammed into a C130 Hercules so tightly we could scarcely breathe.

Soon after take-off, most of the oldtimers immediately went to sleep in the dimly lit cabin, but we cherries were terrified. As the engines throbbed, we craned our necks to look around. Directly across from me, our knees touching, the troop first sergeant and my platoon sergeant sat impassively. For what seemed like hours, we flew "nap of the earth" as the aircrews practiced the low-level, terrain-following flight path that might save our lives on a real combat jump. For us, though, the flight was torture and we all quickly became airsick.

Eventually, even the veteran platoon sergeant in front of me began to look green in the gills. Motioning to the Air Force loadmaster, he was handed a "barf" bag, and in due course we saw him vomiting prodigiously into the bag. Calmly, the First Sergeant took the bag from him and, with a wink, drained the contents. Incredulous, all six of us cherries immediately threw up our dinners all over our equipment, wishing profoundly that some soul would come by and put us out of our misery. It was only later that we learned the bag was filled with vegetable soup, an old trick.

Now it was time to jump, but this was nothing like jump school. Barely conscious, we were hauled to our feet as the aircraft bucked and pitched wildly in the air, knocking several jumpers off their feet. In training, we had been coached to carefully maintain an interval between jumpers to avoid entanglements after exiting. All that went out the window here. After the command "Hook up!" the last man in the stick—selected for his size and strength and referred to as the "stick pusher"—leaned into the stick with his full body weight and we were all jammed into the parachute pack tray of the man in front of us. The idea was to empty the plane as fast as possible, and we did. As the green light blazed on, we flooded out the door, hardly pausing to "stand in the door." I tumbled into the blackness, felt a violent, wrenching opening shock, and immediately found myself smothered in the silk of the jumper in front of me. Fortunately, we drifted apart without entangling. Barely remembering to drop my equipment by its lowering line, I slammed violently to earth and lay stunned. Sick, bruised and stricken, I lay on the ground until a young sergeant came by and kicked me. Snarling, he told me to police up my chute and get to the assembly area, which I did. After that night I learned to confront my fear, a priceless asset for a combat soldier and one reason I always sought to serve with paratroopers.

The Army was changing in that era, but the old ways died hard. We still ran in boots, still wore starched cotton fatigues, and still lined up each payday to be paid in cash. This was a fascinating tradition. Soldiers would put on their dress greens, stand an in-ranks inspection, and then march to an open area between the barracks where a series of field desks had been set up. They would report to the pay officer with a hand salute, sign a roster, and be given their pay in cash (for a private on jump status in 1976, $300). Next, they would be invited to contribute to the Association of the U.S. Army (technically voluntary, but in practice required), followed by the 82nd Airborne Division Association. The first sergeant would then take his cut for the "troop fund," after which the oldest, meanest troopers would gang up to strongarm the cherries for "loans."

Many soldiers would take their pay, head downtown to Hay Street (the red light district in Fayetteville), and literally blow it all on prostitutes, booze, and hotel rooms, living the rest of the month in the barracks, eating in the mess hall, and bumming small loans from buddies. Hay Street was a bad place in those days. Topless bar girls could be seen in the club doorways, uniformed military "courtesy" patrols roamed the area, and a dozen paratroopers a year were killed in bar fights or back alley muggings. I went once, and never went back.

All armies in democracies reflect society to a greater or lesser degree, and the U.S. Army in 1976 was no different. One Saturday the squadron commander hosted a picnic at McKellar's Lodge, the Rod and Gun Club on the edge of the training area. About 1 p.m., the division commander's wife drove by, returning from Sicily Drop Zone where she'd watched her husband jump. As she sped by McKellar's she saw a horrifying sight. On the picnic tables cavorted a collection of Hay Street's finest strippers, surrounded by dozens of inebriated troopers. Inside, one of the troop first sergeants manned a field desk, where in a parody of pay day, troopers would report, lay their money down, and be escorted to a side room for 15 minutes of "jump refresher" with more working girls. Throughout the area, bedlam raged as fights broke out, troopers jumped off tables in formation and cherries did pushups with their feet high up on tree trunks. Free beer flowed like a river.

Thirty minutes later what seemed like the entire 82nd Military Police Company showed up, surrounding the Lodge in their gun jeeps. Our sergeant major, by now too drunk to stand up, was hustled away by a group of NCOs and evaded the dragnet. 1976 was a different time. Every barracks had beer machines. Every brigade had its own NCO club (there were 17 on Fort Bragg), and topless dancers, at the Officers' Club as well, were a standard feature. In the 1980s, all this would be phased out, and the Army would become much tougher on alcohol abuse.

In those days, in addition to its low enlistment standards, the Army was also broke. Training ammunition was scarce, basic supplies were hard to come by, and gasoline and spare parts closely hoarded. Most troopers bought their own toilet paper, as the latrines were always out, and we walked back from the drop zones after jumps (Sicily DZ, nine miles out, was considered a walk in the park; Rhine-Luzon DZ, 33 miles out, was a death march). On the other hand, there were compensations to being in the "Cav." In the field, we often flew in our beloved Hueys, with Vietnam-era warrant officer pilots who treated them like fighter planes. There was still room for individuality then. Many pilots sported handlebar moustaches, wore huge "U.S. Cavalry" belt buckles, and gloried in Stetson cowboy hats in the Officers' Club. Showing up for PT hungover was perfectly acceptable; falling out of the morning run, on the other hand, was not. Formation runs were things of beauty, conducted at a slower pace (because troops wore fatigues and jump boots, not running shoes and shorts), in perfect step ("the airborne shuffle") and done in cadence. By far the best cadence callers were the Black sergeants, usually from the South, with their deep, sonorous voices and rhythmic delivery:

"C130 rollin' down the strip, airborne daddy on a one way trip ..."
"I know a girl who lives on a hill, she won't do it but her sister will ..."
"When my granny was ninety-one, she'd do PT just for fun ..."

As any old paratrooper will tell you, the experience of running on Ardennes Street, through the division area at Fort Bragg, with thousands of fellow paratroopers, all chanting and swaying in time, was almost a religious experience. We felt part of something bigger and more important than all of us. There was much about the Army of that time that was bad, and wrong, and even shameful. But it was an Army that rested on older, deeper, better roots that would not die. You could sense that on Ardennes, on a cool crisp morning, in the company of soldiers.

"I don't know but I've been told, airborne streets are paved with gold ..."

Two months after joining the unit we flew to Fort Stewart, Georgia for a major off-post exercise. While our helicopters "self-deployed," the rest of us conducted an "in-flight rig," donning our parachutes not on the ground but in the aircraft before jumping into the exercise. For a neophyte this was high adventure, but we managed to get on the ground without major mishap.

The highlight of the exercise was door gunnery, a special treat where we tested our marksmanship on the javelinas (wild pigs) who roamed the aerial gunnery ranges. Most of the time, though, the ARPs humped rockets and other ammo for the chopper pilots, pulled police call along the flight strip, and took on all the other boring and unglamorous tasks. The life of the private, I mused to myself, was not all wine and roses.

On the last day, before return to home station, I stood with my buddies at sunrise at "Tac X," an aviation stage field far out in the training area. Although dawn was breaking, the field was blanketed in mist and heavy fog. Soon a Cobra appeared, descending slowly to land. The pilot was a portly young captain named Steve Austin, jokingly referred to by the veteran warrant officers as "the Six Dollar Man" (after the hit TV series *The Six Million Dollar Man*, whose lead character was Colonel Steve Austin). We watched, amazed, as Austin carelessly flew the aircraft into the ground, destroying the helo and almost killing his co-pilot and himself. As we ran to pull the pilots from the wreckage, our company commander, Major Hudson, stood nearby, in tears. He knew it was the end of his career, and he was right.

Soon, I was promoted to Private First Class and began to feel just a bit like a veteran trooper. One morning in late spring, I was told to report to the lieutenant, a short, stocky officer I rarely saw except in the field. With a curt "At ease," he said, "Hooker, it says here you have high test scores. How'd you like to go to the Prep School?" He was talking about the U.S. Military Academy Preparatory School or

USMAPS, a one-year course for enlisted soldiers at Fort Monmouth, New Jersey. If you survived, you got a shot at West Point. If you survived.

I took a few moments to consider. In the past year, I'd decided I liked much about the military, even with its current problems. The prospect of a really first class education, at a world-famous place like West Point, was exciting. If I didn't make it, I'd end up back in a unit as a private, no worse off. In little more time than it takes to tell, I made up my mind and said, "Yes, sir, I'll do it." And that was that.

In early July of 1976, I signed in at USMAPS as a Cadet Candidate or "CC" along with 320 other prospective cadets. We wore uniforms and marched to class, but other than that the program was not particularly military. From 8 a.m. until 3 p.m. we did math and English, and nothing else. Tests were frequent, and students were sectioned and re-sectioned each week based on their grades. The lowest, the "ejection" section, was greatly feared because it meant almost certain disenrollment. Instructors would frequently come into class, touch someone on the shoulder, and that afternoon they would be seen leaving post, doing the "duffle bag drag."

On my first math exam, I scored a 12 percent. After that wakeup call, I threw myself into academics like a man possessed. English had never been a problem. I had edited the school newspaper in high school and enjoyed creative writing. Mathematics was different and a constant struggle. By dint of hard work, with help from a number of compassionate instructors and fellow CCs, I managed to hold my own. I started at free safety on the USMAPS football team, which went 7–2 against small college teams, and as a defenseman on the lacrosse team (I had never played, but most of the team hadn't either; we lost every game but one). By the end of the school year, I was one of three company commanders and had settled comfortably in the top third of the class. By graduation in early June, I was one of 170 survivors, and a month later I reported to West Point for Beast Barracks.

"Beast," otherwise known as Cadet Basic Training, was feared by all. West Point movies, tall tales by old grads, and a rumor mill stretching back to 1802 made it out to be incredibly Spartan and impossibly demanding. But if you were a prior service soldier the scare wore off quickly. On Day 1—Reception Day or "R Day"—I found myself ordered to report to the Man in the Red Sash. I simply said what I had been told to say: "Sir, New Cadet Hooker reports to the Man in the Red Sash for the first time, as ordered, sir!" When told to drop my bags, I dropped them. Simple. But all around me, kids fresh out of high school were screwing up the reporting format, or setting their bags down instead of dropping them, or committing a dozen other minor infractions which caused the cadet cadres to school about them, yelling, screaming, and terrorizing them. A few quit on the spot. Others broke down in tears. Most struggled through the day in a bewildered state.

Here my enlisted experience paid off handsomely. I could already march, shine my shoes, salute, set up my field gear and execute simple orders. I had already been yelled at by the best. My jump wings set me apart from the rest of my classmates as a "real soldier," and the cadre often asked me to call cadence during morning runs or help struggling new cadets. But I had weaknesses too. The biggest was an inability to cut desserts in the cadet mess hall into suitably precise and exact portions. This was an apparently essential military activity, designed to instill in us a proper appreciation of the importance of "attention to detail." I also struggled to remember that on Thursday, if the officer in charge was artillery, my table commandant preferred two ice cubes, not three. I consoled myself with the knowledge that Grant and Lee had also been forced to put up with such nonsense, with no harmful effects.

Some of the minutia of Beast Barracks was actually fun. There were only four acceptable answers for new cadets: "Yes sir," "No sir," "Sir, may I ask a question?" and "Sir, I do not understand!" All new cadets were forbidden to use slang of any sort. All were required to memorize reams of traditional West Point doggerel and spit them out on demand. For instance, when asked "How is the cow?" the correct response, delivered rapid fire, was "Sir! She walks, she talks, she's full of chalk, the lacteal fluid extracted from the female of the bovine species is highly prolific to the nth degree, sir!" I loved the history and traditions, the spectacular beauty of the campus and the panoramic Hudson highlands. Passing by from time to time we saw officers in their tailored greens, their campaign ribbons and brass twinkling in the bright sunshine. The lords of Beast, the high ranking "firsties," or seniors, were even grander in their tall shakoes and ostrich plumes, and their gray, full dress parade uniforms, glittering with brass buttons and a profusion of gold stripes, sabers in hand. Three years seemed an impossibly long time to wait before ascending to such an exalted status, but it was out there, somewhere, if only we could make the grade.

Many of my classmates had come to the academy because of its glamor and prestige. Others came for the free education, or because their fathers had been graduates, or because they had been recruited as athletes. In the beginning, few thought very deeply about West Point's true purpose. As soon as I could, I slipped away from the cadet area to wander through the West Point cemetery. There I found the headstones of men I had heard of—Winfield Scott, George Custer, John Buford—but also hundreds of names unknown except to families and friends. West Point graduates had served in every war since its founding. Every class had gone to war. As a plebe I didn't know much. But I knew that. The grandeur and tradition that surrounded me would never wear off. But there was never a day that I didn't know what lay at the end of it. And it wasn't football games or dress parades on autumn afternoons.

There was also another, darker side to West Point. It had been there for 175 years. The culture permitted and even encouraged any number of petty cruelties, visited upon new cadets for no real purpose other than to humiliate. Dressed up in platitudes about "learning to perform under stress," it was little more than the abuse of power by 19-year-olds over 18-year-olds. In past years it had been far more severe. At the turn of the century Congress had investigated West Point hazing rituals that led to the death of several cadets. Only a few years before, "bracing" (the practice of requiring first-year cadets to stand at an exaggerated position of attention, their chins pushed far back) had been banned because it caused spinal deformation. Yet many traditions remained.

Excessive demerits, often assigned to plebes arbitrarily to "build character," meant hours "walking the area" in dress gray uniform, crossbelts and parade rifle under a burning sun or in near-Arctic winters. New cadets in that era were routinely told to "send out your plate" for imaginary infractions, leading to significant weight loss (I lost 22lbs in the eight weeks of Beast Barracks). Once, forming up for a parade in the sally port, an upperclassman smashed the butt of his M-14 parade rifle as hard as he could into my chest while another braced me from behind. The blow crushed my breastplate, leaving a dark bruise behind. Next, I was ordered to "get those toes in," while two upperclassmen drove their bayonets into my spit-shined leather dress shoes, ruining them. In later years, these indignities would be remembered, sometimes even fondly, as trials we had all endured as part of the West Point experience. And indeed they were. For me, though, a key lesson was how easily authority can be corrupted, and how thin the line could be between setting tough standards and abusing one's subordinates, sometimes for no other reason than the sheer fun of it.

Yet another innovation was the introduction of women at West Point. Mine was only the second class to be "gender integrated" and the Academy was still feeling its way. I'm sure it was difficult for the trailblazers, who in a sense were guinea pigs for the thousands of women who would follow. Many of the upperclassmen resented their presence, but to me it only made good practical sense. There were women in the Army in plenty—one of my black hats at jump school was female—and it seemed only just that if the rest of the Army had gone down this road, West Point should too. In those first years, women were subjected to much trial and error; for example, initially the coattails of the full dress coat were removed from the female version, an awkward look corrected in later years. Female cadets were also required to cut their hair short in bobs more reminiscent of the 1950s (today, long hair is permitted as long as it is pinned up while on duty). As a plebe, my stress level was considerable. I'm sure theirs was higher.

Beast Barracks ended in late August, and in early September we joined our "regular lettered" cadet companies to begin the academic year as full-fledged fourth classmen or "plebes." Now came challenges of a different sort. The "Fourth Class System" was still very much in force. We still "sat up" at table in the mess hall, still "pinged" around the campus at high speed, still flattened against the walls when upperclassmen came by. We were still quizzed incessantly on our plebe knowledge. Most of our troubles came from the "yearlings," until recently plebes themselves, and now intent on passing on the same miseries they had endured. Generally speaking, and with a few notable exceptions, the "cows" (or juniors) and firsties had better things to do than mess with the plebes.[2]

Cadets from all four classes were now consumed with academics, which at West Point were simply ferocious. Plebes took seven classes per day, including English, Calculus, Computer Science, Engineering Graphics, Military Science, Physical Education, and a foreign language. All male plebes were required to box and wrestle, and all cadets played either an intercollegiate or an intramural sport. Formation was held three times per day as the Corps formed up and marched to the majestic Cadet Mess Hall for meals. Even on Saturdays, cadets attended morning classes—after an intensive and dreaded room and uniform inspection that often led to demerits. From reveille to taps the day was filled to the minute. This was the kind of pressure and stress that made sense. Could you manage your time, prioritize your tasks, and juggle multiple competing demands? If you couldn't, you didn't last.

As a plebe, individualism or a rebellious spirit was harshly suppressed, but it was possible to earn the grudging respect of upperclassmen. One day at dinner I noticed a single surviving slice of Black Forest tart left on the dessert platter. Clearly meant for the table commandant, it beckoned irresistibly. I had already had mine, but an overpowering urge came over me and, as the table comm seemed lost in conversation with his classmates, I said—clearly but none too loudly—"Would anyone care for the last slice of Black Forest tart, sir?" Without waiting for a reply, and to the consternation of the two other plebes at the table, I appropriated the delectable morsel.

A few minutes later, the table comm was ready for dessert, but the larder was bare. In righteous indignation he rounded on me, supported by his fellows. The hazing session which followed was epic and demerits fell upon me like an early snowfall. However, I maintained my composure, took it in good humor and swallowed the various punishments inflicted on me without complaint. After an hour or so of rigorous interrogation and creative harassment my captors were compelled to release me—mandatory study barracks had begun—and as I faced about to depart my tormentor gave me a wink. I winked back.

Few cadets of that era managed to avoid walking punishment tours and I was no exception. One night, during study barracks when all cadets were supposed to be in their rooms, my door was thrown open and a shaving cream bomb sailed in, spraying foam all over my uniforms, hung neatly on hooks on the wall. This was a challenge that demanded retaliation. I had identified the culprit during the

---

2   The origin of the expression "cow" is lost to time but is thought to date from long ago when cadets were not allowed leave until the summer between their second and third years, presumably because of the primitive transportation available. Their return was referred to as "the cows coming home"—hence, "cows."

attack, and I quickly filled my wastepaper basket with water and headed for his room, three floors below. En route, I was collared by a senior, who reprimanded me for being outside my room and demanded to know my intentions. With a straight face, I explained my mission. Offering a wry smile, he said, "Carry on, cadet!"

Moments later I stormed into my erstwhile assailant's room and dumped the contents of my trash can on his bed. I retreated quickly and raced up the stairs, only to encounter a small committee of grinning upperclassmen. The inevitable "quill" followed the next morning, and I found myself that Saturday falling in on the area to walk off the four hours of punishment tours that constituted my sentence.[3]

Winters on the Hudson can be brutally cold, and I reported in the prescribed uniform, which included a long overcoat, scarf, and gloves. I had been warned that a rigorous in-ranks inspection would be conducted and, taking no chances, I wore a pair of dress gray trousers with a razor crease, fresh off the hanger from the cadet laundry. This did not save me. The officer-in-charge, a Marine major on exchange at the Academy—uniformed in full regalia, including Sam Browne belt with saber—examined me closely before snarling, "Wrinkled trousers!" More demerits were tacked on to my charge sheet. As I marched forlornly up and down Central Area in a swirling snowstorm, I vowed never to visit the area again if I could help it. Nor did I.

I was fortunate to spend all four years in the Academy in the same cadet company. I-4 was the last company in the fourth regiment, lining up for parades on the extreme left of the Corps of Cadets. I-4 had a unique subculture, emphasizing intramural sports, no cliques, and lack of interest in all things academic; an underclassman doing too well might be "encouraged" to back off for the honor of the company! Esprit was intense. Our rallying cry, "I BEAM," was renowned throughout the Corps. Though we eschewed being "gray" (meaning an excessive affinity for West Point trivia or display) we gloried in all things Army. Virtually all of my company mates selected the combat arms upon graduation, an unheard of thing, and our group of 26 seniors would produce the youngest four-star general in the Army (Dan Allyn, our cadet company commander), five brigade commanders, and 10 full colonels, which must be a record. We remain close, and I count those friendships as one of the most precious legacies of my West Point sojourn.

Some West Point traditions were awe-inspiring and continue to this day. One never looked at the huge eagle, carved into the top of Washington Hall at the entrance to the Cadet Mess Hall, because cadet lore said you would be "found" (kicked out for failing grades). Cadets in danger of being found would steal out to Trophy Point after taps, in full dress uniform, to spin the spurs on General Sedgwick's statue. If not caught by patrolling MPs, this was thought to guarantee passing grades. Flirtation

---

3   "Quill" was cadet slang for being "written up" and assigned demerits.

Walk was the one, and only, safe place to take a girl without fear of being "written up" for "PDA" or Public Display of Affection, since officers obeyed the "Cadets Only" tradition scrupulously. Cadets were almost literally drenched in tradition, and for most it remains a life-long touchstone.

The commissioned officers who taught and supervised the Corps of Cadets were a constant reminder of what lay ahead at the end of a long road. Most were Vietnam veterans, and some were larger than life. The tactical officer for Company I-2 had lost a leg in the war. Company H-4's was so badly shot up that he couldn't really salute. Instead, he would dip his head down to meet his hand halfway. One captain had fought with the Rangers and earned a Distinguished Service Cross, second only to the Medal of Honor, for killing several VC with an entrenching tool. The most impressive was Major (later Brigadier General) Herb Lloyd, a veteran of four combat tours in Vietnam whose uniform sprouted with Silver and Bronze Stars, Purple Hearts, and all manner of other awards. Every instructor in the leadership department was a combat officer with a Silver Star. We were surrounded by role models, and we wanted to be like them.

As I got to know my classmates, stereotypes I'd long held about the service academies began to break down. West Point was nothing if not fair. I found many more sergeants' sons than generals' sons. My classmates in I-4 included the son of a German soldier captured at Normandy, the son of a lieutenant who had served in the Estonian SS division, and the grandson of a Japanese Zero pilot. Most cadets were from solid, middle-class, often blue-collar backgrounds. Many belonged to ethnic minorities. None came from wealthy families, and few were the sons or daughters of doctors, lawyers, or politicians. About 10 percent were former enlisted soldiers like me. These were not kids born with a silver spoon. In later years, I would serve with hundreds of officers commissioned through Reserve Officers Training Corps (ROTC) and Officer Candidate School, like my father and my sons. They would constitute the majority of the officer corps and I would grow to respect and admire their service. But it was never less than an honor to join the Long Gray Line.

All West Point cadets were supposed to be athletes and, although I had started on the Prep School football team, at 165lbs I was judged too small to play varsity football and sent to try out for the "150s." Since the 1950s, 150lb football had been played in the northeast as a varsity intercollegiate sport and West Point had always been a powerhouse. The rules were the same, except that players could not exceed 158lbs on weigh-in days. Most of us had to drop serious weight each week; some of our linemen played at up to 180lbs and would "throw" 22lbs every week (in season, I would eat nothing at all between Sunday brunch and Wednesday dinner). The fact that players at every position were essentially the same size made for a very different game (imagine linemen as fast as backs and you get the idea).

Lightweight football was extremely fast and violent. Injuries were so common that in one game against Navy we lost all four defensive ends on the roster. But the

150s was also "pure" football. We didn't scout opposing teams. There was no spring practice. Most of our coaches were officer volunteers. The 150s sometimes played in front of 5,000 fans, and sometimes there were 50 in the stands. It was football played for the sheer love of the game.

As a plebe I had little hope of getting into games, but practice every afternoon was a welcome respite from the classroom and a chance to work off the tension and stress of cadet life. Our head coach, George Stark, was an icon at West Point and very much an "old school" leader who consciously modeled himself on Vince Lombardi, an assistant coach at West Point in the 1950s. Here I learned real lessons about life. The 150s shunned all display. We wore no names on our jerseys, no logos on our helmets. We had about 12 plays in our playbook, which could be run to either the left or right side. We had three basic defenses. Our quarterback and leader, Dave Farace, was often given to drawing up plays on the turf during the huddle. Our secret was simplicity itself. We were superbly conditioned. We rarely made mistakes. We executed simple fundamentals extremely well. We never quit. And we won, consistently beating Navy and winning the league championship. We made excellence a habit, and we expected to win. I'd apply these lessons in later years to great effect.

One episode stands out in my football career at West Point. In my junior year we played Navy at home, and in the first quarter I was badly beaten on a pass play, giving up a touchdown. It had never happened before and would never again. Downcast, I returned to the bench. My teammates all gathered around, encouraging me that we'd bounce back. At the end of the first half, Navy pushed down to our one-yard line. On fourth down, with time running out, the Navy quarterback rolled out to his left, looking to either run or throw. I pursued and we met in a tremendous collision on the goal line. We had stopped them, and the concussed Navy QB left the game for good.

That evened the score a bit. Still, deep in the fourth quarter we trailed by two, with less than two minutes to play. Navy had the ball, and only had to run out the clock to win. Despite the desperate situation, there was no panic in the huddle. Our captain, defensive tackle Fred Coppola, told us, "I'm gonna get the ball on the next play. Be ready." As the ball was snapped, Fred shot through the line, slamming into the running back an instant after the handoff. The ball squirted into the air, and we recovered. After three unsuccessful plays, our kicker lined up for the toughest kick of his life. It sailed through the uprights, and with seconds left we had beaten Navy by one point.

That earned us the treasured right to wear a gold star on our letter jackets, signifying a victory over our arch-rivals. My football career ended in mid-season my senior year, against Princeton, when I shattered my forearm on another goal line play. I would never play again, but to this day I treasure the camaraderie, the never-say-die spirit, and the winning attitude I learned and shared with my teammates.

It may sound strange, but football is probably the best training in the world for combat. The game is a cocktail of fear, violence, camaraderie, and performance under pressure. It's about taking and holding ground, about teamwork and selflessness, about constant training and extreme physical and mental stress. You wear a helmet and body armor. Fear and aggression come together on every play—fear of failure, fear of injury, fear that you will let your teammates down. In virtually every game there are casualties, and just like combat, some come back, and some don't. Army Chief of Staff General George C. Marshall once said, "I need a man for a secret and dangerous mission. I want a West Point football player."

Academically, my Prep School training stood me in good stead initially, and I finished the first semester with six As and a B. Visions of stars were soon dancing in my head (the top 5 percent each semester were awarded gold stars to wear on their collars and called "star men"). However, my fund of Prep School knowledge soon exhausted itself and I was brought to earth. The academic pace was relentless, and my math and engineering performance began to fall to the B and C range, where it remained for the rest of my cadet career. Only with superhuman effort could I manage even that.

After Christmas, I went out for the sport parachute team, which seemed like fun. After a few static line training jumps we progressed to free fall, and it was here that my cadet career almost came to a quick end. On my first free fall, a short five-second delay, my main parachute malfunctioned, and I was forced to use my reserve. All went well and I landed safely. The next day, the same thing happened (the parachute, a used model obtained as a hand-me-down from the Air Force Academy, was later found to be defective). But this time, disaster struck. My reserve tangled with my main parachute, which had only partially deployed. Jumpers who had exited before me were now high above, indicating how fast I was falling. I went into a violent, disorienting spin as I frantically tried to deploy my reserve.

Soon, I realized it was hopeless, and I gave up. They say your life flashes before your eyes when you are about to die, but all I recall was chagrin that I was about to get killed doing something that was supposed to be fun. I crashed to earth just outside the small town of Central Valley, about 10 miles outside of West Point, in of all places a cranberry bog. Miraculously, the soft ground broke the fall and, though badly bruised and shaken, I had no broken bones. Subsequently, though I continued to jump, I could never achieve the relaxed posture essential to falling "flat and stable." Eventually the coach asked, "Cadet, is there anything else you're good at? Because you're pretty bad at this." I would go on to jump for another three decades, but always as an Army static line jumper. My sky diving days were over.

In the winter of my plebe year, I found myself at the center of an incident still recounted at our reunions almost five decades later. Following a company party held at the old hockey rink, I found myself on clean-up detail with about five of my classmates. Most of the company had departed, but a group of six or so seniors remained behind, intent on draining the last keg of beer. We lowly plebes hovered on the periphery, but in an expansive gesture of generosity we were permitted one last cup of cheap, stale brew. I began to notice one firstie, well into his cups, eyeing me with what appeared to be hostile intent. Suddenly, out of nowhere, he dashed his beer in my face. (To this day I have no idea why, and he probably didn't either, other than for the sheer devilment of it all.) Several of my classmates let out an audible gasp, and even the other firsties seemed stunned into silence. For about two seconds I stood there, beer dripping off my face. Then I threw my beer back in *his* face.

All present seemed to grasp at once the seriousness of the situation. I had committed an unpardonable, egregious breach of discipline and seemed ready to fight the upperclassman, a high-ranking cadet captain to boot. On the other hand, he had provoked the outburst for no apparent reason. I could see the other firsties calculating rapidly. No one looked likely to emerge from this with credit. My classmates quickly corralled me and dragged me away, while the firsties did the same with their man. Later that night we plebes double-timed in formation back to the barracks in the freezing air, singing airborne cadences. Nothing more was heard about the incident, then or later.

Cadet life ground on and the curriculum got progressively tougher. Physics. Chemistry. Multivariable calculus and differential equations. Solid mechanics. Thermofluid dynamics. Probabilities and statistics. Electrical engineering. Almost daily I cursed Sylvanus Thayer, the "Father" of the Military Academy who had ordained in ancient times that "every cadet must be an engineer." By dint of sheer hard work, I managed to muscle my way through the program, working endless practice problems, studying late into the night, and often foregoing the few weekend passes handed out by a miserly administration. I never really understood the engineering concepts my instructors vainly strove to teach me. By osmosis, however, I inculcated an abiding respect for the value of hard work and discipline. Maybe that's what Thayer had in mind all along.

During my yearling (sophomore) year I was one of 50 cadets (of a class of about a thousand) selected to attend the Ranger Course, a 58-day ordeal that represented the toughest training the Army could offer. Ranger School was a hellish experience combining sleep deprivation, starvation, and intense mental stress, conducted in forest, mountain, and swamp settings. The first few weeks were dedicated to weeding out the unfit and unmotivated. I thought I'd seen it all, but I was wrong. Ranger Instructors or "RIs" were connoisseurs of hazing and harassment, displaying an unmatched creativity and originality. Starting with an already hand-picked pool of students, only the most fit and most determined were going to survive.

The training day began long before dawn with long, fast runs, hand-to-hand combatives, obstacle courses, and the notorious "worm pit," a shallow mud-filled trench topped with barbed wire. Students fell out daily due to injury or just plain loss of heart. We learned all about how to plan and lead reconnaissance and ambush patrols, cross streams, and navigate both day and night with map and compass. Ranger students walked to their objectives or were inserted by small boat, helicopter, or parachute, carrying enormous loads of 100lbs and more over great distances, on one C ration per day and little or no sleep. Learning combat skills was important but learning our own limits—how much more we were capable of than we ever thought—was the priceless lesson of Ranger School.

But it all came at a price. One mission called for us to fly from Fort Benning to Eglin Air Force Base in Florida, jump in and conduct a series of raids and ambushes. We rigged in the field, not in the spacious rigging sheds found at Fort Bragg. Most of the students in my class were not experienced jumpers, but a handful of us were. We were dumbfounded to find that the Ranger instructors had issued no lowering lines. Some supply sergeant had forgotten to bring them to the field. This meant that we would "ride in" our rucksacks, weapons, and other heavy equipment. For the machine gunners and radio operators this would be hazardous, especially on a strange drop zone at night. A few of us protested to the head RI. This was not about being "hard." This was about troop safety. We were run off in a profane torrent of invective, and that night six Ranger students suffered broken legs. It was a different Army then.

All through the long, hot summer of 1979 we persisted, watching our classmates drop by the wayside as graduation began to take shape on a distant horizon. I started Ranger School at 168lbs and finished at 133. It had been the toughest trial of my life, but by mid-August it was over. Out of 215 students who began, Ranger Class 503-79 graduated 90, including 42 of 50 West Point cadets. From that group would come a constellation of future combat leaders and Army generals—Dan Allyn, Dave Hogg, and Skip Davis, to name a few, many of whom I'd serve with again and again.

My four long years at the Academy were an unending grind, but there were occasional moments of levity. At the Army–Navy game my senior year, one of my classmates dressed his girlfriend in a cadet uniform and put her in the middle of the company formation, where she marched with the Corps of Cadets on national television! At our graduation parade, unknown to us lofty soon-to-be graduates, our plebes managed to march on to the parade field carrying a scarecrow. At the command "pass in review," the company stepped off, revealing a dummy cadet in full dress uniform firmly planted on the parade field. The tactical officers were furious, but after the parade—when plebes ceased to be plebes forever—we praised them no end. They had done us proud.

A highlight of my cadet career was an informal dinner at my sponsor's house. Major (later Brigadier General) Mick Zais was the son of a World War II and Vietnam hero who had risen to four stars. His young wife Susan was a southern beauty from South Carolina whose grace and charm quickly made her a cadet favorite. Zais had been an infantry platoon leader in Vietnam and now taught psychology. When I arrived at his quarters, I was surprised to see an elderly gentleman, who turned out to be none other than James Gavin, the legendary commander of the 82nd Airborne Division in World War II, where he had been the youngest general since Custer. (Gavin and Zais senior had married sisters, hence the family connection.) For three hours I listened to General Gavin's recollections of the war, some humorous, some colorful, some wistful. It was a profound and memorable experience; one I'd treasure for the rest of my life. In later years, as a commander of airborne units, I would often reminisce with my officers about the time I'd met "Jumping Jim Gavin"—probably the greatest airborne soldier ever.

In my senior year, I found myself posted to the brigade staff as the Assistant Brigade Operations Officer. On a particular autumn Saturday, I was detailed to escort General William Westmoreland, famous as the overall commander of U.S. forces in Vietnam and later Army chief of staff. Now long retired, Westmoreland was at West Point to dedicate a memorial statue and the Corps of Cadets was scheduled to parade in his honor. I looked forward to meeting the general, a former West Point First Captain, not least because my father had been his aide in Vietnam.

Westmoreland in the flesh was as dignified and erect as his photographs showed, but I was surprised to find him painfully introverted and reticent, his expression grave and solemn and his manner almost completely lacking in humor or sensitivity. Embarrassed by his coldness, I lapsed into respectful silence as all four regiments of the Corps of Cadets formed up for the parade. The stands were full as I accompanied the general to the reviewing stand, where a galaxy of generals and colonels stood waiting to pay their respects.

One of my duties was to ensure that the Plain was properly marked for cadet parades, and as I surveyed the field I saw, to my horror, that my team had marked the Plain, not for a full brigade review, but for only two regiments. These markings were essential, as the 36 cadet companies relied on them to line up correctly on the "final line," ready to pass in review. By now it was far too late to fix the problem. There was nothing to be done but brazen it out.

Surreptitiously, I glanced at the superintendent and commandant of cadets. Both were manfully attempting to engage General Westmoreland in conversation and seemed unaware of my gross dereliction of duty. As the Corps streamed out of the sally ports to the beat of massed drums, the right guides—the tallest cadets in each company, posted on the right front of each company formation—snapped to "port arms" and double timed ahead, searching for the small markers in the grass indicating their assigned position on the final line.

This was the moment of truth. I stood trembling, waiting for the entire formation of 4,000 cadets in full dress uniform to dissolve in confusion. Instead, divining correctly that something was amiss, all 36 right guides ignored my incorrectly placed markers and planted themselves firmly where they judged they should be. Their companies fell in on them, the review continued without incident, and as the final unit passed by—my company, I-4—Westmoreland turned to the superintendent and said, "Not too bad. Not too bad. We marched better in my day, of course."

On the Hudson it seemed like academy life would never end, but gradually time passed and graduation hove into sight. By my senior year, I had shared in two national championships as a starting defensive back for the 150s, won two varsity letters and earned cadet captain stripes. In addition to Ranger School, I had been lucky to qualify for Canadian jump wings on a summer exchange with the Canadian Airborne Regiment. As a student I had excelled in the humanities and managed to bull my way through the engineering curriculum to finish in the top 20 percent of my class, making the Dean's List. Several tentative romances had blossomed and crashed. I had made some priceless lifetime friendships, and I was eager to get out into the "real Army" and make my way. In 1981, the world remained locked in Cold War, and most of us expected that, sooner or later, we might tangle with the Russians. Over beers at the First Class Club, we told ourselves and each other that we would not be afraid. But as Yoda told Luke in *Star Wars*, we would be. We would be.

CHAPTER 2

Strike Hold!

Who battled here with bloody hands
Through evil times in barren lands
To whom the voice of guns
Speaks and no longer stuns ...

GEOFFREY BACHE SMITH, *A SPRING HARVEST*

At 0530 on the morning of October 25, 1983, I turned onto the All American Freeway in Fayetteville, North Carolina, just outside Fort Bragg, when the car radio blared out, "Marines and Army Rangers are landing on the island of Grenada." I felt my heart surge in my throat as I turned onto Yadkin Road and headed for the division area, the smell of wet pines hanging in the cool air of an early dawn. For the first time since Vietnam, America was again at war.

I was now a first lieutenant, serving in the 504th Parachute Infantry, my father's old unit. After graduation from West Point and six months of the Infantry Officer Basic Course, I had reported back to the 82nd Airborne Division and been assigned to A Company, 1st Battalion of the 504th. My battalion commander was Lieutenant Colonel Frank H. Akers, a veteran of two tours in Vietnam where he earned a Silver Star and several Purple Hearts for wounds. I knew Akers slightly. He had been a military history instructor at West Point and was rumored to have played some role in forming the Army's elite commandos in the mid-70s. With steel gray hair worn in a short crew cut, Akers possessed a penetrating, unnerving stare and a decided air of command.

I have never forgotten my initial interview. Akers pointed to a black, spray-painted smoke grenade perched on his desk. "See that? The lieutenants gave me that. Around here, the expression is 'pop black smoke at midnight.' You're either straight, or we will pop black smoke at midnight on your ass, the black Chinook will come, and you'll be gone. Gone. Any questions?" I had the sense to mumble "No sir!" and moved out. I soon learned that the colonel wasn't kidding. Akers fired a dozen or so lieutenants in his first year in command. If you couldn't perform on day one, he didn't waste time on you. He didn't confine himself to just lieutenants, either. Every month he would host a jacket and tie "Hail and Farewell" where we would welcome new officers and say goodbye to departing ones. Sometimes, an officer would be hailed one month and farewelled the next.

The old Army was dying but wasn't dead yet. At least in Akers' battalion, tradition endured. On New Year's Day, the officers of the battalion put on their dress blues and called on the colonel and his lady at their quarters on Colonel's Row just off the main parade field. Officers wore "high and tights," stood at attention when addressed by the colonel, rose when he entered the room, spit shined their jump boots and laced every sentence with "Sir."

I was assigned to a rifle platoon and informed that I was the new arms room officer, responsible for the maintenance and security of the company's rifles, machine guns, grenade launchers, and mortars. Under the tutelage of the unit armorer I quickly became expert in the assembly, disassembly and operation of each weapon, as well as the night vision devices and other "secure" items stored in the arms room. I thought I would be greeted as a green second lieutenant, but after a week or two I saw things in a different light. My platoon sergeant was nearing retirement and physically impaired by many years of running, road marching and jumping as well as a broken back suffered in a helicopter crash in Vietnam. My squad leaders, who should have been E6 staff sergeants, were all young E5 "buck" sergeants. I was the only Ranger in my platoon, and one of the few to wear the Expert Infantryman's Badge, earned in the Officer Basic Course as one of 20 (out of 240) who passed the grueling three-day competition. I came to the division with more than 20 jumps and had been a member of the U.S. Army for almost seven years. "Green" I may have been, but much to my surprise, I was more experienced than most of the members of my platoon.

Division was a better place in 1981 than in 1976, but not much. Of 40 soldiers authorized we carried on hand no more than 25. Soldier quality was still low, with too few high-school graduates and too many petty criminals. Drug and alcohol abuse were still common. Still, we were turning a corner. We had a new president who was determined to build up the military. Commanders were given new tools—bars to reenlistment, random drug tests—to weed out the unfit. Alcohol-related incidents were now treated harshly, crime in the barracks was attacked, enlistment standards were raised, and we began to rebuild our standards and our pride in service. Things were looking up.

Meanwhile, we had an eccentric colonel to contend with. Colonel Akers was not a yeller and a screamer, but he had a cold intensity that was terrible to behold. We knew he had a Ph.D., a rarity in the infantry. He was a black belt in karate and was rumored to belong to something called the "First Earth Battalion," a network of military intellectuals harboring strange ideas about future war. Duty officers swore they had glimpsed him in his office, late at night, bending spoons "with his mind." At monthly officer PT sessions, he was in his element, leading us on 12-mile cross-country runs, or crossing streams in mid-winter using one-rope bridges, or running with stretchers and telephone poles. Only handfuls of officers typically finished, and repeated fall outs meant quick reassignment out of the battalion. We jumped often, went to the range much more than I remembered, and trained hard. Akers took the battalion to Germany for the annual REFORGER exercise and to Little Creek, Virginia for amphibious training. This was what I had signed up for. This was cool.

Our commanding general was the legendary Major General James Lindsey, a bona fide war hero and recipient of the Distinguished Service Cross, four Silver Stars, several Purple Hearts and two gold stars on his master jump wings signifying combat jumps while advising the South Vietnamese airborne brigade. He had served much of his career in Division and there was nothing he didn't know about the airborne game. Renowned for his physical prowess, Lindsey would often join one of his units for morning runs and could routinely beat young soldiers and officers in tests of speed and strength.

In one famous incident, Lindsey and his aide de camp fell in on the rear of a rifle company conducting a five-mile run on Ardennes Street. Despite wearing a gas mask, he easily kept up. Eventually the company commander, a young captain, dropped back and ordered the two strangers to get out of his formation. Chuckling inside his mask, the general ignored him. Minutes later, the captain circled back and, finding his orders disregarded, grabbed the division commander by the shoulder and ran him into a telephone pole. Far from losing his cool, Lindsey doffed the mask and congratulated the captain for his decisive and aggressive demeanor—if not his judgment.

A highlight of my young career was the annual "Prop Blast" ceremony where new officers were welcomed into the airborne community. It dated back to the early days of the airborne and, with some modifications, remained essentially the same. "Blastees" endured a day of intense physical training and good-natured harassment, after which the participants repaired to an indoor location equipped with a "mock door." The young officers would be rigged for a parachute jump with full combat equipment, be given jump commands inside the mockup, and exit on command. Next the candidate would report to the president of the Prop Blast Board, usually the brigade commander, as follows: "Sir, Blastee Jones reports to the president of the Board and very meekly, humbly, and respectfully requests consideration for admission into the honorable order of prop blasted jumpers, sir!" The blastee would then be subjected to a series of questions about airborne history and trivia by board members, all senior airborne officers.

None would pass on the first attempt. Many would endure a half-dozen or more trips through the line before hearing the welcome words, "Report to the keeper of the crock!" The young officer would then double time to a large cauldron filled with an abominable grog, down a large portion from the "Prop Blast Mug" (a hallowed piece of unit memorabilia, often very ancient and made of a polished artillery shell outfitted with handles made from rip cord grips), and sign his name in the unit's Prop Blast log. At that moment he would become a "blasted" jumper or "blaster" and join all those who had in previous years endured the ritual for beers and sandwiches. The merriment would go far into the evening, a cherished memory for all. Life in Division was tough, but it had its moments, and this was one of them.

On rare occasions, allowances were made for a lieutenant's "rash, brash" mistakes. As a brand new second lieutenant I was tasked to run a rifle range for the company on a crisp day in early winter. Arriving an hour early to open the range, I climbed up into the range tower, called range control on the radio, and began to brew a canteen cup of hot coffee on a small one-burner camp stove. Just as it began to boil, my platoon sergeant noticed a jeep pulling into the range complex with a large, white star on the red plate fixed to the front of the vehicle. "Get down and report to him," I urged as I frantically tried to prevent my coffee from boiling over. Scrambling down, he snapped to attention in front of Brigadier General Peter J. Boylan, the assistant division commander for Operations. "All the way, sir! Sergeant First Class Allen, Alpha Company, First Battalion five-oh-four parachute infantry, range safety NCO for Range 57, reporting sir!"

As Sergeant Allen began to brief the general in the prescribed format, Boylan looked over his shoulder to see a column of smoke pouring from the wooden tower, layered with about 50 coats of paint since its initial construction 50 years before. In my haste I had knocked over the camp stove, igniting the wooden structure which was quickly engulfed in flames. Rather than burn to death, I launched myself out of the two-story tower, executing a perfect parachute landing fall in front of the general, and snapping to attention with my field jacket smoldering. "Second Lieutenant Hooker, sir, range officer-in-charge!" I barked. A faint smile creased Boylan's otherwise impassive face (no doubt he was recalling similar escapades in his salad days). As the tower collapsed in a roaring heap of flaming cinders and charred timbers, he returned my salute with the obligatory "Airborne!" As I waited for the withering blast which my crimes deserved, he said, "Carry on lieutenant, carry on." With that, he was off in a whirl of flying gravel. I had survived, at least for one more day.

Just a few months into my tour of duty the battalion deployed to Panama for jungle training at the Army's Jungle Operations Training Center or JOTC. For three weeks we chopped our way through the jungle, conducted day and night live fires, crossed the Shagras river on poncho rafts and partied on the weekends in Panama City or Colon. In general, we enjoyed ourselves immensely. Most of the cadre had served in Vietnam and the training was serious, focused and realistic.

On the final day of training, disaster struck. On a long march back to the cantonment area one of my soldiers was overcome by the heat. Lieutenant Colonel Akers personally transported him in his jeep to Fort Sherman, our base camp, for treatment in the aid station. The soldier's weapon and rucksack were placed on his bunk in the platoon living area, which was guarded by an injured soldier who was unable to attend training. (This was a violation of the battalion policy that a soldier should never be separated from his weapon, unless to store it in a secure arms room.) The rest of us continued the foot march back.

After treatment, the soldier returned to his bunk to find his gear and weapon missing. The soldier on guard remembered that a young sergeant had entered 30 minutes before and had left with the items, which the young private assumed were the sergeant's. The battalion was immediately assembled for a 100 percent roll call and the sergeant was found to be missing.

A missing weapon is a serious event, and it now became the immediate priority. Some hours later the sergeant returned, minus the missing weapon. During questioning he denied any knowledge (probably recalling a similar incident in the battalion the previous year, when the theft of a weapon had landed the guilty party in prison).

Akers now swung into action. Taking me aside he said, "Assemble your platoon and have them fill out anonymous statements—it's possible someone may know something." I complied but the responses were predictably negative—the platoon had been road marching during the theft and could not know anything about it. Akers' next order was to truck the platoon back to the start point of the previous day's foot march and repeat the trek, some 15 miles. The men were to search both sides of the road on the grounds that the weapon may have "been lost on the way in."

Though only a second lieutenant, at this point I remonstrated. "Sir, the men have not slept in almost 24 hours. They're exhausted. We know how and when the weapon was stolen. In fact, it came back to Fort Sherman on your vehicle! Why are we doing this?" The colonel set his jaw. "I know what I'm doing. This isn't my first rodeo. Just follow your orders."

On the truck ride back into the jungle I began to understand. As far as I could make out, Akers knew we would not find the missing weapon, but he probably reckoned that the platoon would be so pissed off they would bring intense pressure to bear on the guilty party, who might then confess. This violated everything I had ever been taught about the use of mass punishment, but orders were orders. Akers wanted that weapon back, and I could appreciate that. Angry, hungry, and worn out, my troopers began the long walk.

About six hours later, we arrived back at Fort Sherman. The colonel was waiting at the main gate. "Find anything? Anybody 'fess up?" "Negative, sir." "Right," he barked. "We've moved your stuff out of the barracks. It's over there on the other side of the flight strip in the grass. Tell your men that's their new home. If you want back into barracks, I want somebody to tell me what happened to the damned weapon!"

At this point I broke into open protest. "Sir, we're supposed to fly home tomorrow. The men need to clean and pack their gear. They need to get some chow and rest. In a couple of hours, it's going to pour down rain. We know who stole the weapon. This isn't right."

Akers looked at me coldly. I remembered the black smoke grenade, and the lieutenants all around me who had been fired. It looked likely I'd soon be following them. "Just find the goddamned weapon!" he growled.

That night the other shoe dropped. I was informed by the company commander that Akers had decided to leave us in Panama until the weapon resurfaced. I was to have the suspect grilled by Army Criminal Investigations Division (CID) agents until he cracked. We were to be housed in an abandoned barracks building, eat in the mess hall alone, and in every other way be segregated and shamed until something broke loose.

This was a severe leadership challenge. I had been an officer in the battalion only about 90 days. At a minimum a captain should have remained behind to interact with the brass in Panama. My platoon was seriously undermanned, with "buck" sergeant E5s as squad leaders instead of E6 staff sergeants, and a brand new E6 platoon sergeant in lieu of an experienced E7 sergeant first class. On top of everything else, I faced a lack of adult supervision, myself included.

The next day, we watched mournfully as the battalion drove away in trucks. I still couldn't believe it. My troops began to mutter openly about "doing" the chief suspect, who by now was paralyzed with fear. The CID agents did their best, polygraphing my sergeant (which he failed) and threatening him with every kind of condign punishment. After one tough session with them he came out of the interview room and asked to go to the bathroom. I allowed it, asking another junior NCO to escort him.

Moments later, the escort came running out, white faced. "He's got a knife," he screamed. I rushed in to find the suspect brandishing a steel blade he had somehow obtained and hidden. Blood was gushing from his wrist where he'd slashed it. Holding my hands up, I tried to calm him down, just like they do on TV. He wasn't having it and ran towards me, shouting incomprehensibly and holding the knife across his throat. Just then the lead CID agent barreled in, drew his sidearm and placed it right against my guy's head, hammer cocked. "Drop the knife or I'll blow your goddamned head off," he snarled. The knife hit the floor, the sergeant was immediately cuffed, and the crisis was over, for now.

I assumed that CID would now take the suspect into custody. Instead, I was told, "He's your problem." We drove back to Fort Sherman, where the aid station sewed up my suspect's cuts. I huddled with my young platoon sergeant. "First, I want every soldier thoroughly searched. All bayonets and knives of any kind will be locked away. I want our suspect guarded 24/7 by a sergeant of the guard (SOG). Put him on suicide watch and make sure no one has an opportunity to hurt him." Next, I went to see the lieutenant colonel who commanded Jungle School and to whom we had been attached. "Sir, I feel that I am in over my head here. I'm worried that my soldier is a risk to himself, and at risk from the other soldiers in the platoon. I need some help here."

The colonel waved me off. "Hey, this is not my problem. You've got a bunch of NCOs who can ride herd on this guy. This is between you and the 82nd." Crestfallen, I returned to our empty barracks building, where my troopers slept on cots in a large open bay. In front a desk had been set up, manned by the SOG, with the suspect's cot a few feet away. Thinking I had done my best, I turned in for the night in a small private room off the main floor.

Now things really began to approach the surreal. Around midnight, I was awakened by a loud commotion. Charging out of my room I was tackled by a trio of my own soldiers, who threw a blanket over me and held me down while the rest of the platoon beat my suspect to a pulp. (The platoon sergeant got the same treatment.) After a few minutes we were able to free ourselves and flip on the lights. The platoon scuttled back to their bunks and order was restored.

Later that night, my suspect was escorted to the latrine by the SOG, who failed to enter the stall, however. Minutes later I heard loud shouting. I sprinted to the latrine to see a horrified SOG, and my suspect drenched in blood. He had managed to pry the blade from a disposable razor loose and had slit his arm from wrist to elbow. The platoon medic immediately applied a tourniquet shutting off all blood flow to the limb, and we raced the casualty to the camp aid station where he was stabilized. There he received several pints of blood, and the medical staff agreed to keep him for observation.

By now we had been in isolation for several weeks, and in an era without email or cell phones, my soldiers could not pay their bills. Young wives had no idea what was happening; we had been ordered not to allow access to pay phones and families were in the dark. In daily updates to the battalion at Fort Bragg I stressed our challenges and the dangerously low morale of my troopers. We were a powder keg, set to explode. I didn't know much, but I knew that as a second lieutenant, with my inexperienced platoon sergeant and an indifferent local chain of command in Panama, I was not really in charge. Very soon, events would take matters out of my hands altogether.

Within days, one of my junior NCOs (despite our standing orders), managed to get to a phone and call his mother. Shortly afterwards, a garbled story hit the Associated Press wire. The lurid tale described an Army platoon, "abandoned in the jungle" for weeks, forced to wander aimlessly, its soldiers so distraught that some attempted suicide. This time, it was the battalion calling me. "We don't care how you do it, but get your guys back to Bragg ASAP!" was the message. This was an order I could understand and follow.

The Jungle School colonel was only too happy to provide trucks, and that day we headed down to Howard Air Force Base. Upon arrival I put the platoon in the waiting area of the terminal and reported to the NCO manning the manifest desk. "I'm Lieutenant Hooker, and I've been ordered to bring my guys back to Bragg," I told him. He looked at me with a jaundiced air. "The next open bird doesn't leave for six days. Until then they're all full. Got any orders sir?" he drawled. "No, only verbal," I replied, "but this comes from the top, and if you don't let me on an airplane there'll be hell to pay." Such defiance brought first a captain and then a colonel to show me my place. Stubbornly, I held my ground. Though green, I knew the news story had already gone coast to coast, and that further delay and obstruction would likely bring real heat down on all concerned.

At this point a major uproar erupted in the terminal. Some Air Force master sergeant had ordered my men outside due to their filthy and tattered appearance. With typical paratrooper aplomb, they had then—led by their NCOs—scaled the fence, rushed a transport plane parked on the ramp, and occupied it by force. Base security police with loaded weapons surrounded the plane. The base commander was called in. "Who the hell is in charge of these guys?" he bellowed. I raised my hand. "Don't you have control of your guys?" I hesitated. "It would seem not, sir."

The situation could have gotten out of hand. The Air Force takes safety on the flight line deadly seriously, and though my men had no ammunition, they were in no mood to be left in Panama for a minute longer. Fortunately, cooler heads prevailed. Generals got involved, phone calls were made, and orders miraculously appeared authorizing our flight back to Bragg. The suspected thief remained behind, undergoing medical treatment, and was later court-martialed, though as far as I know the weapon was never recovered. We landed in the dead of night and were driven to the unit area in a bus, with blacked-out windows. The next day the men were reunited with their families, though forbidden to speak to the press.

I went to the headquarters for the inevitable interview with the colonel, full of trepidation. I had resigned myself to my fate, and fully expected to be coldly relieved of duty, as so many others had been in the unit. I had not been involved in the actual loss of the weapon and had done my level best to lead in a difficult and ambiguous situation. But my best had not been very good. Though only a new lieutenant, I knew I had been a party to a great crime: a national news story that brought discredit to the 82nd Airborne Division, the All Americans, America's Guard of Honor. Maybe I deserved to be cast aside.

To my surprise and amazement, Lieutenant Colonel Akers was not angry and did not fire me on the spot. Perhaps his own judgment had been called into question, or he might have put himself in my shoes and concluded I'd made the best of a bad hand. At any rate, I was dismissed after relating the facts and circumstances of our extended stay in the jungle, and returned to duty, if not untarnished at least relatively unscathed. I lived to fight another day. I resolved to make the most of my second chance.

As my tour went on my knees began to give me serious trouble. I had torn ligaments and cartilage in one as a private in the 82nd but had healed well enough to get through West Point and four years of college football. Now I tore up the other on a night jump. Akers' remorseless physical training banged on my knees relentlessly, on top of the jumping, running and road marching common to all infantry battalions in the division. Though I was only 25 years old, my 10 years of football and six years in the military, all as a jumper, had already taken their toll.

The orthopedic surgeons at Bragg examined me and reported bad news. They could go in and fix the floating cartilage that was causing the inflammation and pain. They could do little or nothing about the chronic degenerative arthritis they had found. I asked for a prognosis. "Hard to say," they answered. My knees would continue to degenerate, slower if my lifestyle changed, faster if it didn't. Much would depend on my ability to cope with discomfort and flat-out pain. But a career in the infantry did not seem likely, to them at least.

Colonel Akers was not sympathetic. "Tough break. Have the surgery. I'll give you 90 days to get back to top speed. If you can't, I'll have to move you out." Fortunately, a new procedure could be used: arthroscopy, using a fiber-optic tube instead of opening the knee joint. The surgeons went in four places in the left knee and three in the right. Within a few days I was walking, and within a few weeks I was running hard. As the years went by my knees would get progressively more sore and painful, especially in cold and wet weather, but they would never stop me. Like every other airborne soldier I knew, there would be more injuries, and a delayed price to be paid in retirement. But for now, I could still hang. I stocked up on Motrin and kept driving on.

Though the country was at peace, life in the airborne had its share of dangers. Live fire exercises were dangerous (several soldiers in my battalion would be killed in training accidents my first year). So were night jumps with full equipment (typically we jumped with 140lbs of gear, including the parachute). Even routine training operations could be lethal. One night, I received a call at 0200 to go to the emergency room. My roommate, Fred Hellwig, had been seriously injured in an accident.

Fred had also been my West Point roommate, and we would later be best man at each other's weddings. Fred was an armor lieutenant in the 82nd's light armor battalion, a unit equipped with obsolete M551 Sheridan light tanks. That night he had been standing on the rear deck of his tank, maneuvering it into a night defensive position, when the 20-ton vehicle knocked down a tree. The huge pine fell on Fred, shattering his arm. To this day he carries a steel plate and screws in the arm, a reminder of younger and wilder days. Few of us escaped unscathed. In the airborne at least, it was never a question of if you'd be hurt, but only when.

After only six months, I was put in an antitank platoon in the battalion's Combat Support Company (CSC). Here was trouble. CSC owned the battalion's two such platoons, as well as the heavy mortar platoon and the scout platoon. Normally, lieutenants served for at least a year in a rifle platoon before being given a "specialty" platoon. Though I was older as a result of my prior enlisted service, my new peers were all first lieutenants, hand selected, and full of swagger. They thought I had been jumped up too soon and did not welcome me with open arms.

All of this could be smoothed over by an experienced company commander, but this was not to be. My new captain, an Irish-American officer fresh from aide de camp duty in the Special Forces (SF), had a peculiar approach to leadership. The captain regularly came late, left early, and was often conspicuously absent from morning PT. He regularly fell out of the colonel's runs (rather early, I thought, apparently on the assumption that if you were going to fall out you might as well do it sooner rather than later to spare any unnecessary discomfort). For some reason, perhaps because he was "connected," he escaped Akers' wrath, which left us all in wonderment.

My new job was exciting, however. Though only a second lieutenant, I was now responsible for 13 M151 quarter-ton trucks, the successor to the World War II Jeep, as well as six M220 antitank missile launchers. Called "TOWs" (for "Tube-launched Optically tracked Wire-guided") these could be fired from the vehicles or emplaced on the ground. The missiles themselves were guided to the target by a thin wire. The gunner, peering through an optical sight, held his crosshairs on the moving target and in theory would fly the missile into the enemy tank "with 99 percent accuracy." In practice, there were many problems with this approach. Our jeeps had no protection from enemy artillery. Moving tanks would dip in and out behind rolling terrain, or behind smoke screens. The missile itself was slow, taking 22 seconds to reach its maximum range. And an entire U.S. infantry battalion had only 12 launchers, while the enemy would be attacking with masses of tanks. I knew all this intellectually. In a war with the Russians, we probably wouldn't last very long. Still, when I looked back at a dozen camouflaged vehicles lined up behind me, engines spluttering and long-whip antennas bending in the breeze, I felt great.

Soon after joining CSC, I met my new driver. Specialist Nick Keane could have been a poster boy for the airborne. At 6'3", with wide shoulders and narrow hips,

Keane was immensely strong, extraordinarily competent and even-tempered—except when provoked. Years later, he would save my life, and I would save his. Without compromising the divide between officer and enlisted, we would become great friends, serving together many times in later years. Keane taught me the basics about the antitank platoon and helped me be successful in a hundred different ways. When he'd say "Boss, I think we're getting stupid here," I learned to stop and reconsider.

One morning the commander called me out at the morning formation. Unsure what was happening, I stood at attention as he read out the orders promoting me to first lieutenant. Producing a black magic marker, he colored in the cloth "butter bar" insignia on my shirt collar. We exchanged salutes and I returned to my platoon. Despite the absence of ceremony, I still regard that promotion as my most auspicious. No second lieutenant can ever feel like a salty veteran. Almost all first lieutenants do.

In the fall of 1982, the battalion deployed to Germany for the annual REFORGER (for Return of Forces to Germany) exercise. We flew from Bragg all the way to Bavaria, jumping into the exercise after a nine-hour flight. Once on the ground we hustled off the drop zone to our assembly areas, ready to fight. There we met a chubby captain from the 8th Infantry Division (Mechanized), based in Germany. He informed us casually that all our planes had been shot down and we were all dead for 12 hours. The next day we conducted an air assault raid in helicopters against an "enemy" rear area facility. Again, we were told we had been shot down while in flight. Time after time we would be massacred by the "opposing force," who seemed to know where we were and what we were up to at all times. It began to dawn on us that we were not welcome.

U.S. Army Europe (USAREUR, pronounced "Yoos-A-Yur") at that time was massive, with some 250,000 soldiers, and had garrisoned Germany for 40 years. All units were "heavy" mechanized infantry or tank units, notoriously averse to the airborne, who were seen as prima donnas. In fact, the theater commander, General "Bernie" Rogers, had decreed that no U.S. paratrooper would be permitted to wear the maroon beret in his theater. Rogers didn't really have the authority to do that, as our berets were officially part of our uniform, but in Europe his word was law, and we dutifully complied.

Or almost. Colonel Akers was not the kind of man to take such things lying down. On the last day of the exercise, I was summoned to see him at battalion headquarters. He came right to the point. "I want you to round up all the vehicles in the battalion and road march them to Stuttgart. The maintenance platoon will meet you there. Then you will wash each one thoroughly and prepare them for air movement back to Bragg. And Rich—when you roll out, have the men put on their berets. Questions?" I was stunned. This was really a job for the battalion logistics officer, a captain, assisted by his senior NCOs. Military convoys were strictly regulated in Germany. U.S. units based there trained rigorously to conduct large-scale road movements. We knew nothing of the arcane minutiae of this game; we had no signs, warning lights, or any of the other specialized impedimenta required by USAREUR. Still, orders were orders, and complaining would not do. I saluted and moved out.

Fortunately, I had one NCO in my platoon who had previously served in Europe before going airborne. He proved an invaluable advisor. We consulted the map. Stuttgart was more than 225km away. Our small, underpowered jeeps could make at best about 50 miles per hour in formation. I struggled to remember the little I had learned in the Infantry Officer Basic Course about march tables, pass times and the like. Finally, I announced, "Screw it. We'll leave at midnight. I'll lead in the first vehicle. The motor sergeant will bring up the rear and fix anyone who breaks down. Everybody keep closed up tight. We'll just drive 'til we get there. Oh—and everyone, wear your berets!" A sea of smiles broke out.

So off we went, in a cold, driving rainstorm. In the 82nd, unlike the rest of the Army, our jeeps had no windshields or canvas covers. Our drivers wore plastic goggles and ponchos. Within minutes we were soaked and miserable, our sodden berets drooping sadly around our ears. Out on the autobahn, the German interstate highway system, cars screamed past at incredible speeds in the left lane. We hugged the right lane and chugged along, hour after hour, chilled to the bone.

Soon after first light we passed signs for the town of Ansbach, then the headquarters of the mighty U.S. 1st Armored Division. As we approached the off-ramp, I noticed a cluster of military police vehicles with flashing lights. A green figure detached himself and waved us over. As I coasted to a stop, he confronted me. "Who's in charge here?" he snorted. I quickly noticed he was a lieutenant colonel, wearing MP brass, meaning he was the 1st Armored's provost marshal or senior MP officer. I answered respectfully: "I am, sir. Lieutenant Hooker." "Right," he said. "You're under arrest. Come with me." Leaving my forlorn convoy parked on the side of the road, I climbed into the back seat of his heated, canvas-covered jeep and we drove away.

At the MP station I asked politely what I was being charged with. The MP colonel looked at me triumphantly. "Disobeying a direct order from the theater commander. You guys know you can't wear your berets here. Someone saw you on the autobahn and called ahead." As green as I was, I knew this was dubious. At the very least, I was probably covered by Akers' order. I asked permission to call my commander. Akers came on the line. I briefly explained the situation. "Right," he said. "Put the colonel on the phone." I watched as they conferred briefly. Soon the MP handed me back the phone. "Rich, I just told him you are an idiot and didn't know any better. He thinks you are going to return here for an ass chewing. When you get back out on the autobahn, turn west and continue on to Stuttgart. And put your berets back on. Screw these leg sons of bitches." And that's what we did.

Back at Bragg, life did not improve. Though I thoroughly enjoyed my platoon, things did not get better with time. The captain took to inviting us to his quarters on weekends, where he would get sloppy drunk, play Irish drinking songs, and invariably end the evening weeping. (His career would later end after what the Army euphemistically calls an "alcohol-related incident.") I was disgusted, and soon stopped attending these rituals, which seemed to me to be both unmanly and unprofessional. My fellow lieutenants persisted, however, and it soon became clear that I was on the outside, looking in. More and more frequently, the company commander would hold meetings to which I was not invited. Though I was careful to observe all the customs and courtesies of the service, our cool relationship eventually deepened to something like mutual hostility. This is dangerous for lieutenants. Perhaps I should have been humbler or more politic. Lieutenants should uphold their commander whatever his personal faults, unless and until he crosses an unacceptable moral or ethical line. This I tried to do, but with faltering enthusiasm and sincerity as the days and weeks went by. After six depressing months in CSC, the day of reckoning finally arrived.

It came in the form of the annual Inspector General or "IG" inspection, at that time a significant emotional event in the life of every commander in the division. My platoon was inspected on the first day, and early on Day 2 a runner came to see me. "The captain says the scouts are missing some wiring pliers and he wants yours." The idea was clearly to use the same tool twice, to convince the inspectors that all required items were present and serviceable. I thought for a moment—I knew this was a Rubicon—before answering. "Tell the Old Man no."

Half an hour later, I was standing in the colonel's office, staring at that damned black smoke grenade, my knees quaking. "What's this all about?" he demanded. "Sir, I would rather not say. But I hope you can give me another job. I don't think I can work for my captain anymore."

Akers looked at me searchingly. "Well, look, you've got a good platoon. You've done well in the field. I hate to lose you. But it just so happens that we have to provide an experienced lieutenant to the brigade antitank company, and you're a good fit. Go clean out your stuff. You can report there tomorrow morning. After a year up there, we'll bring you back." I walked out of his office in a daze. I had asked to be moved, but not out of the battalion. Was I being fired? The "OER" or officer efficiency report I received shortly after cleared that up. It was strong and gave me no reason for complaint. It occurred to me that the colonel may have had his eye on the captain after all.

Life in my new unit was good. The brigade antitank company worked directly for the brigade commander, in this case Colonel Henry Shelton (a future chairman of the Joint Chiefs). Shelton was a tall, lanky paratrooper from Speed, North Carolina who had served two tours in Vietnam, one with the 173rd Airborne Brigade and one with Special Forces. As commander of the 504th, the famous "Devils in Baggy Pants," he went by the call sign "Devil 6." (In World War II, a captured German document had referred to 504 troopers as "Devils in Baggy Pants" and the name became the regiment's proud boast, along with its motto "Strike Hold!") Shelton was no wild man. Though decisive and firm, he was reasonable, fair and thoroughly competent. Once, he came to work early to find the brigade staff duty officer, a young lieutenant, sound asleep on the couch in his office. Quietly, he began to go through his in-box. He had been at it for some time when the young lieutenant roused himself and sat up. "Good morning!" Shelton said good naturedly. "Want some coffee?" This story, and others like it, spread through the brigade like wildfire. Colonel Shelton was a commander you loved to work for, and one you prayed you'd go to war with if it came to that.

My new company commander, Captain Bob Hoidahl, had been an offensive lineman at Purdue. Hoidahl was large, charismatic, and tough, with a booming voice, a ready laugh and an ultra-cool yellow corvette. I quickly fell into synch in the unit and began to make myself useful. By now I was seen, and felt myself to be, a veteran lieutenant with real confidence and skills. Soon, there wasn't much I didn't know about antitank units. After 18 months in the division as a lieutenant it was time to face the next challenge, and it was a big one: Jumpmaster School.

Even now, thinking about Jumpmaster School sends a chill up my spine. If Ranger School was the Army's toughest physical challenge, the jumpmaster course was and is the most mentally challenging. The historic pass rate for the 82nd's Jumpmaster Course hovered around 33 percent. During airborne operations, it is the jumpmaster who is in charge, regardless of rank, from the moment a planeload of jumpers assembles for the pre-jump brief until the last jumper hits the ground. Parachute jumping is inherently dangerous, but the danger rises to another level when done en masse, in the dark, at very low altitude, with heavy combat equipment, on drop zones surrounded by tall trees, power lines, and water obstacles. Injuries—sometimes spectacular injuries—are common. Fatalities, sooner or later, will occur. To control the risk, jumpmaster students were subjected to some of the most intense and challenging training to be found anywhere in the U.S. military.

Even seasoned officers and sergeants sweated the course. Students were tested on general airborne knowledge, on nomenclature ("quick fit adapter with the thick-lipped floating bar" still sticks with me to this day, for some reason), and on their ability to give the comprehensive "Jumpmaster Brief" without notes. They were put in an aircraft at night and tested, with live jumpers, on "actions in the aircraft"—the sequence of jump commands and jumpmaster actions required to safely exit a planeload of jumpers. We quickly learned that the jumpmaster motto—"I will always be sure"—was not rhetorical. Grading was merciless and constant. Students were dropped from the course wholesale without pity.

The final examination was the most dreaded. The JMPI (for Jumpmaster Pre-Inspection) test required the student to inspect three jumpers, front and back, in five minutes. The first jumper was rigged "Hollywood," meaning with parachute only. The second wore a parachute with web gear and a rucksack, strapped in front under the chest-mounted reserve parachute. The third jumper carried "full combat equipment," which added a rifle inside a weapons case, hooked onto the main lift web of the parachute harness and positioned under the left arm. Various rigging errors were maliciously inserted, some obvious, some diabolically difficult to detect. My blood literally ran cold as I stepped up to the first man. Racing through the sequence, my hands flew over the jumpers and their equipment almost by rote as I called out the "gigs" I found, one by one, in my test jumpers. As I slapped the third one on the butt, signaling that I was finished, my grader gave me a smug look and held up his stopwatch. I was two seconds over the standard.

I had never felt so deflated. The blow was crushing. Redemption came a moment later when the school commander took me aside. "Because you passed the other tests with flying colors, you're entitled to one retest on JMPI. Get ready." This time, for unexplainable reasons, I felt a sense of calm as I ran through the practiced sequence. When I was done the grader held up his stopwatch again, this time with a genuine smile. I had passed, with two seconds to spare. After graduation, I walked into the company orderly room like I was floating on air.

Some months later, I was detailed to act as jumpmaster for a "mass tac," a training jump involving the whole battalion. The first soldier to board my airplane had had far too much to drink the night before, and after being belted into his seat in the front of the plane, a C141B Starlifter, he removed his helmet, placed it on his reserve chute on his chest, folded his arms and fell fast asleep. It took almost an hour to load the plane to capacity—120 jumpers in full combat equipment. By then my young trooper was in deep REM.

Suddenly, the interior of the aircraft began to fill with smoke. Somehow, a spark had ignited an electrical fire in the wiring running through the roof of the plane. Seconds later the pilot sounded the alarm, a long-sustained blast that meant "evacuate now." Quickly, but calmly, the jumpmaster team helped the fully laden jumpers to their feet, ushering them off the ramp, where they formed up about 50m away. Taking a quick head count, we noticed to our alarm that we were missing one man.

Meanwhile, my drunken soldier regained his senses. Glancing about in the smoke-filled cabin, the emergency evacuation buzzer ringing in his ears, he noticed he was alone. Bolting to his feet, he fell back, still constrained by his seat belt. His helmet fell to the floor. Wrestling out of his belt he managed to stand up, encumbered by the heavy rucksack strapped under his reserve chute and the weapons case rigged under his arm. Panicking, he began to move awkwardly towards the paratroop doors at the rear of the plane.

Seconds later he reached the door. Pausing for a split second, in full view of his fellows, he launched himself into space, shouted "ONE THOUSAND ...," pulled his reserve ripcord, fell four feet to the tarmac and struck his head on the concrete. He was out cold.

An hour later, he woke up in the emergency room to find the colonel and the sergeant major standing by his bedside, his head pounding from a severe concussion.

His first words were "Did the guys make it out of the plane?" The sergeant major assured him that they had. Looking at the colonel he spluttered, "Sir! I must have been the last man out! The plane was so low when I jumped that I could see the treetops! Did the pilots survive?"

As they left the hospital the sergeant major turned to the colonel. "You know, sir, we're gonna have to reassign that boy out of the battalion. He'll never, ever live this one down."

By now I was a fully formed lieutenant, leading my third platoon, with a new set of Senior Parachutist wings on my chest. I had learned my way around the motor pool, the arms room, and the company headquarters, deployed overseas twice for training, and led my troopers through any number of training events, exercises, and inspections. I was fit, able to "max" the PT test and run or road march for miles on end. I could plan and execute a complex airborne operation, deliver a military briefing, run a live fire range, or host a VIP, all on short notice. The division and the Army were coming back. The quality of new soldiers was improving, funding had picked up, discipline had improved, and we had a new bounce in our step. Only one thing was missing. I had never been to war.

That changed when the Reagan administration decided to invade Grenada, a small island about 100 miles north of Venezuela. Grenada was a former British colony that had gained independence in 1974. In 1979, Marxist revolutionaries led by Maurice Bishop's New JEWEL Movement overthrew the moderate United Labor Party and seized power. Cuban and Russian support for Marxist movements in Nicaragua and El Salvador, as well as Grenada, was viewed with alarm by the Reagan administration, an alarm that intensified when Cuban army engineers began constructing a large military airfield at Point Salines, on the southwest corner of the island.

Over the next few years, even more radical elements within Bishop's movement jockeyed for power. The crisis came to a head on October 19, 1983, when Bishop and many of his supporters were arrested, lined up against a wall and executed, throwing the island into chaos. The immediate U.S. concern was the safety of several hundred American medical students now at risk at the hands of a homicidal regime. Frantic diplomacy ensued, as the State Department worked with (some sources say pressured) the Organization of American States to generate a request for military intervention. On October 21, the Reagan National Security Council (NSC) began to seriously consider a rescue operation. The crisis atmosphere intensified on the 23rd when 243 Marines were killed in a terrorist attack in Beirut. That day the division headquarters received an order from the National Command Authority to deploy forces to Grenada as part of Operation *Urgent Fury*.

The 82nd was an obvious choice. Of the 18 divisions in the Army at the time, only the airborne division was structured and trained for rapid deployment. At any given time, one of the division's three infantry brigades was kept in a mission ready status, able to deploy its lead battalion with vehicles, weapons and equipment within

18 hours of notification. Also unique was the 82nd's ability to conduct "forced entry" by parachute assault, usually to seize an airfield to enable follow-on forces to land. The units of the division trained and practiced for rapid deployment regularly, and its formations, from battalion level and up, were led by experienced officers with combat experience in Vietnam. There was only one problem. The division had never actually deployed "no notice" from its home station before.

Urgent Fury was put together so quickly that parallel planning or coordination with other services and units wasn't possible. In theory the Army's two Ranger battalions would parachute at night to seize the Point Salines airfield, after which the 82nd would land its transport aircraft, unload its paratroopers and spread out to control the island. The night parachute assault, however, was pushed back to first light in order to permit the simultaneous "over the beach" landing of a Marine battalion near Pearls airport in the lightly defended northern part of the island, which couldn't be done in the dark. (Somehow, the Marines had wedged their way into the operation.) Hours before, Navy SEALS and Army "special mission units" would carry out several different missions, such as strategic reconnaissance and the safeguarding of Sir Paul Scoon, the British High Commissioner, at his residence in St. Georges. A naval task force at sea, built around the carrier USS *Independence*, would provide aviation and naval gunfire support, and provide a floating headquarters for the overall commander of the mission, Second Fleet Commander Vice Admiral Metcalf. For *Urgent Fury*, Metcalf was designated as commander Combined Joint Task Force (CJTF) 120.

Such was the plan in broad strokes. In practice, much would be haphazard. Maps of the island were not available, so tourist maps were hurriedly procured and overlaid with military grid references (many of which were off by several hundred meters). Intelligence on Grenadian and Cuban forces was spotty. Units would deploy to the island knowing very little—we screened our troopers for Spanish speakers, when in fact the local language was English. Weather, terrain, the enemy order of battle, a communications plan to enable coordinated action with other services, and many other key planning elements were absent. Nevertheless, the operation was aptly named. With all its problems, and they were many, a sense of urgency was not lacking.

As the 82nd swung into action a kind of chaos descended on Fort Bragg. The division's lead battalion rushed to the airfield and was actually in the air only 12 hours after notification, a herculean feat. But thereafter, the fog and friction of war descended. Units went to draw ammunition with carefully packed rucksacks, only to discover that planned ammunition loads would not fit. Troopers therefore discarded sleeping bags, spare boots, rain gear and most of their other equipment to stuff claymore mines, mortar rounds, hand grenades and machine gun ammunition into their rucks. Staff officers meticulously planned aircraft loads for specific packages of transport planes, only to watch helplessly as completely different packages and aircraft types landed. Unit commanders elbowed each other to be moved up in the deployment queue, some successfully and some not. In one case an infantry battalion was deemed not ready to deploy due to its high number of broken or poorly maintained vehicles; it was pushed later into the deployment sequence, causing a ripple effect in the division's finely calibrated plans.

As the "All Americans" took to the air, the special operations forces (SOF) inserted on the evening of October 24/25 began to run into trouble. A SEAL team dropped into the ocean from a C130 was lost and never heard from again. Another attempted to silence the Radio Free Grenada transmitter but was ambushed and driven off. Other SEALs fought their way into Sir Paul Scoon's compound but were encircled and surrounded (they were later rescued on the morning of the 26th by a force of Marines which had landed the night before at Grand Mal, north of St. Georges). A commando mission to assault a headquarters complex at Fort Rupert, near the capital city, was successful but a daylight air assault to free political prisoners at the Richmond Hill prison site ran into heavy ground fire and failed with many casualties and several downed Black Hawk helicopters. Two Marine Sea Cobra attack helicopters were also shot down supporting these attacks, killing three of four crew members.

Probably the most dramatic episode was the Rangers' parachute assault on the Point Salines airfield. The Ranger force was tasked to take the airfield and rapidly push out to rescue the several hundred American medical students located at the nearby True Blue campus. During the flight to Grenada, the Rangers were told to be ready to jump, then to de-rig for an airlanding, and then again to re-rig for a parachute assault. The resulting confusion on board the aircraft meant that many Rangers would jump with no reserve parachutes or rucksacks, as these had been shed in flight and could not be reattached in time. (An alternate story has it that the Rangers jumped too low for reserve chutes to be used anyway.) As the formation of C130s carrying the Rangers approached the drop zone they were taken under fire by several 23mm air defense weapons situated on the high ground overlooking the runway. Seven aircraft were hit by cannon fire, scattering the formation, although fortunately none were shot down.

In a dramatic episode, one luckless Ranger jumped but was hung by his static line, cartwheeling in the slipstream and banging against the aircraft in flight. (A "towed jumper" is rare but does happen. If the jumper is not pulled back into the aircraft or cut away quickly, he will usually die of suffocation or injuries caused by hitting the aircraft frame.) Following the protocol for combat operations, the Air Force loadmaster began to cut him free to allow the remaining jumpers to exit. Realizing that without a reserve he would fall to his death, the Ranger jumpmasters restrained the loadmaster and pulled the dangling trooper back into the aircraft by main force. Forcing the aircraft to "racetrack" for another attempt, they quickly rigged another parachute on the game Ranger, who jumped on the subsequent pass. Unfortunately, he was one of the few who would die on the drop zone that day from enemy fire. It was just not his day.

Once on the ground the tough, resourceful Rangers rapidly secured the airport complex, losing five dead as they drove the defending Cuban combat engineers from the area. By early afternoon of October 25, Point Salines was secure, and the Rangers pushed out to rescue the Americans at True Blue. One hundred and forty American civilians were secured and flown out without incident. The resistance put up by the Cubans, though doomed, was more spirited than expected. Unknown to the Americans, Cuban Colonel Pedro Tortola arrived the day before the invasion to take command of the Cuban defenders. He survived, only to be court martialed by Fidel Castro, demoted to private, and sent to Angola where he perished.

A curious development was the arrival of the 335-strong Caribbean Peacekeeping Force (CPF), a polyglot collection of policemen and paramilitaries from neighboring islands commanded by a colonel from Barbados. Sent to demonstrate regional support, the CPF was given "safe but visible missions," usually to secure key sites once taken by the Americans. The CPF would remain on the island as a security force after the Americans departed. During the invasion itself they played no significant role.

In yet another illustration of how hastily *Urgent Fury* had been thrown together, some of the rescued Americans informed the Rangers that another group of 200 Americans was sheltering a few miles to the north at the medical school's main campus at Grand Anse. This came as a big surprise. At the same time, the first 82nd Airborne units began to arrive. Because Point Salines was still under construction, only a single transport aircraft could be accommodated on the ground at a time. The obvious answer was to drop the 82nd planeloads onto the secured airfield by parachute in order to rapidly build up combat power. However, the 82nd's commander, Major General Edward Trobaugh, decided differently. Slowly and painfully, the arriving battalions were landed one plane at a time, disgorging their cargoes, repositioning and taking off before the next plane could land. This method meant that the six infantry battalions sent by the 82nd to Grenada would take three days to get on the ground. Trobaugh had served with distinction in Vietnam, but (very unusually for an 82nd commander) lacked an airborne background and pursued a cautious course throughout the operation. To this day, Trobaugh's decision rankles in the airborne community and his performance in Grenada—the first real combat operation since Vietnam—is not regarded admiringly. Alone among 82nd commanders of the last 40 years (except for one caught up in an extramarital affair), Trobaugh was not promoted to three stars.

Again acting cautiously, General Trobaugh, with only one day on the ground and lacking helicopters which had not yet arrived, decided to postpone a second rescue operation until the 27th. Overruled by the Pentagon, Trobaugh was ordered by Admiral Metcalf to move immediately. Using borrowed Marine CH46 helicopters, the Rangers flew to Grand Anse and successfully rescued the remaining students, who began to fly home to the States that night on empty military transports. Amazingly, the second group reported that another several hundred students were located east of the airfield on a small peninsula called Lance-aux-Epines (these would not be rescued until the 28th). At the same time, the eastern part of the airfield perimeter was attacked in mid-afternoon by a group of Grenadian armored personnel carriers. Though all were destroyed quickly, the event caused Trobaugh to direct that the 82nd rear headquarters at Fort Bragg continue deploying battalions.

The 82nd suffered its first combat death on the morning of the 26th when a company of its 2nd Battalion, 325th Airborne Infantry was ordered to relieve a Ranger unit near Calliste, not far from the airfield. The company was commanded by Captain Michael Ritz, whom I had met briefly at Ranger School a few years before. Then, he was a recently graduated Ranger student and second lieutenant, held over while waiting for a course at Fort Benning. For some reason he was allowed to serve on the Ranger School cadre, where he delighted in humiliating Ranger students (his signature trick was to push our heads below the water with his boot in the worm pit). On this day, Ritz decided to conduct a "leader's recon" with his lieutenants, despite warnings from the Ranger lieutenant on the scene, First Lieutenant Dave Pelizzon, a Prep School and West Point classmate who had also served in the 82nd as an enlisted man. Advancing towards an occupied building, the party was taken under intense fire at short range, killing Ritz instantly and wounding several others in the party. (Second Lieutenant Mick Nicholson, the West Point First Captain in 1982, distinguished himself in this action and later commanded the 82nd before reaching four stars.) Ritz's actions were described in heroic terms, and a street was even named after him at Fort Bragg. In fact, he was a foolish officer who endangered his own life and those of his men needlessly.

Back at Fort Bragg I followed the operation nervously. My brigade was not scheduled to deploy and antitank units in any case were deemed unsuitable for this specific mission. Echo Company by now had a new commander, Captain Bob Frusha, but he was in Spain doing advance work for an upcoming exercise. We seemed doomed to watch the invasion of Grenada on television. My luck changed on October 26, when a major from the brigade staff strode into the orderly room and called out "Where's Hooker?" I reported myself at once. The major barked, "Got your stuff packed?" I answered "Affirmative!" The major then said, "I'll be back in thirty minutes. Colonel Shelton is sending you to Grenada as the First Brigade liaison officer. Draw your weapon and I'll be back to take you to the airfield."

I was elated, but the other officers were not. I was the senior platoon leader, and the company executive officer (XO), another first lieutenant, had only recently joined the brigade after transferring from the artillery. This likely accounted for my selection, but the XO wasn't having it and insisted that when the major returned it would be him going and not me. (Afterwards, Captain Frusha carried a grudge for months, angry that he had missed his opportunity.) As the saying goes, "there is no rank among lieutenants" and we nearly came to blows. I ordered the armorer to open the arms room and issue me my rifle and night vision goggles, but the XO countermanded the order. Fortunately, I kept a personal weapon, an Army surplus .45 caliber pistol that my dad had used in Vietnam, in the arms room. The XO couldn't prevent me from drawing that, and in a few hours, I was in the air and headed south.

As the C141 Starlifter powered its way towards the Caribbean, I realized I had no idea what my duties might actually be. It seemed clear that the brigade would not be sent to Grenada, although one of our battalions and one rifle company had been deployed under the other brigades. I had a vague idea that I might try to keep tabs on the brigade units that were deploying and make regular reports to Colonel Shelton, if I could find a phone or radio. Other than what I'd been able to glean from the newspaper or TV, I knew little about the operation or about Grenada itself.

We landed early on the 27th in the pre-dawn darkness after a sleepless flight. I trudged down the ramp wearing a flak vest, gas mask and a heavy rucksack and carrying a duffle bag. Guides met the arriving unit and the troopers formed up into squads and platoons, moving off in the darkness. As my eyes grew accustomed to the dark, I noticed several large shapes nearby. On closer examination, I saw they were the hulks of damaged or destroyed Army and Marine helicopters, shot down in the first 24 hours of the invasion and moved to the airfield for transport back to the States. A small row of coffins was also lined up nearby and as the plane emptied, shadowy figures came forward to load them onto the Starlifter. Considerably sobered, I began to walk towards a collection of buildings on the north side of the airfield, where I guessed the 82nd would have its command post.

Almost the first person I met was Colonel Akers, now the 82nd's G3 or senior operations officer after two years in battalion command. Without ceremony he grunted, "What the hell are you doing here?" I explained my purpose briefly. Akers laughed out loud and said, "Well, the First Brigade ain't coming. You're working for me now. Come this way." Bewildered, I stacked my gear in a corner and followed him to a ramshackle table constructed of plywood and 2×4s, on which stood a collection of radios and associated loudspeakers. The time was about 0530. Two officers were hunched over the radios, scribbling on clipboards, while a major stood behind. Akers continued. "We run two radio nets from here. One is division command. Everyone who works for us is on this net. The other is the CJTF net. Everyone else is on that net. The shift change is at 0730. Sit here for the next few hours and watch what these guys do. When the shift changes, you'll take the CJTF net. If you have any questions, ask the major. Welcome to Grenada." With that Akers disappeared into the bowels of the command post. The major chuckled and said nothing.

This may sound unfair. Though an experienced lieutenant, I had never worked above the small unit level before. I knew nothing about the operational plan or how a large headquarters worked. On the other hand, I knew how to follow orders, and to avoid stupid questions. The 82nd took a very John Wayne approach to things: never explain, never complain. At 0730 I jumped into the chair, grabbed the radio handset and went to work.

The job was fascinating and grueling. Every radio transmission had to be summarized in a written log. The calls came fast and furiously from the CJTF staff on the carrier, from Atlantic Command in Norfolk, from Fort Bragg, from the Pentagon. I literally had no time to eat. NCOs would open C ration cans and put them in front of me and I'd wolf down a mouthful in the brief intervals between radio traffic. At first, I had to call in the captains or majors from the division staff frequently, but as I absorbed information through osmosis, I quickly began to fly solo. It dawned on me that as far as the outside world knew, the voice talking on the radio *was* the 82nd Airborne Division.

We quickly fell into a routine. On rare occasions, there was gunfire in the distance, and the odd sniper fire around the airfield. Generally though, the work was not too different from the office back at Fort Bragg. If a call came from the Pentagon, I'd refer them to Atlantic Command, no matter how insistent, to stave off frivolous briefers looking to prepare updates for their general and admirals. Commanders were immediately put in touch with Akers, the assistant division commander (Brigadier General Boylan) or General Trobaugh. Other calls were routed to staff officers, or I'd answer them myself.

A new world opened before me, and I was not sure I liked all of it. Early in the operation, a Navy captain called to say that Admiral Metcalf would fly in the next day in a Navy helo. He then wished to transfer to an Army UH60 Black Hawk, escorted by Army Cobra attack helicopters, and fly to visit a brigade headquarters. The captain insisted that Metcalf be met by a scout platoon in gun jeeps. I pushed back. These were scarce assets, already committed to operations, and it didn't seem right to pull them off the line to satisfy some admiral's vanity. Why couldn't the Navy helo just fly him to his destination? Akers then came on the line and said, in effect, "We're not doing it." Admirals then began talking to generals, and in the end, Metcalf got his way. Though just a young officer, I thought the admiral was a bit of a prima donna. Mostly, we needed the Navy to fly air strikes, and too often even that didn't go right. One Navy strike killed 18 hospital patients near St. Georges on the 26th, and another took out an 82nd Brigade command post a day later, wounding 17 soldiers, one of whom died later.

Still the mishaps continued. A directive was received from the Joint Staff ordering Trobaugh to attack and seize the military barracks complex at Calvigny not later than the 27th, on a peninsula some distance to the east of Point Salines. Trobaugh preferred to wait but his orders permitted no discretion. The area was supposed to be well defended by troops and heavy air defense weapons. Almost no time was available for reconnaissance, planning or rehearsals. Instead, a battalion of Rangers with one rifle company from the 82nd (totaling about 600 soldiers) was hurriedly loaded onto newly arrived 82nd Black Hawks and flown to the scene. Preceded by a few artillery rounds and an air strike, the Black Hawks roared towards Calvigny, expecting to meet hundreds of Cuban and Grenadian fighters. As they approached the landing zone, several Black Hawks collided and many Rangers were thrown from the stricken helicopters, killing three and injuring many others. Unit histories would later make grandiose claims about the "fierce resistance" encountered at Calvigny, but in fact there was none and the downed helicopters were almost certainly lost due to pilot error. No enemy soldiers were captured, and no bodies were found. The raid on Calvigny was a dry hole, dressed up after the fact as a big thing.

It is true that more than a decade of peace had dulled the U.S. military's warfighting edge, but some blame must attach to senior leaders who had withdrawn into comfortable peacetime routines, foregoing hard, realistic joint training. If anything, Grenada was too "joint," in the sense that every service insisted on playing a role. The Marines were a case in point. With two Ranger battalions and six Army battalions on the ground facing a Cuban engineer battalion and a few hundred Grenadian troops of poor quality, adding a Marine battalion proved an unnecessary complication that added confusion and inter-service rivalry to an already complicated plan. (The decision to delay the parachute assault on Point Salines until daylight to accommodate the Marine landing at Pearls is one example.)

Although the Marines were located just a few miles from the 82nd command post (CP) at the airfield, coordinating boundary changes between maneuvering Army and Marine units was nightmarishly bureaucratic. Proposed changes were flown from Trobaugh's headquarters to the carrier for review and approval by the admiral's staff, then flown back to the Marine CP, where a Marine one-star passed them to a colonel and finally to the lieutenant colonel commanding the battalion. (Major General Norman Schwarzkopf, later of Gulf War fame, reportedly served as Admiral Metcalf's deputy for ground operations, but I never saw him on the island and, as far as I could tell, he exercised no meaningful positive influence on our chaotic operations.) The procedure could take up to a day. Angry junior officers confronted each other on the ground, arguing over lines on the map. A much cleaner and simpler solution would have been to place all forces on the island under a single ground commander, but service politics forbade it and the friction continued.

Even within the Army, tempers could flare. Only a few days into the operation, Ranger commanders began to lobby for redeployment, as most combat had clearly ended. One day, a Ranger major accompanied by several captain liaison officers stormed into the 82nd CP, buttonholing my major and demanding airplanes to return to the States. The major replied with some heat. No one had detached the Rangers from the 82nd's control, and he quite properly insisted that he could not act without General Trobaugh's approval. A shoving match ensued, and we all dived for cover as the Ranger officer (very short on sleep and patience, no doubt) went for his .45 as his officers rushed to restrain him. He was dragged away, not to be seen again, but within 12 hours or so the Rangers began flying back to their home bases and Grenada became exclusively an 82nd show—except for the Marine enclave around the capital.

By the end of October, the mission was winding down, the Rangers were leaving, and there seemed little left to do but comb the island for any stay-behind forces. The Marines cleared a few remaining towns and villages and made a few landings to search small islands off the coast, while the 82nd patrolled Grenada's uninhabited areas looking for possible "guerrillas" or "insurgents." As the operation wound down, I fielded a strange radio call from the Special Forces Command at Fort Bragg. Apparently, they had received information about some potential holdouts in the Grand Etang forest, on the high part of the island's center. The officer on the radio informed me that the Special Forces "are coming to drop 150 troopers into the forest to find them and take them out." I relayed that we had received no such information from the CJTF and that it was unlikely General Trobaugh would approve. The SF officer insisted: "We're coming ... tell your boss." After the previous week—*Urgent Fury* had assumed something of a Keystone Cops flavor by now—it wouldn't have surprised me if they did. I passed the information to Akers, who laughed dismissively, and that's the last I heard of that.

In early November, I requested permission to join a unit in the field, as many more staff officers had arrived and I wasn't really needed in the CP anymore. I accompanied a small element of the 82nd's Reconnaissance Platoon on a daylong foot patrol which began with a helicopter insertion onto one of the many small peninsulas which indented Grenada's coastline on the southeast part of the island. Leaving two troopers to secure the landing zone we moved north for several "klicks" or kilometers.

Passing through a small village, I was astonished to see the locals bearing an ancient woman towards us in a chair. As they passed out cans of orange crush, she grasped our hands and thanked us profusely, with tears streaming down her face, for coming to Grenada. Her grandson, a conscript taken for the Army two years before, had deserted and rejoined his family, whom he had not seen for the whole time. High politics aside, we felt intuitively we were doing the right thing.

After several hours of moving, we came upon a small hut in a clearing. The lieutenant in charge sent several more soldiers up the trail to secure the far side of the area, leaving only him, me and an Air Force air liaison officer (ALO), attached to enable direct communication with the AC130 Spectre gunship, a converted transport packed with heavy weapons including a 105mm cannon, orbiting high above.

At this point the patrol leader, a senior lieutenant, motioned to me to enter the hut. Drawing my .45, I crept up to the door. Hearing nothing, I kicked the door in and entered the small, darkened room. The Air Force captain stood right behind me with the muzzle of his rifle close to my ear. Suddenly, without warning, my pistol discharged (I learned later that Dad had modified the weapon with a hair trigger). The noise in the small space was deafening, the surprise so sudden that the ALO jumped back, lost his footing, and fell in a heap on the ground. Sheepishly, I holstered my weapon. The hut was empty.

Suddenly our radio nets sprang to life. Hearing the gunshot, units several miles away called in to ask if we were in contact. The artillery wanted to shoot, Army attack helicopters wanted to launch and even the Navy offered air strikes. Overhead, Spectre came on the net requesting permission to fire on "personnel targets" at our location. Our ALO frantically worked to cancel the request, which had gone to the 82nd's fire control cell in the command post. When asked to authenticate his radio call the Air Force captain couldn't, as he had failed to bring his code book. Panic-stricken, we scattered, knowing we had little chance to escape the terrible firepower of the gunship circling far above. His urgent radio calls recalled those old World War II movies, when the hero gets out of the jam by reciting that year's World Series winner. Fortunately, the division command post refused permission and we lived to tell the tale.

A few days later I logged the following message: "Commander CJTF-120, in consultation with the military commanders, has determined that hostilities have ended." The 82nd Airborne Division returned to Fort Bragg and *Urgent Fury* came to an end. Awards and decorations rained down on its participants, but criticism was pointed. The operation, mounted in great haste, had been successful in removing a radical and violent revolutionary regime, restoring stability to the island, and rescuing hundreds of U.S. citizens. But few would argue it had been well done. Intelligence was execrable, inter-service coordination was poor, command arrangements were flawed, and execution was generally sluggish. Though overwhelming force was used, losses were high given the scanty opposition: 19 U.S. service members were killed with 116 wounded, many by friendly fire.

What had I learned? I had not managed to serve much with troops during the operation, but I had seen and heard much about crisis response, rapid deployment, joint and combined operations and the workings of a large headquarters. I learned that you don't sleep much on operations, excuses aren't welcome, and mistakes carry a high price. I learned that sometimes you're your own worst enemy; the destroyed helos and body bags I'd seen on my first day were caused as much by our own mistakes as by enemy action. Most importantly, I learned that the consequences of error and miscalculation fall most heavily on the troops—and that more often than not, they will find a way to accomplish the mission in spite of almost any obstacle. The entire U.S. military would learn valuable lessons from Grenada and apply them to great effect in future operations.

Back at Bragg, I soon found myself moved up to be the XO for Echo Company. There would be no return to 1/504 for me. Now I was responsible for more than 50 vehicles, hundreds of weapons and radios, the unit budget, the company training schedule, supply operations, readiness reporting to the Department of the Army, and every other administrative aspect. Being the XO was a graduate seminar in running units, especially in such a complex unit, and great preparation for company command. My final year as a lieutenant in the 82nd passed uneventfully, with long hours and little time off. (In one stretch I worked for 26 consecutive weeks on Saturday and Sunday without a break.) I graduated from the Pathfinder course at the Infantry School and continued to jump as often as possible, proudly swapping my Senior Parachutist Badge for Master Wings once I completed 65 jumps. One highlight was the chance to jump with my father, now a full colonel nearing retirement, an event I'd replicate 25 years later with my own son.

All this left little time for a personal life. Meeting new girls took time I didn't have, so I reconnected with old flames a few times, but not much came of that. The problem was more than just limited time to devote to relationships. I was consumed by my new profession, determined to master it, and probably not able to balance the personal with the professional very well. One look inside the house I rented with two other lieutenants was usually enough to scare away any potential romantic partners. The house itself was nice enough. Inside, it was furnished with a card table, four chairs, and a small TV resting on a footlocker. On the wall hung our Academy diplomas and our cadet sabers. Over the fireplace I nailed a gun rack with the weapons my father had passed on to me: an M1 Garand, an M1 carbine, a 1903 Springfield, and most prized of all, a .54 caliber breech-loading cavalry carbine, picked up after the battle of Iuka during the Civil War and handed down, father to son. The refrigerator was stocked with cracker barrel cheese, Vidalia onions and cold beer. On a good night, if we really felt like cooking, we'd heat Campbell's soup on the stove—in the can.

Towards the end of my tour, I drew a choice assignment to lead a platoon and part of the company headquarters on an off-post exercise to Fort Huachuca, Arizona. The company first sergeant came with us, along with the platoon's lieutenant. We flew across country and jumped into the desert, staying in the field for seven days. Afterwards, we came in for a weekend off before returning to Bragg. Housed in a dilapidated World War II barracks building, the men prepared for a night on the town.

By now I was a seasoned officer, and I knew what to expect. I had the men huddle up. "Okay guys, here's the plan. I want you to go out tonight and have fun but behave yourself. Stay in groups of at least four. There are only two bars in town. The lieutenant here will be at one. The first sergeant will be at the other. Curfew is at midnight. I will be here to sign you all in. Any questions?"

It was, I thought, a foolproof plan. At midnight not a single trooper was back. At 0100 hours, a group of NCOs carried the first sergeant in, howling drunk. My young clerk, sitting behind a field desk, politely asked the first sergeant to sign in. Shaking off his handlers, the first sergeant picked up the field desk and hurled it across the room before falling into the first bunk in a stupor. I decided to wait before confronting him. At 0200 the phone rang. It was the post commander, a two-star general. "Are you the man in charge of those damned airborne guys?" he demanded. "Yes sir," I replied, meekly. "Godammit it!" he roared. "The mayor just called. They've got a Lieutenant Hooker down at the jailhouse with about 40 paratroopers. I want you to get down there, round up your guys, get your ass back to Fort Bragg, and never come back!"

This is not good, I thought. Hopping into my rental car I went down to the local police station. Most of my guys were milling around. The lieutenant was in the drunk tank. He had given them my name in the hope that he might escape justice. I asked how it had all started. The fracas began at a bar called the "Sin of Cortez." A corporal with 20 jumps had quarreled with a new sergeant with only 10 jumps over his fitness to hold his rank. Heeding my admonition, they carried the argument outside to the parking lot, followed by the other members of the unit. Forewarned about the presence of a bunch of paratroopers, local law enforcement augmented by several state troopers converged on the scene to arrest the lawbreakers. A melee ensued, with my troopers giving as good as they got.

The following morning, I met with the local magistrate. He was incensed, but willing to let most of my guys go. The lieutenant and four other malcontents, however, were fined heavily. We flew back to Bragg, and I reported at once to Colonel Shelton. As I feared he had already been briefed. He gave me a long look. "Well, Lieutenant, they tell me you lost control of your unit. Is that right?"

I had to agree Shelton was right. Excuses would not do. "Yes, sir," I admitted. "Big time." Shelton paused for a long second. "Well," he drawled, "It happens. Hopefully not again, though. That's all."

Outside of the headquarters I heaved a huge sigh of relief. I would never be called upon to take a bullet for Hugh Shelton. But I would have.

In July of 1984, a classmate called to tell me that we had lost one of our own. Billy D. Hubbard, from Iuka, Mississippi, had been an enlisted paratrooper in the 82nd Airborne and we had gone to the Prep School together. Tall and fair haired with an infectious grin, he had commanded the 3rd Regiment as a senior at the Academy. The son of a convict and raised in poverty, Billy had joined the Army, as so many did, for a chance at a better life. We were close friends, so close that we had spent our graduation leave together visiting my parents in the Philippines, where Billy dated a former Miss Asia! After graduation he went to flight school and became a scout helicopter pilot in the 2nd Squadron, 17th Cavalry at Fort Campbell, Kentucky.

On a routine training mission in the mountains of North Georgia, Billy's bird went down in the trees for reasons that were never fully established. The autopsy concluded that he had lived for some 45 minutes, but he died before a medevac arrived. I was crushed. Billy was the first close friend I had ever lost, and his death robbed us of a life that couldn't have had more potential. He left a young wife and treasured memories that, for some of us, have never faded. In time, almost 10 percent of my West Point classmates who branched aviation would die in training accidents.

Thus, we lived as young lieutenants in the early 1980s. Ours was an Army on the way back. We were getting better and we knew it, could feel it, and wanted to be a part of it. The future beckoned with war, and more war. We likened ourselves to the young French officers we read about in the classic novel *The Centurions* who said, "We like war. We are tooled up for it." In the end, we would get our fill, and more.

CHAPTER 3

Geronimo!

"It makes no difference what men think of war," said the judge. "War endures. As well ask men what they think of stone. War was always here. Before man was, war waited for him. The ultimate trade awaiting the ultimate practitioner. That is the way it was and will be. That way and not some other way."

CORMAC MCCARTHY, *BLOOD MERIDIAN*

ALL THE WAY

In October of 1984, I completed my three-year tour with the 82nd Airborne Division and reported to the Infantry Officers Advanced Course at Fort Benning, the Infantry School. The six-month course was a nice respite from the rigors of troop duty, and a chance to reconnect with old friends and classmates. The idea was to prepare for company command, the next step on our career ladder.

A bonus was the four Israeli exchange officers on my course. Each had been handpicked and would go on to bigger things. Giora Eiland was a veteran of the '73 war and the raid on Entebbe; he would rise to command the Paratroops Brigade and retire as a major general before becoming national security advisor for Ariel Sharon. Mati Harari would also command the Paratroops Brigade and retire as a brigadier general. Moshe Kaplinski, badly wounded in the 1982 incursion into Lebanon in the famous battle for the Beaufort castle, would later command the elite Golani Brigade and become a major general and the deputy commander of the Israeli Defense Forces (IDF).

These three would become good friends and I learned much from them all. The fourth, Amir Meital, was nearest to me in age and we became very close. Amir would later gain fame as the youngest lieutenant colonel in the IDF and commander of a famous special operations unit. In 1989 he would be killed in Lebanon and honored with a book and a movie.

The famously casual Israelis became great favorites with the students but were the bane of the crusty colonel running the schoolhouse. Admonished for refusing to wear headgear, Amir responded by donning a U.S. Marine Corps patrol cap. The others, slightly older, indulged themselves by ostentatiously putting their hands in their pockets, wore sunglasses in class and insisted on addressing the colonel by his first name—all designed to infuriate and all invariably successful. We Americans sat back and enjoyed the fireworks.

When it came to war, however, the Israelis were deadly serious. On one memorable occasion Giora rose, walked up to the stage, took the pointer from the instructor, and proceeded to finish the lecture in front of 800 students. When their practical experience diverged from U.S. doctrine they would speak up and say why. Always, their focus was on accomplishing the mission with the least risk to soldiers. Often our minds would wander as the platform instructor listlessly meandered through his 80 or so viewgraphs. But when an Israeli spoke, we sat up and took notes.

Soon after arriving at Benning, I was promoted to captain. On the date of my promotion, about 80 of us were asked to stand in the huge lecture hall. A colonel intoned "You are now captains. Congratulations. Sit down." Then there began a stormy correspondence with my personnel assignment officer in Washington, who planned to leave me at Benning after graduation to command a basic training company. As I knew well, a training command would hopelessly disadvantage me in competition with my peers. (I later learned that almost every 82nd lieutenant from my year group who had served in Grenada was assigned to a training unit. It was the revenge of the personnel weenies.) I explained that I was perfectly willing to serve anywhere in the world where I could command a combat unit, but that I would absolutely refuse a training command. I maintained my case obstinately, even when the branch chief, a lieutenant colonel, called me personally. Halfway through the course Infantry Branch visited us and I was given a short interview with the colonel.

Brusquely he snapped, "You seem to think that junior officers can give orders to the Department of the Army. I'm here to show you different. Here are your orders to the 1st Basic Training Brigade. Send in the next guy." I looked at him steadily. "I'm sorry you feel that way, sir. All I want is the chance to command a combat infantry outfit. I thought I might lose, so I took the liberty of applying for flight school. Here is my acceptance letter. I'll send in the next guy." Leaving him dumbfounded, I saluted smartly, faced about, and left the room.

A few months later, I was wearing a flight suit as student commander of my flight school class. Flight school wasn't exactly Top Gun, but pilots, even aspiring ones, assumed a certain swagger impossible to miss. The Army Aviation Center, located at Fort Rucker, Alabama, was in the throes of fielding exciting new aircraft like the UH60 Black Hawk and the AH64 Apache. I was thrilled at the prospect of learning to fly and jumped eagerly into the first few days. Then disaster struck. In a routine eye exam, it was determined that I lacked the night depth perception required. I was dropped from flight training for medical reasons. "What do I do now?" I asked. "Call Infantry Branch for an assignment," they answered.

Clearly, I had been hoist by my own petard. Infantry Branch gleefully laid out my choices: command of a chemical weapons storage facility on tiny Johnston's Island in the Pacific, 2,000 miles from nowhere; a job doing cold weather training for the National Guard at Fort McCoy, Wisconsin; or a post as housing officer at Fort Monroe, Virginia, home of the Army's Training Command. I asked for 24 hours to consider my options, and briefly considered the French Foreign Legion. Once I'd fought back my panic, I met again with the post personnel people. The Army had just paid to move me to Fort Rucker. Did it make sense to move me again? Was there a job—any job—I could do as a non-aviator for a year or so, until those bastards at Infantry Branch rotated out? It turned out there was. A battalion adjutant in the 1st Battalion, 1st Aviation Brigade (essentially the personnel and administration officer) had just been fired. I could replace him. The job wasn't glamorous or career enhancing. But I might be able to lay low there for a year or so until the dust settled. Infantry Branch agreed it was a horrible assignment and signed off. I took the job.

Soon after arriving at Fort Rucker, I began attending the First Presbyterian Church in Dothan, a good-sized town about 30 minutes from the post. There I happened to meet Beverly Dees, an electrical engineering student at Auburn University home for the summer. Beverly was tall, slim, beautiful, and smart, a sorority girl with gorgeous, long auburn hair, an easy grace and a warm smile. I was 27 and she was barely 20, but I fell hard for her right away. Now that I was a captain, I upgraded my lifestyle, renting a small but nice townhouse and stocking it with presentable furniture, china, and furnishings. Beverly and I were engaged within six months and married six months after that. We talked at length about what Army life would be like, but neither of us could imagine where our lives together would take us. God has blessed me in many ways, but never more than in bringing us together. Through countless adventures, in good times and in tough times, she has been my rock and the love of my life.

A few months into our courtship, I took Beverly to Washington to meet my folks. Then in the final year of his career, my dad had accepted an assignment as the senior U.S. military officer in Beirut. In 1985, Lebanon was engaged in bitter civil war and Beirut, once the jewel of the Levantine, was now a wreck. Dad traveled everywhere in an armored Mercedes, guarded by Christian Maronite bodyguards. On three occasions he was the target of assassination attempts. He was back in the

States for consultations in the Pentagon, and I wanted Beverly to meet him, just in case. I was shocked at the change. Worn out, he had had aged years in only months, and Mom had too. I wondered if that would be my fate someday, as well.

Over Christmas that year, I traveled to Tel Aviv to visit my Israeli friends at their invitation. While there, Giora Eiland invited me to jump with the Israeli Paratroops Brigade in the Negev desert. Technically, I was in a leave status and no longer on jump status. Should something go wrong, I could end up in all kinds of trouble. Nevertheless, for the honor of the American airborne—and the fun of it all—I accepted, and we drove out into the desert.

Soon after we arrived the Israeli unit, an infantry company, assembled for the pre-jump brief. Conducted entirely in Hebrew, the briefing took about 10 minutes, far shorter than the detailed format we used. I asked Giora (at the time, the chief of staff to the Israeli chief of paratroops and infantry) to summarize. Smiling, he said, "Basically, he is saying to keep your feet and knees together!" A truck pulled up and a small mountain of strange parachutes was thrown onto the ground. Apparently, they were French in origin. Seeing me struggle to don the unfamiliar chute, a young soldier sauntered over to help.

Grinning, he said, "Hey dude, you from the States?" It turned out my new friend was from California. I asked for his story. "Well, my mom is Jewish and after high school I thought I'd come over and check this place out, mostly 'cause I heard Israeli girls are hot! Wouldn't you know it—they drafted my ass! But it's cool."

After dark, a blacked-out C130 landed in the desert, and we boarded. As we gained speed to take off, the Israelis began to stamp their feet, roaring something in unison over and over. Screaming over the howl of the engines, I asked Giora, "What are they saying?" He yelled back, "These are very old planes. They are saying 'Up! Up! Up!'"

As we circled over the Negev it dawned on me that I knew nothing of what was about to happen—not the drop speed, drop heading, the drop altitude, what obstacles might be in the vicinity of the drop zone, and most critically, what markings I should look for on the drop zone. In the U.S., we normally used smoke pots (so jumpers could tell the direction and speed of the wind, crucial for a safe landing), and red lights to mark vehicles and other obstacles. I assumed, or rather hoped, that Israeli jump commands would mirror ours, but I could not be sure. Reassuringly, at 20 minutes out the pilots switched on the red interior lights, just as we did. At 10 minutes, the jumpmasters got to their feet and the Israelis buckled their chinstraps and sat up. So far, so good. All this was familiar.

Soon we began to go through the jump commands. Although given in Hebrew the motions were common enough and I found I could follow along. I was positioned second in the stick, behind the unit commander. As he stood in the door a jumpmaster closed up on me and grabbed my harness—a huge no-no in our system, where it is an iron rule that no one touches a jumper's equipment near the paratroop door. Instinctively I grabbed his hand and wrenched it away. The green light flashed on, the commander leapt out, and I found myself half thrown, half falling out of the aircraft.

Seconds later I was floating down under a full canopy in eerie silence. American paratroopers, though briefed to maintain silence in the air, typically chatter like magpies, usually to warn off fellow jumpers from getting too close and causing mid-air entanglements. The Israelis were quiet as death. There was no moon, no markings at all on the drop zone, and I felt surrounded by total darkness. Ignorant of our drop altitude, I tried to relax my legs to be ready for a landing at any instant. Fortunately, there seemed to be little wind.

About 30 seconds later, I landed safely, sat up and looked around. Should I roll up my chute and carry it to a turn-in point, the normal procedure? All around me, jumpers thudded into the ground, scrambled out of their harnesses, policed up their equipment and double timed away in utter silence. I followed and soon found myself in an assembly area in a shallow depression just off the drop zone.

Shortly afterwards, the brigade commander materialized to give the young Israeli captain his orders. They spoke briefly. The captain moved off to study his map for about 10 minutes, then assembled his platoon leaders for a quick, whispered "oporder." Tucking his map into his cargo pocket, he placed himself at the head of his company. I watched as he took a single compass reading. We began to move.

For the next several hours, we marched at a torrid pace through the darkness. With no night vision goggles, and without consulting his compass once, the commander navigated flawlessly across 18km of rough terrain, changing course headings at least three times. Though I carried only light equipment, I had to hustle to keep up with the heavily laden Israeli paras. Fantastically fit, they took no rest halts. After about four hours, we stopped to form a perimeter in a dry watercourse or "wadi." The captain disappeared into the darkness, I guessed to pinpoint the objective. Returning after a few minutes he briefed his lieutenants, who scurried away to position their men.

The objective was a tank "laager," a group of four shot-up T-55 tanks, scavenged from the '73 war, arranged in a circle behind protective berms. Fifteen minutes later the desert erupted in sound and light as the Israelis fired RPGs (rocket-propelled grenades) and detonated satchel charges. Multiple machine guns laid down suppressive fire, their tracers arcing across the Negev. In seconds, it seemed, the assault was over. Following a whistle blast, the officers huddled for an after-action review, led by the colonel.

Giora appeared at my elbow. "The next mission is a 22km movement to attack an airfield. Are you having fun?" By now I had not slept in 24 hours and hadn't eaten in at least 18. I was on leave, supposedly engaged in rest and recreation! I begged off, and we returned to the makeshift base camp for a hot breakfast. In an impromptu ceremony later that morning, Giora awarded me Israeli jump wings, which I proudly wore for the rest of my career.

Upon my return my battalion commander, Lieutenant Colonel Bill Bauer, called me into his office. "How'd you like to command the pathfinder company?" he asked. In 1986, the Army had a single airborne pathfinder company, an elite unit of one hundred paratroopers specially trained to operate behind enemy lines to set up and run parachute drop zones and helicopter landing zones. Army pathfinders were infantrymen, but closely aligned with their primary customers in Army Aviation and hence based at the Aviation Center. Although an infantry combat unit, they were administratively attached to the 1st Battalion, and Colonel Bauer would have a vote in choosing the next commander. The unit carried a historic designation: Company C (Pathfinder/Airborne), 509th Parachute Infantry.

The 509th had been the first American unit to jump in combat in World War II and had served throughout the war until it was destroyed in the battle of the Bulge. Its motto "Geronimo!" became the battle cry of all American parachute units as they jumped. Its wartime commander, Lieutenant Colonel (later Lieutenant General) William P. Yarborough, had actually designed the parachute wings worn by all U.S. paratroopers and was still alive, serving as the 509th's Honorary Colonel. "Charlie" Company was the only surviving fragment of this legendary outfit.

My heart jumped into my throat. I had expected to serve in purgatory for a year or two before moving on to a "real" infantry job someplace else. Here I was being offered a chance to command an exciting and high-profile unit. I couldn't believe my luck. I accepted gratefully and Colonel Bauer petitioned the commanding general on my behalf.

It wasn't easy. Though an infantry unit, Charlie Company was located at the Aviation School and had often been commanded by an aviator, usually the general's aide de camp or some other favorite son. (Army Aviation as a branch was in its infancy and for decades, army aviators were assigned to "carrier" branches and rotated back and forth between air and ground assignments.) This had led to problems. The former commander had no airborne background, and a recent fatality on an airborne operation had resulted in a nasty investigation, uncovering scores of safety violations. Bauer was able to argue my superior qualifications. I was a master parachutist, well versed in all aspects of the airborne game. I had been the honor graduate of my Pathfinder class, wore a Ranger tab, and had served in combat, a rare distinction for captains in that era. Eventually Bauer's quiet arguments carried the day, and I was given the nod.

When he informed me of my selection, Colonel Bauer told me a fascinating story I never forgot. He had joined the Army at 18 and was flying in combat at 20 as a commissioned officer, earning two Distinguished Flying Crosses in two tours in Vietnam. When the war ended, he found himself in grave danger of being put out of the Army. He had no college degree, no Regular Army commission, and little hope of surviving the RIF—the Reduction in Force—that follows every big war. A letter from Army Personnel informed him that unless he could find a command, and soon, he'd be out of the Army in six months. Bauer scoured Fort Lewis, Washington, where he was serving, only to be told time after time that he wasn't wanted. Hoping against hope, he was granted one final interview. There, a steely old battalion commander told him, "I've been in your shoes, Bauer. I'm going to give you a chance. I only ask one thing. Someday you may have a chance to pass this on. Don't waste it."

Bauer leaned forward and looked at me searchingly. "All I ask, Captain, is that one day you pass this on." Over the next three decades I never forgot Colonel Bauer's story or his admonition. He died of a heart attack only a few years after retiring, but he remains one of my heroes.

Company command in many ways is the best it will ever get as an Army officer. It's the first time you are really in charge, with the power to reward or punish. A good commander puts his imprint on the unit, shapes it, inspires it, pushes and cajoles it, and builds it. In combat he leads it, bearing a crushing responsibility for accomplishing the mission, but also for the lives of his soldiers. A bad commander can wreck a unit, compromising its cohesion and destroying confidence in its chain of command. Unlike all higher levels, a company commander has no staff. He must take on the burden of training, administration, maintenance, safety, property accountability and a hundred other tasks, aided by a first sergeant and executive officer but few others. The hours are long, the pressures many, and the responsibilities grave. But there are compensations.

No matter how young (and company commanders in my era could be as young as 26), you are "the Old Man" when you assume command. The company flag or "guidon" is placed outside in its stand when you arrive in the morning; it is retired when you leave at the end of the day. Sergeants and lieutenants may recommend, but only you have the power to decide. Company command is the last time an officer can know all his soldiers personally by name. Much of the job is human relations, counseling soldiers on their finances, marriages, performance, and prospects. The rest is all about training soldiers for war. I set about it in earnest.

The raw material was excellent. All our junior soldiers were graduates of the Infantry School and the basic parachutist course. Immediately upon joining they were put through the demanding Air Assault course at Fort Rucker, where they learned to rappel from helicopters, rig sling loads, and mark helicopter landing zones. Within a year or two they were then sent to the Pathfinder Course at Fort Benning, a far more advanced and challenging program that taught them to establish and operate drop zones (DZs, for parachute operations) and landing zones (LZs, for helicopter operations), in denied areas behind enemy lines. Many of the lieutenants and sergeants were Ranger qualified as well.

The heart of the unit was our middle-grade sergeants, at that time all career pathfinders with years of experience in these specialized and unique units. A typical mission might be to lift a crashed helicopter, with fuel and explosives on board, out of a swamp. Rigging a "non-standard" load like that, where fuel spills or accidental detonation might occur at any time, took experience and judgment, and they had both in spades. For highly technical missions, the officers stayed in the background, knowing they could not match the sergeants' professional knowledge.

Even so, my officers were a rare breed. First Lieutenant Bob Quinnett was an ex-Navy SEAL and college football player. Second Lieutenant Andy Frank, a giant at 6'5" and about 240lbs, had served as an NCO in the Ranger Battalion and in Special Forces. First Lieutenant Bart Combs was an exceptional athlete who would later become an Army aviator and serve in highly classified special operations units. All would go on to serve with distinction in combat and make great contributions. But with that kind of talent comes individuality and strength of personality. Leading elite soldiers and officers takes a slightly different leadership style, one that accommodates their skills and abilities without giving up the responsibilities of command. Sometimes, giving my lieutenants their heads meant underwriting occasional mistakes, as when Frank, in an excess of enthusiasm, destroyed Fort Rucker's demolitions range. Good commanders know that sometimes the job requires you to take one for the team.

Sooner or later, paratroopers are going to get in trouble and when it finally happened on my watch with Charlie Company it was memorable. The 509th troopers had a favorite bar in nearby Daleville. It wasn't much, just a hole in the wall really, but it was theirs. One Friday, a group of hapless engineers from a nearby unit happened to wander in. One thing led to another, and before long the police arrived to find one of my troopers banging a poor engineer's head on the pavement outside the bar.

Back in my office I arraigned the miscreants. "What happened?" I demanded. Each one responded in kind. "Well sir, there we were, minding our own business, when these engineers came in and started messing with us … and we had to defend ourselves." I knew better. For good or ill, paratroopers like to fight. They tend to be blue-collar high-school athletes, C students who come into the military looking for adventure and a challenge. Paratroopers like to be tested. When mixed with alcohol, this tendency can get out of hand. The trick in leading airborne soldiers is to keep them in line without destroying their natural aggression. I found that winking at bar fights only encouraged more. In this case, I formally charged the worst offenders and took their stripes away. The rest were turned over to the first sergeant for "remedial training."

Early in my command, while jumping with one of my platoons, I had the misfortune to land hard on a concrete runway. I knew right away I was hurt. X-rays revealed I had cracked one vertebra in my lower spine and displaced another. The pain was intense, and the injury was slow to heal. In fact, I would never be 100 percent again. But in a few weeks, I was able to resume my normal routine. As my dad had warned me, getting hurt was part of the deal. It would not be the first jump injury, or the last.

In the spring of 1986, a Special Forces captain wandered in with a request to jump with us. He was at Rucker attending a safety course and needed a jump (paratroopers must jump at least once every 90 days or lose their jump pay). He showed me a copy of the orders placing him on jump status, and a call to his unit verified his story. Everything about the officer vouched for his authenticity. His behavior on jumps with the unit clearly showed him to be an experienced military parachutist. He was affable and friendly, even attending our local church. When he asked to use one of the vehicles from my motor pool for "official business" to visit nearby military installations, I assented.

A few weeks later, my motor sergeant came to see me. The vehicle logs showed only modest distances traveled. But the vehicle odometer showed hundreds of miles. I called the Safety Center. They had no record of the guy in any of their courses. I called him in and asked him to explain these discrepancies. He refused. The next step was to call in the military police and inform my bosses. The MPs were unable to find any information on the captain. There was no Army personnel record on him. His social security number was false. Follow-up calls to his unit phone number revealed nothing; the number had been disconnected. There was no record of fingerprints on file or a security clearance. It was as if the man didn't exist.

This was clearly way above my pay grade and the colonel and general took over. As our suspect continued to stay mum, and there was no evidence proving his status as a captain, he was charged and convicted in civil court, of impersonating an officer and sentenced to a year in the state penitentiary. Out of curiosity, I called the state penitentiary a few months later to follow up. The warden checked his records. "Sure," he told me, "I remember the guy. He was only here a few days when the U.S. Marshals showed up with a transfer order. As far as I know he was shipped out to a federal prison, but I don't know where."

It further transpired that the captain had been visiting deactivating medical, engineer and signal units over a wide area and "signing for" their supplies and equipment, which then disappeared. Was he a former military officer, now working for the intelligence community and helping support the Contras in Nicaragua? That was my theory. But I suppose I'll never know.

Throughout my company command my senior NCO was First Sergeant James Hartsfield, a small, rope-thin infantryman who would later serve as a command sergeant major in the Gulf War. Like many NCOs he was a confirmed smoker. In 1987, the Army, under a Mormon chief of staff, decided to prohibit smoking except in "designated areas." Hartsfield adapted. He had a sign made that read "designated smoking area," which he carried everywhere. Problem solved. In another incident,

Hartsfield was asked to read out the unit history at a black-tie social function. He did a magnificent job until the very end. Finishing with a flourish, he thundered, "And thus we strive to live up to our motto, 'Semper Primus—Always Primed!'"

Life in the pathfinders was fun. But first we needed to get back to some fundamentals. I found early on that while our pathfinder skills were high, our basic infantry skills needed work. We set about improving our physical conditioning, with weekly forced marches and runs, ending the week with an eight-mile run every Friday. The unit didn't shoot well; we scrounged for ammunition and ran more than 30 live fire ranges in my first six months of command. Demolitions, combat first aid and land navigation all received more attention. I worked hard to convince the company that pathfinders don't work in safe, rear areas—they exist to operate in dangerous combat environments where the ability to hide, move swiftly in rugged terrain, and when necessary, fight like hell would spell the difference between success and failure, or life and death.

The basic pathfinder element was six men, enough to set up and run one large DZ or LZ or two smaller ones. Given their bulky pathfinder equipment, which included electronic navigational aids and radios, they couldn't carry creature comforts. Even in cold weather, each man carried only one poncho and one nylon poncho liner; one poncho would be used as a ground cloth, the other set up as a windbreak or rain shelter. Two men would wrap up together in the two poncho liners, relying on body heat for warmth. In this way we could operate without tents or sleeping bags.

Armed only with light weapons, pathfinder teams slept in clandestine patrol bases, essentially hide sights set up in a circular formation, feet toward the center, in hard to find, heavily vegetated areas. Every man slept with his boots on, ready to run or fight. One man remained awake at all times to monitor the radio and watch and listen for the enemy. The site would be protected by several claymore anti-personnel mines (each pathfinder carried one), with the firing wire led back to the radio man, who could detonate them if the patrol base was compromised. Should this happen, the three men facing the intruders would throw smoke grenades and lay down suppressive fire while the rest moved away 50m or so. They would then throw smoke and cover their buddies as they disengaged. In this way, in theory at least, the team might shake off their pursuers and continue the mission. In the field, we carried huge loads, even for paratroopers, including only limited rations. Accordingly, long duration missions or extreme weather were a challenge, and our troopers were often hungry, wet and tired, like infantrymen throughout history.

A harder focus on combat training inevitably ruffled feathers. Though a combat unit, we were based on a training installation, used to using the pathfinders as glorified training aids. Here I had to be stubborn. While continued access to helicopters, ranges and so on required playing nice, Charlie Company was in danger of being swallowed by the training base. I worked out a compromise: while one of my two "line" platoons, with six pathfinder teams each, would provide support to the Aviation

Center when needed, the other would be fenced for training or real-world missions. Every six weeks they would rotate. We also introduced overseas training events like Jungle School in Panama. By the end of my first year, we were regularly jumping from every transport aircraft and helicopter in the Army and Air Force inventory (these included the C141 Starlifter, the C130 Hercules, the C7 Caribou, the UH60 Black Hawk, the CH54 Skycrane, the CH47 Chinook and the venerable UH1H Huey).

Jumping at Fort Rucker was frequently high adventure. Unlike Fort Bragg, with its huge drop zones, Rucker had only small clearings or aviation stage fields, partially covered with active asphalt runways. Tree landings were common, and pathfinders quickly developed skills in maneuvering the steerable MC1-1B parachutes issued to us. On one hair-raising jump, two young troopers collided just after exiting a C130 Hercules, causing both their parachutes to collapse. As the battalion commander and I watched, horrified, they plummeted towards the ground at terrifying speed. At about 300 feet, just seconds from impact, one of the struggling jumpers managed to deploy his reserve, and both heavily laden men crashed onto the concrete runway only yards away from us. Though bruised and stunned, they were otherwise unhurt.

On a separate airborne operation a few weeks later, a helicopter jump from a UH1H, we narrowly averted another disaster. Loaded with eight jumpers, the aircraft approached the drop zone without incident. On command from the pathfinder team below, the jumpmaster exited the four jumpers in sequence on the right side of the aircraft. An inexperienced pilot at the controls, overreacting to the sudden loss of more than 1,000lbs of dead weight on the aircraft's starboard side, rolled the Huey on its long axis dramatically to port, spilling jumpers five through eight into the air simultaneously as he fought to right the ship. The four came out in a tangled mess of static lines in the worst example of high-altitude entanglement I'd ever seen. Remarkably, all four fought free and landed safely, a testament to their training, courage—and good luck.

One big step in refocusing the company on its combat mission was to reintroduce the concept of external evaluations—extended field training exercises graded by outside experts. C/509 had for many years fallen out of the habit of being graded by outsiders, but an honest look by genuine experts was a big part of getting better. At Bragg I had gotten to know Keith Antonia, now a captain commanding the Army Pathfinder School at Fort Benning. He agreed to provide observer/controllers, and we were in business.

We trained for months until finally the big day arrived. The program was ambitious. Lasting seven days, and focused on the six-man pathfinder team as the unit of evaluation, the exercise began with a fixed-wing parachute insertion, infiltration to an objective area, and execution of a standard pathfinder mission such as establishing helicopter landing zones or parachute drop zones for aerial resupply or personnel insertion. As the week progressed the graded phases moved from day to night, testing different techniques like "the Voice Initiated Release System" or the

"Ground Marker Release System." Teams were inserted by small boat, by helicopter rappel, by parachute at night, and on foot. Fatigue, hunger and progressively more difficult missions increased the stress level. Platoon and company headquarters were exercised in tracking, supporting and resupplying the 12 teams operating independently in the training area.

I began the exercise confident that we were prepared and ready. Almost immediately, however, Murphy's Law ("if anything can go wrong it will") kicked in. Early on the first morning, as I stood on the flight line ready to load a C123 Caribou with my men, a major from the brigade staff approached. "Rich, I just wanted to inform you that the colonel will be flying this mission." I looked at him, dumbfounded. "The brigade commander is a helo pilot, and these are Army Reserve fixed-wing birds out of Birmingham. Is the Old Man checked out on fixed-wing aircraft, and is he certified to drop troops?" Clearly startled, the major replied, "He flew them in Vietnam. He's kind of nostalgic. Anyway, he's going to do it."

I pondered for a moment. Vietnam had ended 15 years before, and it was almost a certainty that the colonel had not seen a Caribou since. These were not academic points. If the aircraft was not lined up on the correct drop heading, at the right drop speed and drop altitude, and responsive to course corrections from the ground based on winds aloft, disaster could easily follow. If a mishap occurred as the troopers jumped (for example, if a jumper were towed by his static line or lowering line, or if his reserve accidentally activated inside the plane), serious injury or a fatality could easily follow unless there were perfect reactions by both jumpmaster and aircrew. As my NCOs and jumpmasters clustered around me, I answered evenly, "I'm sorry, but I am the airborne commander. If the colonel wants to fly as co-pilot, and take the controls after we jump, that's fine. Otherwise, we're not boarding the aircraft. Please tell the Old Man … as nicely as possible."

The major shot me a dark look. He knew as well as I did that the brigade commander held the power to blast my career in an instant. But I felt I was looking out for him as well as my men. Even minor incidents on an airborne operation are thoroughly investigated, and to drop troops as an uncertified pilot, especially one not checked out on the drop aircraft, could end the career of even a full colonel. I tried to look cool and calm as the major hustled off. He returned a few minutes later. "Okay. The boss says we'll do it your way." Nothing more was ever said, and at the end of my command he gave me an exceptional rating. Looking back, I admired his heart, but also his common sense in giving way to a junior officer who, on this occasion, happened to be right.

The capstone of my time in company command came in an off-post exercise at Fort Benning, about two hours from home station. The idea was to fly from Fort Rucker, parachute into a simulated "denied" area, and establish a clandestine Forward Area Rearm/Refuel Point (FARRP) for helicopters behind enemy lines. Fuel and ammunition, along with handlers, would be flown in by large Chinook helicopters once the site had been established and marked and covered with large camouflage nets until needed. The entire exercise would be done at night, and only infrared markings and signals would be used, visible through the pilot's night vision goggles but invisible to the naked eye.

Highly complex and dangerous, the exercise scared off every active duty aviation unit we approached. Fortunately, an Army Reserve unit staffed with Vietnam-era pilots jumped at the chance. They were magnificent, flying their Hueys and AH1 Cobra attack helicopters like race cars, approaching the FARRP at high speed, down in the trees, in total darkness, flaring at the last second as they neared their touchdown points. On the ground, pathfinder guides popped out of camouflaged spider holes, unmasked their infrared strobe lights, and directed the helos to their individual rearm and refuel points, manned by other pathfinders. In minutes, the mission was complete, the helos sped off and the pathfinders and their equipment were extracted, again by Chinooks. To an observer, flying overhead without night vision gear, there was nothing to see but an empty field dotted with small bushes and pines. The exercise went off flawlessly, earning kudos from the notoriously taciturn chief of Army Aviation, Major General Ellis D. Parker.

In the course of a long career, I managed to collect a fair share of medals and awards, but the most meaningful accolade came to me, of all places, in a mosquito-infested Alabama swamp in the middle of a moonless, oppressively hot July night. The unit had just completed a night parachute jump with full combat equipment and moved 12 miles by foot to a release point squarely in the middle of a swamp. From there, we broke up into six-man teams to begin a mile-long infiltration exercise, opposed by aggressors with dog teams. The penalty for getting caught was having to walk back to garrison, another 10 miles. Successful infiltrators earned an air-conditioned bus ride.

As the unit broke up into small elements to begin the infiltration lane, a disgruntled soldier—unaware that I stood nearby in the dark—muttered, "This sucks! I hate this goddam company and I hate the goddam captain! This sucks!" His team leader, a young sergeant, replied in a slow southern drawl, "This is good trainin', soldier, and the captain, he's a good captain. He's just tryin' to train your sorry ass for war. Now shut the hell up and move out!" I couldn't help chuckling. Looking back, those are the golden moments that stand out in a long, hard career. This was to know the real joy of soldiering.

And it *was* a joy. Frustrating and demanding and unpleasant and often unfair, the Army was also intensely and personally rewarding in a way I'd never experienced elsewhere. I had now completed my West Point service obligation and was free to depart for the private sector. Many of my peers were leaving. Others were sliding into other parts of the Army in career fields that offered freedom from danger, comfortable office settings, more reasonable hours and lower stress. I didn't begrudge them, but I knew now, with certainty, where I wanted to be and what I wanted to do. I wanted to stay and lead troops.

At the end of my 18 months in command I could look back on a unit that had gone far beyond our starting point. I had learned much about Army Aviation, about troop leadership and about the nuts and bolts of command. Never again would I have the same kind of face-to-face interaction with young soldiers. As my change of command approached, I knew I was leaving important things behind forever. Others would replace them. But nothing would ever be quite the same.

In the summer of 1986, Beverly and I said goodbye to southern Alabama and moved to beautiful Charlottesville, Virginia for two years of graduate school. I'd been selected for teaching duties at West Point, to be preceded by a graduate program in international relations at the University of Virginia. After company command, most officers could expect to serve as recruiters, ROTC instructors or Reserve/National Guard Advisors (the so-called "Three Rs"). Teaching at West Point, with a quality graduate education thrown in, seemed like a much better deal.

The next 22 months flew by at a frenetic pace. Though only required to earn a master's degree, I calculated that by double-overloading each semester and going through Christmas holidays and summer sessions I might—just might—be able to finish a Ph.D. in the time allotted—if I began the dissertation at the beginning, and not the end, of my course work. Knowing no better, I set to work. Unlike other graduate students, I did not have to worry about paying for school or future employment. I could afford, without distractions, to do nothing but work. And if anything, my time in the Army had taught me to work.

After two grueling academic years, my course work and oral and comprehensive exams finished, I was ushered into the presence of my senior faculty, who with beaming smiles informed me that I was approved to proceed to the dissertation phase. A week later I dropped off a finished, 400-page paper on NATO strategy with the head of my dissertation review committee. Dumbfounded, he spluttered, "This isn't allowed—no one finishes in two years. A Ph.D. takes four or five, or more!" (One fellow Ph.D. candidate was in her eighth year, writing on the influence of bullfighting on Spanish politics.) I soon found that the entire committee was against me. What to do?

Here I was saved by my academic advisor, a young Canadian named Neil MacFarlane who would later chair the International Politics department at Oxford. "Gentlemen," he said smoothly, "I've researched our policies and in fact, Mr. Hooker is right. There is no prescribed timeline for awarding the doctorate at this university, only requirements. He has fulfilled all our requirements with distinction. If his dissertation is not up to par, let us say so. But if it is, let's not hold him back arbitrarily. I assure you, he has suffered as much, or more, than any other candidate. His pain has just been more concentrated, that's all!" That drew a laugh, and I was dismissed and told to stand by. Two weeks later I was invited to defend the dissertation inside the famous U.Va. Rotunda. Shortly afterwards I was awarded the doctorate in a gorgeous ceremony on the lawn of "Mr. Jefferson's University."

I looked forward to returning to West Point. Many classmates were coming back to the faculty, and the prospect of teaching impressionable young cadets in such a beautiful setting, surrounded by friends, was exciting. I was slated to join the Department of Social Sciences, or "Sosh," a remarkable institution within an institution. Sosh instructors were handpicked not only for their academic excellence but also for their performance in the field and potential to rise within the Army. A galaxy of future generals came from its ranks, including four-stars like Dave Petraeus, Pete Chiarelli, Wesley Clarke, and Kip Ward, numerous other generals, and even luminaries like Brent Scowcroft (national security advisor for Presidents Ford and Bush) and Heisman Trophy winner and Rhodes Scholar Pete Dawkins. Sosh alumnae could be found in the White House and the inner offices of many senior leaders, both civilian and military, in the national security arena, and were well represented in Fortune 500 companies as well.

On arrival you joined an unparalleled network of bright, talented officers, and you joined for life. The message given on arrival was clear: "We expect your best. We'll do all we can to help you, now and in the future. In later years, when the phone rings asking for your help, we expect a yes." Every year, Sosh sent back to the Army a cohort of young majors, outstandingly successful as troop leaders, but also educated at the best graduate programs in the nation (though the number two public university in the nation, Virginia was considered, if anything, a second-tier school at Sosh compared to Harvard, Princeton, Columbia and the other Ivy League schools heavily represented there). They could write well, think clearly, work hard and make things happen. The downside was that the "Sosh Mafia," as some called it, was widely considered to be elitist. Personnel managers and many inside the Army looked askance at the department, which seemed to have an informal power base all its own that could bypass normal channels. This was largely true. What was also indisputably true was that the Social Sciences Department provided the Army and the nation a continuing supply of talented, hardworking officers able to excel at the highest levels.

For most of my tour on the West Point faculty my office mate was Captain Rick Waddell, raised on a farm in Arkansas. Rick's slow southern drawl and relaxed manner made him easy to underrate. In fact, he was a Rhodes Scholar with a Ph.D. from Columbia who would go on, many years later, to be deputy national security advisor and a lieutenant general. We became good friends, collaborating on research publications and debating the intricacies of strategy and policy far into the evening. To this day we remain fast friends.

My time at the Academy passed quickly, with spectacular autumns in the Hudson highlands followed by harsh cold winters. Junior or "rotating" faculty members carried heavy course loads and were burdened with additional duties. In my case, I served as officer-in-charge of the academy Model UN team (one of the best in the nation) and the Cadet Chapel acolytes, as academic advisor for political science majors and as a volunteer instructor for cadet military training in the summer. Beverly and I hosted cadets from all four classes, a fulfilling part of faculty life. Our two sons, Chris and David, were born at West Point, adding to our joy.

Life in Sosh was nothing if not intellectually stimulating. We argued, debated, attended conferences and wrote articles about tactics, strategy and the future of the Army. I found I enjoyed the classroom and the daily interaction with cadets. It wasn't quite like being with troops, but nothing really is. We were blessed with many new friendships as well as the renewal of many old.

At the beginning of my second year as an assistant professor, in August of 1990, Saddam Hussein invaded Kuwait and the Army was caught up in a frenzy of preparation for war. Most of the junior faculty at West Point were despondent. We had missed the invasion of Panama the previous year, though that conflict lasted a few weeks at most and involved only a relatively small part of the active force. Operation *Desert Shield/Desert Storm* promised to be a massive deployment, going up against the world's fourth largest army. Here we were, safely out of the way teaching cadets, while half the divisions in the Army ramped up for war. I wrote a dozen or more letters, to every former boss I could think of, asking to be sent, but to no avail.

A few months before the start of the ground war, I was approached by the department executive officer, who informed me that the Academy had been asked to provide 25 officers for the war, and that two would be sent from Sosh. Even better, I had been selected as one of the two. My excitement was quickly dashed, however. The next day I was told that upon reflection our leadership had decided that two permanent faculty members would go instead. My dad, by now a retired colonel fishing on the Chesapeake, counseled me to be philosophical. Sooner or later, my turn would come.

After a lengthy buildup lasting six months, the Gulf War kicked off on January 16, 1991, with an intense air campaign lasting some six weeks. On February 23, a massive ground force breached Iraqi defenses at the Saudi border. In four days, the war was over. A shattered Iraqi Army fled north, and Kuwaiti sovereignty was restored. For the first time since World War II, America and her allies had achieved a decisive victory in major theater war.

The keys to our success were not hard to discern. Clear but limited objectives, strong congressional and popular support, willing allies, and overwhelming force carried the day with few casualties at surprisingly low cost. Above all, we were favored by expert leadership, from President Bush on down. In later years, these lessons would be jettisoned by both Democratic and Republican administrations. Instead, we would embark on overly ambitious campaigns with fewer resources, lacking key allies and with far weaker support. For me, then and now, the Gulf War is a clear example of what right looks like.

In my final year I was buttonholed by Colonel Earl Walker, my immediate boss at the time, and asked if I'd be interested in applying for the White House Fellowship.

I knew vaguely that a few prominent Army generals like Colin Powell had been White House Fellows, and that Sosh had been extremely successful at preparing its officers for the competition, which was fierce. I filled out the application (some 50 pages long), and much to my surprise was selected, first for the regional round of interviews and later for the final round. There I was amazed at the talent I had to contend with. More than 4,000 civilian and military applicants had been winnowed down to 35. I was sure I would not beat my own Sosh colleague, Major Rob Gordon, also a finalist and former aide to General Powell as well as an alumnus of Princeton's graduate school of international affairs. Much to my surprise, both Rob and I survived, and late in the summer of 1992 we were off to the White House.

I showed up in the waning days of the George H. W. Bush administration and was assigned to the Office of National Service, the famous "Thousand Points of Light" community volunteer initiative. The office was housed, with most of the president's staff, in the elegant "Old Executive Office Building," the former State, War and Navy Department building immediately adjacent to the White House. Built in the style of the French Second Empire, with high-vaulted ceilings and elegant brass work, it was an awe-inspiring setting. I was thrilled to be there. With the election just nine weeks away, the White House was in a furor, and it was fascinating to see. Though coming off successful interventions in Panama and the Gulf War, the Bush administration faced a stagnant economy and Ross Perot was draining Republican votes away with an insurgent third-party candidacy. Still, Bush's defeat by Governor Bill Clinton came as a shock to the White House staff. Depression and malaise set in, as outgoing staffers scrambled to find jobs in the private sector. Inside the Beltway, government ground nearly to a halt as the "interagency" froze up, deferring all major policy work until the new team could take office.

A few days after the election the entire White House staff was summoned to the East Room, which was soon packed with hundreds of bewildered onlookers. Soon the Marine Band struck up "Hail to the Chief," a cloud of Secret Service agents parted the crowd, and in strode Dana Carvey, waving and pointing in his "Saturday Night Live" persona as President Bush. The president and first lady followed behind as Carvey gave a hilarious short speech. The impromptu event proved a tonic, cutting through the tension and despair of the lost election, reviving spirits and reassuring the president's faithful that life would go on.

President Bush had one more moment in the sun, however, before leaving office. For months, the international media had focused on the human catastrophe taking place in Somalia in the Horn of Africa. American involvement in Somalia grew out of a pre-existing Cold War fear of Soviet intervention in this part of Africa. Emerging from British and Italian colonialism in 1962, Somalia quickly succumbed to tribal strife. Under General Siad Barre, military dictator from 1969 until his ouster in 1992, Somalia embraced socialism and Soviet assistance until Moscow's tilt towards Ethiopia in the mid-80s. Thereafter, Somalia inclined toward U.S.

sponsorship, receiving arms and assistance before degenerating into civil war in 1990. In January of 1991 Barre was defeated by General Mohammed Farah Aidid, leader of the Habr Gidr sub-clan and a product of Italian and Soviet military schooling, with Barre fleeing into exile in Nigeria. A victorious Aidid occupied south Mogadishu, the capital and only major port of entry in the country. For the next year, rival clans battled for supremacy before agreeing to an uneasy ceasefire on March 3, 1992.

By that time, the international community stood horrified at the images of mass starvation beamed into its living rooms by CNN. Up to 300,000 Somalis are thought to have perished in the year preceding the ceasefire. One authoritative government source reported the probable death of 25 percent of all Somali children. In April, a small team of unarmed UN observers arrived to monitor the ceasefire, and in August a major UN-sponsored humanitarian assistance mission began.

Supported by U.S. flights out of Mombasa, Kenya, and a Pakistani troop presence at the port of Mogadishu, the UN mission *UNISOM I* (called Operation *Provide Relief* by the U.S. military) faltered quickly. Although large quantities of relief supplies arrived in Somalia, they were quickly looted or hijacked, while relief workers were assaulted and killed. Aid workers operating inside Somalia reported that food supplies were being intentionally denied to targeted populations and rival clans, spawning a man-made famine of epic proportions. In the fall, the UN reassessed its operations and called for major troop contingents from participating countries to provide military security for the humanitarian assistance mission.

At this point President Bush, above all a humane and decent man, made the fateful decision to lead a large-scale international intervention to halt the mass starvation which had shocked the world. The president seemed personally moved by the vast scale of the suffering in Somalia. As a defeated president, he could garner no political benefit or advantages from intervention in Somalia, and no American vital interests were engaged. But still he acted. His guidance was simple and direct: get in fast and stop the dying. The administration's policy focused almost exclusively on providing security for humanitarian assistance, with no mention of nation building or long-term stability operations.

Beginning in early December, large numbers of U.S. troops began moving towards the Horn of Africa. At month's end more than 28,000 Marines and soldiers from the 1st Marine Expeditionary Force (I MEF) and 10th Mountain Division had arrived. A combined joint task force called UNITAF (for Unified Task Force) was established under I MEF's commander, Lieutenant General Robert Johnston, at the former U.S. Embassy compound; it controlled all U.S. and UN forces. UNITAF fielded 37,000 soldiers from 26 nations, including sizable contingents from France, Italy, India, Pakistan, Belgium, and Egypt. However, the U.S. was firmly in charge, providing the commander and 25,000 soldiers and Marines, in addition to much of the logistical and financial support.

Based in Mogadishu, but with major elements in outlying cities like Bale Dogle, Baidoa, Oddur, Merca and Kismayu, UNITAF quickly established order. The force that went into Somalia that December was muscular and well armed, with liberal rules of engagement that allowed U.S. soldiers to engage any armed Somalis thought to pose a threat.

In addition to overwhelming military force, the American-led intervention featured a small but experienced diplomatic effort, headed by U.S. Special Envoy Robert Oakley. With former assignments as a senior NSC staffer and as ambassador to Pakistan, Zaire and Somalia, Oakley was well known to the major faction leaders and well versed in internal Somali politics and rivalries. Significantly, Oakley's U.S. Liaison Office or USLO (in the absence of a functioning central government there was no U.S. Embassy) was sited near Aidid's personal residence in south Mogadishu and was guarded by only six U.S. Marines.

One morning in mid-December, I was called into the spacious, high-ceilinged office of my boss, assistant to the president Greg Petersmeyer. He came quickly to the point. "I just had breakfast in the White House mess with Dick Clarke from the NSC. He wants to see you. Run up to the third floor and see what he wants." Wondering what this was about, I went off to find out who the hell Dick Clarke was. The last I'd heard, he was the host of *American Bandstand*!

Richard A. Clarke, it turned out, headed the Office of Global Affairs at the NSC. Intelligent, forceful and abrasive, he was renowned as a bureaucratic infighter who made few friends. Our interview was brief and to the point. "I understand you are an infantry officer. Petersmeyer tells me there's not much for you to do these days. Bob Oakley needs a military assistant over there. I want you to catch a plane to Mogadishu tomorrow and link up with Oakley. You'll get everything you need from the Marines once you get there. For the purposes of this mission, you'll be seconded to the NSC. Keep us apprised every day of what's going on. You have any problems, tell them to call this number. Any questions?"

I had about a million, but shook my head and said, "No sir." "Right," Clarke said. "That's all." Dazed, I backbriefed Petersmeyer, who laughed and said, "You'd better get busy." After a quick call to Beverly, I ran downstairs to the White House Medical Office and asked for a complete program of vaccinations. On the way home that night, I stopped at an Army Navy surplus store and bought a desert camouflage uniform. The next day, with nothing else but a shaving kit and a poncho liner, I had Beverly drive me to Dover Air Force base outside Washington.

I'd done Grenada before we met, but this was our first deployment as a married couple. It had come out of nowhere, and I couldn't tell her much—not even when I'd be back. The news coverage of Somalia was awful, and I knew she was worried. Still, with our two small boys in the back of our Saab, she dropped me off with a kiss and a brave smile. She would do it six more times, each time with that same brave smile.

Inside the terminal, a sort of comedy quickly ensued. "Yes," the airman behind the counter told me, "We have a C5 leaving at midnight for Mogadishu and there are empty seats. But you don't have orders or a slot number or anything. You can't just show up and get on a plane and go to Somalia. It doesn't work that way." I asked to see his captain, then a colonel, both of whom said the same thing. Flustered, at this point I remembered Clarke's admonition. "Colonel," I said as casually as I could, "I was told that if there was any trouble to just have you call this number." Reluctantly he took the number and dialed it. A crisp, business-like voice at the other end was heard to say, "General Scowcroft's office." Retired Lieutenant General Brent Scowcroft was the national security advisor. The colonel hurriedly hung up. My bona fides now established, I boarded the plane for the long flight to Africa.

I arrived at the airfield in Mogadishu on December 17 and quickly hitched a ride to Oakley's compound with a group of passing Marines. My first sensation was the smell, a pungent mixture of burning wood smoke and open sewage I would encounter many more times in what we delicately call the "developing world." The short ride to the USLO was shocking. Mogadishu was absolutely ruined. Virtually every building was damaged. Street paving had been ripped up, street signs torn down, windows shattered and even power lines stripped for the copper wiring inside. In the distance, small arms fire crackled as the factions skirmished with each other.

Given the widespread destruction I was surprised to find USLO set up in a nearly intact villa with a charming garden. It was rented from the CONOCO oil company, who had paid off all sides to protect their buildings and physical plant against the day when Somalia might settle down again (that day would be far away indeed). Inside I met a cheerful Air Force colonel, Dick Mentemeyer, who had been seconded by U.S. Central Command (CENTCOM) in Tampa to serve as Oakley's military advisor. With a friendly handshake, he exclaimed, "Didn't know you were coming, but glad to see you! Let's go see the Old Man." In a moment I was ushered in to meet the ambassador.

Robert Oakley was a legend in the Foreign Service. One of only four to hold the rank of career ambassador at the time, he was by far the most qualified diplomat for the job, well known to the players in Mogadishu and in Washington. Tall, spare, angular, Oakley was not an extrovert, but he exuded wisdom, experience and common sense. I quickly came to value all three, as well as the twinkle in his eye which bespoke an innate sense of humor, even in crisis.

"What have we here?" he drawled as I reported myself. "I didn't ask Dick Clarke or anyone else for a military assistant. Still, glad to have you. We can use the help. Tell you what. Get settled in, then head over to the embassy. We'll have you be our liaison to the military while we're here. The colonel here will fill you in. And by the way, Captain. You're not to communicate with the White House for any reason. Any reason. Clear?" Relieved on that score, I gave Oakley a big smile.

First, I had to get kitted out. As directed, I met with the Marine headquarters commandant, explained my situation, and asked for an issue of basic equipment, beginning with a weapon. He indignantly refused. Clearly, inter-service cooperation had its limits. Suddenly inspired, I looked up the Army Special Forces staff element attached to the headquarters, where a very non-bureaucratic sergeant squared me away with some boots and uniforms.

That still left the problem of a weapon. Gunfire crackled non-stop around Mogadishu and to go around unarmed was crazy. I returned to the USLO compound, where the caretaker, an ex-French para named Raymond, listened sympathetically. He was something of a legend. Raymond carried an M79 grenade launcher and a Glock pistol everywhere, accompanied by a dozen fanatically loyal Somalis, all veterans of many years of street fighting. "Did you bring any cash?" he inquired. "About $300," I replied. "Bon. Give it to me and I'll be back in an hour." True to his word, he left for a quick visit to the Bukhara arms bazaar downtown, returning shortly with a 9mm Beretta handgun and a brand-spanking new Israeli Galil assault rifle and three magazines. (I gave them both to Raymond when I returned home, as he probably knew I would. That may explain the discount price!) I felt safer already.

That night, I attended the nightly briefing at UNITAF as usual, when a Marine colonel confronted me. "That is a non-standard weapon. I'm confiscating it. Hand it over." Still smarting from my earlier reception at the hands of the Marines, I resisted. "All due respect, Colonel, but I don't work for you. I'm assigned to the ambassador. And since nobody around here will issue me a weapon, I'm keeping this one."

And so, the adventure began. USLO was staffed with about 25 State Department and USAID staff members. Most were young and hungry but experienced in the region. Many were women. All, it turned out, were fearless and committed. The team slept side by side on cots in a large common room, sharing a single bathroom and coming together for communal meals and staff meetings. I quickly settled into a regular "battle rhythm," attending morning and evening staff briefings at the former U.S. Embassy compound, now occupied by I MEF/UNITAF, coordinating Ambassador Oakley's movements and travel with the military staff, and then briefing Oakley and his staff on the military situation afterwards.

On the ground, Lieutenant General Johnston and Oakley worked closely to coordinate political and military efforts to rush humanitarian assistance to threatened areas. I MEF provided senior, experienced liaison officers to meet regularly with USLO and with UN and relief agencies (one, Colonel Mike Hagee, went on to become the 33rd commandant of the Marine Corps). Both military and civilian representatives worked together in Civil-Military Operations Centers in the capital and in outlying areas to plan and execute humanitarian assistance operations. Somalia was organized into large Humanitarian Relief Sectors, each placed under a capable coalition unit, to ease coordination and command and control challenges. Somali leaders were brought together frequently to hammer out solutions to local conflicts in meetings brokered by Oakley in the neutral setting of the USLO compound.

One of my duties was to facilitate these meetings of local leaders. Mogadishu was more or less partitioned into two armed camps. Aidid's Habr Gidr clan controlled the south. Ali Mahdi and his Abgal fighters ruled the north. The so-called "Green Line" divided the city down the middle. Almost daily I would head off across town accompanied by a young Foreign Service officer and a Somali driver, who carried an AK47 and chewed constantly on the narcotic khat, a ubiquitous Somali stimulant. Interestingly, both driver and vehicle were rented from Mohammed Farah Aidid, victor in the civil war and ruler of south Mogadishu, whose compound was located only 100m from ours. He would later become our nemesis. For now, he was a partner.

Looking back, these excursions seem utterly harebrained. Mogadishu was extremely dangerous, and we traveled about protected by little more than American flags taped to the windshield and our good intentions. On one trip a Somali male in a crowd, missing a leg and leaning on a crutch, pulled out a .45 caliber pistol and fired at me from no more than 10m away. Why he wanted to kill me, or how he missed, I'll never know.

On another occasion we were stopped by a primitive roadblock north of the Green Line. A "technical"—a Toyota pickup truck mounting a heavy machine gun and carrying some eight militiamen—appeared from a side alley. I got out, along with my State Department colleague, leaving my rifle in the vehicle and my pistol holstered. Suddenly a Somali male dismounted and came towards us on foot, brandishing an RPG7 rocket launcher on his shoulder. My diplomatic sidekick yelled something in Somali, but still he came on. At about 50m—"can't miss" range—he brought it up to firing position with his finger on the trigger. I quickly ran through my options. I could shoot him, but he could pull the trigger faster than I could get my weapon out, and his friends would kill us if the rocket didn't. We could run, but my driver would likely be killed (he was Habr Gidr and definitely on the wrong side of town) and we would be cut off, on foot, and isolated. We could try and talk our way out, but my colleague had been doing that for several minutes with no effect. As a crowd formed, I found myself desperately wishing I had about a hundred U.S. paratroopers with me. But I didn't.

Thoroughly frightened, I watched in amazement as an elderly looking Somali man pushed through the crowd to confront the gunman. Carrying a long slender stick, he shouted at my adversary, beating him across the arms and shoulders with the stick. In the distance, his friends laughed merrily. After a moment the gunman sheepishly lowered the launcher and ambled away. Clearing away the roadblock, we continued on our way. That night, Oakley chuckled as I told him the story. "Aw, he was just having fun with you. These boys aren't going to take on the USA unless the big guys tell them to, and that's not going to happen."

Both Aidid and his number two and financier, Osman Atto, participated regularly in these meetings, along with Ali Mahdi and his chief lieutenants. Aidid was tall, lanky, with sharp features and a cunning and intelligent if not intellectual air. Atto was more heavy set, a multimillionaire who nevertheless had a reputation for ruthlessness (he once crossed the Green Line into enemy territory to recover a prized vehicle, a Toyota Landcruiser, stolen from him, killing the thieves personally). At the outset, Somali factional leaders were told politely but firmly that, while the intention was not to impose any particular ruler or system of government in Somalia, no armed threat would be permitted to challenge U.S. or UN troops. All "technicals" were required to be stored in monitored cantonment areas, and no weapons could be carried visibly in public.

The results were immediate and dramatic. By the end of December, massive amounts of food aid were flowing freely and the death toll from starvation had dropped exponentially. Armed clashes between warring factions had declined precipitously and U.S. casualties were low. Although nominally a UN operation, Operation *Restore Hope* was clearly a U.S.-led effort. Both Aidid and Ali Mahdi, anxious to position themselves as future national leaders with U.S. backing, generally cooperated with U.S.-sponsored initiatives to encourage local and regional cooperation. In Mogadishu and elsewhere, joint councils actually emerged to manage port operations, police functions and other forms of public administration. The process was not smooth. Simmering clan tensions and occasional clashes persisted and attempts to encourage cooperation between rival factions failed as often as they succeeded. Still, the primary task of "stopping the dying" was a major success. Throughout December and January, the U.S. approach was consistent and focused: don't take sides, focus on the humanitarian mission, and avoid direct confrontation where possible—and when not, act forcefully and directly.

Early on, it became clear that the port operations, the lifeline of the relief effort, were in chaos. As might be expected, the Navy had assumed control at the outset, but running a large civilian port was actually far outside their expertise. In a planning meeting, I mentioned that I was not a subject matter expert but understood that the Army Reserve included harbor masters for this very purpose. A call went out, and in short order, Chief Warrant Officer Eddie Johns arrived to take charge.

In civilian life, Chief Johns was a harbor master at the Port of Baltimore, where coping with fractious city officials, difficult union bosses, and local organized crime were part of the job description. His transition to our environment in Mogadishu was rapid and high impact. In very short order, Johns had sorted out the local clan dynamics, wage structure, porterage and lighterage, warehousing, stevedore work gangs, port security, customs and excise, pilotage, marine safety inspections, and a hundred other details. He brooked no interference from senior military officers and ran his domain with a cold competence that was awesome to behold. Pilferage declined dramatically and port throughput jumped almost immediately. Here was a very special professional.

As UNITAF expanded out into the countryside, Oakley often preceded military units by flying in the day before to coordinate with local leaders. He traveled with almost no security, but was often accompanied by two young FSOs, John Fox and Don Teitelbaum. Both were incredibly brave. (Teitelbaum was named ambassador to Ghana in 2008.) I developed a lifelong admiration for U.S. diplomats and aid workers, willing to go into dangerous environments with little or no protection. In later years, I would often remind military colleagues, complaining that "State just won't get into the fight," that seven U.S. ambassadors had been killed in the line of duty since the 1960s, though no U.S. generals or admirals had been.

On December 23, several intelligence officers struck a mine just outside Bardera, in the Juba River valley east of the Kenyan border. Three were wounded and one, former special operations soldier Lawrence Freedman, was killed. We learned about the incident from CNN, which frequently moved more quickly than the military or intelligence agencies in passing real-time information. Back home, Beverly was at work with an engineering firm in Washington when a colleague told her, "There's a report that the ambassador's military assistant was just killed by a landmine in Somalia." For six hours she thought she was a widow, until I was able to place an INMARSAT phone call to reassure her. This incident marked the first U.S. fatality in Somalia. It would not be the last.

Meals at USLO seemed to materialize at regular intervals, but I never learned who prepared them or where they came from. At noontime one day, as I returned from a meeting, I noticed an adorable baby goat tethered to a tree in the courtyard. I began to pet and play with the kid until Raymond happened by. "Don't get too attached, *mon ami*," he warned me. "That's your lunch there!"

Christmas Eve 1992 was spent memorably on the compound roof with Fox, Teitelbaum and a group of other young FSOs determined to celebrate regardless of conditions. Though a military officer, I was assigned to the U.S. diplomatic mission and so did not fall under the famous "General Order No. 1" which proscribes alcohol on operations. Though I was careful not to overindulge, we made merry over red wine and cigars late into the evening, as Mogadishu lit up—like every night—in a sparkling crescendo of tracer fire and explosions. We could not be sure what tomorrow might bring. But that night, we enjoyed being young and alive.

A few days later I visited a small village about 40km north of Mogadishu with several USAID officers. There I met Valerie Place, a young aid worker working with Irish Concern, a relief agency focused on delivering food and medical assistance to impoverished Somalis. Valerie was young, energetic and committed, but seemingly oblivious to the dangers of working virtually alone in the middle of a war zone. During a tour of the small village, she said, "Look around. What's missing?" I noted, "Children—there are almost no young children." She said, "That's right. Probably a third die before age five due to disease. And when food is short, the adults eat first. That's Somalia." Seeing my reaction she added, "Don't be too judgmental. People here live close to the edge of survival. In this culture, you can always have more children when times get better. You can't if you're dead." I pondered that for a moment. Though not a Western sentiment, I had to admit that in a curious and maybe twisted way, there was a certain logic in that.

Once a week Valerie would drive down to Mogadishu to pick up the payroll for her Somali employees and consult with her bosses. I warned her that traveling without security was unwise. The cash and her vehicle and radio alone made her a tempting target. She laughed off my concerns, but on February 22, 1993, she was ambushed and killed by bandits on her weekly money run. Valerie was a pure soul, the kind of person you remember long after others fade from memory. But her purity was not enough to protect her in a place like that.

After a few days, Ambassador Oakley began to involve me in more substantive things. More and more often I was asked to draft cables and summarize intelligence reports. We began to see more and more reporting about a shadowy Islamic extremist group trying to establish a foothold in Somalia. One report in particular identified a Saudi Arabian jihadi named Osama bin Laden as a key figure in the movement of more than 5,000 RPG launchers and rounds into the country. Most intelligence agencies discounted these reports on the grounds that the Somali brand of Islam was fairly casual and not receptive to extremist groups. That may have been true at the time. But six months later U.S. and coalition troops began to encounter the RPG in massive numbers.

I also began to attend meetings at UNITAF and to interact with more senior figures. One was Brigadier General Anthony Zinni, the UNITAF J3 or operations officer. Zinni was jovial, a short, square, physically powerful officer with arms like Popeye and a sharp mind (he would move with light speed from one to four stars and would be named commander in chief of U.S. Central Command, overseeing the entire Middle East, only four years later). Zinni was clearly the center of gravity of the military effort, a leader with boundless energy, real charm—and the ability to hide a steel fist in a velvet glove.

Early in January, I attended a meeting of all the major and minor clan leaders in the Mogadishu area at UNITAF headquarters. Zinni politely greeted the Somali leaders before coming to the point. "Gentlemen, we've asked for your cooperation, but several of our convoys have been fired upon in the past few days." He held out an open hand. "Here are some of the bullets taken from our vehicles. We know your young men do not do this without your permission. Please have no illusions. If this continues, we will be forced to act."

On January 7, after another incident, the Marines put up a flight of four Super Cobra attack helicopters and destroyed a cantonment area, killing and wounding more than 30 Somali militiamen. I remember the incident well, as the helos hovered just above our compound while the spent casings rained down around us. The target was in Aidid's part of town, but the incident might well have been carried out by rival tribes hoping to provoke a response. In the surreal logic of Somalia, all understood the deal. The warning had been fairly given. Aidid was expected to control his turf and his men. Unquestionably he had failed to do so, and the response was within the rules. Life was cheap, and a few dozen foot soldiers were easily replaced.

On January 10, things became more personal. Among other duties, I supervised the Marine security detail at USLO, six Marines under a young sergeant, usually posted on the compound roof at night. They relished this detail, as CNN rented the compound next door; the Marines often watched, with excellent night vision gear, the urgent, late-night couplings of amorous reporters and staff on the compound roof. I usually slept topside in the open air, while the ambassador slept in a bedroom below, guarded by four more State Department security officers for close protection.

At about midnight our world exploded when a fusillade of shots erupted, sending dozens of bullets into Oakley's bedroom wall. The Marines hit the ground as concrete chips flew around us, the rounds tearing past just over our heads. The young sergeant screamed, "Two shooters, west side!" I knew that in seconds, one or both would have to reload, and with seven rifles we could put some heavy lead down on them. But the adjacent courtyard would likely have civilians in the line of fire (servants often slept outside). I peeped over the retaining wall encircling the roof, to be answered by a furious burst of fire. "Okay," I shouted, "single shots only. I'll call the QRF." UNITAF maintained a small Quick Reaction Force of four-gun jeeps that could roll in 10 minutes. Moments later I was on the radio to the Operations Center. As our Marines returned fire, bobbing and ducking, I radioed, "This is USLO. We're taking direct fire from close range. Request QRF, over."

A calm voice replied, "Acknowledged. ETA in 20 minutes. QRF call sign is DAGGER 63. Stay on this push. If you need something quicker, contact Marine Sniper Team positioned at K7 on frequency Fox Mike 76:28. Call sign PITFALL. Standing by."

A Marine sniper sounded like just the ticket at a time like this. I changed frequencies and called PITFALL. "You know where we are?" A laconic voice answered, "Negative. It's a big city, Mac." I said "Okay. We're one klick northwest of the K4 traffic circle. Marking my location. Stand by." I had a couple of chemlites stashed in the cargo pocket of my fatigue pants. Cracking one and lashing it to the long whip radio antenna, I waved it frantically. "My signal is out. Can you identify?" PITFALL came back quickly. "Oh yeah. Got you solid." I continued. "See the muzzle flashes just to my west?" "Roger roger." "Great. Please shoot them."

A few seconds later a shot rang out from the roof of the building code-named K7, 800m away, followed by two more. My laconic Marine came back on the radio. "Targets eliminated. Have a nice day." I called UNITAF to cancel the QRF, and hustled downstairs to brief Oakley. He appeared to have slept through the whole thing—or at least, his sangfroid was very convincing. The next morning, we found two bodies lying outside on the dirt road, an 18-year-old male, shot in the chest, and a 16-year-old, shot in the head. I felt bad. These were only kids. Still, they came at us, in the dark, with guns in their hands, trying to kill us. They didn't leave us much of a choice.

For the first time, I now began to deal with real fear—not the rising panic that can happen in the moment, but the fear that comes after, when you have time to think. I was no longer a young, indestructible junior officer. I had a wife, and children, and a steadily growing sense of my own mortality. I had seen, smelled and experienced death. I had heard and felt bullets snapping past, only inches away. I had learned how cheap life can be. I began to be afraid, and the realization disgusted me. Each trip outside the compound became harder, the effort to mask my fear more difficult, my sleep more troubled. I began to doubt myself.

Soldiers as a rule don't talk about such things, and anyway I had no close friends in Mogadishu to unburden myself to. And then, late one night on the roof of the compound, I had a kind of epiphany. There was, for sure, something I feared more than getting killed. My real fear was shame. I realized that to surrender to my fear, to let it win, would cause me to hate myself, to shirk the fight. Close friends would pity me, and my peers would condemn me, behind my back if not to my face. In a long career I would encounter officers who stopped at nothing to avoid combat. You find them in every war. I was sure I couldn't do that. That certainty gave me a hope and confidence that never left. In the years to come I would see more death, more war, and more fear. But it would never rule me. In Somalia, I learned something that every good combat soldier knows. I learned not to value my own life overmuch.

About a week later, I was called to the phone. An irate colonel from the Army staff in the Pentagon was on the other end. He began to harangue me. I had not asked the Army's permission to go to Somalia. In fact, I had not even bothered to inform them. Who the hell did I think I was? I was supposed to be a White House Fellow, wearing a suit and tie, not gallivanting around Mogadishu. I'd better get my ass back to Washington ASAP. If I was not back at work by the inauguration, I would be dropped from the program. Then the Army would deal with me.

I marveled, not for the first time, at how moving to the sound of the guns always seemed to piss off the higher-ups. It had happened in Grenada, it had happened when I tried to go to the Gulf War, and it was happening again. I relayed all this to Oakley, who just smiled and said, "Probably shouldn't annoy the Army too much. After all they sign your paycheck. Thanks for a great job, but you better get back."

That night I listened to the call to prayer, broadcast via loudspeaker all over Mogadishu, as I never had before. I found it beautiful and haunting at the same time. At the Academy I had studied Islam and read some of the Koran. Classical Islamic scholars spoke of two worlds, *Dar al-Islam*—the "House of Islam"—and *Dar al-Harb*—the "House of War." For true believers, only a binary world existed on earth, that part ruled by Islam and all the rest. The task of the faithful was to bring the one into the other. In Somalia, we brought force to counter force, hoping to stop near-genocide. But we had stepped into something like a parallel universe, ruled by laws, beliefs, and cultures we understood only dimly, or not at all. This paradox would haunt me for the rest of my career and beyond.

The trip back involved a small plane to Nairobi and a commercial flight to Washington, with a change in Munich. During the trip I tried to take stock. What had I learned? I had formed a deep respect for the civilian diplomats and aid workers I'd encountered, for the Marine comrades I'd served with, and even for the journalists I'd encountered who in the main worked hard to get a tough story out accurately, under difficult and dangerous conditions. I'd gained confidence that my Army experiences and academic training had equipped me to do high-level, challenging missions, even if they were not traditional military tasks. I'd learned that overwhelming force, clear, simple rules of engagement, unity of command and limited, understandable objectives work best. Finally, Somalia had introduced me, in a way Grenada hadn't, to the notion that real, existential evil exists in the world. To intentionally starve hundreds of thousands of people to death for political ends seemed impossible to imagine. Never again would I imagine a world where good and reason prevailed—at least, not without real protectors. In Somalia, I had seen the Devil walking abroad.

By the end of President Bush's term of office on January 20, 1993, death by starvation had largely ceased and open clan warfare had diminished drastically. Sober analysts believed that as many as 100,000 lives may have been saved. When people remember Somalia today, they recall the trauma and the failures that came after. But *Restore Hope* is an example of what right looks like, with a clear objective, clear political guidance, ample resources, a limited level of ambition and relative freedom of action for military commanders on the ground.

I touched down at Dover on January 19 to hear that my former position at the Office of National Service was under scrutiny. Though the office would remain, the new team had embraced a new vision, focused on paid community service, and denigrating the Bush community volunteer initiative as "not a viable model." I looked about for a new placement, like a number of my classmates who had been reshuffled during the change of administrations. Here my connections proved helpful. Former Sosh professors and retired colonels Bill Taylor and Don Snyder worked a few blocks away at the Center for Strategic and International Studies, a well-known Washington think tank. After a few phone calls I was informed that I would be welcome to join the Arms Control and Defense Office at the National Security Council staff.

At "NSC Defense" I was fortunate to join a wonderful team headed by former Air Force officer and Senate staffer Bob Bell. A protégé of Senator Sam Nunn, a giant in the world of national security, Bell was a moderate Democrat with great gifts, both as a political operator and as a defense professional. Bell ran a small, tight staff that focused on managing the interagency interface between the White House and the Department of Defense. I was asked to work ground force issues, meaning the Army and Marine Corps. Like my teammates I worked hard, drafting dozens of policy memos in my tour at NSC Defense. I learned quickly that the ability to distill an issue to its basic components, find and confer with the experts, and then generate a coherent one-page memo making the case and providing a recommendation, was the coin of the realm.

Bell was a great coach, allowing maximum latitude but stepping in with wisdom and guidance when needed. I still recall the way he schooled me in the ways of Washington. In one instance he called me in to critique a memo I'd written recommending that the NSC nonconcur on a request from the Coast Guard to upgrade a two-star position to three. Just after the end of the Cold War, all the services were being forced to downsize and the request just didn't make sense.

Bell motioned to me to take a seat. In a moment, he was on the speaker phone with the Coast Guard commandant. I listened as the admiral pleaded with Bob for support. Feigning his reluctance, Bell finally gave in. After hanging up, Bell pulled open a desk drawer and said, "What's in there?"

I looked inside, puzzled. "Ummm, paper clips, index cards, manila folders—what am I supposed to be seeing?"

Bob chuckled. "Wrong! That drawer is full of blue chips. I just added another one to my pile. I could care less if the Coast Guard has one less two-star and one more three-star. But someday—and that day may never come—I might need the commandant of the Coast Guard. If I ever do, he'll cash that chip for me. And that's how Washington works, son!" It was good advice and I never forgot it. You make your friends when you don't need them. And you don't make enemies unless you absolutely have to.

At NSC Defense I was surrounded by real pros, but the rest of the White House staff was very much a mixed bag. The Democrats had been out of power for three successive administrations and their bench wasn't deep. In some cases, I found myself working with 20-something NSC staffers from other offices who weeks before had literally been bag handlers for senior campaign folks. The new national security advisor, Tony Lake, was a college professor with limited hands-on national security experience. The new secretary of defense, Les Aspin, was a powerful congressional committeeman but had no experience in managing large executive enterprises. In some cases, career defense, intelligence and foreign service officers found their way into key positions, but there were many—too many—young, ardent ideologues who knew little about national security.

One of my first tasks was to "take care of" a group of generals and admirals who had endorsed President Clinton. This was something of a new dimension in American politics, at least in terms of scale. The professional ethic denigrated openly partisan political activity using one's military status, even for retired officers. Their use of military titles, to many, violated the traditional separation of the military from politics. While so far as I knew no explicit promises had been made to reward their support, there was a clear intent to recognize them in a meaningful way. I was uncomfortable but recognized that I now worked at the interface between military and political affairs. The lesser-known flag officers, mostly long retired one- and two-stars, were rewarded with photo opportunities, seats on presidential boards and commissions, and the like. The leader of the group, former chairman of the Joint Chiefs Admiral William Crowe, had larger ambitions. Angling for a cabinet position, he was offered, and later accepted, the post of ambassador to the Court of St. James. I felt, and still feel, that retired officers should not trade on their military status to openly campaign for political figures, especially with hopes of political reward. But times have changed, and regrettably this seems to be a new norm.

As I settled in my promotion date came around and I woke up one day a major, with no ceremony or fanfare. Coming out of Mogadishu I retained a real interest in our progress there. Although NSC Defense had a hand in Somalia, our influence was not strong. The lead NSC office was "Transnational Threats," a new construct headed by the ever-flexible Dick Clarke, carried over by the Clinton team and chartered to run across the lines of most of the regional and functional NSC directorates.

U.S. policy on Somalia now entered a surreal phase. *Restore Hope* under President Bush had been characterized by a short-term focus, overwhelming force, close cooperation and liaison between its political and military components, clear political guidance and a distinct policy of non-interference in the murky waters of local Somali politics. While attempts were made to support local and national reconciliation to ease clan rivalry and support humanitarian assistance, nation building was never allowed to emerge as a primary goal. In sharp contrast, the new approach (dubbed Operation *Continue Hope* by U.S. military planners) envisioned indefinite time horizons, far weaker military forces, more ambitious and ambiguous political goals and a more idealistic and ideological tone and character. Under Bush the mission was humanitarian assistance. Under Clinton the mission would become far more expansive.

The nature of the U.S. mission in Somalia began to change almost from the day Clinton took office. His national security team lacked experience but not confidence, and within weeks of the inauguration a strong shift in policy began to emerge. The focus now changed from "stopping the dying" to rebuilding Somali national institutions, infrastructure and political consciousness; from the

U.S. to the UN; and from overwhelming military force to the smallest possible American military footprint. On March 26, 1993, U.S. Ambassador to the United Nations Madeleine Albright voted in favor of UN Security Council Resolution 814, creating a successor UN organization in Somalia, *UNISOM II*. Among other things, UN Security Council Resolution 814 committed the UN to more expansive national reconstruction and political reconciliation goals and charged *UNISOM II* to disarm the Somali clans, a fateful step that presaged the failures that would soon follow.

To ensure U.S. control, retired four-star Admiral Jonathan Howe was named to head *UNISOM II* as the secretary general's special representative. Howe had recently served as deputy national security advisor and was therefore experienced in the interagency process and, presumably, read in on the complexities of the mission in Somalia. Polished and articulate, as a military officer he represented both non-partisanship and a willingness to take direction and follow orders. As a recently returned officer with experience on the ground in Somalia I was asked to brief Howe before he left. I forwarded a memo pointing out the dangers, as I saw them, of taking sides in internecine Somali politics. So far as I could tell from my meeting, Howe had not read the paper, but focused instead on minute questions about what kind of clothes he should bring, and whether I thought he should carry a sidearm or not. I left deeply depressed.

To command American troops in Somalia, Major General Thomas Montgomery, a tank officer and protégé of the Army chief of staff, was named as commander of U.S. Forces as well as deputy commander of *UNISOM II*'s military forces (under Turkish Lieutenant General Cevik Bir). Significantly *UNISOM II* lacked a trained military staff and important communications and intelligence systems. Even Montgomery's own U.S. combat forces were placed under CENTCOM's operational control, 7,000 miles away. An ad hoc organization beset with conflicting national agendas, *UNISOM II* was poorly suited to conduct combat operations. Things soon began to go wrong.

Early in Clinton's administration it became evident that Madeleine Albright, the new U.S. ambassador to the UN, wielded a big stick. Albright was primarily an academic and a party fundraiser, though she had worked in the Carter administration in congressional liaison. USUN was her first diplomatic posting and her first major political job. She brought a strong personality to the administration but lacked practical experience and its chastening effects. Her influence on our Somalia policy was at once dominating and doleful.

Driven by a strong desire to pull U.S. forces out, the U.S. troop presence in Somalia declined from 17,000 in mid-March to 4,500 in early June as UNITAF disbanded and the Marines went home. Although many coalition units remained, most of the combat capability in Somalia left with the Americans. This dramatic reduction in U.S. military force coincided with aggressive actions to force various Somali militias to disarm. As Aidid ruled south Mogadishu with his Somali National Alliance or SNA, where UN forces were concentrated, *UNISOM II* pressed the Habr Gidr hard. Predictably, there was resistance and *UNISOM II* began to take casualties. Almost immediately, national contingents began to suspend activities that placed them at risk of reprisal. Increasingly, Howe and Montgomery turned to the lone remaining U.S. light infantry battalion for the hard missions.

On June 5, in an attempt to search one of Aidid's heavy weapons storage areas, a Pakistani unit was badly mauled. In a lengthy firefight, Aidid's militia killed 23 and wounded 59. *UNISOM II*'s Malaysian armor and American troops were unable to intervene in time to prevent the heavy loss of life. From that date, everything changed in Somalia.

Both the UN and the U.S. government reacted heatedly. On June 6, the UN Security Council approved a resolution explicitly calling for the "arrest and detention for prosecution, trial and punishment" of the perpetrators of the attack on the Pakistanis. Despite later attempts to distance the Clinton administration from this action, there is little doubt that the U.S. government not only supported but forcefully promoted this response.

Howe immediately requested special operations forces, and while the administration pondered a response, *UNISOM II* stepped up its operations against Aidid. In mid-June, U.S. forces attacked a radio station and ammunition dumps and attacked targets throughout the city with AC130 Spectre gunships (these were later withdrawn for obscure reasons). On July 12, U.S. forces conducted a major raid on the "Abdi House," scene of a meeting of SNA leaders to discuss UN reconciliation proposals. Many were not in agreement with Aidid and were supportive of efforts to end the tribal in-fighting and encourage foreign aid and investment. Nevertheless, ground troops and Cobra helicopters firing heavy antiarmor missiles destroyed the building with heavy loss of life. Fifty-four Somalis were killed, and in the ensuing rioting four Western journalists attempting to cover the event were killed by the enraged crowd. The Abdi house raid went far to unify Aidid's people solidly against the Americans and raised the conflict to a new level.

On August 8, a remotely detonated antitank mine (similar to the improvised explosive devices or IEDs commonly used later in Iraq) killed four Americans, and similar attacks on the 19th and 22nd wounded 10 more. Mogadishu was fast becoming a free fire zone, and as hostilities escalated, President Clinton approved the dispatch of a 440-soldier Joint Special Operations Task Force (JSOTF).

From my small office in the Old Executive Office Building, I read the daily cables and intelligence summaries with mounting alarm. As good as they were, a few dozen elite special operations troopers were not enough to cope with the several thousand experienced fighters we knew Aidid could muster. Called Task Force (TF) Ranger, this composite unit was built around a rifle company and battalion headquarters element from the 75th Ranger Regiment, a small detachment of elite special operators, and an aviation element from the 160th Special Operations Aviation Regiment (SOAR), equipped with MH60 Black Hawk utility helicopters and MH6 and AH6 "Little Bird" light helicopters. Small numbers of communicators, Air Force combat controllers and para rescue airmen ("PJs"), and a few SEALs were included. Crucially, the AC130s did not return. TF Ranger, led by Major General William F. Garrison, did not report to General Montgomery as commander of U.S. Forces in Somalia. Instead, as a "strategic asset," it reported directly to Central Command in Tampa, Florida.

By this time, I had left the White House for a year at the Command and General Staff College at Fort Leavenworth. The year was busy but not overly taxing, as we prepared for higher responsibilities as staff officers and commanders at battalion and brigade level. Many friends and classmates were there, and the opportunity to mix with friends, old and new, U.S. and international, was a welcome respite from the long hours I'd spent at the NSC. Still, I missed the intensity and the feel of being at the center of events. I remained interested in Somalia, pulsing colleagues whenever I could for updates and following events on CNN and in the newspapers.

I learned that once on the ground, TF Ranger immediately took the field, conducting their first raid against "leadership targets" on August 30. Five other raids took place in September. All were based on short-fused intelligence and followed a similar tactical pattern: an insertion by MH60 and MH6 helicopters, with Rangers forming an outer perimeter and special operators conducting the actual prisoner snatch, supported by a ground convoy to extract detainees and covered by AH6s aloft. These operations met with mixed success. In one, Aidid's financier and right-hand man, Osman Otto, was captured. But others betrayed the spotty human intelligence available to the Americans. In separate instances the Rangers moved against the headquarters of the UN development program and the offices of *Médicins Sans Frontières* and World Concern, leading aid agencies working in Mogadishu. Another raid netted the former Mogadishu police chief, well known as a neutral player and not aligned with Aidid. As with the raid on the Abdi house, poor human intelligence and a lack of situational awareness plagued TF Ranger operations. Significantly, there was little or no coordination between Garrison and Montgomery.

Supporting intelligence structures were also faulty. A CENTCOM intelligence assessment team traveled to Mogadishu in June 1993 and reported that the capture of Aidid was "viable and feasible," though in private, team members described the task as "extremely ugly ... with numerous potential points of failure." Regrettably, the CENTCOM Intelligence Support Element (CISE) in Mogadishu experienced 100 percent turnover in the third week of September 1993. New arrivals were provided an "uneven" transition. CISE support to TF Ranger was therefore minimal, with a poor focus on critical human intelligence.

In mid-September, the commanding general of the 10th Mountain Division, Major General Dave Mead, sent an explosive "personal for" message to the chief of staff of the Army. (This message, a "P4" in military parlance, was not made available to the public.) Visiting his troops in Mogadishu (the *UNISOM II* Quick Reaction Force consisted of a helicopter task force and infantry battalion from the Fort Drum-based 10th Mountain Division), Mead was shocked at what he found.

> Mogadishu is not under our control. Somalia is full of danger. The momentum and boldness of Aidid are the prime concern. The trendlines are in the wrong direction. Thus the mission overall and the security of the U.S. Force are threatened.

Mead went on to describe how hundreds of armed Somalis had attacked U.S. combat engineers and Pakistani tank crews in a major fight along the 21st of October Road in Mogadishu on September 9. In that engagement, two rifle companies from the QRF infantry battalion rushed to the scene, only to be forced back to their compound under heavy fire. Despite heavy losses, Aidid's militia men fought hard and aggressively that day in the face of helicopter gunships, UN armor and several hundred U.S. infantrymen.

As Mead grasped after only a few days on the ground, conditions in Mogadishu had deteriorated dramatically. Aidid was well aware of the American manhunt and the reward offered for his capture. On multiple occasions, he had demonstrated a readiness to take the Americans on directly, despite their advantages in firepower. The national contingents showed no stomach for the campaign to "get" Aidid—a number had in fact negotiated private agreements after the Pakistani massacre. With a limited U.S. force on the ground, *UNISOM II* and its American backers were in real trouble. Mead continued:

> This war is the United States versus Aidid. We are getting no significant support from any UN country. The war is not going well now and there is no evidence we will win in the end. We have regressed to old ways. Our efforts are not characterized by the use of overwhelming force, not characterized by a commitment to decisive results and victory, not designed to seize the initiative, and there is no simultaneous application of combat power, and not a plan to win quick. All this has the smell and feel of Vietnam, Waco and Lebanon …

General Montgomery, the on-scene commander, apparently did not express the same level of alarm in his reports to General Hoar at CENTCOM or to UN headquarters in New York. But he was sufficiently worried to request a major addition to his force, in the form of an American mechanized infantry battalion task force equipped with main battle tanks and artillery. This request reached CENTCOM in mid-month and was refused on the grounds that increasing the U.S. "footprint" in Somalia ran counter to the prevailing trends of policy. Montgomery resubmitted a scaled-down version, now asking for a reinforced company of Bradley Fighting Vehicles and tanks. This time Hoar agreed to pass the request to the Pentagon.

To their credit, the Joint Chiefs of Staff recommended approval and the chairman forwarded the request to Secretary Aspin. The public record does not show that the military leadership pressed hard, however, and given the administration's clear intent at the time to downsize the U.S. presence and hand off the mission altogether to the UN—the hunt for Aidid notwithstanding—Aspin's decision to deny Montgomery's request was predictable.

Even as TF Ranger pursued its search for Aidid, other diplomatic avenues were being explored. One involved an attempt to open a channel to Aidid using former President Jimmy Carter, who supposedly enjoyed a previous "relationship" with Aidid and had volunteered to act as an intermediary. Although a legitimate policy initiative, this approach was never communicated to the military leadership in Washington, at CENTCOM headquarters in Tampa or in Mogadishu. Whether Aidid would have agreed to give up his aspirations to lead Somalia is doubtful; his most likely motives were to buy time, tone down the American pressure and wait for the inevitable U.S. withdrawal. In any case, the Carter initiative died stillborn. Something was about to happen that would change everything.

Mark Bowden's best-selling *Black Hawk Down*, later adapted into an action movie by Ridley Scott, brought the intimate details of October 3 to a national and even global audience. The day began with reports that a number of key Aidid lieutenants planned to meet at the Olympia Hotel, not far from the Bukhara arms market on Hawlwadig Road. Repeating the mission profile that had been used several times previously, TF Ranger launched 160 SOF soldiers (Rangers, special operators, SOF aircrew and a small number of SEALs and Air Force para rescue specialists) in 16 helicopters and 12 vehicles at 1530. (Approximately 110 were inserted by helicopter.) Contrary to some reports, only cursory notification—not preliminary coordination—took place between TF Ranger and *UNISOM II* or the QRF. General Garrison notified General Montgomery of the raid as it was being launched, leaving no opportunity for joint mission rehearsals, exchange of communications plans or discussion of relief operations or link-up procedures under fire.

Confident that the mission would be over in an hour, normal mission essential equipment like night vision goggles, body armor and even water was in many cases left behind. Although operating on the same tactical battlefield, both the Rangers and the Army SMU element maintained separate chains of command, with the senior SMU officer aloft in a command-and-control aircraft and the senior Ranger commander (Lieutenant Colonel Dan McKnight) in charge of the ground vehicle convoy. On the objective, a Ranger captain and SMU captain commanded their respective elements, but neither was designated as the on-scene ground commander. General Garrison exercised overall command from his operations center at the airfield.

Although Somali lookouts reported the launch of the aircraft carrying the raid force, the operation went according to plan until a 160 SOAR Black Hawk, call sign "Super 61," was shot down about 50 minutes into the mission. (The Somalis fired volleys of RPGs at low-flying aircraft throughout the battle with great success, especially against the larger and less nimble Black Hawks.) This event disrupted the orderly extraction of the Somali detainees and gave time for Aidid's militia forces, and for hundreds of angry armed civilians, to flood into the area. Shortly thereafter a second MH60 ("Super 64") was shot down. The lone Combat Search and Rescue (CSAR) helo, "Super 68," was able to insert its medics and Ranger security force at the first crash site but was damaged by RPG fire and returned to base. (There was no viable pre-existing plan to react to a second downed aircraft.)

The raid now became a full-fledged battle, later dubbed "The battle of the Black Sea" by the SNA. The ground vehicle convoy carrying the captured SNA leaders, led by the Ranger battalion commander, attempted to respond but came under intense close-range fire without reaching the second crash site and was forced to return to the airfield with many dead and wounded. A second, smaller Ranger column then moved out from the airfield in vehicles but was beaten back not far from its start point. At this point, one rifle company from Montgomery's QRF was moved to the American-held airfield and attempted to relieve the embattled SOF troopers but could not advance in the furious city fighting and returned to base. Several hours into the mission, TF Ranger found itself clustered around the two crash sites or pinned down inside several buildings along Marehan Road, unable to disengage from the swarming Somali militia and civilian crowds and unwilling to withdraw without the bodies of their comrades in the downed aircraft.

Unquestionably, the SNA militia and the armed civilian irregulars who participated in the battle were underrated by General Garrison and his special operations staff officers and commanders. Although poorly equipped and disciplined to American eyes, many were hardened by years of combat. Their ability to mass quickly and fight in large numbers with determination and courage had been amply demonstrated in the days and weeks preceding the October 3 raid. The local SNA commander, Colonel Sharif Hassan Giumale, had trained for three years in Russia and later in Italy, fought in the Ogaden against Ethiopia and commanded a brigade in the Somali National Army before joining Aidid during the civil war. Several of his subordinates were similarly experienced. Well equipped with RPGs and small arms, they had noted the American tactical pattern and its weaknesses. And they were fighting in their own neighborhoods, in front of their families and their clan leaders. Their effectiveness would be grudgingly admitted after the fight, if not before.

At this point, near sundown, the survival of the raid force was in question. Dozens had been killed and wounded, at least two separate rescue attempts had failed, more armed Somalis were arriving by the hour, and ammunition was running dangerously low. Of the seven troop-carrying Black Hawks available, five were no longer flyable.

Several special operations soldiers died in the field because medical evacuation by air or ground was impossible. Although Aidid's fighters had suffered serious losses they maintained relentless pressure on the Americans through the night. By most accounts, only the dauntless actions of the AH6 Little Bird pilots, flying all night long, kept the besieged Americans alive through the night.

As night fell, General Garrison concluded that the survival of the force was at risk and requested assistance from *UNISOM II*. Over four hours, U.S. liaison officers worked feverishly to coordinate a rescue force consisting of Malaysian armored personnel carriers, Pakistani tanks, and two companies from the QRF infantry battalion of the 10th Mountain Division. The 70-vehicle rescue force, accompanied by special operations personnel from Garrison's headquarters and TF Ranger support units, moved out at 2315 and painfully fought its way to the encircled Rangers and special operators, reaching them at 0155.

Most of the survivors were wounded at this point. Moving in vehicles and on foot, and carrying their dead and wounded, the dazed Americans retreated to a soccer stadium just outside the combat zone as dawn broke over Mogadishu. Though they had fought hard to recover their dead, the bodies of two special operators, as well as the dead aircrew and passengers of Super 61 and Super 64, remained behind. Of the TF Ranger troops who had come to Somalia and entered the fight, 17 were dead. 106 were wounded. The Rangers were hard hit, with almost every participant killed or wounded.

Although General Garrison attempted to portray the mission as a success on the grounds that the targeted SNA leaders had been captured, the raid quickly came to be seen as a military and political fiasco. Almost immediately, the Clinton administration came under fierce criticism. Even as a heavy mechanized force was sent in to stabilize the situation, TF Ranger departed and the hunt for Aidid was quietly dropped. The following spring, U.S. forces pulled out of Mogadishu for good.

From my small study at Leavenworth on the banks of the Missouri, I tried to apply what I had learned to understand what had happened. The causes of failure in Mogadishu, it seemed to me, were not apparent only in hindsight. In many cases they were fundamental, even blatant; they could, and should, have been identified in advance.

At the political and strategic level, the Clinton administration failed to provide specific, coherent goals and objectives that could be translated into concrete tasks and missions on the ground in Somalia. If the policy objective was "the restoration of an entire country," then the trust and confidence placed in the UN were misplaced, while the resources provided by the U.S. were manifestly inadequate. In particular, the decision to disarm the clans, beginning with Aidid, was pregnant with consequence. It forced the U.S. and UN to abandon the neutrality that had helped make *Restore Hope* successful, at a time when American military power was growing weaker every day. And it drew the modest U.S. forces in Somalia into high-intensity combat operations for which they were not prepared or equipped. The June 5 slaughter of the Pakistanis may or may not have been planned in advance, but the battle lines had been drawn between Aidid and the U.S. well before then. Whatever options applied before that date went up in smoke as soon as the extent of the tragedy became apparent. *UNISOM II* now faced only two choices: to retaliate by taking down Aidid, or to get out of Somalia.

Inside the Beltway, an air of detachment had prevailed. No real attempt was made to secure congressional or popular support, an oversight that caused immediate policy failure when casualties mounted. Requests for forces from field commanders were airily dismissed. Long on rhetoric and short on detail, easily distracted by the pressures of domestic politics and other foreign policy challenges and opportunities, the Clinton national security team lost focus on perhaps the most dangerous foreign policy issue then in play. There was a ground truth about conditions in Somalia, waiting to be grasped. The military commanders there saw it clearly. But somewhere between the gutted U.S. compound in Mogadishu and the West Wing, that reality evaporated.

At the operational level, the command relationships established to control forces in Mogadishu proved almost tragicomic. The commander in chief, U.S. Central Command in Tampa exercised operational control (OPCON) of two separate combat forces, Garrison's TF Ranger and the 10th Mountain Division's Quick Reaction Force. Those threads came together only in Tampa. No command relationship existed between the two, though they were located five minutes apart. The commander of U.S. Forces in Somalia exercised no operational authority over any combat forces; at best he could "borrow" the QRF for short periods, subject to CENTCOM's approval. The failure to designate one officer to command U.S. combat forces in Mogadishu stemmed from the desire of the combatant commander to remain "in charge" and contributed directly to the loss of life in the battle of October 3 and 4. The presence of two major generals, each commanding no more than a few hundred combatants, in the same city during the same ferocious engagement, and linked by little more than their good intentions, predictably caused confusion and delay.

Operational level planning and the resources made available based on it were also badly flawed. As General Mead clearly pointed out, the situation in Mogadishu in September had dramatically changed for the worse. The U.S. forces present in Mogadishu were too small and too lightly armed for the mission. General Montgomery's request for heavy reinforcements lends support to this assessment, as does the urgent decision to send them in force days after the battle. General Garrison's request for return of the AC130 gunships is a similar case in point. U.S. forces manifestly required reinforcement, yet military leaders in the chain of command failed to make a vigorous case—with painful and damaging results.

Tactically, special operations forces in Somalia, lacking context and situational awareness, suffered from over-confidence, confusing enthusiasm for capability (Mead's communication shows fairly clearly that the conventional force did not). Virtually all of the advantages possessed by the U.S. military were thrown away: a small force went into a massive urban area, in daylight, without surprise, against greatly superior numbers, without adequate fire support, good intelligence or a strong reserve. Under these conditions a well-trained, well-equipped U.S. force with a clear technology overmatch fought at every disadvantage, suffered appalling losses, and came close to annihilation. These risks were run, not because hard intelligence had located Aidid, but to attempt the capture of a few mid-level subordinates.

Many tactical errors were fundamental. The failure by TF Ranger to adequately brief and rehearse the 10th Mountain QRF; the decision by small unit leaders to leave behind mission essential equipment; the bifurcated command relationships both inside and outside TF Ranger (which ensured that even individual soldiers fighting in the same room reported to different leaders from different organizations); the repeated use of the same mission template, which allowed the enemy to learn and adapt to American tactics; poor operational security which telegraphed the start of the raid; the use of fragile and thin-skinned helicopters at low level over the city in daylight; the failure to plan for the loss of multiple aircraft (not unlikely given the mission profile); the poor intelligence picture on the capabilities and intentions of the SNA; and the hesitation shown in requesting immediate assistance from the UN all reflect poorly on the commanders involved in planning and executing the raid. The American soldiers who fought the battle of the Black Sea deserve every accolade bestowed on them. But they paid dearly for such glory.

The lessons of Somalia were hard but clear. Political leaders must be unambiguous about defining the mission and the conditions for success. Congressional and public support are important and deserve effort and attention. The means provided must be sufficient to the task, in size and capability. Multiple, competing chains of command don't work; a single joint commander should be empowered to conduct operations and trusted, not second-guessed. Senior commanders an ocean away cannot control local tactical operations and should not try. Finally, the soldier on the ground in contact with an enemy deserves every advantage America can provide.

The biggest lesson from Somalia is also the simplest. The fight that took place on October 3, 1993, in Mogadishu was a small unit action, a local tactical operation like several that preceded it. But its effects were devastating, to the administration, to the nation and to American foreign policy. Whenever American soldiers go in harm's way, they carry America's prestige and credibility with them. If they fail, America's enemies are emboldened and empowered. American power and influence can suffer dramatically for years to come, with impacts that reach far beyond the original mission or policy.

Unfortunately, the tragedy of Somalia did not end on October 3. In a way no one expected, it fed into another African holocaust, one of biblical proportion. I had no way of knowing I would see it first-hand. I had no way to know I would spend endless nights wishing I hadn't.

CHAPTER 4

Let's Go!

If you, the gentlemen of this or any other kingdom, choose to make your pastime of contest, do so, and welcome. But set not up these unhappy peasant-pieces upon the green-fielded board. If the wager is to be of death, lay it on your own heads, not theirs. A goodly struggle in the Olympic dust, though it be the dust of the grave, the gods will look upon, and be with you in; but they will not be with you, if you sit on the sides of the amphitheater ... to urge your peasant millions into gladiatorial war.

JOHN RUSKIN, *THE CROWN OF WILD OLIVE*

On April 6, 1994, the Mystère Falcon carrying the presidents of Rwanda and Burundi was shot down by a surface-to-air missile, igniting a long-planned and well-coordinated holocaust that ended in the deaths of up to 800,000 Rwandans. Over the next six weeks, Hutu extremists, led by the Rwandan Army and radical Hutu militias, mobilized the majority Hutu population against the Tutsi minority to execute a bloodbath unequalled since the Cambodian killing fields of the 1970s. Alone among the great powers, the United States possessed the political and military power to organize and lead a rapid military intervention to stop the killing. Yet no one acted.

As the Rwandan tragedy unfolded, I sat in a classroom at Fort Leavenworth, completing my year at staff college. Beverly was pregnant with our third child, and we were preoccupied with family concerns, most importantly where we'd be sent next. I hoped to return to the 82nd Airborne at Fort Bragg and had even received an encouraging note from the division commander, Major General "Iron Mike"

Steele. But it was not to be. I had never been overseas, my number was up, and in due course I received orders for Vicenza, Italy, home of the Southern European Task Force (SETAF), to join the 3rd Battalion, 325th Infantry (Airborne Battalion Combat Team), the famous "Blue Falcons."

An assignment to Vicenza was a real break, a dream assignment for paratroopers. Based in northern Italy, 3/325 was descended from a famous World War II airborne unit. As an independent battalion it was provided with its own logistics company, artillery battery, air defense and engineer platoons and so on, generally called the "slice elements." Most of its officers and NCOs were handpicked. Uniquely, because of its size 3/325 had three majors instead of the normal two; in addition to an executive officer and operations officer it boasted a deputy commander (DCO) as second-in-command, as well as a beefed-up staff. The DCO job would be my new billet.

I joined the unit in early July 1994, at the same time as its new commander, Lieutenant Colonel Mike Scaparrotti. "Scap," as all called him, was a West Pointer from Ohio, son of an Army first sergeant and an experienced airborne officer, already marked out for great things. Slight of build, he was an impressive distance runner, with a calm, courteous personality that set him apart from many of his peers. Though different in many ways, we soon formed a close bond. I was not the senior major, but Scap had picked me as his second-in-command and together we began to get to know each other and the unit. Like all airborne units, 3/325 was optimized for rapid deployment by air and capable of forced entry by parachute assault. We owned our own parachute riggers and could deploy quickly from Aviano air base nearby. Although the Blue Falcons might be called upon to go anywhere in Europe or the Middle East, Africa was at the top of the list.

On my first day in the unit, I was surprised to run into Nick Keane, my old driver from my lieutenant days. Though I was now a major, he still wore E4 rank, as he had 10 years before. Nick had left the service for 10 years, gotten married, and worked as a big game hunting guide, master cabinetmaker and plumber before deciding that he missed the airborne. He reenlisted at his former rank and was sent to the Blue Falcons, arriving a few months before me. A quick word to the sergeant major, and we were reunited as a team.

There was much to do in the first week. Beverly, already seven months pregnant, found a charming house for rent in a nearby Italian village and arranged for some borrowed furniture and furnishings (our car and household goods were on a ship and would not arrive for weeks). A nursery school was located for the boys, and in typical Army fashion the wives of the unit began to swarm around her, offering meals, help with the kids and moral support.

The ABCT had been positioned at Vicenza since the early 1970s, but change was in the wind. Early in 1994, the Army chief of staff had sent a handpicked colonel, James McDonough, to "grow" the ABCT into a brigade. Author of a famous memoir about Vietnam, McDonough was brilliant, eccentric, tough and prickly. The short, wiry former West Point boxing champion was combative, sure of himself, and determined to execute the chief's mandate.

The problem was that the rest of the Army, and in particular the four-star U.S. Army commander in Europe, wanted nothing to do with McDonough or his brigade, which was designated "provisional." He was given no money, troops or authorities—not even an office. U.S. Army troops north of the Alps had been "heavy" (i.e. armor or mechanized infantry) for half a century. The small contingent south of the Alps were paratroopers, "light" soldiers. Put simply, neither group liked the other, and the clash of cultures was and always had been severe. McDonough had been dealt a bad hand.

His first actions were to cobble together a small brigade staff from castoffs and unwanted officers and sergeants. Next, he commandeered an abandoned Italian army base outside Vicenza called Longare for a headquarters. Looking about for troops, McDonough focused on disparate units based in northern Italy but not actually grouped under one combat commander. He managed to gain control of the CH47 Chinook company based at Aviano, 16 brand new D model heavy lift helicopters, fast, rugged and versatile, with crews trained in night and mountain flying and qualified to land on aircraft carriers. Next, he pinched a command aviation company of six old Hueys, along with various other tenant units based at Vicenza. The slice units were next, moving from the control of the ABCT up to the brigade, except for the artillery battery with its six 105mm howitzers.

As a provisional unit the brigade lacked the normal three maneuver battalions normally found in a standard brigade; it would take some five years to grow the brigade to full strength. Perhaps unintentionally, the brigade resembled a Marine Expeditionary Unit or MEU; both were built around an infantry battalion core, but with a command staff led by a full colonel and including aviation, artillery, engineer and logistical formations. Both were capable of rapid deployment and forced entry, in the MEU's case by amphibious assault; in ours, by parachute or helicopter assault. This arrangement gave the European Command an unusually flexible and deployable capability.

With no heraldic designation, the provisional brigade was referred to in official correspondence as the "SETAF Infantry Brigade," an arrangement which pleased no one. (Later, the unit would be designated "the 173rd Airborne Brigade," reviving a legendary unit stood down at the end of Vietnam.) At one point I suggested that we call the unit "Lion Brigade." We wore the Lion of St. Mark, the traditional emblem of the Veneto region, on our SETAF shoulder patches. It seemed apt. "The Lion Brigade" we became, for now.

As the genocide in Rwanda unfolded in May and June, 3/325 waited expectantly for the word to deploy and intervene. An unbelievable bloodletting appeared to be underway. The airborne soldiers could be there in hours, and this was what soldiers signed up to do: to go to dangerous places and save lives. We might not be able to do it all ourselves, but we knew that an entire brigade at Fort Bragg was kept on a short string, with the rest of the division coming in behind (just as in Grenada). No third-rate army from a tiny African country would be able to stop us. Yet even as the slaughter reached epic proportions, no call came.

The background to the genocide was complex. Although tribal intermarriage and blending of ethnic groups had been commonplace in Rwanda for generations, conflict between the Hutu majority and ruling Tutsi elites had marked Rwandan history since long before the Europeans arrived. Originally a German colony, Rwanda was ceded to Belgium after World War I and ruled by a Tutsi monarchy until 1959, when a Hutu rebellion forced the Tutsi from power, killing thousands of Tutsi and ending Belgian rule. The new Hutu government soon found sponsorship from France, eager to retain influence in central Africa in the post-colonial era. Large-scale massacres of the Tutsi recurred in 1963, in 1967 and in 1973. Eventually, more than half the indigenous Tutsi fled to neighboring countries, spawning a resistance movement, the Rwandan Popular Front or RPF, operating from camps in Uganda and Tanzania. Significantly, the RPF included many moderate Hutus longing for a multi-ethnic Rwandan state at peace with itself.

Years of fighting and skirmishing between the Rwandan Armed Forces or "FAR" and the RPF led to the signing of the Arusha Accords in August 1993. Brokered by the U.S., the Accords allowed for the return of Tutsi refugees and a power-sharing agreement to be implemented in stages. Under heavy U.S. pressure, Rwandan President Juvenal Habyarimana began to implement the Accords. His assassination in April of 1994 was almost certainly planned and carried out by extremists bent on sabotaging the peace process.

Within an hour of the crash, FAR units, assisted by Hutu militia (the Interahamwe), established roadblocks and began hunting Tutsi in the capital. Using lists prepared in advance and broadcasting over government radio, the Hutus systematically detained and executed hundreds of Tutsi. On April 7, the Hutu moderate Prime Minister Uwilingiyimana and her 10 Belgian UN guards were killed, along with the president of the Constitutional Court, the leaders of the Liberal and Social Democratic parties, the information minister and the chief negotiator of the Arusha Accords, along with thousands of others. The killing quickly spread throughout the countryside as military, political and militia leaders forced a stark choice on the majority Hutu population: kill the Tutsi or be killed yourselves.

Clear indications of an impending pogrom had existed well before Habyarimana's assassination. On January 11, 1994, UN forces in Rwanda (UNAMIR), under Canadian Major General Romeo Dallaire sent a message to the UN warning that lists were being prepared of Tutsi marked for elimination and that plans to assassinate key government officials were well advanced. From January to April,

Dallaire sent numerous appeals for reinforcements and a broader mandate to prevent the impending catastrophe. That year, senior RPF officials approached Ambassador David Rawson with evidence of the planned genocide. Human Rights Watch and other international human rights organizations issued dozens of warnings prior to April 6. Despite the long history of Hutu-on-Tutsi violence in Rwanda, the UN, the international community, and the U.S. government failed to take notice.

Once the genocide began, UN and U.S. officials were kept well informed of the progress of events. Reports streamed into the UN from UNAMIR, to the Department of State from the U.S. Embassy in Kigali (which did not depart for some three weeks), and to human rights and media organizations from intellectuals in Rwanda. Several dozen local workers at the U.S. Embassy, including Ambassador Rawson's personal driver, were killed in the first few days. Only days after the start of the killings, official memoranda in the office of the secretary of defense warned that a "massive bloodbath (hundreds of thousands of deaths) will ensue." The *New York Times*, the *Washington Post* and other leading newspapers gave front-page coverage to events in Rwanda, specifically detailing the massive scale of the killing. A Defense Intelligence Agency report released on May 9 described an organized, ongoing "genocide" against the Tutsi.

In the weeks that followed, General Dallaire reported regularly on the massive scale of the genocide. Dallaire called for reinforcements to intervene; instead, the UN drew down his force from 2,500 to just above 500, effectively stopping any possibility of effective UN action even in the capital area. Just days after the killings began, the RPF launched major military operations from its bases in neighboring Tanzania in an attempt to defeat the FAR and halt the genocide. But its campaign would take three months to capture Kigali. In the interim, most of the native Tutsi would be destroyed.

The UN Security Council did not take up the matter formally until April 30, when it deliberated for eight hours before issuing a resolution condemning the violence. However, the word "genocide" was specifically omitted, as its use would technically require collective UN action under the UN Charter. Meanwhile, advancing RPF troops precipitated a massive Hutu refugee exodus to neighboring Tanzania and Zaire. Various proposals to insert an African force under UN auspices faltered as member nations squabbled over who would pay to equip and transport the force. Still unable to act, the UN authorized France on June 22 to deploy a force into southwest Rwanda to create a "safe zone." Paradoxically, however, the French operation, code-named "*Turquoise*," was intended to provide a safe haven for FAR forces and Hutu civilians, France's traditional allies, fleeing the RPF—not to stop the killing of Tutsi.

In mid-July, victorious RPF forces overran the territory still held by the FAR, finally ending the genocide. Intact FAR units, accompanied by Hutu militia formations, Hutu government officials and political figures, and hundreds of thousands of Hutu civilians, fled to Zaire in the largest refugee migration since the end of World War II.

Unwilling to act while the genocide continued, the UN and the U.S. government now moved quickly to succor the hundreds of thousands of Hutu refugees massed along the border. In July, a massive U.S. airlift flew in U.S. troops and dozens of non-governmental organizations (NGOs) to provide humanitarian assistance and relief to the displaced Hutu. In Rwanda itself, the expatriate RPF set up an interim government of national unity in Kigali, by now a graveyard in place of a national capital.

To spearhead the relief effort, the U.S. European Command (EUCOM) alerted the airborne troops in Vicenza for immediate deployment. Joint Task Force SUPPORT HOPE under Lieutenant General Dan Schroeder, deputy commander of U.S. Army forces in Europe, was set up at Entebbe, Uganda. The SETAF commander, Brigadier General (later Lieutenant General) Jack Nix, was ordered to deploy to Goma, Zaire, a border town near Lake Kivu where most of the refugees had fled. His mission was to assess the situation and recommend how U.S. military forces could help. Colonel McDonough with his green brigade staff drew Kigali, where he would partner with the UN authorities and run an aerial hub from the airfield there. Scaparrotti with a contingent of 3/325 troopers would base out of Entebbe to act as a flying reaction force should either need assistance.

Though I had been on the ground in Vicenza for only one week, I was ordered to accompany Nix to Goma to act as his primary advisor and staff representative to the UN and NGO aid workers there, based on my Somalia experience. General Nix had an outsized reputation in the airborne community. The only general on active duty to wear two combat jump stars (for parachute assaults into Grenada and Panama), he was rumored to have gotten into a fist-fight with a fellow brigade commander during *Desert Storm* and was often called "Ninja Nix" behind his back. Tall, handsome and charismatic, Nix was all business. Our team was tiny, only a handful of staff officers and NCOs crammed into a C21 jet. Our mission statement would never have passed Staff College muster: "Deploy to Central Africa to conduct humanitarian assistance operations as required." On July 25, after a brief stop at Entebbe, we set down on the old Russian airfield at Goma. Establishing a crude base camp on the airfield, we were quickly joined by a Blue Falcon rifle platoon and a small company headquarters led by Captain Scott Barrington. The Air Force flew in at the same time and began setting up the structures they would need to handle a large military airlift.

With no opportunity to plan in advance, we faced a bewilderingly complicated situation. French troops owned the airfield, commanded by a frosty paratroop brigadier. They had come to harbor their traditional allies, the Hutu, and (we suspected) the Hutu army and militias who had perpetrated the genocide. These were hard-bitten veterans who considered Africa their backyard and they did little to make us feel welcome. We quickly moved to meet with Filippo Grande, the head UN official. Grande was young, experienced, suave and capable. Nix made it clear that we were not there to take charge, but to offer what help we could. "What's your most urgent need?" he asked.

We were stunned by Grande's answer. "We have 6,000 people a day dying from disease, malnutrition and dehydration. We can't bury them. The ground is solid lava flow and we can't dig in it. Tradition will not allow us to burn the bodies, and they are rapidly becoming a massive biohazard. What can you do for us?"

Grande took us out to see for ourselves. Imagine Constitution Avenue in Washington, from the Capitol to the Memorial Bridge, lined with dead bodies—replaced every single day—and you get the picture. The refugees would bring their dead to the one road bisecting the enormous refugee camp each morning, wrapped in their grass sleeping mats. Many were small children, their tiny sandals stacked neatly by their feet. Those of us who were there will remember the smell of thousands of corpses forever. Hell could not be much worse than this scene.

The next day an Air Force C5 Galaxy landed, disgorging four D7 bulldozers, the largest in the military inventory. Frantically they went to work, but the hard lava defeated even them, and within 24 hours all four were broken. Next, we organized locally hired trucks into convoys, and local laborers into details to load the bodies onto the trucks, where they would be transported many miles to the north to be buried in mass graves. Every day, thousands of bodies would be carried away. Every day, thousands would replace them.

Nix had no particular experience in these kinds of missions, but he was decisive and filled with common sense. Overnight he converted his small assessment team into JTF "Alpha." I would function as the J5, both a planner and the JTF interface with the UN High Commissioner for Refugees (UNHCR) and the NGO community. Major (later Major General) Skip Davis, an Academy and Ranger School classmate and until recently an exchange officer with the Italian "Alpini" mountain troops, served as J3 operations officer. A fluent French speaker, he would serve brilliantly. Major Dale Cremesio, a logistician and 82nd Airborne veteran, became the J4 support officer. A borrowed Air Force captain, also a French speaker, stepped in as the J2 intelligence officer. Scott Barrington, in addition to his command duties, doubled as our J1 personnel officer—not that we had many personnel issues. Captain Bob Pierce, Nix's aide, became an indispensable utility infielder, doing everything with enthusiasm and good will. Pulling from Vicenza, Nix had a few enlisted soldiers and communications people, led by an operations sergeant major, quickly flown down. We had no chief of staff, no ponderous bureaucracy, no pre-existing staff procedures. We were so small we could do only one thing: operate.

Very quickly we established a battle rhythm. We'd meet each night to update Nix on the day, and what we expected tomorrow. Skip Davis would pull together our inputs and produce a detailed, daily report explaining our progress and what we needed. It would go to Entebbe, Stuttgart and Washington. Nix established a simple rule. When deluged with silly requests for information (such as "Why did you use 127 more gallons of fuel today than yesterday?"), we were instructed to hang up on the spot. Really important people would call Nix directly. The rest didn't matter.

General Nix focused on managing the three-star in Entebbe, the four-star in Europe, and the Joint Staff in Washington. Cremesio worked the logistics flow into Goma, which quickly grew to more than 75 large cargo planes daily. Davis tied everything together and functioned essentially as Nix's chief of staff, operations manager, executive officer and sounding board. I spent most of my time at the UNHCR building in Goma, and in the refugee camps strung out south of the town for 10 miles or so.

Our immediate task was to stop the dying. The guidance from Washington was to stay small, help where we could, and get out fast—preferably without losing anyone to accident, disease or violent confrontation. Once we got a handle on disposing of the dead, the next urgent challenge was water. Most deaths were from cholera. Infected people were assaulted by copious diarrhea which could exceed 10 litres per day. Those with other ailments—tuberculosis and malaria were the most common—would die no matter what we did. Otherwise, healthy people would survive if we could get more water into them than they lost. Nix broke it down simply. Flood the camps with potable water and we'd win. Fail, and we could lose a hundred thousand in a couple of weeks.

We began with water purification units flown in from Germany, but their equipment was slow, broke easily, and required large amounts of diatomaceous earth as a filtering agent. And with capacities of 15,000 gallons per day they couldn't make much of a dent. A smart young NGO came up with the answer. Fire trucks. When you throw a switch one way, they discharge huge amounts of water. But throw it the other, and they can suck it in in huge quantities. We sent up a flash request. Within days, a C5 transport landed with a volunteer fire company from California. Amazingly, its four trucks could draw a million gallons of water a day from Lake Kivu. The firemen were not exactly svelte paratroopers. But they could work like Trojans, 20 hours a day or more. We were on our way.

Next, we had to purify the water. Another NGO had this answer too. EUCOM had flown down twenty 20,000-gallon water tankers. The firemen would fill them. Then, we'd put in a healthy dose of chlorine, the same used in swimming pools. The chlorine would slosh around in the tankers on the way to the camps. By the time they arrived, it was drinkable. The FDA probably wouldn't approve it, but they weren't there. With our fleet of tankers making multiple runs each day, we began to solve the water problem. The death rate began to drop.

In one of our daily coordination meetings, an elderly American woman took me aside. She had run an orphanage in Goma for decades and was desperately short of clean water. Could we help? I fielded dozens of requests like this every day, but my heart went out to her. Not sure I was doing the right thing, I peeled off one tanker from the last run of the day and accompanied it to her place. Sure enough, there were about 150 small children there, and none looked to be in great shape. We downloaded 2,000 gallons into her holding tanks. But that left 18,000 that would not get to the camps until morning (night runs were banned as accidents were common on the single, two-lane road). Returning the next day, I found the water gone. It had been traded to other NGOs for food, clothes and medicine. It turned out that the orphanage was regularly supplied with drinking water by OXFAM, the British NGO, but only in needed quantities. I'd been played. The decision haunted me. How many may have died because those 18,000 gallons were delayed? I'll never know, but that's a decision I've wished a thousand times I could take back.

As the crisis continued the NGOs, coordinated by UNHCR, were working their own miracles. It isn't easy to feed and care for a million people living in the open. Medical care, tentage, sanitation, and a hundred other things must be provided. The more I lived and worked with them, the more amazed I became. These people moved from disaster to disaster, living in the dirt, often in danger, for low pay and little recognition. Their technical skills were astounding, and their commitment even more so. Many knew each other and knew how to meld their different specialties for maximum effect. What they didn't know, and instinctively distrusted, was the military.

I understood their uneasiness. NGOs don't take sides; they just meet needs. Soldiers definitely take sides, often with extreme prejudice. I saw I would need to break stereotypes if I was to succeed. I began to leave my weapon and webgear in my vehicle at meetings. I'd sit in the back, take notes, smile a lot and let the experts—many of them young women—direct the show. I tried to think like one of them. What could I bring to the table? How could we best fit into the whole? What did we have that they didn't? How could we best help the team?

Our biggest ace in the hole was airlift. No one does strategic airlift like Uncle Sam. Though chartered air was coming in from around the globe, almost 50 percent of the airlift during SUPPORT HOPE would be U.S. Air Force. Working slot times through UNHCR headquarters in Geneva, we could send a request today and watch it land tomorrow, in the middle of nowhere in the heart of Africa. Suddenly, the NGOs became more friendly.

The pace was crushing, but fortunately I had help. Colonel Scaparrotti lent me a French-speaking artillery lieutenant, Sava Marinkovich, who became my deputy. He quickly wormed his way into the confidence of any number of attractive young female NGOs, earning his pay many times over in smoothing out controversies and coordinating the relief effort. Kate Crawford from USAID, a seasoned veteran of six years in Africa, partnered with me to form the "U.S. Humanitarian Operations Center in Goma." It was actually no such thing, but people thought it was, and that made it matter. We began to field queries from Washington. Visitors began to show up to see us. We found a room, put a crudely lettered sign on it, and opened for business. Kate would review my daily reports up the military chain, and I'd look at hers, to ensure we were always singing on the same page. "U.S. HOC in Goma requests …" became a standard litany. "If you build it, they will come …" hadn't been invented, but it worked for us.

Each day I would go with Kate and others to the camps. Slowly, it began to dawn on us that this teeming mass of humanity was more than it seemed. Villages, towns and even cities inside Rwanda had fled to the border as intact communities, under their former Hutu civic leaders. The camps were broken down into *arrondissements* or administrative districts, just as at home. The Interahamwhe or Hutu militia, the same murderous gangs who had perpetrated the genocide, infested the camps and kept the population under the thumb of the *génocidaires*, the Hutu leaders. Just to the west of Goma, the FAR had their own large base camp, supported and guarded by French paratroopers, with their combat vehicles and heavy weapons. (The U.S. military was firmly, and not very politely, warned against visiting the FAR by the French.) The Hutu army and militia are there to this day. For a generation they have destabilized the region and warred in eastern Congo, directly contributing to the deaths of millions of civilians.

We made no attempt to police the camps, as we had no combat troops or military police anyway except for the 40 paratroopers guarding our base camp. The size and scale of the mass of refugees was in any case far beyond our capabilities. One day in early August, on a visit to a World Food Program site, I saw a group of six young Hutu males attack a teenaged girl carrying a box of crackers. With sticks and machetes, they beat and hacked her to death before our eyes. Enraged, I drew my 9mm pistol to intervene. A serious young NGO grabbed my arm. "This happens every day out here. If you get involved, you'll be chopped up too, and so will we. Calm down." To this day I'm not sure why they killed her. I suppose it doesn't matter. No motive could justify her death. I began to feel sick at my stomach. We were moving heaven and earth to save these people. And many of them were little more than mass murderers.

Occasionally, injured refugees would be brought to NGO medical facilities. Along the shores of Lake Kivu an Israeli military hospital had been set up to treat the most seriously injured patients. The Israelis didn't treat diseases, only trauma, their specialty. The hospital was commanded by an IDF army doctor, a colonel, who had literally been through the wars; he carried a Glock 9mm pistol on his hip, loaded with hollow point bullets. As we toured his facility, I was struck by his matter-of-fact manner. "Here is a 30-year-old woman, who lost both her legs and an arm when she picked up a hand grenade. She will live, but not long, because her family will not care for her in this condition." Her sad eyes expressed the loss of all hope. She would not survive on her own, and probably didn't want to.

In another ward, we visited a three-year-old boy, a handsome lad with a ready smile. His head was swathed in bandages as he played with a water bottle. I watched, fascinated, as the doctor gave him a sweet. Instead of eating it, the toddler put the candy inside the bottle of water, swishing it around to sweeten his drink. Still stoic, the doctor said, "He's one of the smartest little boys I've ever seen. We operated on three serious machete wounds to his head. He survived the procedure, but we will not be able to contain the problem of infection. He is in this ward because he will die in the next two or three days." And he did.

All this was hard for me to process. Being immersed in death on an industrial scale is not easy for normal people. I admired my NGO friends for their ability to compartmentalize their feelings, to remain sensitive and compassionate on the one hand, and detached and strong on the other. I didn't feel I was doing as well emotionally. I began to feel, almost subconsciously, that maybe Somalia and Rwanda better represented the real world, and that the suburban, affluent, safe world I'd been raised in was the exception. I'd learned all about the anarchic international system in grad school. I'd read Hobbes' dark warning that for man living in a state of nature, life was "nasty, brutish, and short." At the time I'd considered it all academic. Here it was, stripped of pretense. Somalia had shown me that evil could be part of the normal human condition. Rwanda made me a believer.

This was not war, but danger was everywhere. On a cloudy afternoon I happened to be in the command post at the airfield when a panicked voice came up on the net. It belonged to a young second lieutenant leading a convoy of large tanker trucks returning from a water run. In the middle of Goma city he had encountered a huge riot. "They're swarming my trucks," he shouted, panicking. "We're locking and loading!" As Major Davis worked the radio to calm the young officer down, General Nix shot me a look. Grabbing our intelligence officer (who spoke French), I vaulted into my HMMWV and sped away.

Five minutes later, I rolled up on the convoy. The situation was almost out of control, with hundreds of screaming locals shouting and stamping. The lieutenant and his soldiers were terrified and had reason to be. Every truck was alive with moving bodies. Pushing through the crowd and leaning on the horn, we made our way to the front. Dismounting, our hands in the air, we moved forward. As the intelligence captain engaged the townsfolk in French, I soothed the young convoy commander.

"Turn your trucks around one at a time, and back out of town. Put your weapons away. Do it now." Grateful that someone else was in charge, the lieutenant complied. It wasn't easy but in minutes he had made good progress. The intelligence captain appeared at my shoulder. "They're angry because last night some Zairian soldiers shot two young children. They want us to help. That's why they stopped the convoy."

In the heart of central Africa that made sense. Before I could answer, from the opposite direction, a platoon of four American military police vehicles roared up, led by a lieutenant colonel. Each HMMWV carried a machine gun mounted on top. The gunners, wild eyed, swiveled their weapons back and forth. My blood froze as I noticed their guns off safe, their fingers on the triggers. I leaned inside the window to address the colonel.

"What the hell are you doing, sir?" I entreated. "General Nix didn't send you. Get your gunners down inside the vehicles and get out of here. We're getting this under control." Sent by a nearby maintenance unit who had picked up the radio chatter, the MP officer snarled back. "I'm in charge here. Shut up and get out of my way." This was getting us nowhere. Returning to my vehicle, I raised the general on the radio. Moments later he was on with the MP, snapping peremptory orders. Flashing me an evil look, the MP officer packed up and left.

By now my young intelligence sidekick had almost convinced the crowd that we would look into their problem, and the violent mass looked about to melt away. Suddenly, a Zairian Army officer roared up on a motorcycle and began to harangue the leaders. As we pulled away, I watched the enraged mob tear him apart. "Bad judgment on his part," I thought, and we picked up speed and returned to base. I lay awake for half the night, pondering our close escape. We had come so, so close to disaster.

As I struggled to cope with the enormity of what I saw and experienced, I drew heavily on my friends. Skip Davis and I shared a small two-man tent on the airfield. We slept on cots, set up on a dirt floor, and considered ourselves lucky not to be sleeping on the ground. His friendship and steady, calm demeanor were therapeutic, and he became the anchor our tiny staff revolved around. General Nix provided the clear, firm direction we needed without interfering in the details. He kept the brass off our backs, and his sense of humor and balance were just what we needed from a commander. I consoled myself with the knowledge that we were making a difference, and that thousands would survive who might otherwise die because we were there.

In mid-August, I attended a conference at UNHCR headquarters in Goma to discuss an outbreak of *Shigella* dysentery. The medical experts there projected that, unless decisive steps were taken, the outbreak would become an epidemic. Many thousands would die in the cramped and crowded camps, especially children. One group argued in favor of treating those infected with cipro, a powerful antibiotic and one of the only drugs proven to be effective. An opposing group argued the reverse; many patients would stop taking the drug when their symptoms disappeared, enabling a resistant strain of the bacteria to develop that would be immune to cipro. The debate was chiefly about saving many lives now versus many more lives later. I was able to tell the group that seven million doses could be flown down from military stocks in Europe in a day. But I was glad not to have to make the decision. In the end, the call was made to use the cipro, and we duly provided the medicines. The results were dramatic. Where almost 15 percent of all reported cases initially resulted in fatalities, medical experts were able to reduce the death rate from *Shigella* dysentery to less than 1 percent. But by 2009, more than 70 percent of reported *Shigella* cases in central Africa were resistant to treatment by cipro.

Week by week, the death toll steadily declined, from a high of 6,000 per day to around 400—almost normal for a population of that size in that part of the world. As more and more aid organizations streamed in, our contribution became smaller and smaller. Not every arrival was welcome, however. As I worked in our makeshift operations center at the airfield one day, a young sergeant approached, leading what appeared to be a group of disoriented tourists. Their leader announced himself as Pastor Donnelly from the First Baptist Church of somewhere. "We're here to help!" he proudly exclaimed. Somehow, he and his 10 companions, all clad in Bermuda shorts, T-shirts and straw hats, had managed to get on board a relief flight bound for Goma. I inquired as to their capabilities. Did they have any doctors, engineers, or other relevant experts in their group? No. Did they have a specific contribution they felt they could make? No, not really. Where did they plan to live? "Well, we kind of hoped you could put us up and feed us." I explained politely that we weren't in that line of work, and that while we appreciated their desire to help, we couldn't advise that they hang around. They left in a huff, muttering threats to see their congressman. I had to admire their gumption. But their naiveté was breathtaking.

One night, we heard the crackle of gunfire from the direction of the airfield, perhaps 200m away. Apparently, a squad of Zairian soldiers looking to loot our hangars had surprised the Air Force security police posted there. As General Nix and the rest of us stepped out of the operations center to take a look, we observed our contingent of SPs, supposed to be guarding the flight line, come sprinting past. We watched amazed as they raced to their large wall tent, huddling inside. I accompanied Nix as he confronted their officer. "Lieutenant," he asked sternly, "why did you abandon your post?" "Sir," he exclaimed, "they were shooting at us!" Disgusted, Nix ordered Captain Barrington to send a Blue Falcon rifle squad down to replace them. The next day the Air Force lieutenant flew out, never to return.

Occasionally, the relentless pressure was softened with humor. One of our gate guards approached me one evening to say that two French women were at the main gate. I strolled down to check it out. Sure enough, I found two of the loveliest, pony-tailed NGOs I'd ever seen standing there. I asked them their business in my broken, undergraduate French. Very prettily, they announced that they had come to see Lieutenant Marinkovich for their English lessons, and could I please show them where Sava might be?

As August wore on, we could see that the end was clearly in sight. The daily death toll was now in the low hundreds, the international NGO community had massed on Goma, and the U.S. military's role was decreasing in importance every day. Gradually we reduced our footprint, and by early September we were gone. We left a region that would remain in conflict, a place where many would die in the near future. But redrawing the map of eastern Congo was not our mission. Stopping the dying in that time and place was, and we had helped to do that. On our way out, we cycled through Kigali, a ruined charnel house that looked a bit like Mordor in Tolkien's *Lord of the Rings*. Colonel McDonough had done well with his pickup staff and was redeploying as well. In Entebbe, we boarded C141 Starlifters for the eight-hour flight back to Vicenza and a needed rest.

I was now a seasoned professional, a major with 13 years' service and four rows of ribbons on my chest. If I had learned anything, it was that my calling involved hard choices, life and death choices that might involve hundreds, even thousands of lives. West Point and the Army had prepared me well. I knew intellectually that death in the camps was not my fault. But I also knew that, if I had been smarter, or more experienced, or even just luckier, more might have survived. That's the downside of military life. Your mistakes don't lead to profits or losses. They can be measured in coffins. And if you are an infantry officer, fighting to be sent on operations, you are going to make some mistakes. The best you can hope for is not to make too many, and not to make the same ones twice.

As the months went by, I couldn't shake Rwanda. I was troubled by a recurring dream that I was suffocating under a mountain of corpses. Some people dream in color. In my dreams I was overcome by the ghastly smell of dead bodies, an odor that can't really be described. I would wake up and, for a few moments, smell it on the sheets. Beverly didn't know how to help, and I didn't want to ask for help. I felt, instinctively, I would have to work it out on my own. I'm still at it.

How had we allowed the Rwandan genocide to happen in the first place? That question haunted me for years—in fact, to this day. The Clinton administration's policy on peacekeeping and humanitarian interventions established a long list of criteria requiring "a showing that U.S. interests were at stake, a clear mission goal, acceptable costs, Congressional, allied and public support, a clear command and control arrangement, and an exit strategy." On its face it laid out sensible considerations. Tragically, however, it would provide the excuse for inaction that would guide the Clinton administration throughout the crisis.

As later inquiries would document, the focus of the administration's response to events in Rwanda was not only to forestall any U.S. military intervention, but to limit or defeat any reaction of any kind. At the State Department, Deputy Secretary Strobe Talbott strove mightily to squash any debate about action. At the UN, Ambassador Madeleine Albright worked vigorously to kill General Dallaire's request for reinforcements and in fact successfully brokered the immediate pull-out of most of the UNAMIR force. At the NSC, National Security Advisor Anthony Lake cannot be shown to have taken any particular interest in the Rwandan genocide at all. Richard Clarke, his staff lead for such matters, staunchly opposed intervention, pooh-poohing Dallaire's requests and asserting the infeasibility of any UN military operation to fly into Kigali. Talbott undercut any such plan by declaring, "The U.S.

is not prepared at this time to lift heavy equipment and [UN] troops into Kigali." As the bodies piled up, Lieutenant General Wesley Clarke, the J5 director for policy, plans and strategy in the Pentagon, joked weakly, "Is it Hutsis and Tutus, or Hutus and Tutsis?" Only Prudence Bushnell, a lowly deputy assistant secretary of state, pressed hard for intervention to stop the slaughter.

Even desperate attempts to take minimalist action—jamming Hutu radio broadcasts, for example, or providing obsolete armored personnel carriers to a proposed relief force of African troops—were stymied by bureaucratic delay or inaction by the Department of Defense and the Joint Staff. Secretary of State Warren Christopher refused to even use the word "genocide" until most of the Tutsi population in Rwanda was dead, fearing that its use might activate the legal provisions of the 1948 international Treaty on the Prevention of Genocide, which required intervention by signatory states to prevent the killing of targeted ethnic groups "in whole or in part." In fact, the historical record shows that President Clinton never once convened his national security "principals"—the secretaries of state and defense, the national security advisor, the director of central intelligence, the chairman of the Joint Chiefs, and other leading members of the national security apparatus—to consider the matter.

In March of 1998, President Clinton stopped in Kigali while on a presidential junket to Africa. In a brief address to local notables gathered on the airport's tarmac, Clinton said, "We come here today partly in recognition of the fact that we in the United States and the world community did not do as much as we could have and should have done to try and limit what occurred" in Rwanda. So brief was this visit that the engines on Air Force One never shut down. President Clinton's brief remarks on this occasion represent virtually the sum total of the administration's public comment on the matter. In later years, however, public documents surfaced which showed that U.S. government officials were well aware of the specifics of the ongoing killings.

Why did the Clinton administration, initially charged with foreign policy idealism, so utterly reject all proposals to act to stop the Rwandan genocide? In the months and years that followed the Rwandan genocide, official and unofficial explanations offered since the tragedy center around three themes: that the extent of the killings was not fully grasped until it was too late to act; that a military intervention was infeasible; and that the administration was preoccupied by events in Bosnia and elsewhere.

The first assertion, that the U.S. government was in effect unaware of the genocide, has been definitively answered with the release of many of the internal documents relevant to the case. The second, that military intervention was not feasible, is refuted by the history of U.S. military operations in Africa both before and after the spring of 1994. In January of 1991, U.S. Marines conducted an evacuation of the U.S. Embassy in Mogadishu in the middle of a civil war. In December of

1992, the U.S. intervened in Somalia to stop the mass starvation there, deploying more than 20,000 troops in a few weeks. In July 1994, the U.S. quickly deployed hundreds of troops to cope with the Rwandan refugee crisis. In March of 1996 the U.S. again deployed hundreds of troops quickly into Liberia during the civil war there to protect U.S. lives and property. With a Division Ready Brigade from the 82nd Airborne always on high alert, a parachute battalion in Italy (always focused on African contingencies) in a similar status, and special operations forces from the 75th Ranger Regiment able to move even more quickly, the ability of U.S. forces to intervene rapidly and decisively was never at issue.

Preoccupation with other foreign policy issues, especially Bosnia, undoubtedly confused the issue. But in the final analysis, it is more accurate to say that the leading figures of the Clinton administration *preferred* to focus on Bosnia. There, the scale of the killing was far less. Absent a signed agreement between the contending parties, there was no chance of U.S. intervention on the ground, as the later massacre of the Bosnian men of Srebrenica showed. The real, unacknowledged heart of the matter, however, was not Bosnia. The reason that President Clinton and his principal advisors not only shunned, but abhorred, any discussion of active intervention in Rwanda was Somalia. The administration had been hurt so badly by its political failures in Somalia that it could not risk a reprise under similar circumstances. A disaster in Rwanda on the heels of a disaster in Somalia would have affected the 1994 mid-term elections (where the Democrats were crushed anyway) and threatened President Clinton's chances for a second term in office. In that sense, no number of dead Tutsi were deemed worth risking the president's political fortunes or those of his principal subordinates.

Following the genocide, the advancing RPF, lacking artillery, planes, and tanks, pushed the FAR and Interahamwhe across the border into Zaire, along with hundreds of thousands of Hutu refugees. The U.S. government reacted swiftly, leading an international effort to provide humanitarian assistance to the starving Hutus. In time, many Hutu civilians returned to Rwanda, but the FAR and its militia supporters remained behind. The Rwandan genocide sparked a continuing chain reaction still in motion. In the intervening years, the FAR and Interahamwhe have continued to target Tutsi civilians on both sides of the border, playing important roles in the implosion of Zaire and its successor state, the Democratic Republic of Congo. To date, an estimated two million Africans have lost their lives in the aftermath of the Rwandan civil war in the factional fighting in the Congo. The price of American inaction in Rwanda, at least to the people of sub-Saharan Africa, has been heartbreakingly steep.

Back at Vicenza the train did not slow down. A few days after my return, our third child, a beautiful daughter we named Rachel, was born in the local Italian hospital. As the battalion and the brigade flowed back in and reassembled, we picked back up on an aggressive training schedule, with many trips to Germany to take advantage of the excellent ranges and facilities to be found there. Colonel McDonough pressed hard to train his brigade staff, but as most of the quality was found in the battalion, he found it rough going and he was forced to carry much of the load himself. This led to tension, as on major exercises the battalion often planned and executed both better and faster. Scaparrotti, who had drawn only a limited role in Rwanda, now showed himself to be a superb commander, comfortable with giving wide latitude to his talented team but issuing clear, sound guidance and reserving the final big decisions to himself. His biggest challenge was coping with the friction between Nix and McDonough.

No one rises to brigade command or to general's rank in the U.S. Army without a healthy dose of self-confidence. This is true in spades for paratroopers. Nix was young, ambitious and clearly moving fast. McDonough, though his subordinate, was older, an introverted intellectual with heavy combat experience in Vietnam in contrast to Nix's background of short, in-and-out actions. Both had strong personalities and were conscious of their command prerogatives. It was perhaps inevitable that they would clash from time to time. But the real problem was that despite the superstructure at SETAF, with a general staff and brigade headquarters, there was as yet only a single combat battalion. Scaparrotti had plenty of "help" commanding the Blue Falcons.

These tensions were never fully resolved, but as time went on Scaparrotti's quiet but insistent requests to be allowed to command his unit without excessive interference bore fruit. The team began to settle down. 3/325 gained a huge asset when Skip Davis joined us soon after our return from Africa as S3 operations officer. Nix became more and more preoccupied with a new mission to organize and train the SETAF staff as EUCOM's rapid deployable "light JTF." McDonough began to gain traction with building the brigade into a competent, capable unit.

All levels began to focus now on Bosnia, where matters seemed to be coming to a head. The conflict had begun in 1992 as a result of the breakup of Yugoslavia, driven primarily by Bosnian Serbs seeking to ethnically "cleanse" Bosnia-Herzegovina of its non-Serb populations. Through the fall of 1994 and the spring of 1995, we watched from just across the Adriatic as Serbs, Bosnian Muslims ("Bosniaks") and Croats battled it out in a grinding conflict. All sides participated in atrocities, but the Serbs were in a class all their own, committing the majority of recorded war crimes. The death toll in the Balkan wars could not match Somalia and Rwanda. Still, it was horrific—by most estimates in excess of 100,000. In the early 1990s, the UN attempted to mediate the conflict with a peacekeeping force, called UNPROFOR (UN Protection Force) made up of infantry battalions from various countries. All sides, but particularly the Serbs, held UNPROFOR in contempt. The world watched as the Serbs encircled Sarajevo, site of the 1984 Winter Olympics, in a brutal siege that recalled Leningrad's 900 days in World War II. At different times, UN forces stood aside while the factions took back heavy weapons from cantonment areas, attacked civilians and destroyed key infrastructure. In one humiliating episode, more than 400 UN "blue helmets" were captured and used as human shields to ward off UN air strikes.

UN incapacity led to a growing role for NATO, first with air strikes, and then with planning for ground intervention. Eventually, as Serbia's central role in stoking the conflict became clearer, the U.S. abandoned its position of strict neutrality and began to arm and train the Bosniaks and Bosnian Croats, who united as the Federation of Bosnia and Herzegovina. Through the spring of 1995, the Serbs grew more desperate as their earlier military dominance eroded. Bosnian Serb forces under General Ratko Mladic surrounded the eastern Bosnian enclaves of Srebrenica, Zepa and Goradze and began to squeeze them, preventing supply convoys from moving and shelling the towns.

Watching closely from Vicenza, the Blue Falcons stepped up their training and studied the situation closely, expecting a short-notice mission to go in. In May, the Combat Team was flown up to Germany and began intensive training for a possible mission to relieve the Dutch battalion in Srebrenica. None of us had ever seen anything like it. Dozens of helicopters descended on our training sites at Grafenwoehr and Hohenfels. Other units took over all support details, freeing us to focus 100 percent on mission preparation. Senior generals began to show up to observe our training.

Our preparations were nothing if not thorough, involving several full-dress rehearsals, both day and night. During one iteration I watched through my night vision goggles as a Chinook medium-lift helicopter attempted to sling load a target acquisition radar. The maneuver is dangerous; a soldier must balance atop the load and try to hook a loop onto the helo's cargo hook under the belly. Any number of things can go wrong as the giant helo attempts to hover just above the ground, in pitch black dark. After the third failed attempt, I heard the helicopter crew chief report to the pilot over my radio, "These guys are just not ready for prime time."

Switching radio frequencies, I called Colonel McDonough. "Lion 6, this is Blue Falcon 8 … recommend we call this off for now. The radar crew is not trained up for this … risk is too high. Recommend abort." McDonough was not happy, but went along. This was not the first, or last, near disaster we managed to avoid.

The plan was complex and not at all to our liking. First, we would be flown in UH60 Black Hawk and CH47 Chinook helicopters across the Adriatic to Dubrovnik, where the birds would refuel. (Air Force fighters would escort us and attack any air defense weapons that opened up on us in flight.) Next, we would fly at night through the mountains of eastern Bosnia, through heavily defended airspace, to Srebrenica, at the limit of the helicopters' endurance over distances so great that external fuel tanks would be needed. Once on the ground, we would load the Dutch soldiers and depart. Of course, Mladic could not know our intentions, and might well conclude we were coming to attack him. We prepared as though we would have to fight on arrival.

Even without potential enemy action, the distance and terrain were daunting. The commander of the Apache battalion tasked to support us told me that he expected to lose two or three helos to mid-air collisions alone; while the Black Hawk pilots could fly using night vision goggles, the attack birds used the FLIR (Forward Looking Infrared) system only, which was weather dependent. Davis and I were appalled at the air movement plan, which involved some 13 different serials landing in the dark at the enclave, spaced only minutes apart. The plan, which involved more than 80 helos of all types, was far too complex to survive contact with reality.

If all went well, the first serial would launch from Dubrovnik 15 minutes after last light, while the final serial would depart from Srebrenica 15 minutes before first light. That left no room for Murphy's Law ("if something can go wrong it will"). We prepared mentally to improvise on the ground.

An interesting dimension was the insertion. An option was always to drop the Blue Falcons by parachute, greatly simplifying and speeding up the air movement plan. From the beginning, however, this was anathema to the non-jumpers in Germany who were ultimately in charge. They could only see arguments against a parachute drop and this option was never seriously considered. As in Grenada, the great virtue of parachute troops—the ability to mass them in one location quickly, over great distances—was discounted.

Command and control were just as worrisome. On the ground, Scaparrotti and his assault command post would land at one LZ with a beefed-up rifle company. I would land at a second with a similar force. A small Special Forces element would assist with organizing and moving the Dutch to these two locations for extraction. So far so good. In the air, McDonough would orbit above to coordinate the ground force with the supporting aviation units.

Here it got sticky. The Apache brigade commander insisted on a role, though only one of his battalions was involved. He would also be in the air and insisted that McDonough pass all directives through him. The colonel who owned the Black Hawks and Chinooks was also given a role as commander of the Forward Operating Base at Dubrovnik. A lieutenant general from Germany would be in overall command from a location hundreds of miles away. When you broke it down, the chain of command was cumbersome and ambiguous, virtually guaranteeing friction.

As we trained, intelligence updates grew more and more alarming. The Serbs were squeezing the enclaves hard and it seemed clear that soon they would either collapse or be overrun. The Bosnian war was approaching a climax. Many troopers in the Combat Team began to believe that the mission to bring the Dutch out of Srebrenica was a cover story, and that the real job was to rapidly fly in to defend the enclave from the slaughter that could follow its fall. We continued to rehearse. On several occasions we narrowly avoided mid-air collisions with helos full of troops. Our worries mounted.

As we neared the end of the training program, we participated in several conferences to go over the mission. McDonough was outspoken in criticizing the many flaws in the plan. He was right, but his direct manner offended many of the commanders and generals from U.S. Army Europe in Germany. Abruptly, we were ordered to return to Vicenza and stand by. It seemed, after all this effort, that no one had thought to ask the Dutch, who apparently had no desire to be extracted by the Americans. We continued to monitor the situation closely, half expecting to be called in to save the day. NATO warplanes were now openly supporting the UN, the situation on the ground was deteriorating daily, and we were the closest and most ready intervention force.

On July 6, 1995, the final assault on Srebrenica commenced. Some Dutch soldiers surrendered, while others fired warning shots or flares, but no Serb soldiers or units were ever directly engaged. Over a period of days General Mladic and his "Drina Corps" soldiers slowly crushed the pocket. A few NATO air strikes were attempted but without effect. By nightfall on the 11th, more than 20,000 Muslim civilians had crowded into or near the Dutch UN compound. Eyewitnesses later reported open-air rapes of Muslim women and the murder of several children and infants. Numbers of civilians committed suicide.

Now the unthinkable happened. As a group of some 7,000 Bosniak men attempted to break out on the 12th they were surrounded by Serb soldiers, some in captured UNPROFOR and Red Cross vehicles. Induced to surrender, most were systematically murdered and buried in mass graves. Post-war commissions estimated the dead at between 7,800 and 9,300, including virtually all military-age males in the enclave. It was the largest civilian massacre in Europe since the Holocaust. UN and Bosniak 2nd Corps units in the area stood by helplessly, unable or unwilling to intervene.

As I watched CNN, it was hard not to feel anger and frustration. No NATO decision had been taken to intervene on the ground, but once again the U.S. government had closed ranks to head off any debate. A trained, rehearsed force was ready to go at a moment's notice. The Serbs had previously given ample reason to expect a bloodbath. Could the Blue Falcons have prevented the massacre? With U.S. airpower, I felt the answer was clearly "yes." The Drina Corps numbered perhaps 2,500 soldiers, a very manageable number for our 1,000 troopers. No one had felt right about saving the Dutch so the Bosniaks could be shot down in cold blood. But every 325 soldier would fight hard and eagerly to defend the pocket and the innocent civilians inside. The call never came. Months later, we would be the first U.S. unit to enter Bosnia after the signing of the Dayton Accords. There, in Tuzla, we would encounter the widows of Srebrenica in their hundreds, standing mute outside our wire, staring at us. I felt ashamed. We all felt ashamed. I am ashamed still.

Another enclave, Zepa, fell in July with 3,000 additional civilian casualties, but by now the tide had turned. Bosniak and Croat forces were gaining the upper hand, supplied with Western arms, and trained by U.S. contractors (one company, MPRI, was headed by a former U.S. Army chief of staff). In August, a massive force of 130,000 Croatian troops crushed the Serb defenders of the Krajina, territory populated by ethnic Serbs inside Croatia for several hundred years. Two hundred thousand fled in the largest example of ethnic cleansing of the war. The adjacent Bihac pocket, cut off and surrounded by Serb militias for three years, was liberated along with its 40,000 residents. The war was not going well for the Serbs.

I did not envy the politicians who had to make sense of the Balkans. Balkan politics were byzantine, and we found ourselves forced to align with unsavory characters, like Croatia's Franjo Tudjman, to confront the greater evil of Milosevic. All sides committed war crimes and clean hands were hard to find. Theorists often pointed out that the U.S. had no clear vital interest in intervening in the Balkan wars. Yet the Europeans seemed unable, or unwilling, to police their backyard without U.S. leadership. With 100,000 dead and the UN effort clearly failing, the pressure to act grew stronger.

The Balkan drama unfolded against a complicated historical backdrop stretching back many centuries. Once part of the Roman empire, the Balkans were invaded by ethnic Slavs following the fall of Rome, eventually becoming the fault line between competing Catholic Europe, Orthodox Byzantium and the Muslim Ottomans. They had changed hands many times and violence was stamped into their histories. To this day the Balkans remain a boiling ethnic cauldron. Bismarck had remarked, a hundred years before, that the Balkans "were not worth the bones of a single Pomeranian grenadier." Many in Washington agreed, and we waited in our cantonments as the policymakers pondered what to do.

At the height of the crisis, I was told by General Nix that he had nominated me to be aide de camp to General Crouch, then the four-star commanding general of U.S. Army Europe. Though it was an honor, I protested that I was happy where I was—and Crouch had a reputation for eating his aides alive. Nix insisted. I flew up to Grafenwoehr, in Germany, where Crouch was observing training, and was ushered into the VIP lounge at the modest army airfield there.

I formally reported to the general, a tall, stern figure. Without rising he motioned to a chair, and I took a seat. He came straight to the point.

"So, tell me why you want to be my aide." It came across as a statement, not a question, and I answered it directly.

"Sir, with respect, I'm here at General Nix's direction. I'm happy with the Blue Falcons, and I'm not looking to move."

Crouch seemed genuinely surprised as well as annoyed. "Well, I guess we're done here," he intoned, and without further ado I rose, saluted, and moved out smartly. Back at Vicenza, General Nix was not happy, but I had been honest about my lack of interest in the job and could not be faulted for that. Three months later, the unfortunate officer who was selected was fired.

One Sunday evening in September, I received a call at home from Colonel McDonough. In brief, clipped tones he informed me that I was to catch a Spanish plane out of Dal Moulin airfield in Vicenza early the next morning. I would fly to Dubrovnik, transfer to a British Sea King helicopter, and be flown to Kisseljak outside of Sarajevo. There I would assist a newly created French-British Rapid Reaction Force as a planner.

I remonstrated, as tactfully as I could. As far as I knew, we had no Americans inside Bosnia, which was at war. There were many planners available on the SETAF staff; I was the deputy commander of the Blue Falcons, a "green tab" leader often called upon to stand in for Scaparrotti as he traveled to conferences and site visits. McDonough was unmoved. Finally, I played my ace card. "Sir," I told him, "this is personal, but just yesterday I had a vasectomy. I'm not in good shape. I'm certainly in no condition to deploy." The tough-as-nails McDonough didn't bat an eye. "It's not that bad. Be on that plane. Out here."

The next morning, I found myself flying over the Adriatic in a small cargo plane in extreme discomfort. Upon landing I was taken to a British Sea King, a dilapidated 1960s helo streaked with oil stains and riddled with bullet holes. I comforted myself, as I always do, with the thought that the pilot didn't want to die any more than I did, so it must be safe. Unfortunately, this was a Royal Navy helo, and even though Bosnia is singularly bereft of large bodies of water, my crew chief insisted I wear a life vest, properly worn with a strap routed between one's legs. I demurred; he persisted. Soon our disagreement became a row, until a young flight lieutenant, the pilot in command, intervened. I explained my predicament, earning a hearty chuckle from the young man and a special dispensation. In five minutes, we were off.

The Sea King may have been old and antiquated, but the pilot was not. I'd never flown lower or faster as we weaved and dodged through the mountains. At one point we were illuminated by hostile radar, producing incredible aeronautic gyrations from our young lieutenant. I shouted at the crew chief, "Get shot at often?" He shouted back, "We don't *not* get shot at often!" After an hour or so of these aerodynamic heroics we set down at Kisseljak. I was taken to see the chief of staff, a cheery British colonel, who took one look at me and blurted out, "Good God! Whatever is the matter with you?" After my sheepish explanation he called in his military assistant, a young engineer captain. "Bob, take the major to the guest quarters straightaway. Make sure he's comfortable. I don't want to see him for 24 hours!" Bob the engineer affably whisked me away, presented me with a six-pack of Fosters, and told me to come back when I felt up to it.

The next day I reported in and was assigned to the planning section. No one seemed sure exactly what our mission was. The Rapid Reaction Force was a 10,000-man NATO brigade, operating under NATO rules of engagement, but working for the UN. Some thought its charter was to prepare to intervene across Bosnia where needed. Others saw a narrower mandate to support and protect aid convoys moving into nearby Sarajevo. Still others saw it as a "force in being" whose presence could be a check on Serb intentions. During the day we worked on various contingency plans, though few of us saw much likelihood that they would actually be employed. At night we smoked cigars and relaxed. To me, it all seemed rather pointless.

As September wore on, it became clear that a peace deal was in the works. Diplomats from the contending parties signed a basic framework for a peace accord late in the month, leading to a 60-day ceasefire. I was pulled out and sent home, only to jump right back into serious planning of our own. A comprehensive settlement would soon be signed, we were told, after which a NATO intervention force would be rushed in to secure the peace. The Blue Falcons had been tapped to lead the way in.

Our mission, once the final peace deal was signed, was to fly into Tuzla air base in the mountains of northeast Bosnia, secure it and assist with monitoring and, if necessary, enforcing the agreement. In the early planning stages, it was thought we would be joined by our sister battalion from Fort Bragg, 4/325, the "Golden Falcons," with both battalions under the command of Colonel McDonough. Soon, however, the plan changed. We learned that our brigade would not deploy, and we would fall under the command of 1st Armored Division, based in Germany. This was not good news. 1st Armored was commanded by a general famous for his explosive temper. We doubted this would be a good marriage.

As we finalized our preparations Colonel Scap called the majors and company commanders together. Well aware that the task organization we faced might be problematic, he asked us, "Ever heard of the Chickamauga Rule?" None of us had. During the battle of Chickamauga in the Civil War, as Union General Rosecrans attempted to retreat, General Thomas—later renowned as "the Rock of Chickamauga"—was ordered to hold off the enemy with his corps. He did, but eventually he too fell back to avoid destruction, directing three regiments to form a rear guard. All were out of ammunition, and all were "strays"—regiments not belonging to his corps but "borrowed" for the battle. The rear guard did their best but were destroyed by the advancing Confederates, hence the Rule: when a commander has a choice, he'll give the dirty jobs to the attached force every time, not his own boys. "I expect you all to be professional and do your best—but I expect the Chickamauga Rule to be in effect, so watch out!" Events would bear him out, as we quickly discovered.

Shortly before we deployed the company commanders asked to see me as a group. What followed would change my thinking about leadership and command forever. "Sir," they said, "you know your business and we respect you. But you spend a lot of time busting our chops. How about you let us do our jobs, and focus on helping us solve the problems that we can't at our level?" As I thought about it, I realized they were right. They were a talented group, and most would go on to be generals one day. My job was largely to enable them, not burden them. Colonel Scap, ever the gentleman, had looked to me as his deputy commander to apply pressure where needed, but I had failed to temper that pressure with an equal measure of empathy and understanding. The company commanders were right. Swallowing a large slice of humble pie, I resolved to absorb the lesson and change my ways.

On December 14, 1995, the Dayton Accords were signed, formally ending the Bosnian war, and 3/325 moved immediately to Aviano air base in northern Italy. On the 18th we flew to Tuzla, landing after dark amidst snow flurries, accompanied by veteran CBS journalists Mary Walsh and David Martin and their hardy camera crew. At once the fog and friction of war descended. First, our request to use a small room inside the airport tower to set up a command post was refused by the Air Force. Next, the Danish brigadier in command of the UN force at Tuzla informed Colonel Scaparrotti that he had been instructed not to relinquish command for another 48 hours. As the brass sorted this out, we established satellite communications with our rear detachment at Vicenza. The rifle companies posted security, rolled out their arctic sleeping bags, and bedded down in the open air. Soon our troopers were covered in snow.

The next days were hectic. 1st Armored was in motion, moving its tanks and heavy equipment across Europe to get into Bosnia. Bad weather and high water stalled the division up north at the Sava River, but the division commander and an advance party (called the "division tactical command post") soon arrived by air to take charge. As 1st Armored commandeered the choice real estate, we set up our tactical operations center (TOC) and headquarters in an abandoned, unheated warehouse that had been badly damaged in the fighting. It was brutally cold, hovering around 15 degrees in the daytime and even colder at night. It was worse for the rifle squads and platoons, posted out on the perimeter in the open.

More bad news followed. The C130s which had flown us in were expected to return to Aviano to bring in our tentage, stoves, rations, and other essential gear. Instead, they were diverted in favor of the 1st Armored. This was serious because our paratroopers carried only three days of rations in their rucksacks. Without tents and stoves, our men would suffer cruelly in the intense cold, and soon they would be out of food. Safely ensconced in heated buildings, and enjoying hot food three times a day, the 1st Armored headquarters was sitting in tall cotton. Tensions began to flare.

Meanwhile the UN and NATO were busy working at establishing the framework for stability operations in Bosnia. Pursuant to UN Security Council Resolution 1031, authority to conduct military operations inside Bosnia-Herzegovina was transferred from UNPROFOR to a NATO Implementation Force, or IFOR, with a one-year mandate. Sixty thousand NATO troops began to flow into Bosnia, which was organized into separate sectors. Multi-National Division North was headquartered at Tuzla under U.S. command. Multi-National Division Southeast, under French command, was based in Mostar. Multi-National Division Southwest, led by the British, was located in Banja Luka. In all, 32 countries (many of whom were NATO partners, not members) eventually contributed 54,000 soldiers to the effort, code-named Operation *Joint Endeavor*.

On December 21, the pot boiled over. At 1900, as Colonel Scaparrotti and Major Davis attended the nightly briefing with the Commanding General, the target acquisition battery commander in our TOC hollered out, "Redleg! Redleg! Redleg!" alerting everyone that his Q36 counterfire radars had detected incoming artillery rounds. The previous May, artillery strikes into Tuzla had killed 71 civilians in a single day. We took the threat seriously.

At once, the TOC swung into a practiced battle drill. The fire support officer shouted out the target location (provided by the radars) over the radio and the cannoneers of Delta Battery, our 105mm howitzer unit, laid all six guns on the target azimuth. Simultaneously the battery's fire direction center quickly calculated the elevation and deflection bearings needed to hit the target, and passed them to the guns, along with the desired shell fuse combination ("HE, VT in effect" meaning "High Explosive, Variable Time" or airburst). As the howitzer crews dialed the firing data onto the gunsights, elevating the tubes to the right height and cranking them laterally in the desired direction, the ammunition handlers stood ready to load the rounds.

Hurriedly our fire support officer called the 1st Armored command post for clearance to shoot. Only they could authorize us to fire. There was no answer over the FM command net. We waited anxiously for the incoming rounds to impact. I called the division fires cell on the landline. Again, no response. After several minutes it became clear that the radars had given a "false acquisition," a problem that would plague us throughout the deployment. I decided to go up to Division to sort things out. Taking the radar commander with me I headed up the road on foot.

As I entered the command post, I found the CG already there. (A frightened sergeant had pulled him out of the briefing.) He was red-faced and furious. Rounding on me, he began to shout and curse. As far as I could make out, someone had told the general that Tuzla was under fire, but that 3/325 wasn't monitoring its radios and hence could not respond (at that stage we had the only artillery at Tuzla). I began to explain that he had been given incorrect information, which only made him angrier. As he advanced on me, I retreated, until I was backed into a corner. At this point his deputy, Brigadier General Stan Cherrie, intervened, physically interposing his small frame between us. Cherrie had lost a foot and a part of his right hand to a landmine in Vietnam. A humane and decent man, he had played a prominent role in the Gulf War and was widely admired. "Major, I think you had better move out," he ordered. Humiliated, I left the tent and returned to the command post. Later, Scaparrotti shared with me that the outburst had been, in the CG's words, mostly an act "to keep everyone on their toes."

Days into the deployment our supply shortages became acute. As all paratroopers will, we scrounged and foraged. Some of our platoons occupied abandoned bunkers, first sweeping carefully for mines, which lay about haphazardly. Others rigged windbreaks and "field expedient" shelters. 1st Armored supplies—sandbags, construction materials, shovels, pickaxes—began to go missing. Our engineer platoon did yeoman work constructing shelters and guard posts from virtually nothing. One enterprising company commander discovered a locked bunker full of French field rations, which he quickly shared out to the companies. Our S4 supply officer, Captain (later Lieutenant General) Mike Fenzel, was assumed to be the culprit and dragged to see the 1st Armored chief of staff, a dour colonel incensed at the continuing skulduggery of the Blue Falcons. Mike blandly replied that he was innocent of the charge. Anyway, the troops had to eat something, and it transpired that someone had cagily distributed some of the loot among the 1st Armored staff against just this eventuality. Exasperated, the colonel let Mike go with a stern warning.

Fenzel wasn't done yet. His scouts reported that a shipment of small kerosene heaters had just arrived at the airfield, destined for the Air Force. Mike hustled down to the scene with a large truck. Seeing an Army colonel waiting for a flight, he went up and reported to him. "Colonel, I'd like your permission to take these heaters with me. They're for the troops." The bemused colonel replied, "I'm just passing through, Captain. I have nothing to do with any heaters." Mike persisted. "Sir, could you please just nod your head up and down?" Breaking into a grin the colonel complied. In minutes, the heaters were gone. That night, for the first time since arriving in Bosnia, the Blue Falcons were warm.

The midnight requisitions continued, as our troopers scrounged for anything that could be used to improve their fighting positions and provide shelter from the bitter weather. Eventually the 1st Armored's garrison commander for Tuzla, a lieutenant colonel, came to the command post to complain. As Scaparrotti listened attentively, a young airborne sergeant happened by, noticed the keys left in the colonel's borrowed UN truck, and drove away. Finishing his tirade, the irate garrison commander went back outside to see his vehicle disappearing in the distance. Speechless with rage, he rounded on Command Sergeant Major Picanco, the senior enlisted man in 3/325. Never one to lose his composure, Picanco counseled him quietly, "Well Colonel, if I was you, I wouldn't leave my vehicle unsecured in a common area like you just did!" We howled with laughter as our tormentor stormed off on foot.

Brief moments of levity were one thing, but an already tense relationship between the airborne and the 1st Armored now threatened to unravel. In the mess hall one day, a chubby staff major from the 1st Armored began to loudly berate our mess sergeant over the lack of powdered doughnuts. Our headquarters company commander, Captain Mike Dugan, intervened. Composed but intense, Dugan offered some friendly advice. "Back off, Major, before you get hurt. We've just about had it with you guys."

Scaparrotti was the acme of patience and tact, but the stress began to tell. Most of 1st Armored remained stranded north of the Sava, unable to cross in some of the worst winter weather in decades. Our original mission to secure the airbase perimeter now began to expand and new missions fell on us thick and fast. We provided the airfield departure/arrival control group, ran the mess hall, administered the ammunition supply point for the division and fixed the 1st Armored's vehicles. The battalion was tasked to provide mounted patrols along the Zone of Separation, many miles away, and to man static combat outposts at distant locations. "Escort" missions were assigned almost daily. In effect, we functioned as the general support battalion for the 1st Armored headquarters in addition to manning the perimeter of the large, Soviet-era base complex. Infinitely adaptable as they were, our paratroopers could not be in two places at once. 1st Armored staff officers became irritated as we began to push back on taskings.

In one case our heavy weapons company, commanded by Captain John Lightner, was given a mission to transport two Pakistani officers to their headquarters north of Sarajevo (bad weather had grounded our helos). A furious Lightner came to see me. "I won't do it!" he bellowed. "It's an eight-hour drive one way through the mountains, in the snow. We don't have current minefield maps, and I haven't had a maintenance day since we got here. This is a stupid order. The risk is way too high. Why can't we wait a day or two and fly these guys when the weather breaks?" As Scaparrotti was out, I took Lightner to see the division operations officer, a senior lieutenant colonel. He reiterated the order. Continuing up the chain we visited the chief of staff. His humor had not improved since the Fenzel incident. "Why can't you guys just follow simple orders?" he blustered.

Undeterred, we went to see General Cherrie. Listening patiently, he at once agreed with us and countermanded the order. "Captain, you're right," he said. "There are six million mines in Bosnia, and we don't know where most of them are. I already got that T-shirt. Good call." I learned an important lesson. It should not have taken a stubborn captain to remind me that a good officer should never pass on a dumb order without challenge.

To make matters worse, early in the deployment Scaparrotti and Davis were told that a Russian brigade, due to arrive in late December, had been delayed. The Blue Falcons would have to fill the gap. Pulling soldiers off the line was not an option, as we could barely manage as things were. Taking Davis, a small tactical command post (TAC) with radios, and a handful of HMMWVs, Scaparrotti began a frantic effort to "show the flag" in the Russian area of operations, meeting with local Bosniak and Serb commanders, supervising demining operations, and crisscrossing the sector continuously to bolster the impression that NATO was on the ground. It was dangerous and uncomfortable work. The weather remained miserably cold and wet, the roads were bad and the factions, if no longer at war, remained sullen and uncooperative. Once, Colonel Scap was moving on foot through a supposedly "cleared" area when Sergeant Keane, working with the TAC that day, stopped him. "Boss, look there," he whispered. Just ahead was a tripwire, almost invisible, leading back to a Serbian mine. Another step and Scap and most of his party would have been blown to pieces. I didn't envy my boss.

On most days, the TAC was so far out we could communicate only by satellite radio or "TACSAT." This led directly to another blow-up with the general. The TACSAT could only operate from the halt, when the operator would dismount, set up the antenna, and aim it at the appropriate satellite. Every hour on the hour, Colonel Scaparrotti would stop briefly and call in. Otherwise, he was too far out for normal FM radio comms. One day, the CG stopped by the TOC and demanded to talk to Scaparrotti. Captain Shoults, our S3 Air officer on duty at the time, tried to explain that there was no way to communicate with the colonel while he was moving. Not waiting for the explanation, the CG became more and more aggressive. This time there was no one to intervene. All Shoults could do was wait for the outraged general to wear himself out. Back at Vicenza, Nix and McDonough were tough and demanding. But they were fair, and they drew the line at abusing soldiers. Not for the first time, we wished they were with us.

Ten days into the deployment the Blue Falcons received an order to launch our QRF to secure an IFOR helicopter that had gone down in the hinterlands due to maintenance trouble. The B Company commander, Captain (later Lieutenant General) Bill Burleson, with a small headquarters element and one rifle platoon, raced down to the airfield to board UH60s for the mission. As the troops were moving, Captain Shoults came to me with a request. Shoults, like Burleson a tall, muscular, personable officer, had come to Bosnia with a bugle that had been in his family for generations, carried by family members through both World Wars, Korea and Vietnam. He wanted to sound the charge as the QRF lifted off. "I'll go you one better," I said. "Let's play it over the division command net." And so, we did. Shoults bugled magnificently. The 1st Armored were not amused. But our morale soared. *C'est la vie! C'est la guerre!*

Three days later, Scap called me in for a quick huddle. Bad weather had again grounded our birds. Burleson and his troopers were badly in need of resupply. I was to load up four HMMWVs with food, fuel, and water, move by ground, deliver the supplies and return.

I consulted the map. The downed helo was almost 200km away, in Indian country, in the mountains on the far side of the zone of separation, where no NATO troops had yet ventured. I swallowed hard. Above all, I feared unmarked minefields. This would be no cake walk. Still, there was nothing for it. Our guys needed help, and there really was no other option.

At first light we moved out. About 50km northwest of Tuzla, in the town of Duboj, we ran into trouble—a Serb checkpoint manned by about 30 militiamen. I dismounted and went forward, covered by the machine guns of our four trucks, which were manned but not aimed directly at the Serbs. The Serb officer in charge was agitated. He could not allow us to pass. We would have to come with him.

We needed to hand over our weapons "for safekeeping." I politely declined and asked him to order his men to stop pointing their weapons at us—an unfortunate incident could easily take place unintentionally. I reminded him that the Accords, which had been signed by all parties, allowed NATO free and unhindered access throughout Bosnia, suggesting that his superiors might not appreciate being put on the hot seat over his actions.

The officer continued to rant. Saying that I needed to consult with my commander, I returned to my vehicle and called the TOC. "I'm in trouble," I told Captain Shoults. "I'm in Doboj. I need a couple of fast movers to do a low-level flyover, right now. Can you set that up?" Five minutes later, two Marine F/A 18s roared overhead at 500 feet. Standing on their tails, they shot straight up on their afterburners with a thunderous racket. The Serb commander visibly shuddered, while his soldiers turned white. "I've got firm orders to continue on my way," I said. "Please allow us to pass." Clearly frightened, he motioned to his men and the roadblock was moved out of the way. We mounted up and passed through. Sergeant Keane winked at me. "Sweet, boss. Very sweet."

We moved all day on atrocious roads, often no more than dirt tracks. In mid-afternoon we found ourselves high in the mountains, on a treacherous road barely wide enough for one vehicle, with no guard rails. Looking out my window, I could see wrecked cars 500 feet below. Suddenly and without warning, the shoulder of the road began to collapse under the weight of the heavy HMMWV. We began to slide over the cliff. Horrified, I looked out into space. The right front wheel of the vehicle was in the air. Calmly and without panic, Sergeant Keane muscled us back onto the roadway, saving our lives. Carefully, we continued on our way. Not for the first time, or the last, I thanked the Lord for Nick Keane.

About an hour before sundown, we finally located the downed helo, not far from a Serb mountain village. Four shivering paratroopers stood guard as the snow swirled about us. "Where's the CO?" I queried. A young trooper pointed to a ramshackle barn across the blanketed field. Inside, we found Burleson and his men, toasty and warm, attended by a dozen or so buxom young women from the village with warm bread and hot coffee. Noting my quizzical expression, Bill said, "They're all widows from the war. Looking for husbands, I suppose. Anyway, they're taking good care of us!" I checked around the barn. I found no alcohol. The men's weapons were clean, their equipment stacked and ready to go. Burleson kept a round-the-clock radio watch and a squad ready to react at a moment's notice. I didn't begrudge him finding shelter or taking care of his guys. Handing over the supplies, we called in to the TOC and snugged down for the night. The next day, we made the long trek back to Tuzla without incident. Burleson and his troopers were recovered by helo a few days later when the weather broke, chastened at the loss of rock star status but glad to be back with the team.

On Christmas Eve, the Blue Falcons were treated to a turkey dinner with all the trimmings, flown in at great expense and warmly welcomed. Colonel Scap and Sergeant Major Picanco visited every outpost on foot, an arduous trek they made each night they spent at Tuzla. The tour of the perimeter, often knee deep in mud in bitter weather, took hours to complete and took a physical toll after a long day. But there is no substitute for seeing soldiers where they work, sharing their hardships and looking into their cares and concerns.

The fighting might have ended, but Bosnia remained a deeply traumatized place. The devastation could be seen all around us, in burned-out buildings, in torn-up villages, in the blank faces of the people. One late, dark afternoon, while trooping the lines with Sergeant Keane I came upon a young girl, walking slowly on a muddy road and holding a small boy by the hand. We stopped the HMMWV and I approached her, intending to give her some chocolate and say hello. As I came close her eyes grew wide. Screaming in terror, and half dragging the boy, she ran off in the opposite direction. To her, a soldier—any soldier—was a nightmare to be shunned. I felt the tears start in my eyes. I sensed instinctively that for her there was no innocence left anywhere in the world.

So soon after the war, raw enmities continued to consume many of the former combatants. I recall one particular incident in late December, when I went forward to the Zone of Separation to conduct a negotiation between Bosnian Muslim and Bosnian Serb commanders about removing minefields at a major crossing point. Such things were essential to allow free flow of goods and movement between communities now again at peace. For more than two hours the commanders refused to even speak to each other. Though not a trained diplomat, I knew that one approach was to begin with what we all had in common. Meeting separately with the two colonels, I said, "Look, just like you I'd much rather be with my family right now. But I'm here to try to help make your lives better. We can't do that alone. You have to help, for your children's sake if not for yours."

Pulling out pictures of my wife and kids, I asked to see pictures of theirs. Eventually, the ice melted enough to begin the technical discussion about locating and removing the minefields. The session became even more poignant when the Muslim commander, a former schoolteacher, recognized some of his former students in the Serb party. Soon tears began to flow on both sides. By the end of the afternoon, both sides were openly fraternizing and working collectively to lift and stack the mines. It was a beginning. As I took my leave of the Serb commander, he shook my hand and said, "You are right. We must do this for our children. But for us, the war will never really end. Those people will never forget."

As time went on, we made a great friend in the 1st Armored Division command sergeant major, Jack Tilley. Tilley was a real personality, a first-rate soldier and leader who would go on to become the sergeant major of the Army, the highest enlisted post. Tilley, a tanker, went everywhere in a flak jacket, carrying a rifle and wearing his gas mask—unlike most senior leaders in the division. With a ready smile and a real love of soldiers, his enthusiasm and love of soldiering was infectious. Unlike many 1st Armored leaders, Tilley seemed to take a genuine interest in every soldier working for the command, whether organic or attached. He became our hero when he arranged for our troopers to take showers in the CG's private hooch during his nightly update briefings. We never got caught, but Tilley assured us he would cover for us if we were. Every night, a grimy squad of Blue Falcons would infiltrate general officer country for a welcome hot shower, stealing quietly away before the big guy returned.

In early January, we received word that President Clinton was coming to visit the troops. By now we had endured a legion of visiting dignitaries, and we had our routine down. One of our platoon positions, located near an entry control point, could easily be reached by vehicles and had plenty of hard stand for photographers, protocol people and the hordes of hangers-on who invariably accompany the higher-ups. The platoon leader and platoon sergeant were photogenic, well-spoken sorts who could be trusted not to screw up. We called the place "the petting zoo" and alerted them that they had won the lottery and would have the honor of hosting their commander in chief.

A few days before the visit, the White House advance party arrived. Taken to the large bunker which served as the platoon's living quarters, they noticed the dozens of centerfolds and pinups covering the walls. Embarrassed, the lieutenant assured the team that they would be removed before the visit. "Don't worry," the team leader said. "I think POTUS will appreciate them!"

Finally, the great day arrived. As instructed, the lieutenant had left the bunker décor intact. Unfortunately, as the motorcade pulled up to the petting zoo, the Roman Catholic archbishop of the armed forces stepped out along with the president. With no time to react there was nothing to do but carry on, which the young officer did with aplomb. The archbishop said little, but his expression was priceless. The president, for his part, displayed all the charm and charisma for which he is known, chatting amiably with the troops, posing for photos and taking an interest in their primitive surroundings. As his party congregated around the checkpoint, a foot patrol re-entered the wire in full "battle rattle," exciting a journalistic frenzy of picture-taking and video shots. Shortly afterwards, a young private entered one of the crude field latrines we had constructed nearby. Standing in front of the urinal conducting his business, he was shocked to see the commander in chief join him. "Well, son," Clinton remarked, "now you can tell your kids you took a leak with the president of the United States!"

As the presidential party wrapped up its visit, a sudden burst of rifle fire erupted in the distance, about three miles away. We recognized it immediately as celebratory fire, a common phenomenon, probably a wedding in a nearby village. The Secret Service nevertheless went into hyperdrive, hustling the president away. We turned with relief back to the business at hand.

I was fortunate to have the freedom to range across the U.S. sector frequently to visit our units and happened to be out in the mountains one day checking up on an engineer platoon. The rough trail we were on suddenly ended and I got out of the HMMWV to ground guide Sergeant Keane as he attempted to back out and turn around. As our rear wheels spun wildly in the gravel and mud, I saw with horror that the right rear tire was pressed against a Soviet TM57 antitank mine, rocking up and down on its beveled surface. A tilt rod rose out of its center; if disturbed, the mine would detonate. Designed to destroy a main battle tank, the mine would have obliterated us, the HMMWV, and everything around us for 10m or so. I shouted at Keane, who eased forward out of danger. We marked the mine and called it in. On the long drive back to Tuzla, we sat in silence. There is much for an infantryman to be afraid of, but for my money, landmines are the worst. It took an hour for the acrid taste of adrenaline to go away.

So far, the mission was going well. Across Bosnia, IFOR was succeeding in separating the former combatants, stabilizing the country and enforcing the peace without armed clashes or loss of life. At Tuzla, relations with our tanker brethren remained tense, but workable with the commonsense interventions of General Cherrie and Sergeant Major Tilley. Finally, we were hitting our stride.

On January 19, the Russian brigade began to arrive. We greeted them with mixed emotions. Standing in for them had strained the battalion and we welcomed the relief. On the other hand, they weren't easy to work with. Their officers and soldiers were often drunk—a career-ending offense in the U.S. military, especially on operations—and they were clearly biased towards the Serbs, co-religionists and Slavic cousins. Early on, Major Davis met with the brigade commander, Colonel Alexander Lentsov, a burly, unpleasant fellow, to fill him in on the tactical situation and discuss relief in place operations.[1] Refusing to meet with a mere major, Lentsov left the room while his executive officer took the meeting. Later, Lentsov reappeared and brusquely demanded the use of the conference room. It would not always be easy to work with the Russians, our recent enemy, but with patience and tact—not always easy to muster—the relationship developed well enough to get the job done.

All along the plan had been for 3/325 to serve as the "initial entry" force for 30 days, preparing the way for a long-term mission before redeploying to reconstitute as the fire brigade for the U.S. European Command. As often happened, once a U.S. general got hold of our paratroopers, he was reluctant to let us go. For some

---

1   Later colonel general (equivalent to a U.S. three-star) and deputy commander of Russian ground forces.

time, we weren't sure if and when we would return to Vicenza, but by late January a formal order came, and we began to push our units back to Italy. The ABCT was 100 percent closed at our home station in Vicenza by the end of February and we began to prepare for new missions. They would not be long in coming.

By now, IFOR had taken hold and was succeeding. Simmering tensions remained, but violence had all but ended and the work of reconciliation and political reconstruction could go forward. NATO and EU forces remain in Bosnia to this day, but the job had been well begun. Despite any number of close calls, we came home with everyone safe and sound. We could all take pride in a tough job done well.

What had Bosnia taught me? The Blue Falcons excelled due to a few simple but important factors. We had a talented commander, experienced, possessed of good judgment and even temperament, supported by a well-trained and competent staff. Our small unit leaders were first rate. Our troopers were tough, disciplined and schooled in the fundamentals; they could patrol, observe and report, keep themselves and their equipment in good working order in foul weather, and follow orders intelligently. We had practiced relentlessly on generating crisp detailed orders quickly. Flexibility and a willingness to tackle the mission—any mission—and do it right were hallmarks. And we had focused on Bosnia for months, with ample opportunity to prepare.

Personally, I returned from Bosnia with confidence that I could function well at the "field grade" level in a demanding operation. I was coming into my own. My biggest challenge had been to learn how to interface with partners that did not treat us well. Here I learned much from Scaparrotti, Davis, Picanco, and also from Cherrie and Tilley. I would never quite match their cool, calm, dispassionate demeanor. But I improved and grew. Bosnia had been challenging in many different dimensions. I was learning to command at the next level, from some of the Army's best teachers and from the best teacher of all—from practical experience, on the ground, with soldiers.

I would now face a new challenge. Although happy in the battalion, I was now moved up to the brigade level as the new brigade operations officer or S3. I took the job with mixed emotions. On the one hand, a Brigade S3 slot is a key stepping stone on the way to battalion command, highly sought after and given to only a select few. If I succeeded, I could hope to command at the next level. But I was loath to leave the Blue Falcons. I had been with the unit for 18 months, a true military family where I felt at home and valued. Still, I bent to the task, hoping for the best.

I quickly learned the brigade had problems, but also potential. McDonough had accomplished much with very little. My shop was big, with almost 25 officers, NCOs and junior enlisted soldiers, including an operations sergeant major and a bevy of engineer, aviation, fire support, chemical, ammunition and plans officers and sergeants. My predecessor had been in over his head, but there was genuine talent in this group. Within a month or two, a healthy dose of encouragement, staff training, and reorganization had the shop humming. By then Colonel McDonough had changed command.[2] My new boss, Colonel Glenn Scott, had served in Vicenza many years before. His steady demeanor hid a decisive character and at times a hot temper, judiciously exercised. Secure in the knowledge he would likely never be promoted again, Scott brought a commonsense approach to command, level-headed and unaffected by burning ambition.

Our new commander would be tested right out of the chute. On April 3, 1996, an Air Force executive jet carrying Secretary of Commerce Ron Brown and 34 others crashed in bad weather in Croatia, killing all aboard. Within hours, we received an order to deploy a reinforced rifle company and command element to secure the crash site. Taking the 3/325 "Initial Ready Company" or IRC, Colonel Scott flew to the crash site near Cilipi, linking up with a small Special Forces element led by Brigadier General Mike Canavan, the head of Special Operations Command Europe (SOCEUR). Linked by TACSAT radio, we monitored the operation from our operations center in Vicenza, ready to assist if needed.

As Scott landed in Croatia, we were simultaneously alerted that our embassy in Liberia was threatened by massive civil unrest. Concerned that the U.S. Embassy might be overrun or that U.S. and allied civilians might require evacuation (in military parlance, a non-combatant evacuation operation or NEO), a warning order was issued, and the brigade again swung into action. Though a Marine Expeditionary Unit (essentially an infantry battalion with a small aviation package and command element) was available in the Mediterranean, it would take time to move them by sea to the Liberian coast. In a subsequent meeting of the Joint Staff, the Marine Corps commandant reportedly insisted that the MEU was the "force of choice" for the mission. Asked how long it might take to get them there, he was forced to say "7–10 days," the normal steaming time for the MEU's amphibious assault ships. When asked the same question, the Army chief of staff replied, "I think 3/325 is already in the air!"

Per our standard operating procedure, as soon as the IRC moved to the departure airfield, we alerted the second of the ABCT's three rifle companies to stand up as another rapid reaction force. Throughout the first part of April, we continued to receive updates and plan. This time, LTC Scaparrotti would lead the mission with his assault command post and a reinforced company of 225 paratroopers, commanded by Captain Fenzel (since promoted from his supply officer duties). We moved his force with its equipment and ammunition to Aviano air base in northern Italy. On April 10, EUCOM sent an execute order and the Blue Falcons headed back to Africa.

---

2   After retirement, McDonough would go on to work as a senior official in the White House Office of National Drug Control Policy (ONDCP) and later head both the Florida Office of Drug Control and the Florida prison system under Governor Jeb Bush.

Existing plans called for Special Forces to deploy first and to command the evacuation, code-named Operation *Assured Response*. General Canavan pulled out of Croatia, returned to Europe for briefings and then sped down to Freetown, Sierra Leone, immediately adjacent to Monrovia and designated the Intermediate Staging Base or ISB. Elements of the 1st Battalion, 10th Special Forces Group based in Germany flew with him, along with a small number of special operations helos and transport aircraft. From the ISB, forces would stage for flights into the embassy, while evacuees would be flown from Monrovia to Freetown for processing and onward movement. Special Forces soldiers and a small group of Navy SEALs arrived in Freetown on the night of April 8/9 and immediately pushed forward into the embassy by MH53 helicopter, organizing the first loads for evacuation. Arriving in Freetown early on the 11th, the 3/325 troopers initially formed a quick reaction force, while several of Scaparrotti's officers assisted with ISB operations. Among them was Skip Davis, now assigned to U.S. Army Europe in Germany, who had talked his way into the mission.

On the ground in Monrovia, all was chaos. Rival factions fought it out in the streets, with firing so intense that Canavan forbade helos to land in daylight. One savage faction was led by Joshua Milton Blahyi, known by the nom de guerre "General Butt Naked." Leading his troops naked, except for a lady's wig and sneakers, Blahyi boasted that he prepared his militiamen for battle with human sacrifices, drugs and alcohol. Some wore orange life vests in the belief they would stop bullets. In this surreal environment, the disciplined airborne soldiers proved ideal for the mission, showing great restraint despite extreme provocation. Ably led by Scaparrotti, Davis and Fenzel, the 3/325 contingent—a well-oiled machine after Rwanda and Bosnia—proved themselves as probably the best infantry battalion in the U.S. Army in that era. All three officers would go on to great things.[3]

I was disappointed to be left behind, but with Scott in Croatia and Scaparrotti in Africa there was much to do. SETAF, our parent headquarters, was undergoing its first big evaluation as EUCOM's "Light Joint Task Force Headquarters" and General Nix was determined to go through with the exercise, regardless of real-world distractions. As the exercise scenario was built around an embassy evacuation in a fictional African country, things became confused as we tried to separate real world from exercise play with the same staffs. Incredibly, we were now alerted to send our last remaining rifle company for another possible NEO in the Central African Republic.

---

3   General Scaparrotti rose to be the four-star supreme allied commander Europe or SACEUR, having commanded all U.S. and UN forces in Korea, as well as the 82nd Airborne Division and I Corps. He served three combat tours in Iraq and Afghanistan. Davis retired as a major general, with four combat tours in Iraq and Afghanistan. Mike Fenzel commanded the 3rd Brigade, 82nd Airborne Division and is a lieutenant general today. In addition to combat service in the first Gulf War, he served five combat tours in Iraq and Afghanistan.

In a comic episode, an exercise "greybeard," a retired four-star mentoring General Nix, interrupted the morning brief. "Hold the phone, godammit!" he exclaimed. "Are we talking about Liberia, or the Central African Republic, or the exercise?"

As we worked to recover Colonel Scott's troops from Croatia and outload the force for the Central African Republic, Scaparotti and his troops, along with Davis, were flown into Monrovia on the 12th. One element assumed responsibility for securing the ambassador's residence, while a second conducted a flyaway mission to Bushrod Island, north of Monrovia, to rescue civilians trapped there. On the 14th Scaparrotti and the Blue Falcons assumed responsibility for the entire embassy compound as the Special Forces troopers began to redeploy. Within 24 hours they were gone.

In addition to American citizens, U.S. forces in Monrovia took on the mission of evacuating hundreds of allied citizens as well. By April 20, when General Canavan handed over the mission to the Marines (who had finally arrived after a sea voyage lasting almost two weeks), 2,126 civilians had been rescued, including 436 Americans. Though the Marines would later make much of their role, 97 percent of the civilians ultimately evacuated were brought out by Army Special Forces and 3/325 troopers. The Marines' role would be mostly guarding an empty embassy.

During all this activity we continued to plan and stage for the Central African Republic NEO. Deep in our preparations, I was approached by a Special Forces colonel who announced loudly that he had just flown in from Germany to "take command." Taking him aside, I said, "General Nix commands here. Go see him. Unless he says so, you have no role in this operation, sir." Nonplussed, the colonel disappeared, and I never saw him again.

Following the handover to the MEU, Scaparrotti and his troopers redeployed to Vicenza without incident. By then Colonel Scott had returned with his troops, while an order came in standing us down for the CAR mission. We reconstituted the ABCT and resumed our relentless training. A few months later, Scap and I both rotated out after two years in Vicenza, he for a step up as G3 of the 10th Mountain Division, and me back to Washington. But it was not the end. We would see each other again in the wars of the west.

CHAPTER 5

H Minus!

Here dead we lie because we did not choose
to live and shame the land from which we sprung.
Life, to be sure, is nothing much to lose.
But young men think it is, and we were young.

A. E. HOUSMAN

I was sorry—genuinely sorry—to leave troops and all that I had come to know and love at Vicenza. My next job would be different, translating me from the frenetic world of intense tactical operations back to the rarefied atmosphere of Washington. Here again the Sosh connection played out. In late August of 1996, I reported to the office of the chairman of the Joint Chiefs of Staff (CJCS), General John Shalikashvili, for duty as special assistant. Months earlier I had been contacted by Colonel Joe Collins, a former Sosh professor during my cadet days. He was now the senior special assistant. As so often in the Army, the assignment negated any end-of-tour leave. Beverly, the kids, and I flew from Italy on a Friday, and I reported for work on Monday. Once again, she would have to handle the move alone, an all too frequent side of the life of a military spouse.

Working in the chairman's office was hectic and challenging, but a graduate seminar in strategy and policy at the highest levels. My principal duty was speechwriting. West Point, graduate school and the White House had given me the skills to write quickly and well but writing for "Shali" was not easy. Of Georgian extraction, his grandfather had been a Russian general, while his father had moved the family to

Germany following the Revolution. Shali made his way to the U.S. after World War II and learned English, his third language, "watching John Wayne movies." Shali spoke English flawlessly, but he thought in German, and his spoken delivery was measured and deliberate, not casual and spontaneous. Catching his voice was not easy. I spent many hours listening to tapes, trying to capture his speech rhythms, intonation, and preferred method of speaking. In time I would get the hang of it, but several of my colleagues would not and were sent back down to the staff.

Soon after my arrival a story broke in the national media, alleging that General Shali's father had been a member of the SS during the war. It was not true. His father had served in an ethnic Georgian unit incorporated into the Wehrmacht, and in one operation had fought alongside a Waffen SS formation against the Russians, but he was no SS man. The staff and the inner office were nervous, but the chairman was calm. "Not to worry," he told us in a morning staff meeting, "this will pass soon enough. Now, if they find out I was in the Hitler Youth, *then* we'll have a problem!"

Though only a major, I found it fascinating to be a fly on the wall and to watch the chairman in action. In the U.S. system, the CJCS, though not in the direct military chain of command, is by law the senior uniformed military officer and the principal military advisor to the president and secretary of defense. His seniority and access to the ultimate decision makers, used judiciously, give him real power and influence. General Shali had previously served as supreme allied commander Europe (SACEUR) and was well known and respected internationally. In this, his last year as chairman, he was absorbed with Bosnia, which had been sold to the public as a one-year operation but would clearly take much longer. Shali had gone on record pledging an end to the operation after one year, based on the guidance he had received from the president. Now that guidance changed. The issue was finessed by changing the name: the NATO Implementation Force or IFOR became the NATO Stabilization Force or SFOR. Billed as a new and different mission, the Bosnian venture now became an enduring commitment and the political debate over an "exit strategy" slowly died away.

Though the chairman was a real gentleman, his executive assistant, a tall, acerbic Navy captain named Harry Ulrich, was something of a blowtorch. (Ulrich would later rise to four stars as a top NATO commander in Naples.) With a short temper and a blustering style, he often terrorized the staff. Thanks to a long and close association with the chairman, Joe Collins was generally able to insulate his charges, though occasionally Ulrich would catch us on the E Ring of the Pentagon and give us hell. Not infrequently, he would threaten us with being fired, referred to inside the office as "being put in the penalty box." I tried to be philosophical. Life at that level was stressful in the best of times. It was best to roll with the punches and focus on the work.

The Joint Staff was and is an intensely interesting place to work. Manned by officers from all services, it had benefited greatly from the Goldwater–Nichols reforms of the late 80s, which required the services to send their best. A Navy submariner, Army tanker, Air Force bomber pilot and Marine logistician might share a small room, working on any number of issues unrelated to their backgrounds. You couldn't help but learn and grow in that environment. There were some 30 generals or admirals in the organization, but it was the chairman who called the shots, briefed the president, and presented his "Posture Statement" to the armed services committees each year. Though not a commander, he clearly served as "primus inter pares" among the four-star community.

Drafting the Posture Statement fell to me in my first year and it wasn't easy. Each "flag" officer wanted his pet projects or issues mentioned, and turning them all into a seamless, well-written paper suitable for presentation to the Congress was not easy. In the end, I was able to bring forward a version that satisfied all the players. Attending the chairman's presentation on Capitol Hill, along with the other service chiefs in the capacity as members of the Joint Chiefs of Staff, was a memorable occasion for a young staff officer.

Shali's biggest challenge was coping with the dramatic force reductions following the Cold War which began to bite on his watch. Except for the Marines, all the services took deep cuts, with the Army losing eight of 18 divisions and the entire force contracting by 27 percent. "Managing the drawdown" was the watchword of the day and the inter-service competition was brutal. Here Shali's cool, even temperament and innate fairness made him an ideal CJCS. Rarely rattled, and deeply experienced in the ways of the Pentagon, he steered a middle course that minimized the fallout from what by definition was a crisis in the making.

Speechwriting could at times present unseen minefields. On one occasion General Shali sent back a draft speech, amending a section that quoted a passage from the Bible. I went to Colonel Collins for guidance. "It's your draft," he said with a twinkle. "Take it up with the boss." The next day I went hat in hand to see the chairman, pointing out as respectfully as possible that some might take offense if holy scripture was rewritten by mere mortals. "But it sounds better the way I wrote it," Shali complained. "I'm sure you're right, sir," I remonstrated. "But some people are just going to prefer the King James version!" Fortunately, he relented, and a crisis of faith was averted.

The work was hard, and the pressure was real, but if you like to write it was a special time. I found that all I really needed was a good dictionary, the Bible, and the collected works of Winston Churchill, Abraham Lincoln, William Shakespeare, and Mark Twain. Collins taught us that, whether the audience was five people or five thousand, hearing the chairman was a big deal, and every event should be as good as we could possibly make it. Most of the time we managed it.

At the beginning of 1997, General Shali retired and a "succession" crisis enveloped the Pentagon. The front runner, General Dennis Ralston of the Air Force, had served for four years as vice chairman but had become embroiled in a scandal dating back some years to his war college days, when he had engaged in an affair while separated from his wife. In its wake, a number of other four-star candidates quietly withdrew from consideration. Eventually a dark horse emerged—General Hugh Shelton, my former brigade commander in the 82nd. Shelton was now serving as commander U.S. Special Operations Command, was loving life and had no real interest in the job. He had excelled as commander of the 82nd and later of XVIII Airborne Corps, where he led the Haiti operation in 1995 with brilliant success.

Shelton's candidacy surfaced under the radar and few of us were aware that he was even being considered until we saw him walking the hallways of the Pentagon. A treasured memory was a brief conversation in the men's room with him during his interview period. Apparently, he had been queried in detail about the state of his marriage. He replied that he couldn't imagine anything in his background that would raise questions, except for having been married to two women at the same time! It turned out that as a young Green Beret captain in Vietnam, he had been involved in a Montagnard ceremony that in effect had married him off to the headman's daughter … a union that was speedily dissolved, presumably before consummation, once Shelton received the appropriate translation.

Shelton had credibility and even swagger as a seasoned combat commander and successful leader of big organizations, with a uniform festooned with combat ribbons, skill badges and Special Forces and Ranger tabs. But his Washington and interagency experience was limited. Perhaps because he had not pressed for the job, Shelton was selected to succeed Shalikashvili against all expectations. He would prove an excellent chairman, confident in giving his best military advice, determined to protect the prerogatives of his office when threatened, but deferential to his civilian masters, especially in public and in front of the media.

A new chairman needed a new executive assistant and the man selected was an up-and-coming Army colonel, David Petraeus. Another Sosh alum, Petraeus was fresh from brigade command in the 82nd where he had commanded the 504th, Shelton's old command. The book on Petraeus was mixed. He seemed to have few friends or enemies. His peers on the whole recognized he was different, and they were, if not hostile, at least wary. Of average height and slight of build, he was a fantastically fit officer, intensely ambitious, brilliant intellectually, a workaholic and by repute a demanding boss.

Petraeus had checked all the boxes: company, battalion, and brigade command, and even a tour as aide de camp to the Army chief of staff. His personnel file was rumored to be a "picket fence," meaning an unbroken string of perfect "top block" officer efficiency reports stretching back to his second lieutenant days. Though by no means rare in the late 1990s, a lack of combat experience was seen by some as a blemish on an otherwise spotless military record. Petraeus had also earned a Ph.D. in international relations from Princeton, a rare distinction among infantry officers. Life around Ulrich had been a trial. We awaited the arrival of the much-touted Petraeus with trepidation.

Petraeus in the flesh was both impressive and refreshing. His high energy level and exacting standards proved challenging, but his everyday manner was affable and relaxed, a sea change from the temperamental Ulrich. Petraeus had spent years working in the inner offices of four-stars and he was a master at synchronizing Shelton's official life, which required bringing together public affairs, legislative liaison, legal, trip planning, speechwriting, social and a host of other functions and offices. If Shelton lacked much DC time, his innate common sense, personal touch and vast military experience compensated, while Petraeus and an able staff smoothed out the rough spots.

As Shelton settled in, we gained two new special assistants, both of whom I had a hand in recruiting. Lieutenant Colonel John Antal was a bald, extroverted armor officer with a reputation as a skilled writer and huge brain. Well known for his military writing, he also carried an Army-wide reputation as a superb commander of tank units. Commander Harry Harris was a naval flight officer with remarkable credentials as a graduate of Annapolis, Georgetown and Harvard. Harris was Japanese-American and would later command the U.S. Pacific Fleet and then U.S. Pacific Command, followed by service as U.S. ambassador to South Korea. It was an all-star team and I wondered if I would be able to keep up.

With Bosnia stabilized, the focus in the Pentagon switched to managing the drawdown, "recapitalizing the force" (i.e. finding money to repair or replace worn-out ships, planes and tanks) and, a mounting concern, coming to grips with international terrorism. On June 25, 1996, terrorists attacked U.S. liaison personnel at Khobar Towers in Saudi Arabia, wounding 515 (including 240 Americans) and killing 19 U.S. servicemen. On August 7, 1998, near-simultaneous terrorist attacks on the U.S. embassies in Kenya and Tanzania caused thousands of casualties, including 12 U.S. dead. Osama bin Laden claimed responsibility for the embassy attacks and an intensive effort began, led by the intelligence community, to locate and target him. On several occasions, open sources reported that the CIA had confirmed a precise location on bin Laden but that a presidential decision to launch strikes could not be obtained. President Clinton did approve cruise missile attacks against al Qaeda training camps on August 20, 1998, while specifically denying that bin Laden was the target, but no serious attempt was ever made to kill him, with consequences that would soon be all too clear.

General Shelton was of course intimately involved in these efforts, on at least one occasion (and possibly more) personally pleading for permission to launch. By now, bin Laden stood clearly revealed as a dangerous and bold terrorist leader, rapidly assuming almost mythical status in the world of Islamic extremism. The campaign to hunt him down was, however, affected by a major distraction. In this same time frame the Monica Lewinsky scandal had broken about the president's head, the nation's political apparatus was consumed by the affair, and coherent national security decision making was disrupted. No one who lived through that time in the Pentagon can fail to recall it without chagrin. A classmate and close friend, then serving as Clinton's military aide, called it one of the most troubling and difficult periods of his entire career, tempting him to quit the White House. Professional respect for and commitment to the president, especially in his capacity as commander in chief, runs deep in the military and it is genuine. But this tawdry affair, which saw the president impeached and tried in the U.S. Senate, ignited intense partisan conflict and called into question any national security move, all of which were filtered through the lens of the Lewinsky scandal.

As time went on, tensions began to build inside the office. Though brilliant, Colonel Petraeus seemed to be driven by an inner need to dominate. We were all accomplished writers, but Petraeus regularly kicked back our speeches and written products, inserting corrections and marginalia. On many occasions he inserted language—"ineluctable" comes to mind—that just wasn't Shelton. We began to bump up against and occasionally miss deadlines as the gateway became choked. At one point our senior speechwriter, an Air Force colonel, quit when a major speech was returned for the 10th time—over a semi-colon.

Like many, I spent most lunch breaks working out. On one five-mile run around the Washington monument I encountered Petraeus just as I finished my run. He was headed for the Capitol, a 10-mile round trip, and suggested I turn around and accompany him. By now I knew the drill. Though I was in good shape, he'd leave me exhausted on the side of the road and triumphantly race off into the distance. I respectfully demurred, to his evident displeasure. Though his fitness was truly exceptional, he often used it to demonstrate his superiority over his peers and subordinates.

As part of my duties, I often accompanied the chairman on official trips, and in 1998 I traveled with the official party to Brussels, where Shelton was scheduled to attend a meeting of the NATO Military Chiefs of Defense Staff. The senior American in Europe at the time was General Wesley Clarke, the SACEUR. A Rhodes scholar from Arkansas, like President Clinton, Clarke was hyper-ambitious and political, traits that did not endear him to Shelton. The two were different in every way. Shelton was tall and rangy, Clarke more like a bantam rooster. Shelton affected a country, down-home persona as a farm boy from Speed, North Carolina, while Clarke polished a reputation as an international sophisticate and politico-military expert. Both had served in Vietnam, but Shelton had spent his career in the elite airborne and special forces, while Clarke had specialized in tank forces.

A simple and unaffected man, Shelton traveled with a small party: an aide de camp, a speechwriter, and three or four communicators and security people. After landing in Brussels, we went to the hotel in an unmarked van, with Shelton in a modest sedan. As we attempted to check in, we found ourselves swamped by dozens of Clarke's staff officers, based in Mons (only an hour away by car) but booked into the same hotel. This was a transparent attempt to demonstrate that we were on Clarke's turf, where he was boss. The following morning saw more of the same, as the chairman stood in line behind a horde of NATO people (by my count 48) to check out. Clarke's motorcade was awe-inspiring, and included a luxurious Mercedes armored sedan, another as a decoy vehicle, several sleek buses and a flock of white-gloved motorcycle outriders. After the great man had departed, Shelton boarded his modest sedan and we clambered into our beat-up Chevy van for the trip to NATO headquarters.

Later in the day, one of Clarke's staffers approached with a request for a meeting at 4 p.m. between the SACEUR and the chairman. Shelton agreed. At the appointed time, the SACEUR was nowhere to be seen. Forty minutes later, Clarke sauntered in breezily, claiming that important discussions with the NATO secretary general had held him up. With a look from Shelton, we all absented ourselves, so that the chairman could give it to Clarke "with the bark on." It seemed to me a dangerous thing to offer offense to Shelton needlessly. The chairman is the senior uniformed officer in the Armed Forces, with daily access to the secretary of defense. Clarke clearly thought his entree to the secretary of state and other civilian officials meant he was either outside of or above such things. Hugh Shelton was a fair man and an open-minded one, but never afraid to pull the trigger when necessary. Later, when I heard that Clarke had been removed from his post and retired one year early, I wasn't surprised.

As I began my third year in the chairman's office, I received the happy news that I had been selected to command a parachute infantry battalion in the 82nd Airborne Division. I was euphoric. Command is what all real infantry officers live for. It is the apogee and the consummation of most successful careers, given to only a few and treasured. Even better was my slating to return to "Division," where I had begun as a private 25 years before. I never knew if Shelton had weighed in to have me sent there, but I couldn't have been prouder. To top it off, I would be assigned to the 2nd Battalion, 505th—a famous battalion whose World War II commander had been played by John Wayne in the movie *The Longest Day*. A part of the 3rd or "Panther" Brigade, the unit was colloquially referred to as "2 Panther" and had served gloriously in every 82nd campaign since World War II.

In an unusually generous gesture, the chairman hosted a ceremony that spring in his private dining room to promote me to lieutenant colonel. It was a grand affair. The room was packed with friends, family, classmates, and officials from the Joint Staff. General Shelton gave a short, gracious speech and my father and Beverly pinned on my new rank. After, it occurred to me I'd never actually had a promotion ceremony before!

As I prepared to assume command, the Pentagon became absorbed in a drama unfolding in Kosovo, the southern province of Serbia, inhabited overwhelmingly by ethnic Albanians but administered ruthlessly by the Serbian government under Slobodan Milosevic. The architect of the Balkan wars, Milosevic had been beaten by the Croats and Bosnians (aided by NATO and the U.S.) but continued to cruelly suppress the Kosovars. In 1991, following the breakup of Yugoslavia, an unauthorized referendum of Kosovars voted overwhelmingly for independence. Milosevic responded by outlawing Kosovar local autonomy, including the teaching of Albanian in schools. Ethnic Serbs replaced local officials in most state positions. During the mid-90s the Kosovar Albanians began to raise paramilitary formations, loosely organized as the "Kosovo Liberation Army" or KLA, to take the fight to the Serbian security forces. Financed by the Albanian diaspora and armed with weapons looted from Albanian depots following the collapse of the Berisha government in 1997, the KLA became both increasingly effective and more ruthless. Classified by the U.S. State Department as a terrorist group in 1998, the KLA mounted an effective insurgency that prompted ever harsher reactions from Serb security units in the province.

Here Milosevic fell victim to his own history. Though there was plenty to condemn on both sides, Serbia's role in fomenting the Balkan Wars of the 1990s left it with few friends apart from the Russians. International opinion began to swing to the side of the KLA. After failed peace talks in Rambouillet in March of 1999, NATO began to seriously prepare for intervention. Though lacking authorization from the UN Security Council, the North Atlantic Council approved air strikes against Serbian forces in Kosovo, which began on March 24.

As my change of command date approached, I monitored the evolving situation closely from the National Military Command Center in the Pentagon. Even as the air campaign intensified, ground units began to flow into the region, led by my future command, 2/505 (launched as the 82nd battalion that happened to be on alert status at the time) and the 26th Marine Expeditionary Unit, then afloat in the Med. Initially they staged across the border in Albania and Macedonia, to be joined by a mechanized infantry battalion (1/26 Infantry, commanded by my 150s football teammate Lieutenant Colonel Bob Scurlock) and a tank battalion (1/77 Armor, commanded by Lieutenant Colonel Grady Reese, a West Point classmate) from the U.S. 1st Infantry Division—the "Big Red One"—in Germany. Accompanied by U.S. Army Multiple Launch Rocket Systems and Apache helicopters, and joined by other NATO ground forces, this gathering force posed a credible ground threat to complement the air attacks then in progress.

NATO air strikes initially targeted Serb forces in Kosovo, but the wily Serbs managed to hide their tracked vehicles and tanks well and NATO air strikes were ineffective in finding and taking them out. Within days the focus shifted to Serbia itself and its capital, Belgrade, against "strategic" targets such as military bases, arms factories, road and rail networks, oil refineries, bridges and command posts. Prior to NATO air strikes, the situation had been violent but not out of control. Now Serbia took the gloves off. Up to 850,000 Kosovar refugees fled as Serbian security forces, led by the feared Military Uniformed Police or MUP, responded to NATO attacks with large scale ethnic cleansing and widespread atrocities. In one of the ironies of the Kosovo campaign, it was not until after the bombing began that Serbian atrocities truly escalated. Milosevic refused to follow the script and back down. Supported by the Russians politically, he instead mobilized reservists and fought back.

Serbian air defenses were hopelessly outmatched and only two U.S. jets were lost in combat. Soon things began to get out of hand. Several controversial strikes drew worldwide criticism: an errant attack on the Chinese Embassy in Belgrade, which killed three Chinese citizens; and a deliberate attack on the Serbian national television station, killing 14 Serbian civilians. One errant NATO air strike hit a school bus. Another hit a refugee convoy, killing 50 civilians. "Dual use" sites such as hospitals, schools and radio and television stations would eventually be bombed. Originally planned for one week, the campaign now stretched into its third month. Furious diplomacy, backed up by U.S. and UK threats to deploy ground forces, now took effect.

Once it became clear that Russia would not intervene with troops, Milosevic backed down, signing a ceasefire agreement (called the "Military Technical Agreement" or MTA) on June 3 that would allow NATO to move into Kosovo to supervise the withdrawal of Serbian forces. On June 10, the UN Security Council passed Resolution 1244, authorizing deployment of military forces to Kosovo to monitor and enforce the Serb withdrawal. "KFOR," the 50,000-man NATO Kosovo Force under British Lieutenant General Sir Mike Jackson, commander of NATO's Rapid Reaction Corps, entered Kosovo in force two days later and established its headquarters in Pristina. NATO authorities had designed the operation to unfold in tandem with the Serbian redeployment of forces. KFOR would fall in at key locations as the Serbs pulled out. With luck there would be no direct clashes, and NATO troops would fill the security vacuum as Serb forces departed. The province of Kosovo was organized into five security zones, with the British in the center, the French in the north, the Italians in the west and the Germans in the south. The U.S. sector was in the southeast, initially manned by the Marines' 26 MEU, brought ashore from the Med, and Army forces moved over from Albania, including 2/505. "2 Panther" would later take great pride in being the first U.S. unit to enter Kosovo.

As in Bosnia the Russians proved to be a complicating factor. Without NATO or UN approval, the Russians pulled together a force from its peacekeeping contingent in Bosnia and sent it by road towards Kosovo. The Russians' bid to insert themselves into Kosovo precipitated a dangerous reaction. Arriving in Pristina on June 11, the Russian contingent of 200 soldiers quickly approached the airfield, prompting a furious diplomatic exchange. General Clarke, the SACEUR, sent heated directives, first to the British commander, General Jackson, to stop the Russians—by force, if necessary. When Jackson predictably demurred, Clarke went through U.S. channels to order a rifle company from 2/505 to be flown to Pristina to stop further Russian reinforcements from being flown in. The unit selected was commanded by Captain Matt McFarlane, an extroverted and decisive young officer.[1] When given the order, McFarlane asked, "What exactly am I being ordered to do? Block the Russians? Detain them? Shoot them?" Fortunately for all, cooler heads prevailed, and a diplomatic solution was found. The Russians would not be given a sector of their own. Instead, Moscow eventually agreed to position smaller groups under NATO command in the British, German, French and U.S. sectors, totaling some 3,600 troops.

By then I had signed out of the chairman's office and reported to Fort Bragg. As so often in my career, Beverly was left behind to move the kids and our household goods alone, a process that would take months while we waited on quarters. Just before signing into the division, I got a call from a mentor with some advice. "You've got great paratrooper credentials," he said. "That's why you were slated to command an airborne battalion. But you also have a problem."

"I'm listening, sir," I replied.

He paused before continuing. "You have a Ph.D., and you've written a bunch of stuff in military journals. You're a smart guy. That makes you suspect in the minds of most of the folks who outrank you, and all of your peers. Especially in the infantry."

"Any advice?" I asked.

"Yes … carry an unlit cigar everywhere you go, chew on it constantly, and use the F-word a lot!"

As my battalion was forward deployed, I spent the first few weeks in-processing, lining up post housing and meeting key leaders in the division. The commanding general, Major General Dan McNeil, had grown up in the division, spending most of his career at Fort Bragg.[2] Like me he had also served as a major in Vicenza. McNeil was of medium height, athletic, with a folksy southern accent and a fair portion of charm and charisma. He wore the highly prized gold star on his Master Parachutist wings, signifying a combat jump from the invasion of Panama, where he had served as an 82nd staff officer. Remarkably for an 82nd commander, he did not wear the coveted Ranger tab—but his airborne credentials were impeccable. He greeted me affably enough, but unlike many of my brother battalion commanders in the 82nd, I had never served under him before. Despite my long years of service in the airborne community I would be seen as something of an outsider.

In our initial meeting, he brought up an article I had recently written in *Military Review* called "The Airborne Division in 2010." (The article was written before I

---

1   As of this writing McFarlane is a major general commanding the 4th Infantry Division at Fort Carson, Colorado.

2   McNeil would end his career as a full general commanding all U.S. forces in Afghanistan.

knew of my return to the 82nd.) The thrust of the article was that, since the Gulf War, the division had become too "light." Having lost its light armor battalion and its Apache attack helicopters and equipped with the reliable, but not very lethal, 105mm howitzer, the 82nd lacked the powerful punch it had enjoyed in *Desert Storm*. In the paper I argued for a division structure better able to contend with enemy armor and more lethal scenarios. Should lack of aircraft or the scenario dictate, we could always leave the heavier stuff behind, as we had done in Grenada. McNeil eyed me coolly. "Can't tell you how pleased we are to have you here to tell us how to run the division," he drawled. Ouch. I made a mental note to keep any good ideas to myself unless asked.

The assistant division commander was none other than Dave Petraeus, wearing a new star and happy to be back where he had commanded his brigade. Our prior association gave me confidence that I might have a friend at court, but I knew also that his expectations were high and that he would be as demanding as ever. Petraeus was clearly an officer destined for great things.

My new brigade commander, Colonel Tom Maffey, had served in the division as a lieutenant and captain, but had gone on to serve in the Ranger Regiment before commanding an infantry battalion in the 101st Airborne Division (Air Assault).[3] Like Petraeus, he was small and wiry, not muscular but an endurance runner. Generally referred to as "Panther 6" or "P6," he was newly arrived, like me. As any new battalion commander might, I called around to my friends in the infantry community to learn what I could about him. Although he had served briefly in the invasion of Panama, the colonel had little experience on operations, though he was known to have a powerful senior general as a mentor. My in-brief left me unsettled. Though he was not hostile, there was little of the camaraderie and warmth I had experienced with my commanders in Vicenza. I walked out worried about where this relationship might go. I elected to withhold judgment, reminding myself that it was not his job to impress me, but mine to impress him.

Much to my joy I found that Mike Scaparrotti, now also a full colonel, was the commander of the 2nd Brigade, call sign "Falcon 6." Though not in my chain of command, his counsel and mentorship would prove to be as helpful as ever in the tough times to come.

Expecting to be sent straight out to assume command, I received the unwelcome news that my change of command had been deferred until mid-July. The decision made sense. 2/505 entered Kosovo from Albania as the lead U.S. element on June 12, and moving out its veteran commander, Lieutenant Colonel (later Lieutenant

---

3   The 101st retained the "Airborne" designation but had not been on jump status since 1968. Though non-jumpers, its soldiers still wore the distinctive uniform items—the airborne flash and shoulder tab, the glider patch, and jump boots—worn by all paratroopers, a source of continuing friction.

General) Joe Anderson, at the beginning of a new and challenging mission was clearly unwise. I stifled my impatience and stood by.

As I waited to take command the battalion experienced an event both alarming and comical. A reconnaissance vehicle surveying future positions inadvertently crossed into Serbia, penetrating about 2km. When confronted by a roving Serbian military police unit, our troopers captured the Serbs and brought them back to headquarters. Only then did it become apparent that we had strayed across the border.

What to do? Higher headquarters adopted a novel solution. Insisting that it was the Serbs who had become lost, KFOR scolded the Serb liaison officers harshly, handed their soldiers back with mock indignation, and awarded medals to our errant troopers! For the rest of the deployment, they would perform well, but they were never allowed near the border again.

Finally, in mid-July, the great day arrived, and I assumed command of "2 Panther" in a modest ceremony in the town square of Urosevac. It was the greatest day of my career to date, and I felt both elation and profound gratitude. It took about 30 minutes for my euphoria to wear off. To my dismay, I learned that two of my three airborne rifle companies had been taken away and placed under the neighboring tank and mechanized infantry battalions. It seemed that everyone wanted paratroopers working for them.

In return, I was given a mechanized infantry company (C Company, 1-26 Infantry, the famous "Blue Spaders") and a tank company (C Company, 1-77 Armor), units with far fewer soldiers and with heavy armored vehicles that tore up the rudimentary road network and proved to be maintenance headaches. All three battalion task forces were thus organized similarly, with an airborne infantry, heavy infantry and tank company in each. I kept D Company, my heavy weapons unit (20 HMMWVs with mounted machine guns) along with a combat engineer company from Germany, a 105mm artillery battery that had come with 2/505 from Bragg, an airborne MP squad and other small attachments. I was not happy with the task organization but could see instinctively that roiling the waters right out of the gate would likely be counterproductive.

Once again, I found myself serving under the heavy guys from Germany, in this case the 1st Infantry Division or "Big Red One." Unusually, 1ID was commanded by a legendary airborne guy, Major General John Abizaid, a unique force of nature. Abizaid had commanded a Ranger company in the invasion of Grenada, parachuting onto the runway at Point Salines. He later commanded the Blue Falcons in Vicenza, followed by command of the 504th in the 82nd. Based in Germany, he would be a frequent visitor to Kosovo.[4]

U.S. forces in Kosovo were known as "Task Force Falcon." The on-scene U.S. commander was Brigadier General Bantz Craddock, who had won a Silver Star in

---

4   Abizaid would later rise to four stars as commander U.S. Central Command.

the Gulf War commanding a tank battalion.[5] Small and professorial in appearance, Craddock was level-headed, calm, and intelligent. He had inherited something of a mess but was moving steadily forward to sort things out. Except for 2 Panther, all of his units were from the 1st Division. Nevertheless, he welcomed me to his team.

At first, I thought Kosovo would be much like Bosnia, but I was mistaken. Green, hot and verdant in the summer, southern Kosovo was not mountainous, but featured rolling valleys and sloping hills, in some places spectacularly beautiful. Though the original concern was to save the Kosovars from the Serb paramilitary forces, by the time I assumed command the tables had turned. In the U.S. sector, except for small surviving Serb enclaves in the towns of Stirpce and Vitina, most Serbian civilians in my assigned area of responsibility (or AOR—about 400 square kilometers) had fled along with the Serbian paramilitaries. Only the old stayed. They had lived there all their lives and had no place to go. The KLA (or "UCK" in the Albanian language, for *Ushtria Çlirimtare e Kosovës*) now showed its true colors. Not for nothing had the State Department designated them as terrorists. A spate of murders took place in the absence of any law and order. Elderly Serbs were killed in the fields and in their homes by roving bands of UCK thugs. A favorite sport was blowing up Orthodox churches, so much so that the treasures kept in the centuries-old Orthodox cathedral in Urosevac were evacuated by the Serbian patriarch. We would commit an infantry squad to guard the site throughout our mission. My mission statement directed me vaguely to "establish a safe, secure environment," though I had no police, no judges, no courts, and no detention facilities.

A wise old mentor had once advised me, "Never ask for guidance unless you really need it." Our problems were legion, but we were paid to solve problems, not complain. My working method was to try to solve my problems with what I had, keep Craddock informed, and request more resources or guidance only when absolutely necessary. My first priority was to learn my new organization, my area of operations and my neighboring units and commanders. I found myself blessed with two remarkable majors, Major Bryan Dyer, the executive officer and second-in-command, and Major Casey Griffith, the S3 operations officer. Dyer was quieter, industrious, highly intelligent, and warm hearted—the perfect chief of staff. Griffith was fierier and more intuitive, a strong personality and full of drive. Both were fearless and experienced paratroop officers. Even better, they were close friends, with none of the rivalry often found between majors in an infantry battalion. I couldn't have asked for better.

A welcome addition to the team was Nick Keane, now a staff sergeant. I had earlier made a few calls to Army Personnel to request his assignment to 2 Panther and was glad that we would be partners again. Kosovo would be our

---

5   Craddock would end his career in 2009 as the four-star Supreme Allied Commander Europe.

third deployment together. I assigned him to my headquarters and felt safer just knowing he was around.

An interesting footnote to the deployment was the fact that my task force, which approached 1,000 soldiers, included a single female, Military Police Sergeant Heather Wilson. (In 1999, women were excluded from serving in infantry, armor, or field artillery cannon units.) Sergeant Wilson, a fit, personable mother of two, lived in a ruined building, screened off from her male soldiers by a single poncho taped to the ceiling. Early on I visited her and asked if she had experienced any problems. Grinning, she told me, "Not at all, sir. These are great guys, and besides—I have arrest powers!" She would serve with distinction throughout the deployment and prove an invaluable asset to us all.

Immediately adjacent to me on my western boundary was the Polish 18th Parachute Battalion, with a contingent of Ukranian troops.[6] To the north was the 1st Battalion Royal Gurkhas. I was confident of having good neighbors there. The UCK zone commander based himself in Urosevac (called "Ferezai" by the Kosovar Muslims). Interspersed throughout my AOR were groups of civilian NGOs, roving reporters, visitors from the UN and European Union and God knew who else.

My first real command decision involved the location of my headquarters. A huge base camp called Camp Bondsteel was being constructed in the middle of a large field about 10km from Urosevac, and when I arrived, I found the 2/505 command post and living areas there. The problem was that Bondsteel was far from the action. Commuting to work and being out of touch with the civilian population and its problems and concerns didn't seem to me to be an effective way to operate. Living right next to the "flagpole"—with the staff of my higher headquarters nearby—was also less than ideal. Leaving my logistics support area in place, I moved my headquarters into town. Occupying an abandoned Serb police compound (ironically, only 100m from the local UCK headquarters), we got down to business.

Understanding the culture was an essential, but daunting task. Early in my command a young Kosovar Albanian was detained on a charge of murder. He had killed an old Serb working the fields in broad daylight, in front of witnesses. The case was open and shut. The man freely admitted the murder but denied any criminal intent. In talking with him I could see he was sincere and genuinely confused over his arrest. I later learned that in killing the Serb he was adhering to the "Kanun of Lek," an oral tradition dating back many centuries that regulated, among other things, blood feuds. In return for a Serbian affront, the young man, compelled to revenge the slight, had sought the sanction of his clan elders. His actions, incomprehensible to educated Westerners, were in fact thoroughly in step with the traditional methods of dispute resolution that had guided these people for

---

6 The Polish commander, Roman Polko, would later command Grom, the Polish elite CT unit, and serve as national security advisor as a major general.

hundreds of years. The fact that the murdered Serb was guiltless of any offense was irrelevant; he belonged to the guilty tribe. I could only shake my head. We packed the young man off to Pristina, where he languished in a makeshift prison until a Kosovar court system could be put in place.

The conflict in Kosovo was marked by a tragic custom, common to both sides, whereby Serb or Muslim homes were often burned to the ground. Following the withdrawal of the Serbian military in early June of 1999, the practice almost universally fell on the few remaining Serbian families in the U.S. sector. Frequently, our roving patrols would respond to the scene, but without firefighting equipment and training our efforts had meagre effect. Once, I asked a Muslim father, "Why do you burn homes in the middle of your beautiful neighborhood?" He answered bitterly, "To be sure they never come back." Eventually I directed my troops to stop responding. Too many were racing into burning buildings, and the stress and outrage put many dangerously close to the edge.

How does an infantryman become a mayor, a chief of police, and a county executive overnight, with the added complication of rampant violence and no functioning systems? It would do no good to complain that we were not trained or staffed for the mission. It still had to be done. The first priority was to re-establish law and order, and we went at it with a will.

Our initial mission analysis revealed that most serious violence was committed by UCK fighters against ethnic Serbs. The Serb enclave of Stirpce, just to the west of Urosevac in a beautiful mountain valley, was large enough to provide its own security. With the Poles close by, I elected to post no troops there. Vitina, some 20km east of Urosevac, had a mixed population of Serbs and Kosovar Albanians, with the Muslims in the clear majority. Vitina would be a tinderbox throughout our deployment and beyond. Joe Anderson had positioned his best unit, Alpha Company, in Vitina. Its commander, Captain McFarlane, was told to secure the village and its environs, and to work hard to get the two factions to the table in some kind of shared town council.

My attached tank and mechanized infantry companies were assigned responsibility for securing smaller villages and settlements to the south and northwest of Camp Bondsteel respectively. The artillery battery served as provisional infantry in a similar role. The tanks in particular were limited to major roads due to their great weight (almost 70 tons). The Bradley Fighting Vehicles of the mech infantry company were more mobile and consequently were assigned a larger area to patrol. In Urosevac I stationed Delta Company, my antitank/heavy weapons unit, my scout and mortar platoons, the artillery battery and my tactical headquarters—around 250 soldiers to police a city of some 100,000 inhabitants. We were spread so thinly that the battalion QRF consisted of my tactical command post (TAC), four HMMWVs mounting M240 7.62mm machine guns. If needed the TAC would be led by myself, the S3 or the sergeant major.

As my AOR, extending over hundreds of square kilometers, was impossible to cover adequately with my force, we focused instead on the most likely sources of trouble. This meant the main north/south and east/west surfaced roads (called Main Supply Routes or MSRs), the principal built-up areas (Urosevac and Vitina) and known locations of remaining Serbs, who we knew would be attacked. The idea was to patrol the roads aggressively, setting up mobile checkpoints and searching any vehicle that looked suspicious. In my first few weeks in command, we confiscated large numbers of weapons and the word began to get out that the Americans were serious. Local UCK commanders began to lobby to conduct "joint patrols" or to function as local police forces. I emphatically declined. They had no lawful authority (we did, under the UN resolution), were forbidden to carry weapons openly under the Military Technical Agreement, and were, we knew, the source of most of the violence.

I also took the difficult decision to physically safeguard all known Serb residences in Urosevac. Every Serb who could had fled when the Serbian security forces pulled out, but there were still some 80 elderly Serbs. Without protection their houses would be burned, and they would be attacked. Guarding them was not easy. It meant positioning small units of four soldiers around or even inside their homes 24/7. If attacked my men would have to fight until a QRF could respond, which might take up to half an hour. Remembering my Somalia experience, I also decided that I would locate and secure the civilian NGOs in my area. Though not strictly within my mandate, I knew that their vehicles, cash, and supplies made them targets, and that dead NGOs would be front-page news around the world.

I settled quickly into a standard battle rhythm. I rose each day at 0500, shaved and dressed, grabbed a bite and a cup of coffee, and held a 30-minute staff call to review the events of the preceding night, any orders that might have come in overnight, and the business of the day. Then I was off on "battlefield circulation," moving with my TAC to visit my units, tour the AOR, make face-to-face contact with local leaders and neighboring commanders, or check in with TF Falcon. Several times a week, I went out of sector to visit my soldiers working for the other battalions. In this pre-9/11 era, we had not yet become a "BUB" Army, where commanders at all levels sit for hours in hi-tech "Battlefield Update Briefings" for the big boss. Instead, Craddock held a staff meeting each day at 1800 and commanders were invited to call in by FM radio to provide a five-minute summary of operations. I'd return to my headquarters after dark, receive another short staff update of my own, tackle email correspondence and other paperwork, and huddle with my majors and CSM (command sergeant major). Once a week, but not more, I'd pull in the company commanders for one hour. Often, I'd join my units for late-night patrols, either mounted or dismounted.

All this was not easy with my meagre resources. Within days of taking command the first test came. At 2300 one night, one of my four-man fire teams called in from the other side of Urosevac. "We are on the fourth floor of an apartment building and we are under attack!" The team was guarding an elderly Serb couple from inside their apartment when the UCK burst in. A furious firefight erupted in the living room, with the old people hiding in a back bedroom. As the UCK gunmen burst through the front door, weapons in hand, the fire team leader, Specialist Ryan Adams, fired three rounds into the first man. One hit him in the shoulder, one in the hand, and one passed through his chest. After a few seconds exchanging fire the UCK ran off, carrying their wounded with them. I arrived on the scene with my TAC to find the situation well in hand, Adam's fire team breathing hard and exhilarated at having survived the close encounter. Passing out cigars for all, I congratulated them on a job well done.

Days later, a similar incident took place but did not end so well. At one static guard post a young sergeant, hearing what sounded like an attack in progress, ran on foot to intervene. Racing down an alley he found a local woman bleeding from multiple stab wounds. The victim was quickly evacuated to a U.S. treatment facility at Bondsteel, where she later died.

That afternoon, a team from the TF Falcon CID (Criminal Investigations Division) showed up to arrest my sergeant. I was incensed that they made no effort to inform me in advance. The young man was hustled away to Bondsteel, where his uniform and equipment were confiscated for analysis. Apparently, before she died the victim had described her attacker as wearing battle dress uniform, common for the UCK. The attending physician, hearing her account through an Albanian translator, assumed that the attacker was a U.S. soldier and immediately informed the military police. Going on no more than that, the system swung into action. It took several days of hard negotiating to get my soldier back. CID's job is essentially to police internal crime, and they were determined to do a thorough job. Finally, I reminded the chief investigator that he had no witnesses and no physical evidence, just a garbled translation. Eventually he relented, but the episode left a bad taste in everyone's mouth.

Soon it became clear that our biggest problem was the UCK, essentially a trans-national criminal organization led by in many cases organized crime figures from Albania. There was really only one way to deal with them, and that was through intimidation. A month into our rotation I became aware that a well-known town elder had been kidnapped by the local UCK. As the de facto "town marshal" it was my job to do something about it.

Without asking permission I surrounded the UCK headquarters with 20 gun trucks and knocked on the front door. I was immediately led into the presence of my erstwhile counterpart. We shook hands in a most friendly manner. Over coffee and biscuits, I explained my problem.

"I've been informed that a well-respected and senior elder from Ferezai has gone missing. I need your help. If you could ask your contacts in the area to assist, I'd personally be grateful. I thank you for your time and apologize for intruding without an appointment." The UCK commander promised to look into the matter and the next day the elder was returned to his family.

By now every day was a tough one. Patrols were regularly fired on or mortared. Vitina remained a problem, though McFarlane worked tirelessly to control the situation. On August 9, I got the call that every commander dreads. While pursuing several Kosovars who had fired on his Bradley, Private First Class Benjamin McGill had been killed as he attempted to pull down his radio antenna to avoid some low-hanging power lines. The antenna struck the wires as the Bradley sped by, killing him almost instantly. My teammate, Bob Scurlock, had expected me to take care of his men when they were task organized under me. I had failed. I had made a point of stressing safety but had not considered this particular set of circumstances. I put out an order directing that all antennas be tied down and vowed to pay even more attention to my attached units.

Some problems took real digging to sort out. Headquartered in Urosevac was the Greek 501st Mechanized Infantry Battalion, set up in a large, unused steel pipe factory. For unexplained reasons, the Greeks were based in my AOR but assigned battlespace some distance away. Coordination was difficult and my units kept running into Greek ones at night, "transiting" my area but, as far as I could see, conducting operations in Urosevac. It took several weeks of digging to uncover the truth. The pipe factory, once operational again, would directly compete with a large Greek one in Thessaloniki. The Greek government therefore had a vested interest in ensuring it remained dormant. I pressed the issue. Hundreds of Kosovars could be reemployed if only we could get the Greeks to vacate. I felt strongly about the issue and pressed General Craddock hard, but the politics proved too tough.

Now the issue became surreal. Late one night, as a 2/505 mounted patrol passed the pipe factory, a shot rang out, just missing Staff Sergeant Roderick Morgan riding in the turret. Seconds later a second shot struck him in the head, fragmenting off his Kevlar helmet and embedding in his right hand and arm, leaving permanent nerve damage. With a serious concussion and bleeding heavily, Morgan was rushed to the nearest aid station.

I immediately notified TF Falcon and went to confront the Greek commander. The facts suggested a skilled marksman, unlikely to be a UCK foot soldier. The vehicle had been moving, it was dark, and the shooter had clearly adjusted his point of aim after the first shot to score a direct hit on the second. There was no high ground behind the pipe factory, and the idea that a UCK assailant had somehow infiltrated the large factory complex to shoot at my units seemed unlikely. On the other hand, for a NATO unit to attack another seemed almost impossible.

The interview did not go well. The Greek commander expressed little sympathy for my wounded man, complained that I was interfering with his operations, and threatened to complain to his government. I did not accuse him of directing the

My father, COL Dick Hooker, with his staff, Vietnam 1969. (From the author's personal collection)

The author as a private in basic training, 1975. (From the author's personal collection)

The author as a West Point cadet, 1981. (From the author's personal collection)

Lieutenant, 82d Airborne Division, 1984. (From the author's personal collection)

White House Fellow 1993, with CJCS GEN Colin Powell. (From the author's personal collection)

Special Assistant to the Chairman JCS, GEN Hugh Shelton 1998. (From the author's personal collection)

Graduation from Ranger Course 503-79. (From the author's personal collection)

Returning from the Sinai as Commander, 2d Battalion, 505th Parachute Infantry, 82d Airborne Division 1999. (From the author's personal collection)

Aide de Camp to Secretary of the Army Tom White, 2001. (From the author's personal collection)

Commander, XVIII Airborne Corps Dragon Brigade, Baghdad 2005. (From the author's personal collection)

Destroyed Dragon Brigade vehicle, Baghdad 2005. (From the author's personal collection)

LTC Bob Quinnett at the scene of a Vehicle borne IED attack, Baghdad 2005. (From the author's personal collection)

LTC Ken Hara, Commander 2d battalion, 299th Infantry, later The Adjutant General of Hawaii as a major general. (Courtesy of the U.S. Army)

With COL Ladd Pattillo, COL Carl Reid and COL Arnie Claudio, Victory Base, Baghdad 2005. (From the author's personal collection)

SGT Lee Godbolt, 1st Battalion, 141st Field Artillery, killed in action March 26, 2005, Baghdad. (From the author's personal collection)

With CSM Abdo Zacheus, Victory Base Iraq, 2005. (From the author's personal collection)

Farewell office call with President Bush, with Beverly, Rachel, Chris, and Davis, 2008. (From the author's personal collection)

With MG Mike Scaparrotti, CG 82d Airborne and COL Skip Davis, Bagram, Afghanistan 2009. (From the author's personal collection)

With my son, Private Chris Hooker, Wardak, Afghanistan 2009. (From the author's personal collection)

Exhausted soldier following a firefight, Afghanistan 2010. (From the author's personal collection)

With MSG Nick Keane, Bagram 2010. (From the author's personal collection)

LTG Doug Lute, Senior Director for Iraq and Afghanistan 2007–10 and later U.S. Ambassador to NATO. (Courtesy of the U.S. Army)

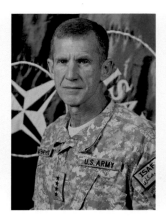

GEN Stan McChrystal, ISAF Commander 2009–10. (Courtesy of the U.S. Army)

GEN Dave Petraeus, MNF-I Commander 2007–9. (Courtesy of the U.S. Army)

GEN John Shalikashvili, CJCS 1993–7.

LTG John R. Vines, CG XVIII Airborne Corps and MNC-I, Iraq 2005. (Courtesy of the U.S. Army)

Meghan O'Sullivan, Deputy National Security Advisor for Iraq and Afghanistan 2004–7. (Courtesy of Washington Institute for Near East Policy)

COL H. R. McMaster in Iraq 2005 (later, National Security Advisor 2017–18 as a 3 star). (From the author's personal collection)

shooting (which I recognized was highly unlikely), but it seemed clear that either a Greek soldier had taken it upon himself, or an unknown assailant had gotten inside the Greek perimeter to do the deed. I stressed that as allies in a common effort, we must work hard to ensure both our common success, and our soldiers' safety. Fortunately, Sergeant Morgan made a good recovery, and was even presented the Purple Heart by General Shelton during a subsequent troop visit to Camp Bondsteel.

Though challenging, my mission so far had enjoyed the steady support and understanding of General Craddock, an intelligent, dignified and extremely competent boss. Now my luck changed for the worse. Craddock rotated out, to be replaced by a tall, overweight, newly promoted brigadier. As some commanders will, he obscured a lack of confidence with bluster. His first act was to revise the mission statement to read: "TF Falcon assures force protection while ..." followed by a mass of verbiage that few of us, much less our solders, could understand and repeat. The new general's mania for force protection at the expense of all else offended us, as the only way to ensure it was to stay in the base camp. Instead of checking in by radio every night, commanders were now forced to endure daily two- and three-hour "commander's updates" in person. It wasn't long before I had my first run-in with the new boss.

It began with an order to "report to the commanding general immediately!" Once in his presence, I was surprised to be addressed not by the general, but by his staff judge advocate (i.e. military legal advisor), who clearly had an attitude. Looking at a paper he sneered, "It says here that you have been stopping and searching civilian vehicles without probable cause. This may be a crime. I need to read you your rights before we proceed." The general leaned back in his chair with his hands behind his head. I raised my hand. "There's no need."

Looking at the lawyer I said, "We're not in the United States. Under international law we are the occupying power, and we have certain obligations, among them to provide law and order. U.S. search and seizure protections that apply in the States don't apply here."

I continued. "I have no police, no courts, and no jails. To stop the killings, I need to control the streets and confiscate the guns. So yes, I let my company commanders search pretty much anyone who looks suspicious. They do it professionally, but they do it, because it works. We only rarely find weapons anymore, and killings are way down. General, we know what we're doing. If you order me to stop, I guarantee you'll have dead Serbs by morning."

The general grudgingly relented, but a week later we went from dumb to dumber. After a soldier in a neighboring unit was killed in a vehicle accident, he ordered a 100 percent "safety stand down." Every soldier in TF Falcon was to report to Bondsteel for safety training. I responded with some intensity. "This isn't garrison. We're on a real-world operation. If I uncover my Serbs, they'll be burned out or killed in hours." Despite my protests the order stood. Before my last platoon had even made it to the base camp, an old man was knifed to death just minutes after his U.S. guards departed.

I was frustrated, but experiences like this are all part of a commander's education. Most bosses I worked for in my career were competent and hard working. Many were exceptional. But occasionally, you'd come across one who was both incompetent, and lacked the values and instincts that are so essential to successfully commanding in complex and dangerous environments. Here was the poster child for this kind of boss. Somehow, he had become a general without commanding a unit in actual operations. That lack compromised his ability to command in a difficult operating environment like Kosovo.

Our commander's lack of situational awareness was linked to one bad habit—he rarely left the headquarters. This trait trickled down to his staff. In one staff session, the G2 intelligence officer, a lieutenant colonel, briefed the general that the local UCK zone commander had been replaced in an internal power struggle and had fled the country. I raised my hand. "I don't think that's right," I remarked. "Where are you getting that from?" The G2 shot me a dark look. "From my sources," he retorted. "Well, I'd check them again. The guy took a vacation in Italy and returned yesterday. We had coffee together this morning. My intel shop sent that information to you more than six hours ago. It would be nice if you actually read what your units are sending you. It would be even better if you got out of the headquarters more often." Throughout my tour in Kosovo, I would beg the TF Falcon operations and intelligence officers to visit us in the field, but without much success. This I attribute to the commander, whose reluctance to get out and about and whose obvious distrust of his units permeated his staff.

I was aware that my direct ways were not winning me many friends back at Camp Bondsteel. On occasion, I was probably too direct and unsubtle. On the other hand, I trusted my instincts and my experience and felt strongly that directives from my higher headquarters that put either my soldiers or my mission at risk should be challenged. Years before, my father had given me some sage advice: "Command on your own terms. You won't get do-overs when bad things happen. Don't let them happen if you can possibly avoid it." Problems had been rare under Craddock. Now they were mounting.

I was, however, reassured by General Abizaid's frequent visits from Germany. Often, he would show up with little fanfare, always supportive and helpful. I soon learned that he was well informed of affairs in our neighborhood, and my confidential requests for help—with spare parts, personnel replacements from the rear, or an adjustment to goofy guidance from Bondsteel—were usually met swiftly and quietly. It was a blessing to have the top cover of a truly talented general who spoke our language and genuinely wished to help.

Abizaid showed his quality one night when he stole into my headquarters unannounced during a staff call. Sitting in darkness in the back of the room, he listened quietly as I asked the staff for solutions to a pressing problem. In the course of our operations, we had discovered many unburied bodies, most of whom were Kosovar Albanians, but some Serb. Most Serb residents in Ferezai had fled, and the Kosovars would not bury Serb corpses. We had no mortuary units with us, and I did not want to ask my paratroopers to moonlight as grave diggers.

Speaking quietly with me after the meeting, Abizaid confided, "Traditionally in the Balkans the Roma often perform this role, since they belong to neither ethnic group. You might consider them. Also, you should be aware that they have been historically persecuted by all sides. Within your capabilities, you might keep an eye out for them too." The Roma were Gypsies, an itinerant people who had originated in northern India many centuries before.

Grateful for his insights, we followed his advice with success. And he was right. For reasons I never fully understood, the Roma were hated and discriminated against by all parties in the Balkans with equal vehemence. As firmly as I could I instructed local leaders that any targeting of the Roma would be dealt with harshly.

For all our difficulties, commanding 2 Panther on operations was immensely satisfying. My troopers were impressive, taking on incredibly difficult tasks like they were born to it. Second lieutenants and even young sergeants would be put in charge of villages, far from help or support, and told to "figure it out." Almost invariably they did. Though shootouts and mortar attacks continued, our luck held. None of my men died. But the command challenges kept coming without let-up.

One bright sunny morning, my battle captain interrupted a commander's call with an urgent message. Signaling my S3, I jumped into my HMMWV and drove to the grid location the captain had scribbled on a slip of paper. As we pulled up, I almost couldn't believe my eyes. To my front were railroad tracks, laid across the two-lane road I was driving on. At the point of intersection was a huge pile of sand, obviously dumped there by the engineer platoon standing nearby. Moments before, a British troop train loaded with troops going on leave had come around the curve and slammed head on into the sand pile, derailing the locomotive and injuring scores of soldiers, some seriously. The young lieutenant sat in his HMMWV, paralyzed. I nodded at Major Griffith, who immediately got on the radio and called in every military ambulance and helicopter for miles around. Our medics converged on the spot and began treating the wounded.

I knew someone had screwed up badly but did not learn all the details for some time. Apparently, some locals had complained that the raised tracks damaged their cars when they drove over them. Without informing me, the engineer brigade located nearby had sent a dump truck and a lieutenant to solve the problem. His solution was to dump the sand over the raised tracks, and then grade it over. This was just dumb. No one had conducted a site assessment, checked the train schedule, or thought to post warning signs or road guards to warn oncoming rail traffic.

As we worked feverishly on the mass casualty evacuation, several British vehicles approached. A tall British colonel wearing red tabs stepped out, flanked by two large military policemen. "Who's in command here?" he demanded. I saluted. "That would be me, sir—Lieutenant Colonel Hooker." "Right," he growled. Turning to his escorts he snapped, "Place this man under arrest." Twice in one career! As the two beefy MPs stepped forward, a stentorian voice from just behind me boomed, "I don't think I'm going to let you arrest my colonel today."

I turned in astonishment. Somehow Sergeant Keane had materialized from nowhere. He was standing in full kit, carrying an M203 grenade launcher at port arms across his chest. At 6'3", wearing helmet, body armor and a grenadier's vest festooned with grenade rounds, he looked a bit like an angry NFL linebacker. He stepped forward menacingly, his weapon at the ready. It appeared we had a Mexican standoff going.

In times like these it's important to defuse the tension in a way that allows the other guy to save face. I faced the angry British colonel. "Sir, I will be glad to accompany you in your vehicle to headquarters where we can sort this out. My S3 will remain in charge here to care for your men."

Back at Bondsteel, I let the British officer blow off steam. He was the KFOR provost marshal, sent by General Jackson, the KFOR commander in Pristina. He had every right to be upset. Many British soldiers had been needlessly injured, and the incident would be national news in the UK. The engineer staff blustered, but they were dead wrong and knew it. Not to inform a commander that an outside unit was operating in his area broke a cardinal rule. Had we known, I would certainly have sent my CSM or a staff officer to oversee the project. Fortunately, no one was killed. However, the locomotive—the only operable one in Kosovo at the time—was destroyed. U.S. forces in Kosovo fell several notches in the estimation of our allies.

Almost immediately after this unfortunate event, a similar one took place that again only narrowly avoided tragedy. One of my foot patrols moving through Urosevac in the middle of the night bumped into a UCK element, obviously bent on evil of some sort, and was fired upon. Sensibly, the patrol leader deployed his men under cover, returned fire, and called for backup in accordance with my standing guidance to "clearly dominate every tactical situation." The battalion QRF was dispatched, led by my S3, and within 10 minutes the four gun vehicles had closed in on the site of the incident.

Combat veterans know that linking up with friendly units under fire, at night, is tricky at best. Generally, the converging units first establish radio contact, and then mark themselves in some way while unit leaders talk through the linkup, exchanging information about friendly and enemy locations and the situation. In this case, as the QRF approached from one direction, a U.S. Special Forces unit, also mounted in HMMWVs, came barreling in from the other. Unable to communicate with my troops (we operated on different radio frequencies) and unaware of the situation, the

Green Berets waded into a confusing mess. Bewildered, the UCK quietly decamped, leaving U.S. forces to blaze away at each other.

Friendly fire, or "green on green," is a commander's ultimate nightmare. It happens in every conflict and can never be entirely avoided. But in this case, just about every rule in the book, as well as common sense, had been disregarded. It was only by the grace of God that loss of life was averted. The 2/505 soldiers on the scene ceased firing and were eventually able to wave off the SF troopers with flares and signals. This time, things had gone too far.

The next day I demanded a meeting with the local Special Forces commander, a major, and the TF Falcon chief of staff. I began by recounting the previous night's events, then broadened my critique. "These guys are here supposedly to 'advise' the local UCK commander, as though he were a friendly allied unit. He isn't. He's our biggest problem. They operate in my battlespace, but don't coordinate their movements with my command post or share information on the UCK. They live in a 'team house' on the outskirts of town, shacked up with a bunch of so-called 'translators,' all beautiful young Albanian women picked up in refugee camps. They stroll around town without helmets or body armor, which are required by TF Falcon order. They are out of control. And if you don't get them under control, someone is going to get killed."

"What do you want?" the chief of staff asked. "I just want the rules enforced," I answered. "I want an SF liaison NCO in my headquarters 24/7. When someone comes into my area, I need them to contact my op center, explain their mission, and monitor my command frequency. We should coordinate with and not ignore each other. We should exchange all relevant information. If I say stop because they are jeopardizing one of my operations, they should stop. I'm the battlespace owner and that's supposed to matter. And there should be one uniform standard for all U.S. forces, not one for us and none for them."

The chief nodded. "That all makes sense. Major, what do you say?" The SF commander twisted in his seat. "I don't work for him." The chief of staff came right back. "He's not saying that you do. He is saying that he owns the ground and you should coordinate your operations with him. And he's right." That night, a written order went out which largely solved the problem.

As summer transitioned into early fall, every day remained tough, but there were occasional interludes. To break the tension, we sponsored a barbecue on Sundays and invited commanders from neighboring units, journalists, NGOs, and other guests. My maintenance warrant officer, a Puerto Rican, would go out on Saturdays with a few mechanics to hunt feral hogs that had been left to run free when the Serbs departed (the Kosovars, mostly Muslim, would have nothing to do with them). An expert cook, he would roast a huge hog in the ground for 24 hours. My cooks would prepare the trimmings, and in the late afternoon, I would host our guests around a huge outdoor table made of plywood. Usually, a few lieutenants would be invited to host the attractive young female NGOs who often showed up. The party would last until well after dark, enlivened by non-alcoholic "near beer" and cigars. For days, my troopers would feast on barbecued pork, and the good will engendered among our civilian counterparts went far to fuel active cooperation.

Unexpectedly, Kosovo offered spiritual refreshment as well. Midway through the deployment, Major Griffith asked me to take a ride with him. We drove for almost an hour, on roads and trails almost impassable even for a HMMWV. After climbing a difficult hill, we broke out of the underbrush to see a charming village nestled against a beautiful alpine vista. This was Stubla, home to one of the few surviving Catholic communities in all of Kosovo.

As we toured the village on foot we were approached by a priest, who offered us lunch and filled us in on the history of Stubla. Kosovo had been Christian since Roman times, but following the Ottoman invasions of the Middle Ages, most of the ethnic Albanian population had been converted to Islam (the Serbs had dwindled over the centuries but remained Orthodox). For whatever reason, perhaps because of its remote inaccessibility, Stubla had not. The priest assured us that the Virgin Mary had provided her special protection through the centuries, and for all I know she had. The surrounding towns had been shattered by the years of fighting, but Stubla was pristine and untouched, a kind of Balkan brigadoon, as if it existed in a time warp. Though only a small village, it was populated by dozens of priests and nuns, and even a bishop. The church was small but lovely, with a wonderful choir. Often, I would return and sit in the pews, watching as the young girls of the town would come to light candles and pray. Kosovo then was an intense furnace of ethnic hatred and enmity, but here was a little piece of heaven on earth.

At a staff call one day I posed the question: how do we give the local population confidence that normalcy is returning? NATO had now been on the ground for several months, but little had so far been done to reconstitute civil society. We had made strides to limit violence, but governance was a different matter altogether. My fire support sergeant spoke up. "Why don't we set up shop in the city hall and just do it? I mean, just do it! Little by little we can involve them more and more, until the civilian side gets its act together." "Go on," I said. "Well, they all want to be compensated for the damage done before we came. We'll set up an office, ask them to fill out a simple form. Then we'll stamp it and file it and ask them to come back in 30 days. When they do, we'll have civil affairs give them a partial payment for their cow or tractor or whatever. That way, they'll see progress. They'll see that we give a damn. It will give them some hope. And we can buy some time until things get organized again." It was a fine idea and we ran with it. We formed a provisional city council to give us advice and provide a forum for discussion. I started up a Sunday radio program. With the help of a few European police trainers we began to stand up a local police force. Things were looking up.

On frequent occasions I would patrol the streets of Urosevac, either on foot or mounted in our HMMWVs, late at night when the bad guys were most likely to be out. One evening as we moved across a dirt field, we were fired on from the second story of a building about 50m away. We all flattened against the ground except for Major Griffith, the S3. Calmly taking a knee he flipped up his night vision goggles, pointed to where the fire came from, and sent a fire team to sweep the building. Excitable in debate, Griffith was cool as ice under fire. He would later command a paratroop battalion of his own and, as a full colonel, all U.S. troops in the Sinai.

In every military career there are golden moments that stand out, and the visit of my neighbor, commander of the British Gurkha battalion nearby, was one. I had invited him for dinner one warm summer evening, and he had shown up with the battalion's pipes and drums to stage an impromptu concert in front of my headquarters. Gurkhas are Nepalese soldiers who have served in the British Army since before Victorian times. They are small, tough, invariably good-natured troops with a great reputation for endurance and ferocity in war. Each Gurkha officer and soldier, from the commander on down, carries a kukri, a curved dagger unique to the Gurkhas. British officers serving in Gurkha units are required to learn and speak Gurkhali. Every Gurkha battalion features a Gurkha major, a vastly influential personage who has risen through the ranks to become the colonel's senior advisor of all things Gurkha. As I stood with my British friend and his subedar major, listening to the screeching bagpipes, I made some friendly conversation.

"They really are wonderful pipers, aren't they?" I offered helpfully. My colleague looked askance at me and said slowly, "Nooo, I imagine they are the worst pipers in the British Army." I tried again. "Well, it must be a real honor to be a piper in a Gurkha battalion." Now he stared at the ground, scuffling the dirt with his boot while the subedar major looked skyward. "Actually," he drawled, "in Nepal only low caste people are musicians. We have to pay them extra to be in the band." Exasperated, I blurted out what was really on my mind. "Why in hell does a Gurkha unit have bagpipers anyway?" Now a big smile creased his face. "Well, about a hundred years ago we had a Scotsman for a colonel. He liked the pipes. So, we've had them ever since."

I laughed out loud and looked out over my small domain. On the road running past my headquarters, the locals began to gather, first in dozens, then in hundreds, to hear our summer concert in the open air. They brought their children and smiled. As the Gurkhas marched to and fro, in perfect step to the drums, the crowd began to laugh. Their lives had turned a corner. "This might work," I thought to myself. "This just might work."

Across Kosovo, NATO forces had gripped the situation firmly and created a safer and more stable environment. Large-scale violence had mostly ceased, local governance began to return, and aid and development organizations began to gain traction. In the 2 Panther sector we had hit our stride. Attacks on our troopers had become less and less frequent and some sense of normalcy returned. We began to look forward to redeployment, scheduled for late September. My XO, Major Dyer, began intensive planning. It would not be easy. Dozens of large metal containers containing our equipment, as well as our many vehicles, would have to be moved to the port of Thessaloniki in Greece by road and rail. The troops themselves would move down to Skopje in Macedonia to be flown home. All this would be done during the transfer of authority (TOA) to our replacements, the 3rd Battalion, 504th Parachute Infantry, or "Blue Devils."

This process is always tricky. The transfer should appear seamless to the outside world, as though nothing had changed. Incoming units needed to be shown the ropes, normally during a week-long "battle handover." These could be uneventful with good will on the part of the incoming and outgoing commanders and staffs. Otherwise, the transition could be rocky. I had been exchanging emails and training tips for weeks with my replacement, though we had never met in person. I looked forward to a collegial and professional handover with a brother commander from my own division. It was not to be.

Lieutenant Colonel Mike Ellerbe was built like a college linebacker and crackled with intensity. A former aide to an Army three-star, he was pugnacious, and his charm wore off quickly. Arriving about 10 days before takeover with his advance party, he immediately began to ruffle feathers. Incredibly, his two majors loathed each other so much that Ellerbe kept them physically separated. Though forbidden by standing orders to conduct his own operations until taking over, Ellerbe sent his advance people on "recons" throughout the U.S. sector without coordination, angering our sister units. On several occasions his senior NCOs dished out reprimands to 2 Panther troopers for violating "Blue Devil standards," provoking instant retaliation from my own senior NCOs. Styling himself "the most combat experienced officer in the U.S. Army" on the basis of his time in Somalia as a staff major, Ellerbe did not walk—he strutted.

Soon after his arrival, Ellerbe pointed out the large apartment complex across the street from my headquarters. "You could put snipers in there. I want that gone," he demanded. Hundreds of civilians lived there, and demolishing the structure was quite simply impossible. I was dumbfounded. Kosovo could be dangerous, but violence had steadily decreased through the summer. The principal threat by September of 1999 was organized crime. This was no longer a war zone, yet Ellerbe seemed determined to view this as a combat mission. His hyper-aggressive approach permeated his battalion and filled me with foreboding. The UCK needed to be dealt with firmly, but they would always back down if confronted with determined force. The local people were not a threat, and a sensitive and measured approach was critical. We had worked hard to build mutual trust and confidence. All this now seemed at risk.

After several days I spoke with Ellerbe. Aware that he had been in command for longer than me and was something of a golden boy, I spoke politely but directly.

"Mike, let's get something straight. Until we change command, you're not in charge. Stop giving orders to my soldiers and stop roaming around Kosovo without permission. You're pissing people off, and you're making the 82nd look bad. And another thing. This isn't a combat mission, it's a security mission, and there's a difference. We've made that clear in all the message traffic we've sent you through the summer. You need to be careful but not provocative. I recommend you calm down and calm your troopers down."

This did not sit well. Ellerbe's subordinates stopped harassing my troopers. But my suggestions made little impact otherwise. Ellerbe had prepared his unit for a combat environment, a view that suited his temperament, personality and predisposition. The Blue Devil motto with Ellerbe in command was "shoot 'em in the face." He genuinely believed that a hard, aggressive manner would cow the locals and cement his authority. I thought this attitude presaged disaster. As a brand new commander, not well known to the brass back at Bragg, I lacked the confidence and perhaps moral courage to share my concerns with my bosses back home. We would all come to regret it.

As we approached our transfer the logistical challenges of moving troops and equipment became consuming. The 3/504 main body was now on the ground and, though I was technically still in command, most of the day-to-day operations were being conducted by the new unit, with my leaders overwatching. Two days before the transition, I was called in to see my portly commander. With a conspiratorial air, he motioned me to sit down.

Clearing his throat, he began. "I have come to the conclusion that there is a high chance that the Serbs will attempt to reoccupy Kosovo. Therefore, I have decided that I cannot allow you to redeploy to Bragg. I will need you here to help defend the U.S. sector. Your movement orders are therefore canceled." This news hit me like a sledgehammer. "Sir," I protested, "most of my troops and all of my heavy weapons—my artillery, mortars and antitank launchers—are already in Macedonia or on the way to the port in Greece. Our aircraft have been laid on and will arrive in two days. I've got nothing and almost no one to fight with. And I've heard nothing about the Serbs coming back. That would mean war with NATO. With all due respect, this is crazy!"

The general refused to budge. I left in a daze. I'd seen much in my career, but this beat all. A few secure phone calls to friends on the Joint Staff and in U.S. Army Europe confirmed that there was no intelligence to back up the general's assessment. It seemed likely, then, that this was a ploy to retain control of two paratroop battalions instead of just one. What to do?

I took a deep breath. Conflicting loyalties played out in my mind. Strictly speaking, I owed the general obedience as my superior. But I was now convinced he was playing a double game. Many of my soldiers had made plans and spent money on leave plans in accordance with the original timeline for return to Fort Bragg. A detailed training plan had been drawn up involving ranges, ammunition forecasts and a thousand other details that would now have to be scrapped. I was sure that the scenario of Serbs reoccupying Kosovo was fantasy. What should I do? Bypass the general and appeal to Abizaid? Or to General McNeil?

In the end, I did neither. On a secure line I called Harry Harris in the chairman's office, explained the situation and asked if they were aware of the change in plans. Orders to move, or cancel movements, from a theater of operations to home station must be approved by the Joint Staff in the Pentagon. That had not happened. I did not specifically ask for the chairman to intervene. I didn't have to. Within hours, Dyer called me back. "I don't know what happened, but our birds have been turned back on. We're back to the original plan." The general's chief of staff called later that night with the same word. On schedule, we loaded our planes in Skopje and began the trip back to the States. After six months of hard duty, 2 Panther was coming home.

What had Kosovo taught me? During the flight home I reflected that, while we tend to use past experiences as a guide to future action, each deployment is different. We had done well in many ways, but I had missed any number of cultural clues, misread the signs from time to time, and allowed some bad things to happen on my watch. We had narrowly averted disaster when the SF ran into one of our fights. I should have watched them more closely. The railroad accident weighed on me. I should have insisted, earlier and more strongly, that no one operate in my area of responsibility without my knowledge. And the handover with 3/504 had been tense, to say the least. A better, wiser commander might have found a way to work through it more successfully. Still, we had come through more than 30 firefights and mortar attacks with no fatalities, saved many civilians from death or injury, and left our sector much more stable and calmer than before. That at least was something.

In early October of 1999, after a too-short period of leave, we reassembled in garrison to begin re-training for war. The battalion went through a six-week "intensive training cycle" in the field, beginning with individual weapons training and progressing through squad, platoon, and company-level live fire exercises, both day and night. The final week was the big show, an external evaluation proctored by General Petraeus. It began with the battalion jumping at night from 23 C130s to simulate seizing an airfield, followed by a series of follow-on missions: search and attack, movement to contact, and finally an air assault and deliberate night attack.

The evaluation was challenging, as we had scant opportunity to prepare beforehand. I was helped immensely by Dyer and Griffith, by a great set of company commanders and first sergeants, and by a cohesive and proud unit that had done well in Kosovo and knew it. I also found that my schooling under Scaparrotti stood me in good stead. We kept our plans simple and clear, gave the smaller units time to plan and rehearse, and stayed out of their business as they executed at their level. Though the pressure was on, I enjoyed the chance to maneuver the whole battalion in the woods. The opportunity to practice with all the pieces—artillery, engineers, air defense, the fuel handlers and truck drivers, Army Aviation and military police—was great fun. I felt that I had professionally arrived.

In January of 2000, news from Kosovo hit us like a hard punch in the gut. A 3/504 NCO, Staff Sergeant Frank Ronghi, had apparently slipped away from a foot patrol and raped and murdered an 11-year-old Albanian girl. The subsequent investigation revealed other incidents inside the battalion, all directed against Albanians, apparently encouraged by an over-aggressive and dehumanizing "command climate." Court martial proceedings began, and the Army initiated a four-star investigation. As Ellerbe and his leaders lawyered up, we began to see press reports blaming it all on the division for "not training us properly." I was shocked. 2/505, under my predecessor, had had no mission-specific training for Kosovo at all. But Joe Anderson had built a disciplined unit, well able to cope with complexity and restrained in its use of force. I had only continued in that direction. Ellerbe, on the other hand, was advantaged by reading my regular situation reports and training suggestions. We'd painted a clear picture. It appeared my reservations were right. The Blue Devils came to Kosovo looking for a fight. Without a willing opponent, they had taken it out on the locals.

As the investigation and court case wound on, investigators began to show up in my area. One defense offered by Ellerbe and his soldiers was "we didn't do anything the guys before us didn't." Dozens of my troopers were interviewed. Every document was reviewed. After a painful scrubbing lasting months, it was determined that not a single case of 2/505 misconduct could be found. The 82nd took a beating in the national and international press. Ellerbe's excuse that "we are trained for combat—it wasn't our fault" gained traction. The narrative shifted from him and his leaders to the division and the generals who had failed to prepare the battalion properly. Even the secretary of defense joined in. This was unfair and inaccurate. The real error was not seeing through Ellerbe's persona. The division and the whole Army paid a high price for that mistake. Ellerbe would finish his command tour before all the investigations were complete, but the fallout would be career ending for him.

I felt sick. It was now clear I should have said something. One of the worst crimes a commander could commit in the 82nd was to disgrace the division. We now had probably the worst scandal in the 82nd's history going. I felt complicit. I might not have been listened to. But I should have made the attempt.

On the horizon the following summer was another six-month deployment, this time to the Sinai desert with the Multinational Force and Observers or MFO. But first we faced a three-week rotation to the Joint Readiness Training Center at Fort Polk, Louisiana. JRTC was where the Army's light forces went to train and be evaluated on a fully instrumented "battlefield" with a live opposing force or OPFOR. Except for a real-world deployment, JRTC constituted the toughest test for a commander of light forces. Like the National Training Center at Fort Irwin,

California (a similar training installation for heavy forces), JRTC was not meant to be fair. Most units were defeated in every engagement by an adversary who knew the terrain intimately and practiced relentlessly. This was accepted and expected. JRTC would be an invaluable opportunity to train for war. But we would not, I vowed, go there to get our ass kicked.

The rotation turned out to be demanding, but an unqualified success. Most units followed the script, applied Army doctrine faithfully, and lost—not because they were bad units, but because the OPFOR held most of the cards. We played a different game, never showing the enemy what he expected to see. Well drilled in the fundamentals from the Kosovo deployment, we planned quickly and executed violently, pushing our combat power down to junior leaders whenever possible. Many units suffered cruelly from simulated mines and mortars. We had encountered both in Kosovo and treated them with respect, locating and clearing them as high priorities. In the final battle, the attack against the Shugart-Gordon urban complex, we fought alone after our sister battalion was destroyed on the approach march. Despite high casualties we took the town, an unprecedented achievement for a single battalion.

As we cleaned our equipment and prepared to return to Fort Bragg, a young Observer/Controller captain sidled up to me. I recognized him as one of our junior staff officers in Vicenza some years before. Shyly he took me aside. "Sir, you didn't hear this from me. Officially, we don't grade training battalions here. But off the record, 2 Panther was the best of 20 infantry battalions to rotate through here in the past 12 months. The best. By far. Your guys should know that."

That knowledge filled me with quiet satisfaction on the long bus ride from Louisiana to North Carolina. All that really mattered was that we had learned and gotten better over the past few weeks. We would earn little in the way of public recognition for our exploits at Fort Polk. But our generals knew a good battalion when they saw one, and they would remember. 2 Panther rode through the night in a deep slumber, sleeping the sleep of the contented.

Back at home station we were given one treat. Because 2/505 had led the division in reenlistment for the preceding quarter, we were given a "Hollywood" jump, meaning a jump in daylight, with no combat equipment. These were rare and highly prized, as the division jumped almost exclusively at night, with equipment, as part of a follow-on tactical exercise. (In my career I would make almost a hundred night, combat equipment jumps.) The troops boarded the planes in good humor, joking and skylarking on a brilliant, sunny spring day. As we approached the drop zone and began to run through the jump commands, the safety near the ramp of the aircraft blew into his open palm and held up his thumb and forefinger in a "zero" sign, meaning "no wind on the drop zone." As the first jumper in the first plane, the prerogative of the ranking man, I stood in the open jump door and took it all in. This was truly living the dream! As the green light flashed on, I leaped into the slipstream, enjoying every second until I came to earth with a surprisingly soft landing.

After rolling up and turning in my chute I trotted over to my vehicle, where my driver sat monitoring the drop zone safety officer's frequency. He shot me a concerned look. "The DZSO is reporting a serious injury. It's Sergeant Keane." The news seemed incredible. Keane was one of the most experienced jumpers in the battalion, in great physical shape. We had no wind that day, and no heavy equipment to complicate things. I hopped into the command HMMWV and we hurried over to the scene. As we arrived, I could see Nick sprawled out on the ground, his face white with shock, his body lying awkwardly astride an erosion ditch. The medic on the scene had cut away his battle dress trousers to reveal a shattered femur, the compound fracture protruding under the skin. It was the worst jump injury I had ever seen. The wound was bleeding heavily, rapidly swelling the space around the fracture as Keane was put on a stretcher and loaded into a field ambulance.

I stopped the senior medic. "How long will it take to get him to the emergency room?" I asked. "Twenty-five to thirty minutes." "Negative," I fired back. "That's too slow. Bring in a medevac." In minutes, a UH60 aerial medevac landed, loaded Sergeant Keane and sped off into a darkening late afternoon sky. I followed in my HMMWV, calling Beverly en route. She met us at the hospital, and we went in together. I was immediately taken to a screened-off area where Keane was being prepped for surgery. He smiled and gripped my hand, but it was obvious he was in bad shape. "What's the prognosis?" I asked the attending physician. "Not sure," he replied. "He lost a lot of blood. He probably would have bled out if he had come by ground. We've transfused him and he's stable. We'll go in and replace his thigh bone with a titanium rod. It will be a year or so before he is fully mobile again. Not sure if he can stay in the Army or not. One thing is sure, though. He will never jump again."

In the months and years to come, Nick Keane would confound the doctors, recovering quickly and jumping again in only nine months. As 2/505 would deploy shortly to the Sinai, he was moved to 2nd Brigade under Colonel Scaparrotti, whose life he had saved in Bosnia. In 2003, he would participate in the invasion of Iraq as a medical platoon sergeant with the Falcons, earning a Bronze Star and Combat Medical Badge. In his late 40s he would complete the year-long Special Operations Medic course, an incredible achievement given his age and medical history, and serve three combat deployments in Afghanistan as a special operator. I said goodbye to Nick with real regret, grateful for his service and friendship over many years. But it would not be the end for us. Not yet.

As I neared the end of my first year in command, I decided that it was time for a Dining In, a formal mess night modeled on British military tradition where officers would enjoy a formal dinner, celebrate the history of the battalion and enjoy a festive night out. By custom, each of the companies would put on a humorous skit at the end of the evening. I was excited when General Yarborough, our Honorary Colonel in the 509th and probably the greatest living World War II airborne hero, agreed to attend. Near 90, he regaled my young officers with tales of derring do in the days when "men were men, and giants roamed the plains." The evening was all I'd hoped. The unit skits were hilarious, poking fun good-naturedly at the senior officers. As midnight approached, the time arrived for the final skit.

Unexpectedly, the commander of my Delta Company put in a previously taped video in lieu of a skit. I watched in mounting horror and anger as the presentation grew more and more profane and filthy. Finally, when two of his lieutenants began to simulate oral sex on screen, I pulled the plug. Calling an end to the evening, I ordered the captain to report to me in the morning, with the video in hand.

My humor had not improved by the next day. The audience had included not only General Yarborough, but also our unit chaplain and a young female captain who would accompany us to the Sinai the following month. Dining Ins are often marked by a relaxation of formal discipline and even by somewhat risqué comedic routines. But I had specifically directed that professional decorum be observed in respect of our guests. The video had gone far beyond the pale. As we reviewed the tape, the captain, by now clearly worried, attempted to argue that the video *seemed* to portray oral sex between two officers, but in fact showed nothing more than a shoe polishing scene. This was absurd. A subsequent formal investigation by a major from the brigade staff produced distressing conclusions. All five Delta Company platoon leaders had sworn, under oath, that the captain had directed a portrayal of oral sex. Three had refused to participate in the video, including a former West Point First Captain and son-in-law of a famous Army four-star. Two had agreed under duress. The captain himself was cited in the investigation for having lied in writing and under oath. Worse, he had attempted to influence his lieutenants to do the same.

This raised the incident to a new and very different level. The video had been bad enough. It had showed poor judgment and disregard of my instructions that would concern any battalion commander. But an integrity violation of this magnitude was almost unheard of. Certainly, I'd never encountered one like this before in my career. I consulted with the brigade commander. I saw no alternative but to request the captain's relief, a career-ending sanction. It seemed impossible that he could effectively command his unit, having pressured his subordinates to lie under oath and been caught doing it. Clearly uncomfortable, the colonel agreed. Only the division commander could direct the relief, so we went to see him.

By now General McNeil had been promoted to command of the XVIII Airborne Corps. His replacement, Major General John R. Vines, would not report for duty for two more months, and so the division was temporarily under the acting command of Brigadier General Stanley McChrystal, the assistant division commander (General Petraeus had also moved on to become the Corps chief of staff). I had met McChrystal on a number of occasions and, like most of my peers, was tremendously impressed. Tall, lean, and handsome, he was personable, even gregarious, with a great resume that included command of the 75th Ranger Regiment. The son of a general and the brother of an Army chaplain, McChrystal was clearly marked out for great things. I considered the case cut and dried and expected the meeting to be a formality.

It turned out to be anything but. The general I now encountered was annoyed and combative. Clearly briefed in advance, he flashed on me, dismissing my version of events. "Dining Ins are where you let your hair down. There's a lot of alcohol. People do stupid things. You're overreacting." Patiently, I repeated my case. This wasn't about drunken shenanigans. The video had been taped days before the event. The request for relief was based upon a serious integrity violation, indeed one that could hardly be more serious. McChrystal became more irritated. Finally, he ended the meeting. "I don't agree. The relief is not approved."

I left the headquarters, shocked. The brigade commander had said almost nothing throughout the interview. I could not account for McChrystal's decision. Later, I was told that my captain had served under him in an earlier assignment and had been a favorite. I was never able to verify the story, but it seemed irrelevant. Now I had two problems. I had insisted on a relief for cause and been rebuffed. This would be common knowledge by the time I reached my headquarters, and my own command would be, at the very least, compromised. Also, I had angered the general, and he would not forget. Caught between a rock and a hard place, the brigade commander was far from pleased as well. Command was turning out to be very hard indeed.

As I considered the incident my resolve hardened. As a cadet I had been drilled on "the harder right instead of the easier wrong." I didn't wish to appear self-righteous, but I couldn't square what had happened with any conception of an officer's duty that I recognized. Knowing the likely consequences, I decided that if there was ever a time to take a stand, this must be it.

The young commander's annual officer evaluation was now due and in it I cited, word for word, the conclusion of the investigating officer. This was fatal for the offender, and by law I could not be ordered to change my evaluation. Nevertheless, the report was returned to me several times for "reconsideration." Each time I resubmitted the report with no changes. The report finally went to Washington, and within six months the captain was out of the Army.

Had I done right? I thought I had. Many mistakes can be forgiven, especially in younger officers. But in any Army worth a damn, officer integrity matters. Lives can depend on it. The officers, sergeants, and soldiers I had known in a career spanning more than three decades were overwhelmingly honorable and truthful men and women. In fact, that was one of the chief joys of soldiering. But all Army leaders will encounter ethical dilemmas in their careers and be forced to resolve them, one way or another. This was a particularly tough episode, but a part of command. I put it behind me and looked ahead.

Meanwhile, the Sinai beckoned. The MFO had kept the peace between Egypt and Israel for 20 years. Composed of three infantry battalions—U.S., Colombian and Fijian—plus support troops, the MFO manned a series of observation posts or OPs in the Sinai desert, which had been returned to Egypt as part of the Camp David Accords under President Carter as a demilitarized zone. The U.S. sector was in south Sinai, headquartered in Sharm el Sheik on the Red Sea. 82nd battalions had been serving in the MFO since its inception.

In June 2000, after a period of specialized training, we boarded our chartered aircraft and flew to Sharm el Sheik, arriving at the MFO's "South Camp" at midnight in oppressive heat. The battalion was herded into a gym, where we were briefed by Herb Brav, an MFO civilian who ran the athletic and morale programs there. The men were exhausted after the long plane flight and wanted nothing more than to turn their weapons into the arms room and get some sleep. What they got was an electrifying presentation that most would never forget.

Herb was one of the most remarkable people I ever met. Humble and self-effacing, his life could easily be turned into a feature movie. Herb had joined the Army at the end of World War II as a paratrooper in the 101st Airborne Division. In Korea, he had jumped with the 187th Airborne, been captured, escaped and walked some 200 miles to freedom. In Vietnam, he had served as command sergeant major of a Special Forces Group and had been intimately involved with Project Phoenix, the highly classified "kill or capture" program that targeted high level Viet Cong operatives. Herb had ended his eminently successful military career in the 70s as CSM of the 8th Infantry Division (Mechanized) in Germany.

But there was much more to this amazing personality. A tiny man, barely 5'6" and weighing about 130lbs, Herb had once been a three-hundred-pound heavyweight power lifter (he had the pictures to prove it). His office displayed pictures signed by JFK, Muhammad Ali, Frank Sinatra, Donald Trump, and many other famous personalities as well as an amazing constellation of four-stars, all inscribed with variations of "To my good friend Herb." Herb had won $13 million in the Florida state lottery but lived simply in a trailer at South Camp. On his birthday he would swim to Tiran Island in the Red Sea, 12 miles away, until at 72 he was attacked by a shark. In his late 70s now, he ran the open water international lifeguard certification program at South Camp, and regularly "smoked" our best young swimmers in the rough seas near Sharm. Herb had boarded the chartered DC8 carrying MFO soldiers home which crashed in Gander, Newfoundland in 1986, killing all 256 soldiers on board—but was bumped in Cairo by a higher priority passenger and so survived. Each story sounded more improbable than the last—but all were true.

Herb's welcome speech was supposed to be a safety briefing. Instead it was a primer on a life well lived, Herb-style. By the end he had five hundred paratroopers screaming along with him: "We set the example high! Where the will is strong, everything is easy!" I soon learned that Herb was far more than the guy who ran the gym. He was Yoda. His wisdom seemed unbounded, his care and love of soldiers genuine, his advice and counsel treasured by every commander who came to the MFO. Within a week Herb would identify the problem soldiers, the troubled ones, and ask if they could be assigned to duty in the gym. Then he would go to work, teaching them to box, to smile, to care again, to soldier. Invariably, he would fix them.

Herb was a little strange, it was true. I would often hear him at 0430, walking by my trailer on the way to the beach for his lifeguard training, mumbling to his ancient bicycle. Herb seemed to eat almost nothing and could often be found at "Herb's Beach" hanging upside down like a bat from the pull-up bar. His quirks however were harmless, while his virtues were legion. When he died in 2012, he was eulogized from the floor of Congress, and soldiers around the world mourned.

Very quickly we got organized, pushed out to the desert OPs and relieved the departing battalion. Until we acclimatized, the heat was almost unendurable, more than 125 degrees in mid-summer. As soon as I could, I flew to North Camp at El Arish, some 400km away, to meet the MFO commander and staff. The Force Commander was Norwegian Major General Tryggve Tellefsen, a veteran of a few small UN monitoring missions. Thirteen different nations contributed to the MFO, most with small contingents. I soon learned that, though the U.S. avoided a high profile, every staff section was anchored by a U.S. deputy as well as the chief of staff, all the logistics, and the aviation detachment, flying creaky old UH1H helos left over from Vietnam.

To my surprise, I quickly found that the worst thing you could do was report an actual treaty violation. These were not unusual, and generally involved a stray aircraft or patrol boat venturing where it shouldn't. If reported, an involved process was required to bring the Israeli and Egyptian sides together to resolve the violation. No one wanted that. Even the phrase "suspected treaty violation" was banned. Short of a tank brigade charging across the desert, the mission was really to "observe" and not "report." This seemed a strange way to run a railroad, but it had worked for years, and we fell into line like all the battalions before us.

At the end of our first month, I took a phone call from the aviation detachment out at the airfield, about eight miles away. A contingent of U.S. officers from North Camp, led by a full colonel, had just flown in by fixed-wing airplane. They were demanding helicopters to fly them to Tiran Island in the Red Sea, manned by a squad of paratroopers. I could guess what this was about. Because of a line on a map, soldiers serving on the island were entitled to hazardous duty pay, but everyone else in the MFO was not. Americans from North Camp would typically fly in on the last day of the month for a "staff inspection," stay the night, and return. They would then draw danger pay for two months. I had often seen the same thing in the Balkans. I ordered the aviators to stand by and drove to the scene.

When I arrived, the American colonel was seething. "I am giving you a lawful order. Release the damned helicopters now!" Keeping my cool, I responded pleasantly. "Sorry sir, but you're a staff officer. I work for the Force commander. And south Sinai and everything in it that is American works for me. I'm pretty sure this is all about defrauding the government, but I'm willing to submit the matter to the lawyers or the inspector general to get a ruling. I'll make you a deal. If you and your staff officers want to visit every OP every month, including the island, I won't object." This meant driving hundreds of miles in the deep desert over three or four days. In no good humor, the colonel declined. They all left, and the "pay day follies" ended.

For my troopers in the rifle squads and platoons, life in the Sinai was forbidding. They spent most of the deployment in isolated locations, in fierce heat, looking at a beautiful and austere, but mostly empty, desert. Boredom was a constant enemy, and we did not have the technology that would later enable soldiers to connect with families and friends from almost anywhere. Sergeants and lieutenants kept them busy with physical training, correspondence courses and hands-on training with weapons, tactical skills such as call for fire or combat first aid, and leadership training. Every six weeks or so, troops would rotate back to South Camp for a brief R&R, followed by intensive combat training at the squad level. General Tellefsen visited once to observe several squads conduct a live fire exercise at night to enter and clear a trench line using live ammunition and hand grenades. The event seemed so dangerous and stressful that he never came back. Over almost 20 years, a huge backlog of training ammunition had accumulated, and we resolved to fire all of it off during our six months. Some soldiers were able to qualify with their assigned weapons six or seven times, raising the number of "experts" in the battalion to above 90 percent. Throughout the deployment, CSM Padilla forced the pace, keeping the men busy and sharpening their skills.

As commander in south Sinai, I also hosted an Italian naval contingent, the "MFO navy," which manned three U.S. World War II surplus minesweepers. Commanded by a naval commando named Francesco—a graduate of U.S. Navy SEAL training who insisted on being addressed as "Frank"—their task was to monitor the peace on the Red Sea. Frank and I became good friends, and one day he invited me to join him for a cruise.

Knowing little of naval matters, I was fascinated by the shipboard routine. At one point the officer of the deck, scanning the horizon with his binoculars, sounded off in English. "Sir, surface contact, bearing 255 degrees, range one mile!" Frank took a quick look himself before barking, "Come left to 255, increase to flank speed!" As we closed the range at a lumbering 15 knots—best speed for the antiquated vessel—Frank quietly ordered, "Stand by to render passing honors!" This provoked a flurry of activity. As we came alongside, bosun's pipes shrilled, flags were run up, and the crew manned the rail at attention, all saluting. Seeing my confusion, Frank handed me his binoculars. I laughed out loud. The target of our protocol was a dive boat, populated by a bevy of topless Italian girls.

Running a multinational operation involved many such cultural challenges. South Camp in the Sinai was maintained by a small cadre of British civilian contractors, many of whom were ex-military, and all of whom were talented and prodigious drinkers. They maintained a small pub, outfitted with portraits of the Queen, British flags, and soccer paraphernalia, which did a lively business each night after work. One fellow was a fixture. An elderly man, he would show up each day at about 6 p.m., take his accustomed perch on a corner seat at the bar, and drink beers until closing time, rarely joining in the usual camaraderie. Eventually the inevitable happened, and one night he quietly passed away at the bar, beer in hand. In his honor, his mates left him seated, grasping his beer mug, until closing time before calling the doctor. All agreed he went out as he would have wished.

Several months into our rotation the Second Intifada began, spurred by an ill-advised visit by Ariel Sharon to the Temple Mount (there is also evidence that the uprising was planned in advance by Yasser Arafat following the failure of the Camp David Accords). In the first week of unrest, almost 50 Palestinians were killed by Israeli security forces and almost 2,000 were wounded. As a consequence, the character of our mission changed overnight. All weekend cultural trips, except to the Israeli port city of Eilat, were canceled. We were directed to begin contingency planning to reinforce the U.S. Embassy in Tel Aviv if needed. Force protection was stepped up and we hunkered down. Our mail, which came by air to Tel Aviv and then by road through the Rafah border crossing in Gaza, was interrupted. An already challenging mission became more difficult—and less fun.

In that same fall the U.S. presidential election came to a head. As the desert began to cool down, we watched on CNN as Bush and Gore battled it out. I had taught political science at West Point, but even I had difficulty explaining the election outcome to our international comrades in the MFO. We soldiered on in our lonely outposts, spending Christmas in Sinai before finally completing our tour. Towards the end of the mission, we underwent a three-day exhaustive evaluation by MFO headquarters and finished with the highest scores in the history of the MFO. In mid-January, we returned to Fort Bragg, well satisfied with ourselves and ready to see our families again.

We had much to do to regain our war-fighting form, but we began with some real advantages. The battalion was in terrific physical condition, as PT was one thing you could do a lot of in the desert. We had stressed road marching, working up to 25 milers with rucksacks, and could outperform most if not all our sister battalions in this area. 90 percent of the battalion's troopers had qualified "expert" with their assigned weapons, and we were fully trained on infantry battle drills at the squad level. We looked forward eagerly to a short leave, and six hard weeks in the field to regain our form at the platoon, company and battalion level.

I thoroughly enjoyed the final six months with the battalion, though my dealings with my boss remained problematic. No officer can assume that he will gain the next step in command, and so I tried to lead 2 Panther as though I would never command again. After two overseas deployments and a Combat Training Center rotation, by now I was tried and experienced. In training I could maneuver the battalion task force confidently and manage its resources expertly. We were among the best battalions in the division in physical fitness, in marksmanship and in airborne operations. We had proved ourselves in Kosovo and the Sinai and were in fact the most deployed battalion in the entire U.S. Army. I felt I had come into my own, and whatever happened next, I could take pride in what we had accomplished.

Physically, though, I was beat up. I'd cracked a couple of ribs on a jump, separated my shoulder for the fourth time, and the chronic arthritis in my knees had worsened. I could still "max" the PT test, but the life was taking its toll. As a prior enlisted officer, I was older than my peers, and it was starting to show. Twenty-five years of running, jumping, road marching, and living in the woods with little or no sleep was catching up with me.

As I approached my change of command, I had one more dramatic episode yet to come. I took pride in continuing to perform jumpmaster duties as a way to set the example, remain proficient and stay close to the troops. Late one night in April of 2001, while serving as a "safety" on a night mass tactical jump, I stood behind Staff Sergeant David Jordan, controlling his static line in the open door as he leaned out to make his final door check before exiting his stick. Just as he pulled himself back inside the aircraft his reserve parachute accidentally deployed. In a fraction of a second, he was snatched out of the plane as his reserve inflated, striking the edge of the paratroop door on the way out. Horrified, the Air Force loadmaster slammed the jump door shut and our pilot broke out of the formation to return to the airfield.

As we flew back to Pope Air Force Base, we all sat, enveloped in gloom. I had no communication with the ground and would have to wait until we landed to learn about my jumpmaster's fate. Sergeant Jordan, a short, squat antitank specialist, had served with me in Vicenza and was popular and well liked. He had a family, a wife and kids. Reserve deployments in the aircraft were often fatal, as the jumper would usually strike something at fantastic speed on the way out of the aircraft. After landing, the C130 taxied up to the parachute packing shed and dropped its ramp. As I filed off, the battalion's S3 Air officer met me with a big smile.

"Sergeant Jordan's all right, sir!" he beamed. I couldn't believe it. "He broke his shoulder and three ribs, but after landing he policed up his chute, flagged down a farmer and made him drive him to the drop zone. He checked in with the DZ safety officer before the third pass had even jumped. He's in the emergency room now. He'll be fine."

"Well, I'll be damned," I thought. "That is one hard dude." Jordan was back in the saddle four months later, working at full speed. I took great pleasure in pinning on his Master Parachutist wings after his recovery—this had been his 65th and qualifying jump, one he would remember forever.

There were many such stories in 2 Panther. These were hard men. We were not all Americans. The battalion had soldiers from 24 different countries. The native-born

Americans were largely from the Mid-West and the South, many from military families like me. My troopers were not the sons of doctors, lawyers, politicians, or wealthy businessmen. They were tough blue-collar kids. Most were high-school graduates, but few were college bound. Many had played football or other sports in high school. They were used to hard physical work, being yelled at by coaches, and making sacrifices for the team. They wanted adventure. They wanted to fight. Some would stay on for a career, though many would not. But all would answer the call. I was the luckiest man in the world to command them, and the joy and pride that gave me would last a lifetime.

Now it was time to consider next steps. Battalion commanders in the 82nd often moved across post to work in the XVIII Airborne Corps headquarters, and my preliminary inquiries revealed that I was programmed for a plans job in the Corps G3. Serendipitously, the phone rang in my office one day. The caller was Colonel Joe Schroedel, the executive officer for the incoming Secretary of the Army, Thomas White. I had known Schroedel on the Joint Staff and accepted his offer to interview as Secretary White's new senior aide de camp. The interview went well and soon after I was informed I had gotten the job.

The orders arrived quickly, and I found myself summoned to see General McChrystal once more. I had worked hard, and on the whole successfully, to avoid seeing much of him since our last encounter. I doubted this would be fun. In fact, I expected what the British called "an interview without coffee," and that's what I got. Somewhat stiffly, McChrystal returned my salute and offered me a seat. For a few minutes we exchanged desultory conversation about the battalion. Then he came to the point.

"I'm told you sought out an assignment in Washington. You know, we had other plans for you." In a neutral tone I answered, "Actually sir, it was the secretary's XO who called *me*. But I'm happy to go and work for him. He seems like a great guy, and I'll learn a lot. Bev's company is based in DC and this will work well for her. Schools for the kids are great in northern Virginia, and my folks are getting older and live nearby."

McChrystal continued. "That's a horse holder's job. Kind of a Courtney Massingale thing, don't you think?" This was a reference to *Once an Eagle*, a classic military novel about two fictional officers whose careers intersect over four decades as they rise in the service. We'd all read it. Sam Damon is the hero of the piece, a compassionate soul, a dynamic combat leader and hero in the World Wars and a character combining all the positive qualities of the perfect officer. Courtney Massingale is the quintessential scheming staff officer, shunning combat, climbing the social ladder, toadying his superiors and rising to the top of the military hierarchy. All good officers wanted to be Sam Damon. To be compared to Courtney Massingale was a calculated insult, and I said so.

McChrystal's offhand remark bit home, as he intended. Even my enemies would not describe me as a sycophant. I had served in the invasion of Grenada, fought in Somalia, dodged mines in Bosnia and been shot at in Kosovo. All this seemed a bit raw. Still, there's not much point arguing with a general. After a lengthy, cold silence McChrystal dismissed me.

My final out brief with Major General Vines, the 82nd's commanding general, was altogether different. Vines was a tough guy (his unofficial nom de guerre was "Viper 6"), with a renowned combat record, but rigorously fair and objective. Perhaps not as polished as some generals, he was much more down to earth. Well aware that we had been the most deployed battalion in the whole Army, Vines complimented me on my two years in command, looked me in the eye and said, "I rate you as number 5 of the 24 battalion commanders I rate. You've got a legitimate shot at brigade command." I was grateful. There were several commanders in the division that I knew were better than me; I might have rated myself a notch or two lower, in fact. He wished me well, thanked me for my service and we shook hands. Though I could not have known it, we would serve together again and my admiration for this talented commander and good man would only grow.

I was sad to be leaving command, but it had been a grueling two years. I had not seen much of my wife and children and the pressure and stress had worn on me. As I trooped the line during the change of command ceremony, I wondered if I'd ever serve with soldiers again. I thought it more likely than not that I'd end my career as a staff officer somewhere in the Pentagon. I stood and watched as my troopers passed in review, jaunty in their maroon berets and battle dress, regretful that it all might be coming to an end. But it was not—not yet. Though I had seen 26 years in uniform, all that had gone before was just preamble. The real fight was still to come. It goes on still.

CHAPTER 6

Sky Dragons!

There is a sobbing of the strong
And a pall upon the land
But the people in their weeping
Bare the iron hand
Beware the people weeping

HERMAN MELVILLE

It was a glorious sunny morning as I stood at the Pentagon's River entrance, waiting to greet my boss. A hot August had given way to a beautiful September, a cool breeze wafted in off the Potomac and a bright, blue cloudless sky promised a perfect day. Soon the Lincoln town car pulled up and Secretary of the Army Tom White stepped out. Cheerful as always, he bounded up the steps and I hurried to keep up as we made our way towards his office. The date was September 11, 2001. Very shortly, the whole world would change, and my life with it. All that had gone before, all my service, all that I had learned and experienced, would be a precursor to the events that would follow. That day America would embark on the Global War on Terror.

"What's on the schedule this morning?" he asked. "Sir, you've got the balcony brief at 0730 in the Army Ops Center, then the Reserve Forces Policy Board at the Army Navy Country Club at 0930. I'll accompany for that one. Here's your read-ahead." White flipped the pages as he strode purposely down the hallway, offering a friendly greeting as staff officers and civil servants streamed past.

I'd been on the job for 11 weeks and loved it. Tom White, the son of a bus driver from Detroit, was a West Point graduate and Vietnam veteran who had risen to one-star rank in the Army before starting a second career in the business world in Texas. While there he had become a supporter of Governor George W. Bush. When Bush became president, he brought White to Washington as the Army secretary. In his short few months on the job he had made a great start, invigorating the Army staff with a series of new initiatives designed to increase efficiencies, outsource non-core functions, and improve conditions for soldiers. White was popular and personable, meshing well with the senior generals on the Army staff and infusing the headquarters with enthusiasm. Considerate with his personal staff, he was an ideal boss.

Getting off to a fast start, Secretary White was soon being talked about as a possible replacement for Secretary of Defense Donald Rumsfeld, who had been President Ford's SECDEF almost 25 years before. Amazingly, Rumsfeld had been resurrected and brought back through the efforts of Vice President Cheney, whom Rumsfeld had mentored long ago. Rumsfeld was difficult, abrasive, and controlling and soon the newspapers were running stories about his poor management style and unhappy subordinates. It was thought he might not last out the year. Rumsfeld's deputy was Paul Wolfowitz, a cerebral academic who had been the number three in the Department of Defense in the Gulf War. Sure of his own brilliance, Wolfowitz amplified Rumsfeld's weaknesses instead of filling in for them. Here lay seeds of disaster. But for now, the Bush national security team was still new and falling into place.

At 0725, we moved down to the Army Operations Center, deep underground in the Pentagon, for the daily update. Called the "Balcony Brief" because of the configuration of the briefing room, this updated the secretary, Army chief of staff, and their principal subordinates each day on the status of Army units and soldiers around the world, highlighting any fatalities or newsworthy incidents. On this day the brief was routine, and at 0800 we returned to the secretary's office. I began to go over the details of upcoming travel for the secretary, as CNN blared in the background.

Just before 0900, reports began streaming in that an aircraft had struck the World Trade Center in New York. Our initial reaction was that a private plane must have collided with the building by accident. Minutes later a second aircraft, this one recorded on video in real time, slammed into the second of the Twin Towers. We now realized that two airliners, filled with innocent passengers and crew, had slammed into the complex, killing everyone aboard and probably hundreds more inside the structure. It was surreal, unbelievable. We had all seen the attack on the USS *Cole* in Yemen in October of 2000 and the embassy attacks in Tanzania and Kenya in August of 1998. But a terrorist strike of this magnitude, here in the homeland, seemed impossible. We were stunned, as though we had been hit on the head. Whatever it meant, one thing seemed certain. There would be retribution. We were once again at war. A familiar jolt of adrenaline pumped through us.

Colonel Schroedel snapped us all back to reality. "Rich, let's huddle with the boss." We briefly discussed whether Secretary White should keep his meeting with the Policy Board. White remained firmly in control. "We'll probably be needing these guys soon. I think I should go," he told us. I quickly called the Pentagon security office and asked if there was any threat to Washington or the Pentagon on the radar. They replied "negative," and we walked quickly to the town car. Minutes later, we pulled up outside the Army Navy Country Club and I walked the secretary into the building, where he was met by a coterie of distinguished-looking gentlemen, all with looks of grave concern.

The meeting began and I moved back to the car to call the office. At that moment the driver muttered, "Jesus Christ!"

I looked up to see a wide-body jet scream over, its wings rocking, low and fast. The airplane, a Boeing 757, disappeared behind a low hill, and moments later American Airlines Flight 77 slammed into the southern wedge of the Pentagon, killing all 59 passengers and crew as well as the five hijackers aboard. Entering near the spaces occupied by the Army personnel chief, Lieutenant General Tim Maude, the impact and resulting explosion vaporized Maude and his office staff. In .8 of a second the aircraft penetrated the E, D, and C rings of the building, wiping out the Navy Command Center and killing 125 military and civilian workers.

I scrambled back inside and, taking the secretary by the arm, gave him the news. I looked for signs of panic or internal distress but saw none—this was a guy who won the Silver Star as a lieutenant in Vietnam for clearing bunkers personally with a .45. "Let's go," he said. Once inside the car he ordered, "Take me back to the Pentagon." We sat in silence for the few minutes it took to drive back. White broke in. "Call your wives now. In a few seconds, you won't be able to. Tell them you're all right but won't be home for a while."

I managed to get through to Beverly. Working in a secure facility, she knew about the World Trade Center attacks but not the strike on the Pentagon. We'd discussed in detail what to do if something ever happened to me while deployed, but not this. "I'm fine," I told her, "but I'm not sure when I'll be home."

As we approached the River entrance, we could see thousands of people streaming out of the building. White was determined to go in. As we neared the wild-eyed security guards, they drew their handguns and waved them at us. "I'm the Secretary of the Army!" White roared. "Either shoot us or get out of the way!" We made our way quickly to the Army Ops Center, then staffed by a brigadier general and about 12 officers and NCOs. Reverting to his former days as regimental commander of the "Black Horse," the 11th Armored Cavalry Regiment, White barked, "This is the Army Ops Center. Let's operate!" For an hour we struggled to gain situational awareness. How badly had we been hit? What were our losses? What was going on in Washington? The rest of the country? The world?

The stark truth was that al Qaeda had dealt us a crippling blow and our national security apparatus was disrupted—though not shut down. The president was in the air, in touch with the White House and Pentagon but unable to meet face to face with his senior staff and commanders. The National Military Command Center continued to function even as the building burned. General Shelton, the CJCS, was on international travel, as was the chief of staff of the Army, General Erik Shinseki. Wild reports circulated of more hijacked airliners, of bombs going off next to the State Department, of civilians jumping from the World Trade Center to avoid being burned to death. I had an eerie feeling, much like a football game when the momentum inexplicably changes, and your opponent comes charging back with blood in his eye. You choke down the panic rising in your throat even as it rises back up. We worked hard to focus on the task at hand. But 3,000 people had just been murdered, right on CNN.

At about 1100 that morning, an Army colonel showed up and announced, "I'm from Secretary Rumsfeld's office—the SECDEF wants to evacuate you and the other service secretaries to Site R." White expostulated, but the colonel insisted the order was peremptory. Minutes later, we boarded Air Force "white top" Huey helicopters along with the Navy and Air Force secretaries, Deputy Secretary of Defense Wolfowitz and a three-star from the Joint Staff. The flight to the "undisclosed location," a seldom-used emergency operations center, took about 45 minutes. Once inside, we were dismayed to find that we lacked secure video teleconference capability. At some point, one of the secretaries turned on a television. There in all his glory was Rumsfeld, carrying a stretcher, chatting with the media and, in general, grandstanding while his senior subordinates fretted, out of sight and out of mind and to all appearances having fled the scene.

Furious, the secretaries remounted the helos and sped back to the Pentagon. En route, we noticed a pair of F-16s with Air National Guard markings flying alongside. The pilots seemed to be making frantic gestures. At this point Secretary White, a combat helicopter pilot in Vietnam on his second tour there, hollered over his headset, "Hey, PIC (for 'pilot in command'), are you on Guard?" Embarrassed, the young captain immediately switched to the Guard frequency he should have been monitoring all along. At once we heard an angry fighter pilot screaming over the radio, "Identify yourself at once or we'll blow you out of the sky!" (Apparently, in the haste of the moment no flight plans had been filed, and all air traffic approaching Washington had been shut down.) Hurriedly the confusion was sorted out and we were permitted to land once again in front of the Pentagon's River entrance.

Still the Pentagon burned furiously. Most of the damage was contained to one side or "wedge" where the aircraft struck, and there the casualties, both civilian and military, were heavy. (It would be days before the Army could account for its 38 dead, mostly career civilians.) Unknown at the time, the fire had spread to the wiring inside the walls and from there throughout the building. It would take days to contain and suppress. For months afterwards, the Pentagon smelled like acrid smoke, a vivid and sobering reminder of our new reality.

Two days after 9/11, I accompanied Secretary White to New York, where we toured Ground Zero. Army National Guard troops were already on the scene assisting city authorities and the Army Corps of Engineers was alerted to provide technical help where required. As we wandered through the rubble of the Twin Towers I was struck by a familiar and hideous odor—the smell of decomposing bodies. Inside the wreckage, hundreds of corpses lay buried and unrecovered. We were shown a fire station near the site, its coat hooks holding the jackets of dozens of firemen who never lived to reclaim them, its walls covered with photos of kids and wives and families. A few hours later, we were taken to a pier housing the city's emergency operations center, reconstituted overnight after the original, located in the basement of the Twin Towers, was destroyed. It was enormous, dwarfing the Pentagon's National Military Command Center. There White was taken to see Rudy Giuliani, New York's high-profile mayor.

The meeting lasted less than five minutes. White's offer of "anything the Army can do to help" was dismissed with a curt "Thanks—we'll call you if we need you." Our party was hustled off the premises and driven to LaGuardia. On the short plane ride back Secretary White was pensive. It was hard to shake off the sense of shock. What had happened was so far outside our experience that comprehending it would take time. One thing was sure, however. Somebody was going to get punched in the face, hard.

The next weeks and months were a blur as the Army and the nation went to war in Afghanistan. Dubbed Operation *Enduring Freedom* (or "*OEF*" for short), the campaign focused on al Qaeda and bin Laden as the targets, along with their Taliban hosts. Within days Special Forces units were on the way, along with strong Air Force elements and CIA paramilitaries. Linking up with the "Northern Alliance"—mostly Tajik fighters based in the remote northern parts of the country—this hastily assembled task force took the fight to the Taliban and its al Qaeda allies. At first the Taliban tried to mass and fight off its attackers, only to be pummeled from the air. In barely two months, Taliban resistance collapsed, and Kabul fell.

Following closely on the heels of the special operations troops, the Army's 10th Mountain Division headquarters deployed to Karshi-Khanabad (K2) in Uzbekistan on December 12 as the locus of "Third U.S. Army Forward." (Third Army, commanded by Lieutenant General Paul Mikolashek, was the designated "Land Force Component Command" under U.S. Central Command and was based at a forward command post in Kuwait.) K2 was a large, Soviet-era air base not far from the northern Afghan border. 10th Mountain was not an ideal choice. Its leaders were among the best in the Army, but the division had only two infantry brigades instead of the normal three. The division was widely dispersed, with one brigade in Kosovo, a battalion in Bosnia and another in the Sinai. Only half of the division staff was present at K2, while neither of the two one-star deputy division commanders was available to participate. On February 13, the division moved forward to Bagram, about 30 miles north of the capital city of Kabul, as Combined Joint Task Force (CJTF) Mountain, accompanied by a single infantry battalion. 10th Mountain was handicapped by the fact that much of its intelligence staff section had been left behind, as well as its support units, key components whose absence would be sorely missed in the fights to come.

In the same month, Special Forces analysts identified enemy concentrations massing in the Shahikot valley, some 150 miles south of Bagram, thought to be a haven for al Qaeda fighters fleeing the fighting. Earlier efforts to corner enemy troops, and even Osama bin Laden himself, in the Tora Bora region had failed, and planners in Washington now saw an opportunity to inflict a heavy blow on an elusive foe. Accordingly, the 10th Mountain commander, Major General Frank Hagenbeck, drew the mission to assault the valley to find, fix and destroy the enemy located there.

Initial estimates placed the number of enemy fighters at 150 or so. That plan that evolved included a bewildering array of U.S. and coalition conventional and special operations units (including Army Special Forces, CIA paramilitaries, Army Rangers, and Navy SEALs), British Marines, Australian, New Zealand, Norwegian, and German SOF units, in addition to Afghan irregulars and Air Force, Navy and even French combat aircraft in support. Although the controlling headquarters for the conventional part of the fight, General Hagenbeck had only one infantry battalion, 1-87 Infantry, from his own division. A Brigade Combat Team from the 101st Air Assault Division had been sent to Afghanistan and would come under 10th Mountain for the operation, along with a single Canadian infantry battalion. However, the 101st brigade lacked its organic artillery battalion and came with only six of its normal complement of 18 AH64 Apache attack helicopters.

A further complication was that the U.S. infantry battalions lacked one of their three rifle companies, casualties of an arbitrary "troop cap" imposed by Secretary Rumsfeld. It was, as Secretary White commented at the time, a "dog's breakfast"—a fantastically complicated mix of forces, largely unknown to each other at this early stage of the conflict. Confusingly, the conventional and special operations forces would operate under separate chains of command. Although designated the overall joint commander as the senior U.S. military officer on the ground in Afghanistan, General Hagenbeck "owned" only the conventional ground forces present.

The general idea was to insert the conventional forces onto the ridgelines overlooking the valley by helicopter as a blocking force, while a mixed force of Afghan militia and U.S. Special Forces troops advanced into the valley in vehicles. Ideally, the small enemy force that was expected would be caught between the two forces and destroyed. The night before, special mission units would establish observation and sniper positions overlooking the valley. Strike aircraft were available in ample numbers, augmented by the fearsome AC130, an orbiting gunship armed with a

105mm cannon and smaller 40mm Gatling guns. Despite the plan's complexity, the force seemed overwhelming considering the few enemy forces anticipated.

On March 2, the operation commenced, and chaos immediately descended. Monitoring from the Army Operations Center, we watched as the first reports came in. The advancing Afghan militia and their Green Beret advisors were mistakenly engaged by an AC130 gunship, killing or wounding more than a dozen U.S. and Afghan soldiers. Confusion over garbled radio calls resulted in the suspension of bomb strikes, leaving half of the originally scheduled targets unscathed. Ultimately the Afghan militia absconded, scuppering the plan. The 10th Mountain troops air assaulting onto the ridgelines encountered much fiercer resistance than expected; the intelligence picture was badly in error and the valley was occupied not by 150 enemy fighters but by upwards of a thousand. Very quickly, maintenance problems and battle damage reduced the six Apaches present to only three. Although strike aircraft were present in plenty, Air Force insistence on controlling them from the air operations center in Qatar and restrictive control measures prevented quick response against enemy targets maneuvering close to friendly positions. Now the absence of field artillery, and a local decision to leave heavy mortars behind due to space limitations, began to bite deeply. Despite their massive advantage in technology and fires, U.S. troops on the ground once again found themselves in a desperate, close-range firefight armed mostly with small arms and hand grenades.

Throughout the long day the battle swayed, its outcome in doubt. Follow-on waves of reinforcing infantry were delayed by the intense ground fire. Wounded troops could not be evacuated by air until sundown. Heavy enemy fire prevented some units from reaching their assigned blocking positions, and by the afternoon many were pinned down and running low on ammunition. An attempted insertion of a small SOF reconnaissance team in the dark resulted in the downing of an Army Chinook helo and the loss of seven SOF troopers, with another six wounded. Day 1 of the operation, code-named *Anaconda*, ended depressingly, with plenty of bad news and somber faces. It had quickly become apparent that faulty command arrangements, the arbitrary troop cap, failed intelligence and inter-service rivalry had all combined wretchedly. The one bright spot was the magnificent courage shown by the troops in the field. As in Somalia, their valor redeemed an otherwise dismal outing.

In the next few days, close air support procedures were adjusted, damaged Apaches returned to the fight, heavy mortars were flown in and the U.S. units in the area were resupplied with ammunition and water, while wounded soldiers were flown out for treatment. By the end of March 4, the valley was declared "secured," with hundreds of enemy dead claimed. However, only 23 bodies were found, and it seemed likely that many enemy fighters had escaped. Scattered fighting would continue for some days. The final reported casualty count was eight U.S. dead and 82 wounded, with two CH-47 Chinooks destroyed. An undetermined number of enemy fighters, possibly including bin Laden himself, escaped.

As *Anaconda* unfolded, I could see and sense that Secretary White and Army Chief of Staff General Eric Shinseki were dismayed. An official Army assessment later concluded that "virtually nothing went according to plan" in *Anaconda*. Directly and indirectly, Secretary Rumsfeld had pressured the Army to go into Afghanistan with a small footprint, capping troop numbers in such a way that deploying units were denied critical capabilities. That in turn forced soldiers into situations where our inherent advantages—fire support and intelligence most importantly—were absent, leaving them to fight it out on much the same terms as the enemy. Inter-service rivalry also played a role, as the seamless and effective use of close air support—the one way to rapidly adapt to a distorted intelligence picture and unfavorable force ratios—was badly disrupted by procedures intended to reserve control of the strike aircraft to their parent services and not to the on-scene commander.

Air Force aircraft were forbidden to descend to lower altitudes where they could see enemy and friendly locations. Army forward observers were not permitted to control close air support strikes, which were centralized under Air Force control located a thousand miles away. Air Force enlisted controllers (called JTACs or Joint Terminal Attack Controllers) were required for that, and they were not present in anything like the numbers required. Communications snafus, coordination failures, divided command and plain incompetence all had their day. A dog's breakfast, indeed.

General Hagenbeck later attempted to identify these shortcomings in an article published in *Military Review*, drawing the ire of Air Force generals and instigating a fierce inter-service imbroglio. He had coped with any number of unnecessary difficulties and was absolutely right, but the backlash was intense, and he was left chastened by the experience. Relations between the Army leadership and Rumsfeld, which had never been smooth, now became positively frosty.

Part of the problem was that Rumsfeld was frankly parochial. A reserve naval officer, he harbored a strong prejudice against the Army, which he viewed as "non-transformational" and hide-bound. Fascinated by video clips of "Special Forces on horses," Rumsfeld and his senior aides adopted the view that small forces, airpower and Afghan proxies were the answer. Army protests about breaking up units were airily waved aside. Contributing to the problem was that Tom White, a gregarious and charismatic leader, had enjoyed a good press in the months preceding 9/11 and was even rumored to be under consideration as Rumsfeld's replacement, as the prickly SECDEF had alienated most of the Pentagon leadership and rank and file in his first year. In the coming months, this dynamic would metastasize rapidly.

In all of this, CENTCOM Commander and Army General Tommy Franks and Chairman of the Joint Chiefs General Richard Myers proved unable or unwilling to engage or push back against Rumsfeld's intrusive and overbearing management style. Franks, a profane and outspoken general, was openly contemptuous of the service chiefs but surprisingly meek when pressured by Rumsfeld. Myers, a gentlemanly officer, was well liked but not seen as inclined to defend the prerogatives of his office. Rumsfeld had set the Department of Defense on a fixed course towards "Transformation," a vision of warfare as a highly orchestrated, networked exercise in delivering precision fires based on near-perfect intelligence enabled by sophisticated technology. Lost in all the buzz words and PowerPoint presentations were timeless verities. War is fundamentally a clash of wills, a very human endeavor as much about passion, uncertainty, and friction as it is about target sets and chains of supply. On land, war is about seizing and holding ground, a manpower-intensive chore that seemed anathema to the civilians running DoD. For many Army and Marine Corps officers, "Transformation" was a push from the Air Force and Navy to reduce land wars to a mere targeting exercise. Many of our generals knew this. Few were prepared to risk their careers over it.

As we moved deeper into 2002, the situation in Afghanistan began to stabilize. Stunned, the Taliban leadership and most of their surviving fighters sought refuge across the border in Pakistan, beyond our reach. Battered but not destroyed, they would regroup and return. Following a national "Shura," Hamid Karzai emerged as Afghanistan's new leader. Though his nascent government was weak, its reach confined mostly to Kabul, heavy fighting dissipated, and civilian and coalition organizations began to flow in. Warlordism abounded, but to most it seemed that the terrorist safe haven that had been Afghanistan was eliminated. Almost before we knew it, Afghanistan moved to the back burner. Something else was in the wind.

That something else was Iraq. Within days after 9/11, Rumsfeld and his sharp-elbowed deputy, Wolfowitz, began to talk up Iraq as a key threat. They alleged that Iraq harbored a dangerous and growing arsenal of chemical and biological "weapons of mass destruction," along with a nuclear program they judged to be nearing completion. Iraq was identified as a "nexus of terrorism," tied in some mysterious way to al Qaeda and 9/11. Intelligence to back this up was scanty or absent altogether, but contrarian views were ruthlessly suppressed. Soon it became apparent that forces were being husbanded for an eventual invasion of Iraq and withheld from Afghanistan. We lost the bubble, as Iraq became the vortex attracting most of the Department's energy and focus. A new word began to dominate the conversation on the E ring. That word was "invasion."

From my vantage point inside the secretary's office, it was clear that the Army and the military in general had serious reservations. Afghanistan had been represented as a clear-cut success, but bin Laden had escaped and the Taliban, while routed, had not been wiped out. *OEF* would continue, and the prospect of launching a second and probably more demanding campaign was daunting. Many of the Army's leaders had served in *Desert Storm* and understood the difference between that operation's limited objectives and invading the whole of Iraq. The proffered justification—that Iraq possessed a lethal hoard of WMD—seemed weak. So did Iran and Syria. Later studies would show conclusively that the reservations of mid-level intelligence analysts were watered down or dismissed by their superiors, themselves under intense pressure from the vice president's office and Rumsfeld's people. Even the formidable Colin Powell, now serving as Secretary of State, would prove unable to halt or deflect the unstoppable momentum now gathering behind invasion.

In this critical hour our generals, though not enthusiastic, did not push back. A National Defense University study commissioned a decade later would conclude, "We do not find in the record convincing evidence of vigorous debate or respectful dissent from senior military leaders on the key questions" relating to the invasion of Iraq. Even students in our war colleges pointed out that invading Iraq was far different from occupying and administering the country, and that, given Iraq's conflict history and fractious ethnic divisions, the only real winner in the end would be Iran. Even under the odious Saddam, Iraq stood as the Sunni counterweight to Iran, an implacable opponent of the U.S. with ambitions towards regional hegemony some three thousand years old. Academic and policy objections were carelessly waved aside. Paul Wolfowitz would estimate the costs of the campaign at less than $50B, "paid for by Iraqi oil." (The final accounting is now well over $2 trillion.) For inexplicable reasons, the Department of Defense had become enamored of Ahmed Chalabi, a shady and corrupt expatriate Iraqi with dreams of running a post-war Iraq. Wanted for arrest in Jordan for financial crimes, Chalabi fed the Pentagon reams of false "intelligence" and pledged that he could raise an army that could replace U.S. forces after the fall of the regime. Virtually all his intelligence would prove false, while his "army" would never materialize.

All of this took on a surreal air, but the determination of the "neo-cons" to implement this agenda was no fantasy. Service chiefs and service secretaries judged to have faint hearts were marked out for destruction. For the Army, matters came to a head when General Shinseki and Secretary White were called to testify before Congress on the impending invasion. In response to direct questioning, Shinseki estimated the operation would require "several hundred thousand soldiers." White supported this view. History would bear them out, but their testimony incurred the enmity of Rumsfeld and Wolfowitz, who publicly rebuked them. Thereafter, both lost most of their influence. White was peppered with criticism about his former association with the Enron Corporation, supposed travel irregularities (later ruled unfounded) and a lack of enthusiasm for "Transformation." Shinseki's successor was announced 14 months in advance of his retirement, neutering the Army chief, while White was clearly living on borrowed time. I recall escorting Secretary White and General Shinseki back from a meeting with Secretary Rumsfeld around this time. Shinseki, an officer of real dignity and composure, looked shaken. White, an ebullient personality, was angry and morose. "The chief has left body parts scattered all over Southeast Asia (Shinseki had been badly wounded as a young officer in Vietnam). When the SECDEF insults him to his face he insults the whole damn Army and every soldier in it."

The end came in a political battle over the Army's Crusader field artillery system, a modernized self-propelled howitzer intended to replace the Army's ageing M109 platform. Crusader was in many ways almost revolutionary. Improved technology gave Crusader greater accuracy, range and rate of fire, with a smaller crew. The root problem was that Rumsfeld and his Transformation team felt that field artillery in general was something of an obsolete concept—surely airpower, which we had in abundance, could do the job? Patiently, Army leaders explained that weather, range, weapons load, pilot crew rest requirements, competing service doctrines and a host of other factors created real distinctions between what airpower and artillery could and could not do. The Army had relied on field artillery since the Civil War for its responsiveness, all-weather, day/night capability and crushing combat power. The artillery community was one of the strongest in the Army, and Army chiefs of staff and corps and division commanders were as likely to be artillerymen as infantry or armor officers. These views were disregarded. Crusader was ruled "too heavy" and a "legacy" system and was killed. To this day, a much-reduced artillery establishment carries on with the M109, first fielded in the early 1960s and now in its seventh "upgrade."

Soon after, General Shinseki retired and Secretary White was dismissed. Bypassing every active duty Army four-star, Rumsfeld selected retired General Peter Schoomaker, a Green Beret and the former commander of U.S. Special Operations Command (SOCOM), as Shinseki's replacement. Intended as a snub to the Army's leadership, the move sent shocks throughout the service. As we geared up for what now looked like certain invasion, the Army reeled in the fallout of these bitter disputes. This was no way to begin a war.

By then I had completed my tour as aide de camp and had enrolled as a student in the National War College in Washington. My admiration for Secretary White remained high. He had served our Army and the nation honorably and well in turbulent and difficult times, never more so than during 9/11 and its tumultuous aftermath. I had learned much about the Army in my tour as the aide. In more than 40 trips with the secretary, I had seen many of the Army's posts, camps, and stations all over the world, been immersed in the workings of the Army staff, and met many of the Army's current and future leaders. My appreciation for the Army's many capabilities, its resilience and versatility, and the steadfastness and patriotism of its soldiers, NCOs and officers had only grown.

My year at the War College flew by quickly, as we watched the U.S. military prepare to invade Iraq. As might be expected the student body, which included six Arab officers, debated the pending invasion and its details endlessly. We were sobered by the lack of support shown by close allies France and Germany and alarmed at the SECDEF's continuing insistence on a small footprint and a quick handoff to some sort of ill-defined transitional Iraqi government. *Desert Storm*, for most of us, had been a nearly perfect campaign, with clearly defined and limited objectives, strong support from Congress, the electorate and allies, and overwhelming force. The invasion of Iraq in 2003 promised a different case altogether. Like most of my peers, I foresaw a relatively quick military campaign ending in regime change, to be followed by great uncertainty and danger. As veterans of the Balkans, we knew that "stability operations" were manpower intensive and required an enduring presence. It was hard to imagine an "in and out" operation like the one being discussed in the media, and we worried that we were taking our eye off the ball in Afghanistan, by now clearly a "back burner" operation.

The invasion of Iraq commenced on March 20, 2003, and—as expected—the Iraqi Army was quickly smashed. The nation and the world fully expected that, as relentlessly promised by U.S. leaders, large stocks of WMD would be uncovered by advancing American and coalition troops. Perplexingly, that never happened. While Baghdad fell in just over a month, the invasion force faced unexpected resistance from irregular "Saddam Fedayeen" units and suffered from a lack of route and rear area security, a consequence of the "light footprint" approach. (Where the *Desert Storm* coalition totaled just under a million troops, the 2003 invasion force numbered well under 200,000.) Most tellingly of all, once "major combat operations" ceased on May 1 it became quickly apparent that we had no real plan for occupying the country. Tactical units attempted to secure key infrastructure such as hospitals, government ministries, and water and power stations. But with too few troops, much was left unsecured and mass looting ensued. At this critical time, a series of blunders ensured that we would become mired in Iraq for years to come.

Early planning envisioned an "Office of Reconstruction and Humanitarian Assistance" that would oversee a rapid transition to Iraqi control, but in less than a month that office was replaced by something called the "Coalition Provisional Authority (CPA)." Headed by Ambassador Paul Bremer and staffed by a pickup team, with many young volunteers, CPA reported to DoD, not the State Department. With breathtaking naiveté, Bremer (who had no background in the Middle East) swiftly implemented a comprehensive "debaathification" program that removed almost all of Iraq's technical experts. The Iraqi Army was dismissed, throwing its large officer corps out of work and driving many into the ranks of an already emerging insurgency. An Iraqi transitional council was set up, composed mostly of dissidents and expatriates with little actual influence inside Iraq.

Inexplicably, at this critical juncture Secretary Rumsfeld decided to place the Army's most junior three-star, Lieutenant General Ricardo Sanchez, in command of the military component in Iraq. (Rumsfeld would later deny any role in Sanchez's selection, a position described by one biographer as "not remotely credible.") The original war plan called for Third Army, now led by the deeply experienced Lieutenant General David McKiernan, to stay on following the invasion to superintend the initial occupation. Third Army boasted a large, well-trained staff that was intimately familiar with Iraq. Sanchez, in contrast, had just been placed in command of

V Corps, a much smaller headquarters based in Germany with little understanding of the mission. Personality conflicts with Bremer prevented the kind of seamless cooperation required to succeed in such a difficult and complex setting. We had, we thought, won the war. Now we set about losing the peace.

As graduation approached, I learned that I had been selected for promotion to full colonel, but my next assignment was up in the air. At one point I was ordered by the Army to interview as military assistant to one of the assistant secretaries of defense, a job which held no appeal. (I had long since adopted the view that any job title which contains the word "assistant" more than once should be studiously avoided.) Purposely flunking the interview, I was next sent to interview with Scooter Libby, chief of staff to Vice President Cheney.

Libby would later be convicted of obstruction of justice and perjury in the aftermath of the Valerie Plame affair, but I thoroughly enjoyed the interview and found him both personable and engaging. He had reviewed my CV and expressed interest in an article I had written dissecting the German invasion of Russia in 1941. We spent an hour talking about Operation *Barbarossa* and little else, and soon after I was notified that I had been hired as special adviser.

Excited about a return to the White House, I bought five new suits and began a deep dive into Middle East issues, my new portfolio. Only days before reporting, Libby's assistant called me at home.

"The Army chief of staff wants you assigned to his office, we're told. What do you want to do?"

Many years before, I had been told to stand clear when the elephants were stomping around the yard, and I replied dutifully, "Thanks very much. When my orders show up in the mailbox, I'll follow them." Those orders materialized the next day. A week later, I reported for duty to the Army Staff, this time for an assignment in the chief of staff's office as an "Army Planner." The term was something of a misnomer, as the service staffs were concerned with manning, training, and equipping the force—the so-called "Title 10" functions—and not actual operational planning. Each of the four military services had three 06 officers assigned to the service chief's office with responsibilities for joint matters. In his capacity as a member of the Joint Chiefs of Staff, the Army chief attended weekly JCS meetings in the "Tank"—the JCS conference room—and his Army planners were responsible for preparing him for those sessions. All joint issues sent to the Army for consideration and comment passed through the planners, who alone (except for the chief and his three-star operations deputy) had the power to sign off on joint actions with the official "Army position." It was a responsible job which again afforded me regular contact and interaction with the Army's top leadership, as well as a deep understanding of the joint world and its many areas of friction.

I assumed these duties in the summer of 2003, only days before General Shinseki's retirement. For a few months General Jack Keane, the Army's vice chief, served as the acting head until General Schoomaker came out of retirement. Schoomaker had enjoyed a successful career as a special operations officer and former commander of the Army's premier "high end" counterterrorism unit, rising to command SOCOM in the Clinton era. He now found himself staring down the muzzle of a double-barreled shotgun.

Any Army chief would be challenged by the requirement to support not one but two shooting wars, on top of the Army's other worldwide commitments. But Schoomaker had been specifically selected to champion "Army Transformation" as well. Here the idea was to reorganize the Army into "modular brigades," by deemphasizing the division as an echelon of command and by restructuring maneuver (infantry and armor) brigades. Modular brigades would "own" their own artillery and support units, which had formerly been assigned to the division. Crucially, the brigade's three maneuver battalions were reduced to two, while a Reconnaissance, Surveillance and Target Acquisition (RSTA) squadron (essentially a small battalion-sized reconnaissance unit) was added. Overall, the brigade grew in size, but in terms of actual combat soldiers—"boots on the ground"—the decline was marked, some 1,000 soldiers. Central to this concept was that the Brigade Combat Team or "BCT" would now be the "Unit of Action," a "plug and play" entity that could in theory work under any division headquarters or none at all.

The basic idea was lifted from *Breaking the Phalanx*, a book written by a renegade Army colonel then working in Rumsfeld's Office for Transformation. Conceptually, the modular brigade was full of holes. First, the idea was rushed through before the Army could generate doctrine or training programs to give commanders and staffs some idea of how to employ it. The loss of combat strength could not be overcome by the greater "situational awareness" provided by the high-tech but weak RSTA unit, whose systems were in any case poorly suited to our low-tech opponents in Iraq and Afghanistan. Ultimately, maneuver units must seize and hold ground and there were now far fewer soldiers to do that. Sending brigades to the fight willy-nilly, under division commanders and staffs they had never met or trained with, was simply foolish. Finally, reequipping and reorganizing every brigade in the Army during active conflict proved wrenchingly difficult and problematic.

Virtually every division commander in the Army opposed this approach, seen to be both flawed and untested. (Later, the Army would revert to the three-battalion format and reempower the division level.) On the Army staff, we marveled that the Marine Corps—organized on similar lines—was not subjected to such heavy pressures for radical change. It soon became clear that the new chief would embrace Army Transformation enthusiastically, and Army generals dutifully fell into line and resolved to make the best of a bad bargain.

In the spring of 2004, I received word that one of my former officers in 2 Panther had been killed in action. In the wars that followed 9/11 I knew a lot of officers who were loved and respected by the soldiers they led. But I never knew a man as beloved as Captain John F. Kurth from Beaver Dam, Wisconsin.

Captain Kurth was a rifle company commander in the 1st Division, the "Big Red One." He had led his unit, Company B of the 1st Battalion, 18th Infantry, all through the training and preparation for deployment to Iraq. He was only 31 when the "Bushmasters" deployed, yet he carried a sincerity and an affection for his soldiers that made people want to follow him.

"I would have followed that man through hell," said one. "He was everything I wanted to be." "I think of you every day," said another.

Kurth seemed a born soldier. Tall, rangy, and handsome, a high-school wrestler and football star in Beaver Dam, he was called "Hans" by his friends. At West Point his infectious sense of humor, willingness to lend a hand and never-failing optimism made him legions of lifetime friends. As one classmate put it, "I never told you this because we were too full of pride and the stubbornness of youth, but I loved you like I love my own brother." "You were the best of us."

After graduation he went to the 82nd Airborne Division. It was my good fortune to have Hans in my battalion. He was supremely competent, but then many of the lieutenants were. What set Hans apart was an unaffected and genuine love of his fellow man, a sense of empathy and compassion for all that filled a room. There was no ego or bluster about him. Self-confident and assured, with a wonderful fund of humor and good fellowship, he could make both soldiers and peers feel special. It was a rare and precious gift that we all wished we had.

A few years later, I ran into Hans in Germany. He was frustrated, waiting on the staff for his turn to command a company and lead soldiers again. Eventually his chance came. He worked hard to get his troopers ready. Morale was high. He had trained the unit well, and they were all eager to show what they could do.

When the time came, B Company flew into Iraq and pushed up to its assigned area of operations near Tikrit. Then it happened. Hans' convoy was hit by small arms fire from the rear. Seconds later a roadside bomb detonated with crushing force, destroying his HMMWV. Kurth was killed, along with his driver, Specialist Jason Ford, from Bowie, Maryland. Three other soldiers in the vehicle were wounded, one seriously.

For Captain Kurth's soldiers and for his friends and loved ones, it was as though a small piece inside died that day, a piece that would never come back. Like so many, his death was random. He did not die leading an attack against great odds or carrying a wounded trooper to safety. There was no glory in his death or the way he died. But there was something else. Kurth's death mattered because his life mattered, in large and consequential ways. He had touched us all in ways we would not forget. A bereaved comrade wrote later, "I breathed for you and my breathing wasn't good enough. I miss you. My life is not worth your death."

After recovering their dead and tending their wounded, his company mounted their vehicles, moved off and got back to the war. It was Day 1 of their tour.

As I grieved for the loss of Hans Kurth, the Army was beset by reports that NFL football star Pat Tillman, who had joined the elite 75th Ranger Regiment after 9/11, had been killed by friendly fire in Afghanistan. At the time, Tillman was the most famous soldier in the Army, celebrated for walking away from millions of dollars to serve on the front lines of the Global War on Terrorism. Initial reports attempted to obscure the facts and—most seriously—Tillman's commanders recommended him for a Silver Star for heroism in combat against the enemy. The officer who signed the citation was Major General Stanley McChrystal. It quickly became clear that he had signed the award in the full knowledge that it was false.

McChrystal in 2004 was commanding an elite headquarters exercising operational control over Tillman's Ranger unit in Afghanistan. A former commander of the Ranger Regiment, he had enjoyed a storied career. Subsequent investigations by the Pentagon's inspector general concluded that McChrystal and others had submitted "inaccurate" and "misleading" information in an attempt to obscure the circumstances of Tillman's death. A separate investigation by General William Wallace would spur a later Army secretary to conclude that the incident "called into question the Army's credibility ... and strikes at the very heart of Army core values." As one of the Army's most high-profile commanders, McChrystal attracted intense media attention and the story consumed Army leaders for months. Across America, the Army took a beating. The IG recommended "appropriate corrective action" against McChrystal and other officers involved, and some were severely disciplined (one general responsible for administratively processing the award was demoted in disgrace). However, McChrystal himself escaped formal censure and would go on to further promotion and celebrity. For its part, the Army would endure years of criticism and painful congressional scrutiny over the Tillman incident.

As though cursed by the decision to invade Iraq, an even more devastating blow fell upon the Army at the same time when photos surfaced in the national media depicting torture and inhumane treatment at the Abu Ghraib detention facility in Anbar province in Iraq. The photos were shocking in the extreme. A small group of Army Reserve soldiers led by Specialist Charles Graner had subjected Iraqi detainees to multiple forms of mental and physical abuse, much of it documented in dozens of photos. In many cases, the abuse was calculated specifically to offend the religious sensibilities of the detainees.

Subsequent investigations revealed that just about everything that could go wrong at Abu Ghraib did. Lines of responsibility between military intelligence interrogators and military police detention units became hopelessly blurred. Civilian contractors enthusiastically applied "enhanced interrogation" techniques pushed by the White House and Secretary Rumsfeld. From General Sanchez to the most junior officer in the chain of command, oversight and supervision of detention operations was virtually non-existent. Graner, the ringleader, had been enlisted in the Army Reserve despite a troubled record as a civilian corrections officer. Abu

Ghraib was a perfect storm of bad leadership, flawed and ethically questionable policy guidance, and plain inhumanity. To this day, when people think of Iraq, they think of those pictures. They are a stain on the Army's honor, and the nation's, that may never really wash away.

As the Army leadership convulsed over the Tillman and Abu Ghraib crises, I received a cryptic message to report to the director of the Army Staff. A personal interview meant one of two things. It could be good news. Or it could be very, very bad. I responded with alacrity and soon found myself seated in front of his secretary.

"The general will see you now."

I rose from my seat in the general's outer office, thanked the secretary and walked into a large office decorated with the memorabilia of a long and successful career. In the corner stood an American flag and the large red three-starred banner signifying a lieutenant general. Standing at attention I saluted.

"Sir, Colonel Hooker reports as ordered."

Not knowing what this was all about, I tried to keep a neutral expression. Though my conscience was clear, one never knew what to expect from touchy senior officers. I stood, motionless and expressionless, as he returned my salute. Rising from his desk he strode forward, hand outstretched and smiling. Instinctively I relaxed. Shaking my hand and motioning me to a large leather easy chair, he sat down beside me, leaning forward intently.

"I've got good news. You're being offered brigade command. At Fort Bragg. Congratulations."

I paused for a moment as a thousand conflicting thoughts raced through my mind. I had done well as a battalion commander, and since. But I had served exclusively with paratroopers—something of a liability in an Army that prized diverse career assignments—and some of my assignments had been outside the mainstream of the Army. I had hoped, but not expected, to get a brigade. I felt momentarily overwhelmed.

And there was one other thing. There were only three infantry brigade commands at Bragg, all in the 82nd Airborne Division. I was well aware that all three were filled. Had someone been fired, or more likely, badly injured on a jump?

The general waved my question aside. "You're not going to the 82nd. You're going to XVIII Airborne Corps. You're getting Dragon Brigade. And you're going downrange, to Baghdad, about six months after you take command."

I bit my lip. To be selected for brigade command was a real accomplishment. Of a hundred lieutenants, fewer than 10 might gain brigade command 20 years later. On the other hand, few would call Dragon Brigade, or more formally the "XVIII Airborne Corps Combat Support Brigade," a premier slating. None of its previous commanders had ever been promoted to general, and this development probably meant I wouldn't either. Dragon Brigade had been created some 20 years before to provide command and control for a number of unaffiliated "separate" units located at Bragg that lacked a full colonel as commander. In its time it had included air defense, signal, explosive ordnance disposal, psychological operations, garrison, public affairs and many other battalions and companies. What it did not include was infantry soldiers. Dragon Brigade was a consolation prize in the eyes of many, not a command sought by fast movers. Officers assigned to command the brigade often developed "medical" issues that would see them re-slated, hopefully to a more desirable command, the following year. In fact, that had happened this time around; the original pick had developed "cardiac" problems that somehow did not prevent him from being later assigned to brigade command in the 1st Cavalry Division.

On the other hand, Dragon Brigade was an airborne organization. I'd be back on jump status, serving with paratroopers again. The unit was going into the combat zone by year's end. And the corps commander was Lieutenant General John R. Vines, "Viper 6," my old boss from battalion command days. Perhaps this had not been an arbitrary selection after all. As for promotion—well, declining a combat command would earn me the disapproval of everyone I respected most in the service. I didn't see that as an option.

The general must have seen this internal debate in my expression. A harder tone crept into his voice. "Well, do you want it or not?"

I straightened up and looked the three-star in the eye. "Sir, I'll need to talk to my wife tonight and get her blessing. Can I give you my answer tomorrow morning?"

A faint look of disapproval crossed his face. "Fine. Let me know first thing. That's all."

As I left the office, I knew what my answer would be. But I owed Beverly a chance to speak her piece. After putting me on the airplane many times before, to Somalia, and Rwanda, and Bosnia, to Kosovo and the Sinai, she deserved that. With a full-time job as an engineer, and three kids at home, she carried a heavy burden. And there was more. None of my previous deployments had exceeded six months. This would be a full year. And while I had been shot at before, Iraq was different. We were losing hundreds of soldiers every year, in a war with no real rear area. Most casualties were caused by improvised explosive devices (IEDs), homemade bombs of enormous size that could cause catastrophic injuries. Temperatures in Iraq rose above one hundred degrees for seven months of the year. This would be the hardest, most dangerous year of my career. By far.

That night we held hands and talked about the future. By now we knew each other bone deep. Beverly knew that if she asked me to stay I would. But she also knew that I would always regret it. Our relationship would be changed, just as my parents had been when Dad returned to Vietnam. We brought the kids in to the discussion. The boys were 16 and 14. Rachel was just 11. They were frightened as children always are. But they were also Army kids. They knew this was Dad's job. The next morning, I sent word that I'd accept the command. A few months later we found ourselves back at Bragg.

As Beverly settled us in on Colonel's Row, I began my initial assessment of the unit. The outgoing commander had led Dragon Brigade to Afghanistan, where it had served as headquarters commandant for the corps commander. The brigade had done well but had functioned essentially as a small headquarters support element, with few troops under its command. In garrison, Dragon Brigade had often been a repository for castoffs from other units, and in general its personnel lacked the quality found in the other brigades located at Bragg. Adding to the gloomy prognosis, the unit was far understrength. There was one bright spot however: the Brigade Command Sergeant Major, CSM Abdo Zacheus. Universally known as "Z," Zacheus had previously served as sergeant major of an artillery battalion in the 82nd Airborne, was Ranger and master parachutist qualified, and had fought in the Gulf War and in Afghanistan. A Puerto Rican, quiet and self-effacing with strong nerves, he would emerge as the backbone of the brigade in the stern test we would soon face.

Early on I met with General Vines. Since our last encounter he had battled a life-threatening illness, an experience which had visibly aged him. Though physically less robust, Vines still vibrated with innate common sense and good humor. We quickly re-established rapport and I left confident in his support and care for my unit and for me personally. A subordinate can't ask for more.

The first order of business was to start building the team. In the first few weeks I made mental notes of key officers and NCOs I'd trust to go to war with or wouldn't. As most of our home station units (mostly tenant units grouped under the brigade for command and control) were not slated to deploy with us, I soon learned that the brigade executive officer, a bright signal officer named Lieutenant Colonel Jeff Ellis, would stay behind to lead and support them. For now, we did not have a specific mission. More importantly, I needed a deputy, an executive officer, and an operations officer, in addition to a whole slew of more junior staff officers and NCOs. In garrison, Dragon Brigade had a far smaller staff than a normal combat brigade. We would have to double in size to be ready.

The corps commander obliged us by tasking his units for augmentation personnel, and in this way, we built up the intelligence, operations, logistics, engineer, and signal staffs as well as the administrative echelon required. Many of our "fillers" were reservists with unique backgrounds. The new brigade S2 intelligence chief, for example, was an attorney in civilian life. Over the next 90 days the staff began to fill out as new people arrived almost daily.

Early on I was thrilled to learn that Major Hugh Shoults, my S3 Air 10 years before in Vicenza, was now serving at Fort Bragg. With a little string pulling I was able to have him assigned as the new Brigade S3. As brigade executive officer, I hired a West Point classmate and now a lieutenant colonel in the Army Reserve. He had been gravely wounded the year before in Iraq but reported himself fully recovered and ready for duty. Though we had not seen each other in many years, he appeared in my office one day and asked for the job. Now all I needed was a deputy brigade commander.

As there was no Regular Army colonel available, I consulted a long-time mentor, Ladd Pattillo, a retired Army Reserve colonel, to help in my search for a quality officer. A former assistant attorney general in Texas and a successful businessman, Ladd was 10 years older than me and politically well connected with the Texas contingent in President George W. Bush's White House. To my surprise, Ladd volunteered for the job himself.

At first, I didn't know what to think. Ladd had always been far senior to me. Though an infantry officer and master parachutist in his youth, he had not served with troops for many years, and had never deployed. How on earth could we recall a retired reserve officer, place him on active duty, have him assigned to the brigade, and deploy him to a combat zone? It seemed impossible. Even if we could, could he stand the pace? Nearing 60, was he up to the job in a combat zone? An added concern was the fact that his son David was a lieutenant, fighting with the 101st Airborne Division in Tikrit. That was asking a lot of his wife, a retired Air Force reserve colonel in her own right. For guidance, I consulted now-retired Brigadier General Mick Zais, my old sponsor from cadet days, who knew Ladd well. His son Bradley was a young trooper in the 101st serving up north in Iraq.

Zais came right to the point. "Look, Ladd is not the guy to lead a brigade movement to contact, but you know that. You will need him for many other things, not least to help you with the many general officers, contractors, Iraqi counterparts, visiting congressional delegations and God knows what else. And he will help round off some of your hard edges. He will be loyal, smart, and capable. I'd take him in a minute if I were you." A few days later I called Ladd to say that I'd be glad to have him, if his wife agreed, but that I had little confidence I could pull it off. "You leave that to me," he chuckled. His political connections apparently cut through the red tape, and I had a deputy commander. It was a choice I'd never regret.

As the brigade staff began to take shape, I faced another major challenge. Dragon Brigade had traditionally run the Corps Rear Command Post, essentially a logistics and administrative headquarters far from the front, and word soon reached us that we would likely draw that mission this time around as well, probably from Kuwait. This would not do. Over the next few weeks Major Shoults and I drew up a detailed proposal that would place the brigade in charge of all base security and base operations for the Victory Base Complex (VBC) in Baghdad, the sprawling collection of 10 base camps that surrounded Baghdad International Airport (BIAP) and home to the four-star Multinational Force-Iraq and three-star Multinational Corps-Iraq staffs, as well as dozens of tenant units. (Our own XVIII Airborne Corps under General Vines would soon rotate in to replace III Corps.)

Our proposal was in fact ridiculously ambitious, and I had no reason to think Vines would approve. But I hoped that he might take an interest in some parts of it—the base security mission appealed to me in particular—and that we might accordingly be allowed to join the Corps in the fight inside Iraq. Shoults gave a masterful presentation, replete with charts and graphics, and to our amazement General Vines quickly agreed. The concept of a single "belly button"—a single commander he knew and trusted to free him and the Corps staff from the details of defending and running the huge complex—appealed to him. Shocked, Shoults and I walked out of the headquarters, worried that we had bitten off more than we could chew.

In brief, the general concept was as follows. For base operations, an Army Reserve garrison command under a full colonel would be task organized under us, with lieutenant colonel or major "mayors" who would fall in on each of the 10 base camps, each with a small staff. They would oversee troop billeting, real estate management, mess halls, power and water, construction and road maintenance, and the hundreds of smaller details involved in installation management. To secure the huge perimeter (some 45km in circumference, in all about 200 square kilometers), three battalions would be placed under our operational control: a combat engineer battalion from the Texas Army National Guard, an infantry battalion from the Hawaii Guard, and a field artillery battalion from the Louisiana Guard. All would function essentially as infantry for the deployment.

The brigade staff itself would operate the Base Defense Operations Center or BDOC, tied into these units and to all tenant units at VBC. In addition to manning perimeter defenses, our units would run interior and exterior patrols on a continuous basis and maintain QRFs, able to respond to attacks or penetrations on short notice. Fortunately, VBC was surrounded by a 12-foot-high concrete wall from the Saddam era, equipped with more than 150 towers for observation. Six entry control points provided the only ways in or out. The largest, ECP1, was located on the famous Route IRISH leading into BIAP. Some 800m deep with three successive layers or belts of access control, it was the crown jewel and the biggest target.

A special concern was the XVIII Airborne Corps Special Troops Battalion, part of the brigade and tasked to look after the Corps staff as "headquarters commandant." Downrange, the STB would also be responsible for the care and feeding of the four-star Multinational Force–Iraq (MNF-I) headquarters, as well. Both were located in the huge Al Faw palace at Camp Victory. The idea was for the Force to handle the politico-military, high-level business while the Corps handled the actual fighting. Together these staffs comprised more than 2,000 soldiers, mostly officers and NCOs, including more than 30 generals. This was a tall order, especially considering the small size of the STB staff. The unit was commanded by an imposing officer, Lieutenant Colonel Timotheus Graham, a combat veteran of the Panama invasion and a Ranger and master jumper. Graham was flinty and reserved, traits that would both help and hurt on the deployment, but he was competent, hardworking, and willing. His would be a very tough task.

During our mission analysis, I decided that one additional, non-standard staff section would be required, a "Force Protection" cell charged to continuously monitor all aspects of this important function. Much went into this that overlapped the operations, intelligence, engineer, and other functions. Reaching into the past, I located Bob Quinnett, the ex-SEAL who had been my lieutenant 20 years before. Quinnett was now teaching in inner-city Chicago but retained a reserve commission as a lieutenant colonel. Though it had been years since we spoke, Bob accepted my offer immediately. His shop would grow to include a major, a captain, a warrant officer, and a master sergeant and would prove essential to our mission success.

There was one additional dimension to our mission that I hadn't counted on. Virtually all Army forces (except for special operations forces) would be task organized under General Vines and the Corps. Many separate units required a colonel-level commander to process their awards, administer military justice, approve their leaves and so on. These units would be placed under my administrative control (called ADCON in Army doctrine), not for operational employment but for administration only. Some of these units, such as the Explosive Ordnance Disposal (EOD) or Psychological Operations battalions, supported the entire theater and only their headquarters were located at VBC. In time, Dragon Brigade's task organization would grow to include nine battalions, nine separate companies or detachments and the Garrison Command, all under my operational (OPCON) or administrative control. Eventually more than 6,500 soldiers would fall under the brigade, making us by far the largest Army brigade in Iraq. But all this still lay in the future.

As an experienced commander I knew that we would have to refine this concept based on conditions on the ground, but events were to show that our planning had been sound and with few modifications we were able to execute the original plan throughout the deployment. For now, we focused on reception and integration of our new soldiers and mission preparation and training. There was much to do and not much time to do it. Equipment had to be containerized and shipped by sea and air, soldiers readied for a year-long deployment, and staffs trained and rehearsed for combat operations. Through the fall of 2004 we worked tirelessly to get ready. Just before Christmas we put our soldiers on leave and prepared to deploy just after the New Year.

By now, the war was not going well. The initial invasion had faced stiffer resistance than expected, but Baghdad fell in relatively short order in 2003. Rumsfeld's original intent had been to transition quickly to some form of Iraqi control, but that policy had faltered under the mismanagement of the Coalition Provisional Authority (under Ambassador Paul Bremer) and the irreconcilable differences of Iraq's warring ethnic groups, now unleashed through the disintegration of the Iraqi state. Rumsfeld had made fundamental mistakes by discouraging preparations for post-war lawlessness, opposing a four-star headquarters to oversee the occupation, and halting the flow of additional ground forces once victory over the Iraqi military was assured. A virulent Sunni opposition flared up in Anbar province, just west of Baghdad, amplified by a dangerous and brutal al Qaeda offshoot led by Abu Musab al-Zarqawi, a Jordanian terrorist. On the Shia side, different factions jockeyed for dominance, some supported by Iran. Internal Iraqi politics was a mess, national reconciliation was failing, and U.S. and coalition casualties were mounting. Though we did not officially admit it, a powerful insurgency had taken root in Iraq. Every movement in the capital and throughout most of Iraq was a combat operation. Mentally, I prepared to lose soldiers and take losses. At best, this would be a long, hard year. At worst, we might lose the war.

Christmas came and went and soon enough I found myself at the departure airfield. Beverly and the kids accompanied me to the hangar, smiling bravely but sad and worried inside. I thought back to how I felt each time my father deployed to Vietnam. There are really no words to describe that empty feeling. In a real sense, you are leaving for the unknown. In the back of your mind you fear failure, death or injury, defeat, and the prospect of endless days away from your family and loved ones. You are surrounded at that moment by hundreds of soldiers and family members going through the same thing. There are many tears and few smiles. You feel the heavy burden of command, but also pride, and determination, and confidence, in your troops and in yourself. I had spent 30 years preparing for this moment. Commanding troops in combat was the whole point of my professional life. In a real way I felt torn. But as the plane neared the theater of operations a transition took hold. For the next 365 days, Baghdad would be my new home. By the time I landed, my head was on right.

As the brigade flowed into theater the first task was to settle in and establish a battle rhythm. A complication was that we fell in on a very different system. Under III Corps, the VBC footprint and perimeter was not organized under a unified command. Instead, different units "owned" different parts of the whole. Dragon Brigade, for the rest of the deployment referred to as "Task Force Dragon," occupied a small compound previously used by Saddam's internal guard force at Camp Victory. A small National Guard Rear Area Operations Center or RAOC, located at Camp Liberty, adjacent to Camp Victory and home to the Multinational Division-Baghdad (or MND-B), operated the BDOC, but it had no operational control of assigned force protection units. Instead, it functioned essentially as a monitoring and reporting headquarters.

This was a faulty arrangement, and a terrible suicide attack near Mosul the month before proved the point. There, a suicide bomber had entered the mess hall at Forward Operating Base Marez and killed 18 Americans. At Marez, the BDOC was responsible for base security, but had no control over any units based there. As a consequence, onerous or annoying force protection policies were routinely ignored. I did not want to repeat the mistake.

During the transition I visited the BDOC, a small affair in a cramped room, and was horrified to see officers tracking units and significant activities (SIGACTs) literally on yellow post-it notes stuck to a wall map. Drawing on the resources of the Corps Rear CP, we had deployed with a full suite of computers, flat screens, tentage and associated equipment. Within a week we had established a fully modern command post, automated and linked to both Division and Corps with secure voice and data communications. Soon we moved the BDOC into a hardened building in our compound with a reinforced concrete ceiling, proof against mortar rounds. Over the next few months, we increased our capabilities with some of the most advanced technology available to the U.S. Army. Overhead, a large, tethered dirigible, called an "aerostat," mounted a variety of cameras and sensors that could see miles in every direction, day and night. Along the perimeter, we mounted motion sensors, television cameras and night vision systems feeding into the BDOC. There, the on-duty battle captain could monitor 24 different views simultaneously or reduce them to a single view on a huge, wall-sized screen. Never in my Army career had I enjoyed such situational awareness.

As for communications, the BDOC was equipped with line-of-sight secure FM communications as well as satellite comms, but much of our work was done on CPOF, short for "Command Post of the Future." CPOF was a system that allowed us to talk securely direct to higher, adjacent and subordinate units and to pass photos, imagery and maps instantaneously. All of VBC's many tenant units were hooked in. We were, in a sense, like a Borg collective—totally wired in and aware. Whether voice-to-voice or in real-time chat rooms, we could operate at top speed with full cognition.

Early in the deployment we organized the staff into day and night shifts of 12 hours each. Earlier in my career I had experimented with different approaches, including three eight-hour shifts or changing up daytime and nighttime assignments periodically. I had learned that shifts develop strong sub-cultures of their own, as well as gaining rapid expertise through repetition with the same staff members. These soldiers worked seven days a week, 12 hours on and 12 off, and were not rotated for the entire year. (All soldiers were however given a two week "mid-tour" leave back in the States.) Shift changes took place at midnight when enemy activity was most likely to be nil. To ensure no loss of situational awareness, the outgoing battle captain held a formal shift change brief. Every hour, each of our 40 tenants was required to acknowledge a secure comms check, which was recorded in the operations log. The battle captain was assisted by a battle sergeant and three radio operators, in addition to intelligence, operations and signal sections manned continuously with an officer and several enlisted. In addition to the command group (myself, the CSM, the DCO, and the XO), the Brigade S3 operations officer, his operations sergeant major and a single assistant S3 captain did not pull shifts. Lieutenant Colonel Quinnett's Force Protection Cell, which ranged far and wide across the giant footprint, was also not limited to shift work. Our days typically lasted 18 or more hours. The only break was Sundays, when we did not hold internal staff meetings or other avoidable activities; Sunday was a "light" day for church and rest, when the enemy or higher headquarters did not intervene.

Our arrival coincided with Iraq's first hesitant steps towards democracy in the form of national elections, held on January 30, 2005, to elect a National Assembly that would then draw up a new Iraqi constitution as the "Iraqi Transitional Government." Our commanders and diplomats had two principal concerns: would violence disrupt the elections? And would all three factions turn out and vote? On balance, the elections were a qualified success. While dozens of polling sites were attacked, fatalities were relatively low (44 civilian deaths across Iraq, including 20 in Baghdad). Turnout among the Shia and Kurds was strong, but Sunni voters largely boycotted the election, casting some doubts on its legitimacy. A leading Shia politician, Ibrahim al-Jaafari, was selected by the national assembly to serve as prime minister while Jalal Talabani, a senior Kurdish leader, was named to the largely ceremonial presidency. While perhaps not ideal, the election produced a functioning Iraqi government, chosen by Iraqis and not appointed by U.S. and coalition leaders (as had been the case with the interim government). Factional infighting would bedevil Iraqi politics throughout the U.S. presence and beyond, but it was a beginning.

As we settled in, I took time to get to know our subordinate units. Except for Lieutenant Colonel Graham's Special Troops Battalion, all were from outside organizations. I was fascinated by the three National Guard Battalions, each with a rich and unique history. The 2nd Battalion, 299th Infantry (Hawaii Army National Guard) was composed overwhelmingly of Asian Americans, many descended from soldiers of the famous Nisei 442nd Regimental Combat Team in World War II, the most decorated unit in Army history. (The 299th also included one company of Alaska Scouts from the Alaska Army Guard.) The 1st Battalion, 141st Field Artillery (Louisiana Army National Guard) traced its lineage to the "Washington Artillery," a famous Civil War unit. It had served proudly in both World Wars and *Desert Storm*. The 111th Engineer Battalion (Texas Army National Guard) came out of the 36th Division, famed for its tragic but heroic attempted crossing of the Rapido river in Italy in World War II. The Texas and Louisiana units were halfway through their year-long tour, while the Hawaiian unit had just begun theirs.

Serving with National Guard units was a new experience and at first, I was taken aback by what, to a Regular Army officer, seemed to be incongruities. Many Guard soldiers were far older than their regular counterparts. The CSM of the 111th, for example, had served as a private in Vietnam—in 1966—and was well into his 60s. One junior enlisted soldier from the 299th was a 54-year-old attorney from Honolulu. In the same battalion, the son of a company first sergeant was a company commander in another company. Many Guard enlisted soldiers were far more accomplished in civilian life than their officers. All of this took some getting used to. I quickly learned that each of these three battalions had undergone an intensive six months of training before deploying. All were manned by eager volunteers. All would serve with distinction in the grueling months to come.

The Puerto Rican Garrison Command was a bit different. They were not a combat unit and did not have combat responsibilities, but they operated in a combat environment where rocket and mortar attacks were a common occurrence. Attempts to breach the perimeter with suicide attacks had happened and would happen again. The base camp mayors had a tough job enforcing basic rules on tenants they had no real authority over. We could help there.

Among the many units we inherited was the "Three Niner Deuce," or Detachment 3 of the 92nd Chemical Reconnaissance Company, a 60-soldier Army Reserve unit out of Jonesboro, Arkansas. Commanded by First Lieutenant Eric Goff, a former enlisted soldier in his early 30s, the unit would unexpectedly become one of our prized possessions. Equipped with 10 up-armored HMMWVs armed with light machine guns, the unit had little to do in the way of chemical reconnaissance. Instead, it became our dedicated VIP shuttle service from Camp Victory into downtown Baghdad.

This mission was both dangerous and exacting. Ground travel in downtown Baghdad was high risk, and the many generals who needed to go there every day could not always travel by helo. We needed a highly trained, professional unit that could take on this "no fail" mission and execute to a high standard. At first, senior officers balked at putting their lives in the hands of chemical troops, traditionally regarded as rear area types, not combat soldiers. Your first trip with Goff would dispel any such notions.

The trip would begin with a safety briefing from the boss. I would sometimes attend, just for fun. Addressing his party of generals, the young officer would bellow, "I am Lieutenant Goff, your convoy commander. During this trip, you will be my precious cargo. My soldiers and I will get you to your destination and bring you back safely, or die trying. During transit you WILL wear your ballistic helmet, hearing and eye protection, seat belt and shoulder harness, and body armor at all times. You will follow all instructions from my NCOs and me. You will not give instructions to us. In the event we are attacked, you will remain in the vehicle, and we will deal with the situation. Do I make myself clear?"

Off duty, Goff was friendly and outgoing. On duty he was intense and highly professional, exuding confidence and competence. Early on I stopped inspecting his vehicles and weapons, as all were immaculately clean and well maintained. His unit was always on time, always in radio communication, and never experienced navigation problems. To see them on the road, moving at high speed, gunners scanning their sectors as the drivers weaved expertly through and around civilian traffic, was almost a thing of beauty. Through hundreds of missions, on the most dangerous road in the world, "Three Niner Deuce" would never lose a vehicle or a passenger. In 2005, it would win the Sibert Award as the best chemical unit in the U.S. Army, and Goff would earn not one but two Bronze Stars, unheard of for a junior officer. To this day, I consider them one of the best units I ever saw.

In our first weeks, based on my prior experience in Kosovo, I directed a 100 percent inventory of each unit's basic load of ammunition, with emphasis on high explosive ammo such as hand grenades and antitank weapons. My concern was that these dangerous weapons would not be stored and secured properly, posing a threat to the more than 30,000 soldiers and contractors housed at VBC. Our three combat battalions passed with flying colors. But the Garrison Command had been issued, then lost track of, dozens of hand grenades and AT4 antitank weapons drawn in Kuwait. (Why their commander drew them in the first place remained a mystery.) An intensive room-by-room search turned up grenades stored in wall lockers, desk drawers and unsecured vehicles. The antitank weapons had apparently been given away to a passing Marine unit, with no documentation. Accordingly, I relieved the Headquarters Company commander and demanded that the garrison commander, a full colonel like myself, do his job properly.

I had seen this before. On operations there can be a strong temptation to relax basic safety precautions on the grounds that "this is combat." In fact, those precautions assume even greater importance in an environment where everyone is armed 24/7, perpetually short on sleep, and worried about the enemy. We would be almost fanatics about safety and force protection, and many of our tenant units would come to resent our inflexibility. But many would return home safely because we did not cut corners.

My previous experiences had also taught me the importance of continuing to train even while deployed. For our entire tour, starting in the first month, we organized large scale mass casualty (MASCAL) exercises involving all the relevant players. Vehicle-borne suicide attacks, downed aircraft, serious vehicle accidents, accidental ammunition explosions, and other scenarios were practiced and rehearsed. We ran weekly firing ranges and insisted that all units departing outside the wire test-fire their weapons. More than once we would be called upon to respond to real world MASCALs and this preparation proved invaluable.

A serious threat was the network of canals that crisscrossed the Baghdad area. These were about 10 feet deep and perhaps 20 feet wide. Many soldiers in adjacent units died when their vehicles drove or slid into a canal, inverted and quickly sank, drowning the occupants. Often, tragedy ensued when our heavy vehicles collapsed the shoulders of the unimproved dirt roads alongside many canals. The problem became so serious that the Corps considered providing emergency oxygen bottles for every vehicle.

I attacked this problem as I had always been taught. Soldier safety is a commander's responsibility, and never more so than in combat. Any fatality due to accident or a safety violation would be seen as a command failure and dealt with accordingly, without exception. Standing orders in Dragon Brigade were: never traverse a road at night that hadn't been reconned in daylight; never use excessive speed, even in pursuit; never use an untrained or unlicensed driver; and when in doubt, select an alternate route. We took great pride in our safety record and never lost a soldier due to accident in our year in Iraq, an unusual and even unique distinction.

So, the word went out. If you were caught in a tactical vehicle without an NCO or officer as vehicle commander, without your ballistic helmet strapped on, or without your seat belt you risked having your vehicle impounded. At each entry control point soldiers were required to dismount, present identification, and clear their weapons into a firing barrel; accidental or "negligent" discharges were handled severely. Vehicles with senior occupants were not waved through but were carefully inspected like everyone else. Inside the VBC perimeter, rounds could not be chambered. Roving patrols spot checked relentlessly. Calmly but persistently, I responded to a flurry of complaints from scores of commanders and angry staff officers.

As time passed this tension between force protection and the petty irritations it engendered threatened to boil over. I decided to attack the problem with humor. Every night I was given a few minutes to brief the generals in the nightly update. Without alerting the commanding general, one night I played a short video instead.

In it I sat in an ornate, Saddam-era gold-leafed chair, staring belligerently at the camera. "You want answers?" I bellowed. An off-camera officer replied, "I think I'm entitled!" "You want answers?" I shouted. He shouted back, "I want the truth!"

Leaning forward from my throne, I exploded. "YOU CAN'T HANDLE THE TRUTH!"

The crowded room erupted in laughter. Everyone recognized the signature courtroom scene from the feature film *A Few Good Men*. I pressed on.

"Son, we live in a world with walls, and those walls have to be guarded by troops with guns. Who's gonna do it? You?" By now even the general couldn't keep a straight face.

I went on. "Deep down in places you don't talk about in the mess hall, you want us on that wall! You NEED us on that wall! We have a greater responsibility than you can possibly fathom. You have the luxury of not knowing what we know; that force protection saves lives, and our existence, while annoying and irritating to you, *saves lives*. We use words like "force protection," "standards," and "compliance" as the backbone of a year spent defending something. You see them as a pain in the ass!"

I rose up out of the chair. "I have neither the time, nor the inclination, to explain myself to people who rise and sleep under the blanket of the very protection we provide, and then question the manner in which we provide it! I would rather you just said, 'thank you,' and went on your way. Otherwise, I suggest you pick up a rifle, and get your butt in a guard tower. Either way, we don't give a damn what you think you are entitled to."

Now the room grew quieter as it dawned on my audience that this wasn't all humor. I turned to the general.

"Sir, I'll be followed by the next briefer."

The general surveyed the room for a long moment. Then, laconically, he said, "*Word.*"

Once more the audience cracked up. And life at the Victory Base Complex got better.

One concern was command relationships. Baghdad came under 3rd Infantry Division (3ID), the "battlespace owner," commanded by a two-star division commander. For the base defense mission, it only made sense for Dragon Brigade to be task organized under him. However, XVIII Airborne Corps saw me as a Corps asset, and for the base operations mission that also made sense. The solution was to split the baby and, in a sense, require me to report to both. I would remain "organic" to the Corps for base operations, but for base defense I would be placed under the tactical control of the division (called TACON). This was somewhat non-standard, but with tact and good will we made it work.

This arrangement began awkwardly with an order from 3ID to relocate the BDOC from Camp Victory, near the corps headquarters, to Camp Liberty, adjacent to the division headquarters. Although at first housed in a large wall tent, we had plans to move into a mortar-proof hard stand facility very soon. We had just completed the arduous process of installing secure and non-secure computer and landline telephone networks at great cost—and the move would only improve my response time to Division by five minutes or so at the most. I had vowed to never use the three-star against the two-star unless absolutely necessary, but as my admin and logistic nodes, as well as my troop living areas, were all at Camp Victory I decided to appeal to a higher authority. The issue was resolved amicably, and we stayed put.

Early on I was surprised to find that Camp Victory included three swimming pools, left over from the Saddam era, all fully functional and staffed by contract lifeguards. This offended me on a number of grounds. First, the pools were mainly used by staff officers assigned to the major headquarters; the junior enlisted soldiers in the combat units were too busy for pool breaks and not welcome there anyway. The pools were therefore seen, and rightly, as essentially officer perks. In fact, the outgoing unit had left a sign that said "no bikinis or speedos"—their idea, we supposed, of discipline in the combat zone. I also learned that to maintain and staff the pools cost several million dollars per year, money that could be better spent on force protection. Lastly, the sight of male and female staff officers lounging about in the middle of the duty day, in a theater of war, was just too much. In fact, the whole operation, with its Pizza Hut, Green Bean, Burger King, and beauty salons, smacked too much of the rear and its garrison mentality. Only the largest bases in Iraq enjoyed such amenities, which meant that most soldiers would rough it out for their 12-month tours. I couldn't change all of it, but the pools closed almost immediately. My decision generated scores of complaints from annoyed staff officers, all of which we weathered.

Our most serious challenge at the outset was manning. We simply had too few soldiers to properly defend our huge perimeter. My commanders acknowledged the problem but couldn't help; Secretary Rumsfeld's rigorous "troop caps" had put the entire theater in the same boat. I was told to "accept risk." We therefore adopted a "layered" approach. Exterior mounted patrols circulated more or less continuously (we would log almost 10,000 in our year-long mission). The perimeter guard towers represented the next layer. As fewer than half could be manned, we rotated these randomly each day and covered them with camouflage netting so that enemy observers watching from a distance could not detect which were occupied and which weren't. A regular series of constantly circulating internal mounted patrols formed the next layer. Finally, locations designated as "critical infrastructure" were guarded by static, dismounted soldiers drawn from tenant units. As an emergency measure, each battalion was required to maintain a four-vehicle quick reaction force. (My tactical headquarters constituted the brigade QRF.) Staged at the unit headquarters on a 10-minute alert status or "string," each QRF had a predetermined location, specified in standing orders, to move to on issue of a code word indicating a serious threat to the perimeter. At least weekly, the BDOC would randomly exercise the alert plan, posting officers or senior NCOs at these sites to confirm that our units were on their toes—or weren't.

In Iraq, no one was permitted to venture "outside the wire" in less than a four-vehicle element. These were remarkably uniform. The standard vehicle was the "up-armored HMMWV," typically manned by a driver, a vehicle commander, and a gunner, leaving two seats for passengers. All soldiers from general to private wore complete body armor with water, ammunition and first aid kit, along with a tourniquet. Initially, most vehicles were standard M998 HMMWVs carrying bolted-on, "hillbilly" armor; later we began to receive some custom-built M1114s with better armor and stronger suspensions. Each vehicle mounted an automatic weapon in the turret, usually an M249 light machine gun, M240 medium machine gun or M2 .50 caliber heavy machine gun. (Each of my TAC vehicles mounted both the M2 .50 cal, and an M249, presenting a fearsome appearance.) Every vehicle carried extra ammunition, water, and medical supplies, as well as a spare tire mounted externally and signs in Arabic warning the locals to stay well clear. All were equipped with radios and antennas. Often, one of the four "trucks" would carry a high-powered jammer, intended to defeat IEDs set off by radio, as well as a tow bar for immediate recovery of a damaged or broken-down vehicle.

Both a second lieutenant platoon leader and a two-star division commander would thus move in a formation that looked the same. There was no nonsense about plates with generals' stars or antenna pennants in Iraq. The streets were far too dangerous for that. The 3ID commanding general, Major General "Fuzzy" Webster, wore body armor and carried an M4 rifle as well as an M9 pistol whenever he left VBC—not as an affectation, but as a tactical necessity. (We all did.) Our vehicles were rugged and dependable, bullet proof with "run flat" tires and equipped with air conditioners vital to operating in Iraq's intense heat. For fear of being rammed by vehicle-borne IEDs (VBIEDs) we moved at high speed on the roads and did not permit civilian vehicles to approach us closely, warning them off with horn blasts, flares, warning shots and aggressive driving techniques.

In Baghdad at that time, any immobilized vehicle was likely to draw unwelcome attention from the enemy, and so we took great care with vehicle maintenance. At home station, the driver would normally conduct a basic "dash 10" or operator level inspection before use. Trained mechanics would perform scheduled "dash 20" maintenance checks at less regular intervals. In Iraq, half of our mechanics worked a night shift, and no vehicle left the perimeter without a by-the-book technical inspection by a certified mechanic. Any fault was corrected immediately, or the vehicle was replaced with a spare. While laborious and time consuming, this approach assured that vehicle breakdowns were rare. My maintenance people were condemned to round-the-clock operations for a solid year, but they worked uncomplainingly. We owed them much.

On occasion a vehicle would be damaged or destroyed, usually by an IED, and we would spring into a practiced battle drill, initiated with the code words "broken arrow." Some units would evacuate their casualties and abandon the vehicle, only to see footage on al Jazeera of insurgents dancing on it a few hours later. In Dragon Brigade we formed a perimeter, called in the QRF, alerted higher headquarters, and dispatched a vehicle recovery team with security from the base camp. Secure radios, night vision devices and other sensitive items would be secured as soon as casualties were treated on site and evacuated. Even totally destroyed vehicles would be recovered. As finding an enemy to fight face-to-face was always a problem, we welcomed the opportunity to stay and fight, knowing we could build up combat power much faster than the bad guys.

But exactly who were the bad guys? On arrival, we weren't given a "playbook" spelling out the local tribes, insurgent and terrorist networks, or criminal gangs who often attacked coalition soldiers for payment. Often, we had no idea who was firing mortars or rockets at us, or sniping at our guard towers, or ambushing our mobile patrols. In the greater Baghdad area, we faced al Qaeda in Iraq (led by the notorious Zarqawi), Iranian-supported Shia militias, Baathist remnants, pissed-off tribesmen indignant over some real or perceived affront, and everything in between. We had taught these groups not to talk on their hand-held radios, which we monitored. Accordingly, our knowledge of their whereabouts and intentions was weak at best. Some of our best information came from interpreters, local tribal leaders or Iraqi Army commanders we managed to befriend. Very little came our way from our own intelligence chain or intelligence agencies back in the U.S.

As soon as we got settled in, I instituted a weekly awards ceremony to recognize deserving soldiers from across the brigade. A common practice, we added to it by taking a picture of each soldier receiving his or her award and sending it, with a short note, to the awardee's parents. I often received heart-warming responses. Across the nation, thousands of mothers and fathers had entrusted to us the most precious things they could possibly offer. We all saw leading these wonderful young people as a sacred trust, as it surely was.

As we got our teeth into the mission, I grew increasingly concerned about the soldier's load. Since the World Wars, basic soldier equipment in many ways had evolved only slowly. We still wore or carried a helmet, web gear, canteens, first aid pouch, ammunition, and so on. In the 1980s, based partly on our experience in Grenada, the Army went through a light infantry "renaissance" and staff officers got serious about lightening the soldier's load. It was decreed that the load for the "approach march," which included a heavy rucksack, should not exceed 72lbs, while the "combat load" should be no more than 48lbs. These standards greatly reduced the burden on the infantry soldier and were graded events at our combat training centers.

After 9/11, however, the introduction of body armor capable of stopping rifle bullets greatly increased the weight of our ballistic vests, originally much lighter and intended to stop shrapnel and pistol rounds. Our rifles were lighter than in past wars, but we carried more ammunition. Many items of equipment were added that never existed before, like close combat optics for every weapon, "camelback" water bags, GPS hand-held navigational devices, night vision goggles, bulkier first aid kits and much else. Although our soldiers often moved mounted, for dismounted operations and foot patrols their fighting load regularly approached 100lbs, and for machine gunners, mortar men and combat medics, often much more. In practice, this meant that our soldiers usually fought standing up, as getting into the prone firing position and back up, over and over again, just wasn't possible. As a commander, and not burdened with hand grenades, a grenade launcher, a machine gun, or a sniper rifle with their heavier ammunition, I would carry just under 90lbs—the *lower* limit for an infantryman in that war. I would rarely accompany a unit on foot for more than a few hours. Many troopers carried far heavier loads for many hours every day.

Though well intentioned, each new item penalized the combat soldier, now less mobile and more quickly fatigued, especially in the extreme temperatures found in Iraq. A lightly equipped enemy was generally able to break contact and elude us at will. Better protection undoubtedly saved lives, but the casualties we suffered because our troopers could not move under fire were surely significant. Unfortunately, we did not have discretion to leave behind heavy body armor or other items deemed essential. The few commanders who tried were sternly rebuked. Later, the Army would discover that some 40 percent of infantrymen came out of Iraq or Afghanistan with chronic back injuries. Two thousand years ago, the Romans wrote of "the toil, the incredible toil, of the march." Not much had changed since the time of the legions.

On earlier deployments the state of our technology had limited us to infrequent phone calls to our families, but by 2005 all that had changed. Soldiers could now talk daily to the rear, and they did. This was widely seen as a morale booster. Beverly and I, however, kept to a weekend schedule. I found it impossible to live in both worlds simultaneously. I'd look forward throughout the week to our weekend reconnect, and she was careful not to burden me with the small crises that I couldn't influence anyway. For my part, I did not share my worries and cares, not wanting to import that trouble and strife into her world. It was enough to hear her voice and see her smile, and to chat with the kids for a few precious moments. It worked for us.

In spring, summer, and fall the temperature rose well above 100 degrees Fahrenheit, regularly exceeding 120 in mid-summer. Rainfall was unknown. Many soldiers worked outside on 12-hour shifts, seven days a week, wearing full equipment. Soldiers wore gloves with their sleeves down to protect against the searing heat and possible burns from touching scorching metal. NCOs checked them constantly to ensure they were properly hydrated, rested, and rotated into shade where possible. But the strain was intense, and some soldiers simply broke down.

As part of the daily routine, we would be told by our EOD commander when to expect to hear programmed detonation of unexploded ordnance (UXO). Almost every day, our forces would encounter live IEDs or other booby traps. They would call in EOD, who would defuse and transport the explosives to a safe location and set them off. Knowing when this happened was helpful, as it helped to distinguish between real explosions or attacks and controlled detonations. Typically, we'd be told "UXO 20/50" or some variation thereof, meaning that any loud explosion at 20 minutes past the hour or 50 minutes past would not be enemy generated. These timings would be varied each day to ensure the enemy did not mask a real attack during these events. Each day I would write these numbers on the back of my hand with a sharpie for easy reference. Throughout our year-long deployment I'd often be asked by visitors, staff officers or my superiors to explain the strange numerals on my hand, which would change every day. Always, I'd provide a humorous explanation ("Oh, that's the number of days until my next colonoscopy"). I never revealed the mystery, contributing to a growing reputation for inscrutability.

Although our soldiers were sometimes shot at in the towers (usually by snipers or small arms, but on occasion even with rocket-propelled grenades), the greatest threat inside the sprawling VBC perimeter was from indirect fires in the form of rockets or mortars. The standard rocket was a 122mm weapon, looted from old Iraqi Army stocks. The 122 could be set up quickly using an improvised bipod, enabling the firer to escape immediately after launch. It had a flat trajectory, was extremely fast, and impacted with an ear-splitting crash. And it could be devastating. In one attack on Camp Liberty, a single rocket killed one soldier and wounded 22.

Drawing on my experiences in training, after every rocket or mortar strike, we immediately dispatched an assessment team to do crater analysis to determine both the exact type of weapon and its direction of fire. By carefully tracking this data we quickly built a picture of locations and timings for all rocket and mortar attacks, showing when, where and with what the enemy was likely to strike. VBC was also home to a number of counterfire radars that in theory could track mortars and rockets in flight and locate their points of origin. We could then focus our intelligence and surveillance assets in those areas and either target the shooters, or at least force them to move around and change their "pattern of life." Over time, we were able to reduce these kinds of attacks by some 50 percent but rockets and mortars would continue to plague us throughout the deployment.

One attack in particular proved exceptionally devastating. When off duty, soldiers lived in trailers protected by 10-foot-high cement barriers. (Congress had forbidden us to construct hardened buildings to ensure there would be no "permanent presence.") These protected them well against flat trajectory rockets, and as most mortar attacks were fired from small 60mm tubes, usually with only two to three rounds to ensure a fast getaway, casualties were rare. In this case, however, a concentration of twelve 82mm mortar rounds impacted squarely in a troop living area, demolishing a trailer and gravely injuring the six female soldiers living there. I arrived on the scene just minutes later to see our combat medics evacuating the worst casualty. As I rolled up and dismounted, the smell of high explosive still hung in the fetid air. Soaked in blood, the wounded soldier was strapped to a backboard, an IV forced into one arm and a breathing tube inserted. As she was loaded in a field ambulance the senior medic gave me a quick update: "She's litter urgent, in shock with multiple lacerations, a collapsed lung, head wounds, blood loss and a fractured femur."

Translated, his terse summary meant that she would die in less than two hours unless she received advanced trauma care. Accordingly, she was flown by helo to the "Level III" facility in the Green Zone in the center of Baghdad, staffed by some of the military's best trauma surgeons. There she was stabilized. That night, she was placed on a fully equipped "Nightingale" fixed-wing medevac plane and flown to Landstuhl Medical Center in Germany, and ultimately on to Walter Reed Army Hospital in Washington. Hundreds of badly wounded soldiers would make that flight, and most would survive—a testament to the skill of our medics and surgeons. In Iraq, if you were not killed outright, you had a fighting chance of survival no matter how badly you were hit.

Two months after we arrived, the 3rd Armored Cavalry Regiment arrived at VBC, led by an iconic colonel named H. R. McMaster. Famous as the hero of the Battle of 73 Easting in the Gulf War as a young captain, McMaster wore a Silver Star and was also the author of a best-selling book about command failures in Vietnam. A former West Point rugby player, the brawny, bullet-headed cavalryman crackled with intensity. We had been friends for years and the reunion was a warm one.

In his first week, McMaster lost his sergeant major to an IED strike. What followed was unlike anything I had seen before. McMaster pursued the insurgents responsible for hours, massing tanks, attack helicopters and everything he could muster, finally driving them to ground and wiping them out. He broke crockery doing it, crossing unit boundaries, uncovering other sectors and in general raising hell. Monitoring his radio nets, I was impressed by his driving forcefulness, even ferocity. Here was someone very special.

McMaster soon found himself at odds with the Corps, for complex reasons. For months he had trained to operate in Baghdad, only to learn soon after arriving that he would be pushed up north to Tal Afer. The Corps planners began to dismember his regiment, slicing off one of his three ground squadrons and making a play for his aviation squadron as well. Any commander would be frustrated if dealt this hand.

H. R. was however cut from sterner stuff, and he pushed back hard, alienating his paratrooper bosses. At the price of angering the generals he held on to his helicopters and forced the Corps to give him more infantry. During his tour he would be injured in an IED strike that upended his vehicle, but he remained in command for the duration. His "clear hold build" approach to operations in Tal Afer proved enormously successful and was adopted by the White House as our strategy for all of Iraq, infuriating his superiors. In retaliation they damned him with faint praise on his command reports, hoping to side-line him from future promotion. Though he would always have detractors, his many admirers, of all ranks, recognized his talent and he would rise to three stars, concluding his career as national security advisor. For my part, I considered McMaster probably the best battlefield commander in the Army, and certainly the most interesting.

In May of 2005, I fielded a phone call from the current head of the Sosh department, who offered me the services of six Sosh captains. I took my obligations to the department seriously and wanted to help. Still, I proceeded cautiously.

"How long can I have them for?" I asked.

"Thirty days," was the answer.

It was all I could do not to slam down the phone. The idea here was clearly to "credential" these officers with a combat patch and a campaign ribbon or two before bringing them back for the fall semester. They would hang around my headquarters for a few weeks offering advice, but not much more. I felt a visceral distaste for military tourism and said so. It would be some years before I would be invited back to the annual Sosh reunion.

As our year wore on, we battled rockets, mortars, small arms fire, and IEDs, but the most terrifying threat of all was the suicide bomber. As we had seen in the Marez attack, a single individual on foot and wearing a vest could cause incredible damage. A vehicle-borne suicide attack could be truly catastrophic, as an enormous weapon could be housed in the vehicle. Invariably, suicide attacks were carried out by Sunni fighters affiliated with al Qaeda in Iraq (AQI). Most were foreigners recruited to carry out "martyrdom operations." Every day we carried on a cat-and-mouse game with the enemy to prevent a high-profile suicide attack inside our thinly guarded perimeter, knowing that a successful strike would generate international headlines and cause massive loss of life.

Here we took no chances. Civilian vehicles could enter at only two of our six control points; the rest were restricted to U.S. military vehicles. At an outer station, the occupant would be stopped at a barrier and instructed to dismount and come forward (soldiers manning the checkpoint would remain under cover some distance away). He would be searched, checked for official MNF-I issued ID and temporarily held inside a concrete barrier. A handler and dog would then carefully circle and inspect the vehicle.

In this battle the Army threw every kind of technology at the problem: electronic sniffers, "Z Backscatter vans," infrared systems and much else besides. In the end, nothing worked better than our military working dogs. Highly trained and incredibly sensitive, they simply could not be fooled, though the enemy tried. In the course of our mission, we encountered vehicle-borne explosives rigged inside ice, surrounded by blood bags, or shrouded in animal carcasses. Nothing worked. Invariably, the dog would alert on a vehicle carrying any explosive—even loose rifle bullets stored in the trunk. At that point, the driver would be detained, EOD would be summoned, and the vehicle would be blown in place.

Most working dogs were German Shepherds or similar breeds, unsuited to extremely high temperatures, and their handlers went to great lengths to care for these precious animals. In hot weather the dogs were rotated every 20 minutes into air-conditioned kennels in military vehicles. The animals wore leather booties to protect their feet from the searing concrete as well as "doggles," specially fitted tinted goggles to protect their eyes. Inseparable, handlers and dogs ate, slept, and worked together, and given the high stress they operated under they served six-month and not 12-month tours. TF Dragon was given 20 teams, but we could have used twice that number.

Our challenge was greatly complicated by the fact that more than 2,000 Iraqi civilian workers and scores of large trucks entered the VBC perimeter daily. Here we could not accept risk, no matter how inconvenient our safety measures might be. Every morning our soldiers searched every entering Iraqi carefully. If found with weapons, cell phones, cameras, or fake IDs (literally a daily occurrence), they were turned over for interrogation and possible detention. Trucks entered at a specifically designated entry point and were taken into a large sterile holding yard where their cargoes were downloaded and searched by dogs. Only then were they uploaded onto our own trucks, which never left the perimeter, and taken to the job site. During our deployment, several large bombs were found in this way that, if detonated, could have killed and wounded hundreds. All of this was laborious and time consuming, but it was the only way to be sure.

A few months into the deployment, my force protection cell came to see me with an unusual request. After careful study they had concluded that we could improve our observation of the area if we constructed large towers in the four corners of the base complex. A month later they were in place, paid for with force protection funds and erected by one of the large contractors present at VBC. Each was 10 stories tall, equipped with a .50 caliber machine gun, a .50 caliber Barrett sniper rifle, FM and landline communications, and a large telescope. Atop each was a sensor suite of television and IR cameras which fed into the BDOC. The towers were roofed and manned by four soldiers, led by a junior NCO, at all times. The first nine stories were simply an iron framework, with an interior stair, but the top story was essentially a small room surrounded by a 4-foot bulletproof wall. A rope and pulley system enabled the occupants to bring up heavy items like water, rations, heavy weapons, and ammunition.

The towers were imposing and gave us the ability not only to see for miles in all directions, but to place heavy fires along the perimeter if needed. Early on, however, we identified a challenge. In the dust and dirt and wind, our sensor lenses quickly became obscured and required regular cleaning. This was both difficult and dangerous, as climbing atop the tower roof 10 stories high required strong nerves. CSM Zacheus gave the task to the brigade signal section. Fashioning safety harnesses out of modified parachute straps they happily took on the challenge.

Much of our work was constantly checking up on our units, in keeping with the old saying that "the unit only does well those things the commander checks." During one of our nightly spot checks, the duty officer happened to find two soldiers sound asleep in their tower, wrapped up in poncho liners and oblivious to all else. This was a serious dereliction of duty in a combat zone, and I directed the deputy commander to convene a court martial. Soldiers from each unit were directed to attend, and Colonel Pattillo served as the presiding officer. An attorney in civilian life, Ladd understood we needed to send a strong message to the command. Opening the Manual of Courts Martial, he read out the maximum penalty for "sleeping on one's post in time of war"—"death, or such less penalty as a court martial may direct." Gasps could be heard in the courtroom, while the defendants literally turned white. Both were reduced in rank to E-1, heavily fined and sent to Kuwait for confinement. An account of the proceeding was published in daily orders, and no more incidents of this kind happened for the rest of the mission.

As the brigade commander, "battlefield circulation" was an almost daily practice as it was for all commanders of combat units. In this way I could visit my units, see soldiers where they lived and worked, maintain situational awareness, and keep informed in ways large and small. (By standing order, all brigade staff officers were required to accompany units outside the wire at least once per week to stay involved and aware of the challenges faced by our soldiers.) Each movement began with pre-combat inspections (PCIs), a tactical brief, and a short group prayer. Like every other combat unit in Iraq, my TAC had a tacit understanding, seldom discussed but always in force. Should the day go against us, we would not allow any to be captured alive. This was not bravado. We had all seen the gory videos and knew what would happen if we did. In both Iraq and Afghanistan there were cases where small groups of soldiers and Marines fought to the bitter end, but surrender was almost unknown. These wars were different.

We would then mount our vehicles, strap in, check our communications and prepare to move out. A typical radio message as we rolled out would be "Sky Dragon Main, this is Sky Dragon 6 … SP-ing for the IZ with four victors and 12 pax, time now, over." A rough translation is: "Command post, this is the commander … I am starting movement to the International Zone with four vehicles and 12 personnel at this time … please acknowledge." During movement, we would call in checkpoints as we passed so that the BDOC could track our movement. Like all military units, we used jargon and "pro words" to speed communication without loss of clarity. To the uninitiated, military radio traffic is virtually unintelligible. A trained ear is necessary to tune out the radio static and background noise, while military acronyms and verbal shortcuts can sound like a foreign language.

In early March of 2005, we became embroiled in an ugly incident highlighting just how hard coalition warfare can be. A month earlier, an "unembedded" Italian journalist, Giuliana Sgrena, working for the communist newspaper *Il Manifesto* was kidnapped by insurgent forces near Baghdad. As they had often done in other conflicts (for example, in the Balkans and in Somalia), Italian authorities negotiated her release through a large ransom payment. Without informing U.S. authorities, Italian secret service officer Nicola Calipari attempted to transport Sgrena to Baghdad International Airport in a civilian vehicle, a hazardous and foolish excursion. Approaching a U.S. checkpoint at high speed, Calipari's vehicle was fired on by U.S. troops belonging to the 69th Infantry, an adjacent National Guard outfit out of New York, after ignoring warning signals. Calipari, an intelligence major general, was killed in the incident, igniting a firestorm in the Italian press.

In the ensuing outcry the Italian authorities and media worked hard to obscure or distort the facts, alleging that Calipari and another agent, Andrea Carpani, were "murdered" in an "ambush." Denying that any ransom had been paid or that prior coordination was not conducted, the Italian authorities dismissed the results of the U.S. investigation and later attempted to charge American soldiers in Italian courts.

In fact, Calipari encountered a mobile checkpoint established to protect the movement of U.S. Ambassador John Negroponte that day. At that time, Route IRISH was known to be perhaps the most dangerous road in the world, with almost daily attacks. (One *New York Times* report chronicled 135 attacks on the road in the four months up to early March of 2005, including 15 suicide car bombs, 19 roadside bombs, and 14 attacks with rocket-propelled grenades.) The 69th would sustain heavy losses during its year in Baghdad and had in fact lost two soldiers in a catastrophic explosion nearby only two days before. Brigadier (later Lieutenant) General Pete Vangjel from the Corps staff was tasked to investigate the incident and his report was comprehensive and accurate. 69th soldiers on the scene were well versed in the Rules of Engagement and had employed searchlights, laser pointers and warning shots before engaging the careening vehicle.

Following the incident, Italian Prime Minister Silvio Berlusconi's government came under great pressure, threatening Italy's continued participation in the coalition and damaging the military-to-military relationship seriously (Italy would withdraw from the coalition in 2008). On the ground, we were equipped with more and better barriers, signs, and warning devices, while our soldiers were exhorted to be even more "aware" and "sensitive." At the tactical level, however, the threat remained critical. We could not and did not retreat from a bedrock principle—the fundamental right of self-defense.

Soon after, I would experience this tension and this agony first-hand. On occasion I accompanied subordinate units on mounted or dismounted patrols, and on this evening, I joined a squad from the Hawaiian infantry battalion as it moved on foot after dark through the Ameriyah neighborhood. An hour into the patrol, a civilian vehicle entered from a side street and began to accelerate towards the rear of the patrol. This was unusual, as by now all Baghdad residents knew not to approach any U.S. patrol in anything that looked like a threatening manner.

As with the Calipari incident, here was a life-or-death situation which called for split-second decisions from the young soldier bringing up the rear. A vehicle-borne suicide attack could wipe out the entire patrol and kill many civilians in nearby buildings. But how to be sure? Taking no chances, in mere seconds the trooper executed the "escalation of force" sequence that by now was almost second nature. First, he fired two warning shots into the air, immediately followed by two shots into the pavement in front of the oncoming vehicle. When it continued towards him, he fired two more into the engine block. The car continued to charge right at him, and now out of options, he engaged the driver directly with a burst into the windshield at a range of no more than 20 meters.

Tragically, his rounds flew between the driver and passenger and struck a 10-year-old boy in the back seat, fatally wounding him in the head. The driver, his father, was from Anbar province and simply panicked when he came up on the American patrol. We rushed the boy to our aid station in my vehicle, his blood drenching its floor. He died 30 minutes later.

I returned to the BDOC and sat in my command chair, unmoving, still in my body armor and soaked in sweat. Around me the night shift worked quietly, standing apart, sensing my anguish. After a few minutes the battle captain thoughtfully turned out the lights, so that no one could see the tears running down my face. For an hour they worked by the light of their computer screens, the silence broken only by the soft staccato of the radio nets. A young sergeant, unobtrusively posted by the entrance, kept all visitors away. For what seemed an age I wrestled with myself in the dark, until I gave up, exhausted. My armor had never felt heavier, or more useless. At that moment, the war didn't make sense to me. Not really.

That night, I thought about a talk with my father, years before. Then, I was a grad student, my head filled with lofty notions of international politics. I asked him what it felt like to fight in a war with no clear path to victory. Puffing on his pipe, he waited before answering. Then he said, "They gave me an area to work. My job was to kill as many of the enemy as I could and bring home as many of my men as I could. That's what I did. All the rest was somebody else's business. We go where we're sent. And we do what we're told. It's pretty awful sometimes. But that's the job." Not much seemed real to me that night. But that did.

My young soldier was inconsolable, though a subsequent investigation concluded that he had followed the correct procedure to the letter. Only two days later, a similar incident not far from VBC resulted in eight dead Iraqi soldiers and 20 wounded. This time, the threat was real. This was the reality of war among the people. We knew that every incident of "CIVCAS" would be turned against us to alienate the locals. Yet our forces were constantly attacked inside populated areas by an enemy that dressed like civilians and hid among them. We did all we could to avoid harming non-combatants, but batting 1.000 was simply not possible. All we could do was try to live with the consequences when we failed. We live with them still.

Three months into the mission, on March 26, a catastrophic explosion shattered the calm of the BDOC as our radio nets sprang to life. Our tower guards quickly reported in and we trained our dirigible-mounted TV cameras on the scene. Zooming in only seconds after the blast, we saw a HMMWV in flames only yards outside the perimeter wall. A small blue pickup truck had slammed into the vehicle and detonated, burning two Louisiana Guardsmen to death and seriously injuring two others. Within seconds CSM Zacheus and I were rolling to the scene, while the BDOC staff rushed field ambulances to the site and reported to higher.

By now we had learned that an observer was usually in the vicinity to video the attack. An alert battle captain, expertly manipulating the aerostat cameras, located the observer and shifted the field of view to track him as he fled with his camcorder in a small white car. We began to vector QRFs onto the fleeing insurgent. If we could catch him, we would likely learn much about his network. Suddenly, without warning, the camera view shifted violently back to the burning wreck. Officers in our higher headquarters had overridden the BDOC and taken control of the cameras. Fascinated by "war porn," they watched the dead and wounded being carried away as the attacker escaped. Later, I argued hotly with the staff at 3ID. Voyeurism was not an excuse for crippling an operation in progress.

On the scene, I was briefed by the 111th Engineer Battalion sergeant major, over 60 and a veteran of the Ia Drang battles in Vietnam. He was tough, composed, and in charge. Apparently, the targeted unit (a small patrol from the 1st Battalion, 141st "Washington Artillery"), had stopped to pick up an interpreter, as they did each morning at the same time and place. A thinking and adaptive enemy had observed this patterned behavior and acted on it.

In a curious postscript, the remains of the suicide bomber were left on the scene, in full view of our towers only yards away. We summoned the Iraqi police, but they refused to evacuate what was left of the body, arguing that as he wasn't Iraqi it wasn't their job. How they determined nationality wasn't clear, as there wasn't much left that was recognizable. With no other options we called in graves registration soldiers to do the job.

The incident hit the 141st hard. Behind every death in war lies an unspeakable human tragedy that will never really end for the families. In the midst of war, Sergeant Lee Godbolt from New Orleans had thoughtfully sent his aunt, Mae Hagan, a birthday card. It arrived two days after his death. Godbolt had some college behind him and had worked hard to better himself. Service in the Guard was part of that. Sergeant Isaiah Sinclair from Natchitoches left a widowed mother. His father, twice wounded in Vietnam, had died at 55. Both were young Black men, handsome junior noncommissioned officers marked out for better things. A few short months later, Hurricane Katrina would batter and smash their hometowns. Denise Godbolt, Lee's mother, would lose his medals and the flag that draped his coffin in the disaster. The 141st would redeploy from a year in Iraq and without rest go straight into disaster relief on an epic scale. This one hurt. The unit was crushed.

When we lost a soldier, the unit would hold a memorial service whenever possible. On a crude stage, the soldier's helmet would be placed atop a rifle, which was stuck into the platform by the bayonet, along with a pair of boots. The soldier's dog tags would be hung from the rifle and a picture of the soldier in uniform would be placed nearby. As many soldiers as we could spare from the unit would attend. A chaplain would offer a prayer. The company commander would speak, often accompanied by short remembrances by the soldier's close friends. Taps would be played.

Often, no bugler could be found, and Major Shoults would do the honors. As he had in Bosnia and Liberia, as his forebears had done in both World Wars, Korea and Vietnam, Hugh would play the mournful notes of the Army's most beautiful song on his battered instrument. Soldiers would file by for a last goodbye, caressing the dog tags, often leaving small mementos. Always, there were many tears. From general to private, to say goodbye forever is heart breaking. For me, the experience would never become easier. We would bury our dead as full-grown men or women. But I often recalled an epitaph, written on a child's grave: "Walk softly, stranger, for here lie dreams." Everyone was some mother's child. For her, the world would never, ever be the same.

Later, at the airfield, a separate ramp ceremony would take place. An honor guard would solemnly carry the flag-draped casket into the transport plane. The general, the colonel and the captain would follow, disappearing up the ramp behind the metal box containing the remains. Again, the chaplain would pray. It was an intimate experience, deeply moving and always wounding. I hoped the families would know that we had done all we could to honor their soldier.

The war ground on. On April 2, 2005, the detention facility at Abu Ghraib, about 15 miles to our west, experienced a major coordinated attack unlike any we had seen before. The assault itself involved dozens of al Qaeda attackers, who attempted to breach the main gate with a massive truck bomb. Thirty-six Marines, soldiers and civilian detainees were wounded or injured in the attack, which continued for some hours. Aerial and ground quick reaction forces sent from VBC encountered fierce resistance on the main routes leading to Abu Ghraib. Several Apache gunships were forced down at Baghdad International Airport with battle damage, and for the first (and only) time our forces encountered surface laid antitank mines on the highways. Route TAMPA, the MSR leading up from Kuwait, was closed during the attack and many large convoys were diverted into VBC for safe harbor. Our situation maps exploded with SIGACTs, which crackled all around the western part of the huge perimeter. All of our 20 QRFs were stood up, and we directed the entire base complex and its 30,000 soldiers to go to Force Protection Condition (FPCON) Delta, the highest stage of alert meaning "combat is imminent."

In this instance all of our training and rehearsals paid off handsomely. Every tenant unit command post reported in and maintained constant communication with the BDOC. Medical treatment facilities went to full alert, empty towers were manned, and a dense network of patrols scoured the area. It was, in a sense, a full-dress rehearsal for a major attack.

Abu Ghraib, unfortunately, lay astride the boundary between the Marines, who owned Anbar province, and the Army, who controlled the Greater Baghdad area. Because the Marines were not formally task organized under the XVIII Airborne Corps (they reported instead to the senior Marine at USCENTCOM in Tampa and were only required to "coordinate" with the Army), the attempt to synchronize a response proved difficult. A service boundary is a non-trivial thing. Secure radio "fills" (cryptological codes) are different, disrupting communication. Jargon and terminology also differ, while flying and shooting across service boundaries (never mind unit boundaries) can be problematic. All of these sources of friction happened during the attack, and it began to dawn on us that the enemy might be more than just brute terrorists. A major attack (undoubtedly intended to free prisoners) conducted right along a major coalition "seam" was highly intelligent and well prepared. We resolved never to underestimate the opposition and redoubled our training and planning.

Shortly after the Abu Ghraib attack, in May 2005, Lieutenant Colonel Ken Hara, commander of the 2nd Battalion, 299th Infantry (Hawaii National Guard), came to see me. "Sir," he said, "we're confident we have a bad guy right under our nose, inside the wire. He runs a small shop, approved by the last regime. We've had him under surveillance for some time. We assess he's a genuine threat, and I'd like to raid his place and search it." We went over the details, and I approved the operation. I listened to his briefing and was impressed. Hara's troopers often operated in the city, but this time the enemy was closer to home.

A few days later, the "Two Niner Nine" moved in and hit pay dirt. The small trailer was cordoned off, the target was detained, and the unit began the search, assisted by members of the Army's CID and the Air Force Office of Special Investigations. Led by First Lieutenant Charles Neumann, the members of the search team fanned out, videotaping the operation as they went.

What they found was staggering. Inside the trailer were classified documents, drugs and a prohibited cell phone. On it were phone numbers, some of which later traced to known al Qaeda affiliates and insurgent personalities. And cash. Lots and lots of cash—$750,000 in all—in bags and backpacks and safes. The Iraqi vendor was hustled off for interrogation and detention, and the inventory began. The lieutenant and his team began to painstakingly count the money.

Suddenly, a CID agent intervened. "This will take forever. We have a machine back at headquarters. We'll do it there." The bags of money were loaded into his vehicle, and he pulled away. A few hours later, I received a call from the CID commander. "$50,000 is missing and my agents are initiating an investigation. Right now, it's focused on the 299th." I was dumbfounded. The operation had been thoroughly supervised—even filmed—right up to the point that CID intervened. No one had ever been alone with the cash, except for the CID agent. I objected but was warned brusquely not to interfere. As I briefed general officers to express my concerns, I was warned: "Be careful. CID is talking about obstruction of justice."

For weeks, the soldiers involved in the raid were grilled. Pulled from operations, they were subjected to many hours of interrogation and threatened with long prison sentences. Frightened, most eventually sought defense counsel. Early on, I brought Hara in. "Ken, what do you think?"

He set his jaw and said, "My guys are innocent. I'd bet my career on it." I grimaced. "Brother, I think you just did." My next step was to consult with Colonel Arnie Claudio, a close friend and the Corps provost marshal. Claudio had served for years in Colombia, fighting the drug war, and was well known for repeatedly risking his life as he roamed across Iraq with his beloved Military Police. "Let the investigation take its course," he counseled. "When the final report is in, let me know." A cloud descended over the unit, with rumors swirling that they had staged the operation to make off with the cash. There was a war on, and this was a distraction we didn't need.

Some weeks later the report hit my desk. I read it with a sinking feeling. "We conclude that First Lieutenant Charles Neumann likely committed felony theft in the amount of $50,000. It is recommended that the command take appropriate action." No witnesses or other pieces of evidence were cited. Neumann was duly "titled" (found by "a preponderance of the evidence" to have more likely than not committed the crime), appearing in law enforcement databases and losing his security clearance in the process. Facing court martial and imprisonment, the young officer was disconsolate.

I called Hara in. "What now, boss?" he asked. "I'll go as far as I possibly can for my officer. We can't let this stand. Let's go see the general." Taking Hara by the shoulder I said, "First off, I'm not going to charge the lieutenant. Someone else might, but not me. Let's see what the provost marshal has to say."

A few hours later, I sat with Arnie as he read the report. "Okay," he said, "I'll take it from here." Twenty-four hours later an expert CID investigative team consisting of a senior chief warrant officer and a sergeant major was in the air, headed for Baghdad. We soon found ourselves meeting with the Corps chief of staff, an irate brigadier. He'd heard about the team. Who did we think we were? Were we trying to cover for the culprit, or ourselves? As he ordered Claudio to turn off the investigation, the provost marshal spoke calmly and carefully. "Sir, this is an internal CID matter, and one we take very seriously. With all due respect, you don't really have a vote here."

Angrily, the general turned to the staff judge advocate, the senior legal officer for the corps, who nodded solemnly. Shortly afterwards, General Vines weighed in with his support. Within 48 hours, the CID team had located the cash in the bank account of the agent's brother in the U.S. Shortly afterwards, the provost marshal general of the Army "un-titled" Neumann—something that had not happened, we were told, in years.

In the end, justice was done. As I pondered the outcome, my thoughts wandered, not to the CID agent—once in a great while, even the best organizations have a bad apple— but to the actors in this drama and their unshakable integrity. Neumann held his head high throughout the ordeal, maintaining his innocence and that of his soldiers to the end. Hara, who would go on to command the 29th Infantry Brigade and then serve as the adjutant general for Hawaii as a major general, found himself under heavy fire but risked his career and never wavered in defending his troopers. Claudio, the provost marshal, acted without hesitation and fearlessly to ensure that his organization lived up to its reputation for honesty and probity. His superiors acted swiftly to do the right thing.

Fortunately, the lieutenant returned home to be promoted and continues to serve honorably in the Guard today. As we put the case to bed, I found my faith in our Army strengthened, not weakened. With hundreds of thousands of soldiers, perfection is the ideal, but often we will fall short. When we do, our values and our leaders usually come to the fore. Most of the time, they choose the harder right instead of the easier wrong.

Over time I grew to love the Guardsmen who served with us, but the 299th earned a special place in my heart. One of their affectations was the "Shaka" sign, a hand gesture of friendly intent often associated with surf culture, roughly translated as "hang loose." Among their other duties, the famously casual Hawaiians provided a security platoon at the Al Faw palace and its many generals. On one particular day, I found myself summoned to meet Major General Webster. He was hot.

"Goddammit Colonel, I want you to get those National Guard types under control. I was down at the palace today and they all but flipped me off. I don't think a simple hand salute is asking a lot. Get this fixed now!"

I knew exactly what he was talking about. Webster was an outstanding officer and general and would soon be a three-star. But he could be temperamental, and there was some context here. "General, the 299th guys mean no disrespect. They're excellent soldiers. This is a cultural thing and just their way of showing friendship."

Webster was having a hard day and wanted none of this. "Just get this fixed!"

That night I met with Hara, who grimaced. "This won't go down well." I commiserated with him but told him the order was firm, and to his credit he passed it along immediately. Two days later the *Honolulu Advertiser* ran a front-page story complaining about the Regular Army's cultural insensitivity and poor treatment of the National Guard. The day after that, General Webster fielded a call from the office of Daniel Inouye, the senior senator from Hawaii and a one-armed, Medal of Honor recipient from World War II—informally referred to by the 299th as "the Shogun."

Soon after, a very pleasant General Webster called. "Rich, I may have been a little hasty the other day. Please tell the boys I rescind the order, with my compliments." Within minutes the Shaka was back, and if the stories are true, even Webster himself might have flashed it once or twice thereafter.

As the weeks flew by, we began to experience chronic problems with the special operations forces (SOF) resident at VBC. These came in two flavors. Army Special Forces ("Green Berets") were originally formed in the 1950s to train and lead indigenous forces behind enemy lines. In 2005 the Army had fully 15 battalions of these troops, plus another six in the reserves. These reported only to the four-star theater commander. Army Rangers, select SEAL units, and the Army's Special Mission Units stood at the top of the heap as America's most elite military formations. Their sole business was "direct action," essentially hunting, killing or capturing enemy "high value targets." They reported only to the CENTCOM commander in Tampa.

Since the 1980s and the formation of U.S. Special Operations Command, SOF had become stovepiped, walled off from the rest of the force. As a result, we rarely saw, trained with, or interacted with their community in peacetime. What we did experience was a constant skimming of our quality NCOs, painfully eroding the conventional Army. (As a battalion commander in the 82nd Airborne, I lost 16 NCOs in a single year to Special Forces, a crippling blow.) Understandably, relations between the two communities were cool at best. They now began to crater altogether.

The high-end units mostly operated out of BIAP or Balad, an hour north of Baghdad, and we saw little of them. A Green Beret battalion, however, was headquartered at the Radwaniyah Palace, a lavish complex with lush green lawns, air-conditioned villas and swimming pools wrested from Saddam's forces during the invasion. Given their special status, they were exempt from many of the inconveniences visited on conventional units. They did not man towers, provide QRFs, attend force protection meetings or conform to the uniform standards required of everyone else. Unlike our soldiers, who pulled repetitive year-long deployments, the Green Berets rotated every six months. Much to our annoyance, Dragon Brigade was required to provide a round-the-clock guard force at Radwaniyah, seriously depleting our limited manpower.

Several incidents highlighted the nature of the problem. In one case, Special Forces officers in civilian clothes and driving a civilian vehicle were fired upon at one of our checkpoints after refusing to stop. In another, one of their vehicles was searched and found to contain beer, scotch, and whiskey in large amounts—a serious violation of "General Order Number 1" banning all alcohol consumption throughout Iraq. On one Saturday morning, several hundred Iraqi males rioted at ECP1 after being turned away from a recruiting session for the Iraqi commandos run by the SF battalion. The Green Berets dispersed the crowd with "flash bang" stun grenades and warning shots. In the absence of any coordination with us, the 80-man guard force at the checkpoint assumed the worst and we barely avoided a major "green on green" friendly fire disaster with our own Special Forces.

The worst was yet to come. In late May of 2005, I was called to the phone by a staff officer from 3ID. One of their brigadiers informed me that a SOF unit would be conducting a raid early the following morning in my battlespace. I needed to have a reaction force standing by in case they ran into trouble, and ready my aid stations to receive casualties.

I remonstrated. "Sir, with all due respect, I've seen this movie before. I'm not doing anything unless there is proper planning and coordination beforehand. What unit is carrying out the mission? Who is the target? How am I supposed to link up, under fire, at night, without exchanging call signs and frequencies? We should be better than this." A moment later the division commander came on the line. "Rich, this is way above your pay grade and mine. Get your guys ready. Out here."

The next morning at 0400, a SOF element kicked in the door and arrested Mohsen Abdul-Hamid, head of Iraq's largest Sunni Arab political party and former president of the since-dissolved U.S.-backed Iraqi Governing Council. Hamid was well known to us: pro-American, he was one of a very few senior Sunni politicians calling for a peaceful political solution to ward off an impending civil war. Taken into detention along with his sons, his arrest provoked a storm of media attention, landing on the front page of the *Washington Post*. The White House was not pleased. As happened so often, U.S. SOF had been hoodwinked into targeting Hamid by his political opponents. Even cursory coordination would have avoided this public relations disaster.

In keeping with the best traditions of the Army, I was called to the palace and arraigned by an irate general. "You're the battlespace owner here. You are responsible. You're not doing your job!" Jumping to my feet, I responded hotly. "No sir, you've got it backwards. I tried to stop this mission and was given direct orders to shut up and color. You let these cowboys run around in our areas with no supervision and no coordination, and when things go south you go after the local commander. Who's not doing their job?"

The general wasn't going to take this from a colonel, and he began to shout and threaten. Clearly, some major heat had descended on the Corps from Starfleet level. The general raved on for some time. When he paused for breath, I interjected. "Sir, this isn't getting us anywhere. I'd like to see the three-star, right now."

As I expected, my belligerent general backed down. "He's too busy for this stuff. You just remember what I said. Now get back to work." I walked back to my compound in suppressed fury. I hoped that matters would improve. But for many years after, the refusal of U.S. SOF to integrate and coordinate in both Iraq and Afghanistan seriously compromised our strategy and our operations. I would see this play out again and again in my career.

One hot morning, as I adjusted the headphones under my helmet, I heard my driver, Private First Class Wooliford, chatting over the vehicle intercom with the trail vehicle. "Looks like this will be a long one, guys … the Old Man is packing three cigars today!" Over time, my wily driver had figured out that we tended to stay out as long as my cigars lasted! Every day, he would remind me of the peacetime regulation against smoking in military vehicles—before offering me a light.

Battlefield circulation was usually uneventful, but not always. Midway through the deployment, the Louisiana Guard battalion rotated out and was replaced by an artillery battalion from the 101st Air Assault Division (the 2nd Battalion, 5th Field Artillery), out of Fort Campbell, Kentucky. Used as provisional infantry, the battalion was responsible for the western portion of the VBC perimeter, out to a north-south canal about 2km beyond the perimeter wall. As my TAC rolled towards the canal one afternoon, we heard a tremendous boom, followed by a torrent of radio chatter. Picking up speed we raced to the scene, to find a mounted patrol of four 101st vehicles clustered near the canal, led by a second lieutenant platoon leader.

His lead vehicle had struck an IED, which took off the entire front of the HMMWV and badly injured all three occupants. Two could not move and were being treated by the platoon medic. The young officer, somewhat in shock, was attempting to call in a medevac while his platoon sergeant, his jaw wrapped in a field dressing drenched and dripping with blood, worked to position the remaining three trucks for all around defense. A thousand yards away, three Iraq males stood on the roof of a building surveying the scene, one through binoculars.

As we rolled up, I dismounted and approached the lieutenant. At once I could see that my presence only added to his distress at a difficult time. As gently as I could I said, "Lieutenant, I have four gun trucks with me. You're in charge. Where do you want them?" My sergeant major conferred with the platoon sergeant, who refused to be evacuated although he was quite badly hurt with a fractured jaw and concussion. Barely able to speak, the blood-stained NCO sank to a knee and pointed to the Iraqis in the distance. Zacheus trained four .50 cals on them and appointed a squad leader to take over and prep a landing zone for the medevac chopper, now appearing in the distance. Soon after the helo landed to evacuate the wounded, while the lieutenant and his battered sergeant returned to base with their remaining vehicles. We stayed on the scene until the battalion QRF and recovery assets arrived. Later, as always, a team from CEXC—the Combat Exploitation Cell tasked to analyze IED sites—showed up to do the forensics.

At this stage of the war our medical understanding of traumatic brain injury was limited. Soldiers involved in IED attacks would normally be checked out for symptoms, but if all seemed okay, they might be back on the road in two to three days. In some cases, soldiers might experience multiple IED events on the same tour. Eventually military medicine became aware that the blast wave could cause permanent damage not immediately apparent, and soldiers exposed to IED attacks would be restricted to inside the wire or sent home.

In a similar way our understanding of how to use tourniquets to stop blood loss evolved during the war. Early on, military physicians feared that overuse or misuse of tourniquets might lead to needless loss of limbs, and only trained combat medics were authorized to employ them. With time we learned that rapid medical evacuation was almost always possible, and that death from massive blood loss was a much greater threat. As a consequence, everyone from general to private was issued an Israeli-made tourniquet, as well as pressure dressings, and trained to use them. These simple measures saved countless lives.

These kinds of details were a constant reminder of the danger that enveloped us. In a painful and poignant incident, we experienced the loss of four of our interpreters or "terps" in a single day. All four were local nationals, Christian women who spoke excellent English and worked inside the wire to help us communicate with our many Iraqi counterparts. For cultural reasons, they declined to live in the base camp, preferring to stay with their parents in Baghdad and commuting to work each day in the same vehicle. Knowing the danger, we entreated them to let us protect them, but always they politely declined. On one fateful day, as their car idled in the queue to enter VBC, it was struck by a suicide bomber and all four were killed instantly. The message was clear: work for the Americans and you'll be targeted. We felt genuine grief for these courageous young women and their families, and rage at the cowards who regularly murdered the innocent in the name of religion. An old Vietnam expression now began to gain currency, overheard on radio nets, in the mess halls and motor pools and troop billets—"Get some."

Veterans of the conflicts in Iraq and Afghanistan know well that civilian contractors have become omnipresent and indispensable to the war effort, but we found them a double-edged sword. There was almost literally nothing they couldn't do, but they charged the government accordingly. (The biggest, Kellogg, Brown, and Root or "KBR," collected a $48M "annual performance bonus" from the U.S. government in Iraq for 2005 alone; its revenues ran into the billions.) In theater, they were often represented by recently retired generals, whose personal relationships with current generals—often their former subordinates—gave them real leverage.

This reality was driven home to me forcefully one day when a KBR representative appeared uninvited in my office. A standing requirement for all contractors was to provide security guards to overwatch the third country nationals or "TCNs" that made up much of their work force. TCNs were cheaper and worked under conditions no American or European would accept. We knew that TCN vetting was hit or miss, and we worried constantly that terrorists might infiltrate the contractor work force and strike from the inside—hence our caution. Now, KBR had decided they had had enough. Their representative demanded that we "waive the requirement."

I politely declined, explaining our rationale. In a huff, the KBR messenger, a retired colonel, stormed out of my office. A few hours later, I was summoned to the palace by the chief of staff, who had just been visited by KBR's senior official in Iraq, a recently retired three-star. "I don't know what's going on down there in Task Force Dragon, but you need to stop picking fights with the contractors. We need them and this isn't helpful. Whatever they're asking, just give it to them and stop bringing me problems."

I responded with deference. "Certainly, sir, no problem. I'll just need you to put that in writing." Reddening, the brigadier immediately escalated. "You're just trying to cover your ass!" "That's right," I replied. "I made a decision for good reasons. You're overruling me. That's your right, but I can't accept the responsibility. I'll need that in writing with your signature." I was confident he would balk at that, and he did. The rules remained in place.

Among my many tenants at VBC was Saddam Hussein, Iraq's former dictator. Most important detainees were housed at Camp Irish, one of the 10 camps inside the perimeter, but Saddam was held in a high-security facility by himself, guarded constantly by a military police platoon. He would eventually be tried and executed, but before then he became something of a tourist destination for VIPs. Despite the secrecy surrounding his whereabouts, very senior civilian and military officials could and did demand to observe him through the window in his cell door. I found this distasteful but, like much else, these decisions rested far above my pay grade. I personally never laid eyes on him, nor would I permit any officer or soldier under my command to visit his location except for good reason, and then only with written orders.

At one point I was directed to brief a visiting general officer on our security arrangements. They were comprehensive, including external and internal roving patrols, rooftop guards, patrol dogs, special hardening of the structure which housed Saddam, sensors and a specially trained and equipped internal guard force. Almost farcically, the general expressed grave concerns that a rescue force might evade layer after layer of our security and spirit Saddam away. After an hour spent trying to soothe his fears, I gave him up as a nervous Nellie and terminated the briefing. He flew out that night and was never seen again. In December of 2006, Saddam was executed by hanging.

By now we were deep into the deployment. I couldn't have been happier with my deputy, command sergeant major and operations officer. Pattillo was all he'd been promised and more. Zacheus was the best CSM I'd ever seen, brave as hell and impervious to pressure. Shoults was full of energy and competence, a master of operations and always situationally aware. All three worked in harmony and with good will. Bob Quinnett was working miracles in force protection and proved a valuable and popular leader. The staff officers and NCOs in the BDOC were well trained, hardworking and on the ball.

One exception, however, was my executive officer. At the brigade level the XO functions essentially as chief of staff, charged to coordinate staff operations and to interface with the staffs of our subordinate battalions and higher headquarters. He had come to me and sought the job, and though aware of his many strengths I had some initial misgivings. Earlier in his career, as a company commander, half his company had perished in the Gander Newfoundland crash returning from the Sinai. He left the Army and dropped from sight for years, only to resurface after 9/11 as a reservist. Without knowing the details, I was aware that his marriage had collapsed. As the saying goes, he had a lot of rocks in his rucksack. Before hiring him, we had a heart-to-heart. I said, "All our lives we've been friends, classmates and equals. But in Dragon Brigade there can be only one commander. I've got to know you can function as a willing subordinate." Pledging his loyalty, he assured me he could function happily as my junior.

At home station my executive officer had been invaluable in preparing us to deploy, working overtime and often sleeping in his office. I felt we owed him much. Once downrange, he seemed an entirely different person. Chronically fractious and irascible, he was overbearing to the staff, often berating Major Shoults in public. Arguments with Lieutenant Colonel Graham became a common occurrence. In one instance, his crushing rudeness drove an easy-going Bob Quinnett, my former Navy SEAL, into a near-murderous rage. Something was clearly wrong here.

Matters came to a head in the summer of 2005 when Skip Davis showed up in my office. Now also a full colonel, Skip commanded a training support brigade tasked to advise an Iraqi National Police Division in Baghdad. Unfortunately,

Skip's organization lacked the support structures common to most brigades. He had come to me for help.

"Rich," he confided, "I've sustained some serious losses in recent days, including one of my battalion commanders. I have a mission to go to Ramadi tomorrow and I'm short two gun trucks and crews for my TAC. Can you help?"

No one was allowed to travel outside the wire with less than four gun vehicles, and for Skip to be in such a bind as a full colonel meant he was really struggling. I instantly agreed. "You've got them. And I'll go you one better, Skip," I vowed. "My maintenance guys are yours. Use them whenever you need to. And I'll pay for the spare parts." Davis shook my hand earnestly. "Thanks, brother!"

Soon an infuriated XO burst into my office, boiling mad. Shouting, he excoriated me for not consulting him, insisting he "did not approve." "Our guys might get killed," he growled, "and Ramadi isn't our mission." Threatening to "inform the Corps," he demanded that I recall our soldiers.

Rising to my feet I shut the office door, motioned for my executive officer to sit down, and ordered him to lower his voice. Leaning forward, I said quietly, "First, you don't get to give me orders. We've been over that. Second, as you'll learn if you ever command in the future, when your brothers ask for help there is only one answer: yes. Full stop. Third, you're supposed to be my chief of staff. Instead, you're terrorizing my staff and my units. My staff, not your staff. That's going to stop. Fourth, if you ever threaten me again, I'll relieve you instantly and send you home with a performance report that says you failed in combat. Are we clear?"

Stunned, he sank back in his chair. Now it was time to build him back up. "XO, you're a critical guy and we need you. We need your experience and talent. All of us are carrying a heavy load here. Think about how you can help, every day, and we'll be fine." Shaking his hand, I escorted him from the room. For the rest of the deployment, he was a contributor, not a detractor.

That night I lay in my bunk and pondered. My XO had given much for his country, all voluntarily—his blood, his marriage, his youth, and whatever innocence he may have once possessed. He had been changed forever by war. Fundamentally he was a good man, a patriot, and a brave officer. I resolved not to judge him harshly, but to try to get the best out of him. Ultimately, he would be promoted in his own right to colonel and return to the wars, where he would serve with distinction.

At the height of a searing summer, I fielded an urgent radio call from ECP1—also the entrance to the international airport. In five minutes, Sergeant Major Zacheus and I were on the scene. I found a young lieutenant facing down one very angry Iraqi brigadier general, backed up by a dozen or so combat vehicles and more than a hundred Iraqi troops. Taking over from the young officer I asked the Iraqi commander to state his business.

"I have orders to go to the airport. Get out of the way now, or my men will open fire. This is our land. I am warning you," he growled.

Iraqi politics were often opaque, but I knew right away that this was not what it seemed. The airport belonged to the Ministry of Transportation. These were Ministry of the Interior troops, known to be heavily infiltrated by Iranian special forces and reporting to a corrupt and ruthless minister. My initial assessment—later confirmed—was that this was some kind of power grab.

I needed to make a decision, and I had no idea what to do. Although outnumbered for the moment, my soldiers were stationed behind concrete barriers and could probably stop any determined attempt to push past. But if things got out of hand and shooting started, both Americans and Iraqis would be killed and our whole presence in Iraq might be undermined. In that event, my own chances of survival didn't look promising. Looking over the general's shoulder, I saw his troops tensed and ready to fire.

Playing for time, I politely told the brigadier I must first report to my commander and get his guidance. As I walked to my vehicle, Sergeant Major Zacheus strode into the mass of Iraqi soldiers, hand outstretched, a big smile creasing his worn face. As I stood dumbfounded, he began to shake hands, greeting them in pidgin Arabic. Soon he was surrounded and almost lost to view. But I began to see rifle barrels drop, and smiles breaking out all around.

I soon raised General Webster on a secure frequency. Quickly briefing him on the situation, I asked him to send help and advised that he have General Casey, or the ambassador, call the Iraqi prime minister immediately to call off the Ministry of the Interior. Webster quickly agreed and signed off.

Returning to my irascible brigadier, I soberly told him, "My orders are clear. No one is authorized to pass without clearance, and nothing has been coordinated in advance." Getting a bit ahead of myself, I added, "I understand the prime minister is speaking to your minister right now about the matter. I suggest you contact your chain and sort this out." Simultaneously, the 299th's QRF arrived, to be joined soon after by two M1A1 main battle tanks sent by 3ID. We now had a clear overmatch.

It was clear to me that the general had been given explicit orders to take the airport, but his position was now untenable, and he had few options left. Scowling at me, he mounted his vehicle and sped off as I snapped to attention and saluted. Seconds later, Zacheus ambled over.

"Thought I'd lost you there," I joked. "Aww, I just talked to them like soldiers," he rejoined. We shook hands, and I took a deep breath. For the rest of the tour, we kept the tanks.

Days later, I sat in the BDOC and watched an operation in our outside battlespace at about midnight. Though pitch black, we could see the unit clearly from the thermal imagery mounted on our aerostat. As four soldiers stacked up to enter a building, Major Shoults nudged me. "Hey, isn't that Z in the middle of the stack?"

Pulling out my Iraqna cell phone, I speed-dialed the sergeant major. We watched as Z pulled his phone out and whispered, "Sergeant Major." "Z," I answered. "Where are you?" He whispered back, "I'm overwatching that 299 op in Ameriyah." We howled with laughter as the lead man kicked the door down and Z signed off with a hurried "Gotta go." That man engendered much more than respect in all of us. We loved him for the great soldier and great human being he was. We remain close to this day.

At one point I took a call from Lieutenant Colonel Hara, requesting permission to put his battalion in the "hot weather" uniform. I recall the temperature that day was 126 degrees. I immediately agreed. The change was not much, only untucking uniform trousers from inside the boots and unbuttoning the cuff of the shirt sleeves, but it increased air circulation and gave some relief. On a net call, I told all my commanders they could do the same, as long as the whole unit was in the same uniform.

About 30 minutes later, the XVIII Airborne Corps command sergeant major called me. He had just passed through a checkpoint and noticed the change. The sergeant major was hot. "Uniform changes are my business," he scolded. "Next time check with me. Put 'em back in the normal duty uniform. Now."

His tirade struck a nerve. In the U.S. Army, we often refer to our NCOs as "our secret weapon" or "the backbone of the Army." And so, they are. Few armies can call upon a stronger or better cadre of junior leaders. At times, however, we gave them too much rope. Throughout my career I had seen NCOs mock young lieutenants, often to their face, without correction. On occasion, first sergeants or sergeants major would establish alternate NCO chains of command that would undermine the formal chain. Prior to Vietnam, command sergeants major had only existed at the battalion level. Afterwards, the Army placed CSMs in every formation up to four-star headquarters as "senior enlisted advisors." At the highest levels they were placed in general officer housing and given personal staffs of their own. Most conducted themselves professionally, but some were seduced by their high station and assumed the powers of the commanders they advised. This was an example.

I pushed back. "Watch yourself, Sergeant Major. I don't take orders from you and taking care of soldiers is absolutely commander's business. Next time you talk to me I'd appreciate a little professional courtesy, not an ass chewing. My troopers are staying as they are. Now, I've got work to do, so—out here." I hung up.

As I expected, within 10 minutes I was called back to the phone. An infuriated chief of staff began to pile on, accusing me of "disrespecting" the CSM. The conversation grew heated as he ordered me to follow the CSM's guidance. I refused. We both knew the incident was far too trivial to waste the three-star's time, and as I expected, after further hectoring he angrily hung up. Our relations remained cool, but I knew that stepping on my prerogatives as a brigade commander over small things would inevitably lead to more of the same. With faith in General Vines, I stuck to this line for the rest of the deployment.

In the seventh month of our deployment, I was again called to the command post for an emergency, this time involving Blackwater, the private security firm that provided contract guards for our diplomats. Because Secretary Rumsfeld had refused to provide soldiers for this important duty, the State Department had been forced to hire contractors at exorbitant rates. The crisis began when a team of four Blackwater security guards pulled up to "Flying Man," an Iraqi statue at the entrance to the airport, to wait for an arriving VIP.[1] Moments later, a large tractor trailer driven by a confused Filipino contractor entered the military-only lane. Ignoring shouted commands to stop, he pushed past the first barrier and was fired upon by the soldiers manning the checkpoint.

At this point, the Blackwater guards began to fire wildly in the general direction of the driver, igniting a murderous free-for-all. Dressed much like Iraqis, in civilian clothes, sunglasses and the checkered tribal scarves favored by the locals, they were taken for the enemy and engaged by our security troops. A later investigation concluded that, in addition to wounding several civilians caught in the crossfire, the Blackwater contactors also killed an off-duty Iraqi lieutenant colonel.

As the responsible commander, after overseeing the casualty evacuation and reporting to my higher headquarters, I traveled to the embassy compound, looking for answers and some accountability. My first stop was the regional security officer (RSO), the State Department official charged with supervising all security matters, including Blackwater personnel. I knew he kept a log of all escort missions, and accordingly I asked for the names of the Blackwater guards involved. He adamantly refused. All subsequent attempts to fix responsibility and to coordinate Blackwater movements with the U.S. military to preclude future disasters like this were stonewalled. For some years, the bad blood between the State and Defense Departments in Iraq had stunted effective cooperation, at great cost to the mission. Now, we paid the price on the street. Later, that price would rise dramatically.

Often, late at night before turning in, I would gather around the fire barrel and smoke cigars with CSM Zacheus, Ladd and Hugh Shoults. Over "near" (non-alcoholic) beers we'd swap war stories and revisit the events of the day. Looking back, those were some of the most memorable experiences of my career. I hold fast to those memories as touchstones of a life that, if marked by hardship and war, was also tinged with laughter and comradeship. I'll forever be grateful to have served with such men.

One night, as we puffed away, chatting about nothing in particular, Baghdad exploded around us. Thousands of tracers lit up the night sky, streaming across the

---

1   The statue commemorated Abbas Ibn Firnas, a legendary Muslim scholar from Cordoba, said to have built a primitive glider in AD 875.

heavens in long, lazy arcs. Dumbfounded, we looked at each other in amazement. Was this the massive attack we were forever being warned against? What the hell was going on?

Seconds later, all those rounds began to fall around us like monsoon rains. Startled out of our reveries we sprinted to the relative safety of the BDOC. Inside, the battle staff worked the phones and radios. After a few moments, the battle captain strode over, beaming. "Hey sir, guess what? The Iraqi national soccer team just beat Qatar. The whole city is celebrating!" I burst out laughing, but there was a serious side as well. That night 12 American soldiers were treated in our aid stations for gunshot wounds, including one lieutenant with a 7.62mm bullet embedded in the side of his skull. Fortunately, no one died.

As part of my normal duties, I was often invited to participate in meetings with the command group—the Corps commander and his principal staff officers. One of these was a weekly video teleconference or VTC with the Army Staff in the Pentagon. In one session General Vines suggested a need for improved body armor. "The enemy has started using armor piercing 7.62 rounds that our SAPI plates can't stop." (SAPI meant "small arms protective inserts.") "We need something better."

A short, fat logistics general chirped up on the screen. "That won't be easy, General Vines. But what if we just taped on another SAPI plate, front and back, instead?" The suggestion was absurd. Our body armor alone already weighed some 30lbs, tripled by the weight of weapons, ammunition, water, and other kit carried by every soldier in Iraq's crushing heat. I'd have bet real money that the staff general, who looked a bit like Danny DeVito, had never worn body armor in his life. Normally controlled, Vines began to turn purple. Diplomatically, a staff officer pulled the plug out of the wall, ending the VTC. Vines later called the Army vice chief of staff directly, and within months we had a new enhanced or "ESAPI" plate that could do the job.

Better body armor was a blessing, but sometimes it wasn't enough. Midway through our deployment we began to see reports of U.S. fatalities that were clearly the work of trained snipers. Wounds just above or just below the body armor were a dead giveaway. One began to achieve near mythical status. Operating mostly in central Baghdad, he seemed to break all the rules, often engaging targets at closer ranges, sometimes from street level, and at other times from atop buildings. On occasion he would not relocate, a rarity for trained snipers up against American technology and training. Days might go by without incident, followed by multiple shootings in a single day. Pattern analysis, the key to locating and eliminating enemy snipers, wasn't working.

Ultimately the powers that be brought in an elite counter-sniper team from one of our high-end special mission units. Patiently stalking their prey, they eventually located and killed the shooter, a Chechen terrorist and true believer who had come to fight and die in Iraq. We celebrated his death, but on some level, you had to respect his commitment and skills. This guy was for real.

In mid-July, a beefy colonel appeared in the BDOC and, without introduction, ensconced himself next to my CSM during the nightly battle update brief. This was a clear violation of protocol and following the brief I invited the officer to explain himself. Throwing out his chest, he announced that he was the commander of a 39-man National Guard RAOC, and he was here "to take over."

Inviting him to my office I asked what he meant. "My TAG sent me here to run base defense for Victory Base. I'm your relief." I suppressed a chuckle. I asked to see his orders. He had to confess he had none, except verbal directions from his state "TAG" (for "The Adjutant General"). A quick phone call to the Corps G3, Colonel (later Lieutenant General) Ben Hodges, confirmed my suspicions. Corps was considering how to use the RAOC but taking over the BDOC halfway through our tour wasn't on the menu. This guy was hunting for a juicy mission. Reminding him gently that state TAGs don't control federalized Guard units in war zones, I suggested that he visit Hodges, who would tell him where his unit might best contribute.

I forgot all about the incident, but days later I fielded a call from the Corps inspector general. "Sorry Rich, but we've been asked to respond to a congressional inquiry involving this RAOC commander. Apparently, he complained that he isn't being treated right. I'm going to need you to come in and give a sworn statement, and I'm going to need to see any relevant emails."

By now, I had begun to understand the culture of the National Guard. Regular officers are full time professionals and resent the implication that "one weekend a month and two weeks a year" is enough to master the military art. Guard officers for their part often resent what they see as the arrogance or condescension of the Regulars. Much of this tension can be resolved by working together and learning about the strengths, and weaknesses, of both organizations. But there is another wrinkle that came into play here.

In the National Guard, advancement to colonel and above at the state level is an inherently political process, and senior Guard officers are often linked to political personalities, if not parties. (In 2005, the North Carolina deputy TAG was fired for conspiring with his brother, the speaker of the state house of representatives, to unseat the TAG and take his place by planting false stories in the media.) "Playing politics" to reach your objective is therefore second nature for many Guard officers but is anathema to the Regulars. Once federalized, Guard organizations are in theory the same as Regular organizations—part of one "Total Army"—but in practice their cultures remain intact and operative.

Viewed in this light, the actions of my RAOC colonel seemed understandable, if not laudable. Someone at Corps level "apologized" for any "unintended insensitivity" and assured the colonel's congressional representatives that he would be assigned a mission appropriate for his rank and skills. Orders were cut sending him up north to the back of beyond, in serious Indian country, where he might run a BDOC of his own on a small forward operating base in the middle of nowhere. That night he was back in my office.

"I think we got off on the wrong foot," he remarked. "On second thought, we would be happy to work for you here at VBC. Maybe my guys can fold into your staff, and I can be one of your deputies—what about it?" I thanked him for the offer and reminded him that I wasn't responsible for task organizing the Corps, and that it would probably be best if he complied with his orders. He departed mournfully and that was the last I saw of him.

Almost daily on my visits to the palace I would check in on the Special Troops Battalion. The STB had been given a tall order, to support both the Corps and the Force headquarters, both located in the same large building. With a staff that never exceeded 15 officers and NCOs, Tim Graham was supposed to keep 32 generals and admirals and more than 2,100 other folks happy. It was a herculean task. Given the enormity of the mission, as well as its sensitivity, I banned Graham from anything not directly related to the headquarters commandant mission. As an aggressive infantry officer, this did not suit him, but it was necessary. There were a few ways that I could fail in command of Dragon Brigade. Screwing up the palace was near the top of the list.

A big part of Graham's task was to make senior officers do things they didn't want to do. The previous unit had ignored property accountability altogether, resulting in millions of dollars in losses. Graham was a fanatic about monthly inventories, hand receipts and the like and he was right. Often, he would have to deal with spurious leave requests, unjustified award recommendations, pressure to overlook misconduct and so on. Graham could be flinty, even prickly, and not everyone liked it. It wasn't always pretty, but the alternative was a collapse of standards that we knew the commanding general would not appreciate. As much as I could, I backed him and tried to shield him. Both of us took plenty of scolding from the brass. That went with the territory. Later, I gave Tim a strong performance report and urged the commanding general to do the same. Unfortunately, and unfairly I thought, Graham would not be promoted to full colonel. But the nation and the Army owe him a debt of gratitude for the selfless officer he was.

At mid-tour my Puerto Rican garrison command rotated out and much to my surprise, the 18th Field Artillery brigade headquarters out of Fort Sill, Oklahoma replaced them. 18th FA was commanded by my classmate Carl Reid, an alum of the West Point Gospel Choir and an officer of impressive reputation. This was awkward to say the least. Both of us were centrally selected brigade commanders of equal rank (in fact, Carl's deputy, Dan Ragsdale, was also West Point Class of 1981). Carl's artillery battalions had been chopped away on various duties all over Iraq, leaving his headquarters available for the garrison command job. His staff was first rate—well-trained professionals with plenty of prior combat experience.

In my first meeting with Carl, I admitted to my embarrassment. It didn't seem right to be placed over a peer in this way. In fact, I knew of no such precedent in the whole Army. I offered to go to the Corps and request a change of mission, giving 18th FA the base operations piece independently while Dragon Brigade retained responsibility for base defense. Carl demurred. "Let's not upset the apple cart," he confided. "You guys are in the groove. I know we'll work well together, and you know these airborne guys much better than I do. Let's keep things as they are." We shook on it, and 18th FA jumped on the garrison command mission and excelled.

One of the most difficult parts of my job was casualty tracking and reporting, and at one point it became clear that there was a problem in the EOD battalion. Though not under my operational command, I did have administrative oversight of the unit, which rotated every six months instead of the normal 12-month cycle. An EOD battalion consisted of 18 three-man EOD teams plus support personnel, and the key element in each team was the staff sergeant team leader. (In the Hollywood action picture *Hurt Locker*, the male lead is an EOD team leader.) Three of these experienced, key leaders were killed in a two-month period, a crippling blow.

I was aware that, although trained to defuse explosives by hand, the preferred method for EOD personnel was to send a camera-equipped robot to the IED location and blow it in place with a small charge attached to the robot. In this way we hoped to minimize the danger to our highly trained and scarce EOD cadre. In each fatality, the EOD team leader had disregarded procedure, gone forward and attempted to disarm the IED manually. In each, the IED was in fact a decoy. Buried underneath, a far larger weapon was command detonated by an observer watching from some distance away. The idea was to target the team leader, known by a wily enemy to be a precious and rare commodity.

I engaged the battalion commander on the matter, not as his boss but out of genuine concern for his losses. I found him deeply distressed. "I know what right looks like," he explained. "I've done all I could think of to avoid this. But it's what these guys do. If the robot breaks, or the camera malfunctions, they go do what they've been trained to do. It's who they are." I learned that the most recent fatality had been gravely wounded in Afghanistan the year before and come straight back to the fight.

I had seen this before. Combat, or any dangerous activity like parachute jumping, can be terrifying. But it is also exhilarating. Soldiers experience an adrenaline surge that heightens the senses, and over time they may come to welcome and even desire it. A few become consumed by it. Decompressing after combat can be hard, often driving bad choices. All commanders in wartime must confront this reality and try to balance the need for aggression and willingness to face danger with the need for good order and discipline. At all times it is an uneasy balance. Sometimes, there is no balance at all.

In these cases, the buried IEDs weren't going anywhere, and the smart play was to bring up another robot. I urged the EOD commander to issue a blanket order that only a company commander could approve a manual disarm, and to have replacement robots ready to go on short notice. He complied and we lost no more EOD soldiers for the rest of our tour. We named the new VBC gym after the dead sergeant and got on with the war.

We soldiered on through a long, hot summer with temperatures above 120 degrees on most days. The war was not going well. Bremer's disastrous CPA had given way to a more conventional embassy operation in the Green Zone, a massive operation boasting more than 1,000 diplomats and half a dozen ambassadors filling senior staff roles. The theater commander, four-star General George Casey, commanded a coalition of more than 30 nations with a huge MNF-I staff. Still, we could not solve the political morass we had created when Saddam was overthrown. For some 80 years a small, Sunni minority had lorded it over much larger Kurdish and Shia communities, savagely repressing them on many occasions. Now the genie was out of the bottle, aided and abetted by an Iran determined to undermine U.S. influence on its border. Rumsfeld's idea of a swift transition to a successor government composed of the three factions had been shown to be fantasy. Hatred and mistrust were rampant on all sides, fueled by horrific violence from Zarqawi's al Qaeda in Iraq (AQI) and, increasingly, by Shia insurgent groups sponsored by Iran's Quds Force, the external arm of the Iranian Revolutionary Guard Corps.

The signature weapon of the Quds Force was the EFP—short for "Explosively Formed Projectile." The EFP was a devastating shaped charge weapon, far more lethal than normal IEDs and capable of destroying the heaviest armored vehicles. (In 2005, the EFP would be used in only 2 percent of IED attacks but account for 48 percent of our fatalities.) Triggered when the vehicle crossed an infrared beam, the EFP didn't miss, and there were few survivors. Our soldiers justly dreaded this fearsome device, made worse by our inability to identify and target the Shia networks that employed them.

In late August, a spectacular explosion at ECP1 stunned the battle staff in the BDOC, though we were at least a thousand yards away. As the battle captain swung into a practiced battle drill, I glanced around the command post. All our radio nets frantically came to life, and the giant video screen displayed graphic images of ruined vehicles, dismembered bodies, fire, and smoke. It later transpired that a suicide bomber, sitting in the queue, had detonated his VBIED when approached by another civilian. His action killed and wounded dozens of innocent Iraqi civilians waiting to be searched before entering the airport. Sheltered behind concrete barriers, my troopers were dazed by the blast wave but unhurt.

As I donned my body armor to go to the scene, I saw a young female intelligence officer gazing at the screen in shock and horror. Only a second lieutenant and a reservist, she had volunteered for Iraq straight out of the officer basic course with no prior experience in a unit. In recent months she had become an invaluable member of the intelligence section, sunny, resilient, and hard working. Now I could see what we asked—demanded—of these young people. It wasn't fair, or reasonable, or right. As we roared to the scene it occurred to me that she might never be the same person again.

By the time I arrived our ambulances were already loading the wounded, while combat medics worked feverishly to triage the most seriously injured. As the local officer in charge filled me in on what had happened, a short, wiry civilian strode forward. I recognized him immediately as Steve Crowsley, a British national and former special operations officer now working for a UK security contractor at BIAP. A veteran of the Falklands War and many tours in Northern Ireland, Steve had worked in Iraq for more than two years and was unflappable. We had become good friends. "Bloody hell," he remarked with a quizzical smile. "This wanker's head came sailing through the air and landed right at my feet. Imagine that."

As the scorching summer gave way to the promise of a cooler autumn, U.S. forces in Iraq began to prepare for the constitutional referendum, set for October 15. Detailed plans were issued to help the Iraqi Army and police secure the city for the elections, as we knew AQI would try to disrupt the process. With growing concern, I scanned the intelligence reporting for any sign of specific threats but saw little.

On the evening of the 10th, I took a cell phone call from an Iraqi counterpart I had befriended, informing me that the city was rife with rumors about impending attacks the following day. Many of our translators reported the same thing. Consultations with the Corps intelligence people gave me nothing, but a sixth sense warned me that the local buzz was probably right—the enemy knew we would lock Baghdad down tight a day or two before the referendum, so the timing looked propitious for large-scale attacks.

Accordingly, I warned my units to curtail all non-essential ground traffic for the following day, and to move in force and with extreme caution otherwise. At sunrise the next day we heard the first loud explosion, a large IED going off about 2km to the east in the city. All day long they continued, until by nightfall we had counted 20. From my headquarters we watched columns of black smoke rising skyward for hours. The combat radio nets burned with excited contact reports, urgent calls for quick reaction forces and medical evacuation. We stood to on full alert, but no attempts to breach the perimeter took place. Next door, 3ID lost a company commander, then another, then a battalion commander. It was to be the bloodiest single day of our year in Baghdad.

A few days later, the constitutional referendum took place as scheduled, followed in December by fresh elections, but it did not mean peace. Iraqi politics remained as roiled as ever, riven by sectarian and tribal and confessional strife, abetted by Iranian and Syrian influence. The civilian death toll continued to mount.

In November, I was summoned to the BDOC following a report from the Joint Visitors Bureau. One recurring feature of our tour was a steady stream of visiting congressmen (called "CODELS" for "Congressional Delegation"). Most of the time, the DCO handled these; as a veteran of years serving in Army Legislative Liaison as a reservist, Ladd Pattillo was a past master at these sorts of things. I hurried to the command post expecting to hear yet another story about a disgruntled member—or more likely, a disgruntled staffer. This time, however, the news was far worse.

I spoke directly to the lieutenant colonel in charge. "Sir, about 30 minutes ago we dispatched a van and escort officer to meet a CODEL at the airport. On the way back the van was run off the road by a large contractor truck coming the opposite way. The vehicle flipped. One of the congressmen is being evacuated right now. He's reported litter urgent. Sir, the member is Ike Skelton."

I felt like I'd been shot. Ike Skelton was the ranking member (later chairman) of the House Armed Services Committee, a legendary politician respected and even loved by the military. He was a giant. Now well up in years, he had suffered from polio as a child, losing much of the use of his arms and shoulders. Elderly and disabled, Congressman Skelton was unlikely to survive serious injury, and his death would be a serious blow to the war effort, the U.S. Congress and the nation. Fighting down a wave of panic, I reached for the landline and called General Casey directly, something I had never done before. I told him what I knew, and he headed straight for the helo pad to fly to the Green Zone. I promised to meet him there in the emergency room.

While my staff backbriefed General Vines I jumped in my TAC and roared down Route IRISH. Twelve minutes later, we arrived at the Level III trauma facility, and I sprinted inside, expecting the worst. To my surprise and joy, Skelton was sitting up on an exam table, to all appearances none the worse for wear. Though a little shaken when the van flipped, he escaped injury and was wisecracking with the young combat medic taking his vital signs. Breathing a huge sigh of relief, I reflected on how often first reports turn out to be wrong. Here we had dodged a huge bullet.

By now we were well into the fall and redeployment began to loom. It soon became apparent that our replacements would not adopt the same approach to base defense. As the only Army corps headquarters with a "combat support brigade," XVIII Airborne Corps enjoyed a luxury the new corps could not afford. As best we could we shared lessons learned with several units who would inherit pieces of our empire. I wasn't happy, but as I had no vote anyway, I approached the coming handover philosophically.

Our final month passed uneventfully, marked by occasional rocket or mortar attacks but with no casualties. December was busy, filled with briefings, close-out reports, and logistics work, but by now we were a hardened and experienced outfit in the home stretch. My biggest worry was that we might let down and relax our guard, and much of my time was spent on constant visits to my units to keep them on their toes.

On one of our last nights together I took a moment to address my commanders and staff. By now we had become more than a team. As I gazed around the command post I felt a welter of emotions: gratitude, pride, affection, and sincere regret that it was coming to an end. We had begun as a motley collection of regulars, reservists and guardsmen of all branches and specialties. Over time we had grown into a remarkable organization, expert in our mission, used to pressure and at home in the crucible of war. I spoke from the heart:

> Ladies and gentlemen, I want you to take a moment and look around the room. This is a special place filled with special people. Years from now you'll look back at this time and I promise—you will treasure it. It will always be a part of you. In the next day or so this team will begin to break up and we will never be together like this again. Remember this moment. Remember each other. I know I will.

As our tour came to an end, we began to send our troops home in waves. In early January, I officially handed over and boarded the plane with the last of my troops for the tedious flight back. As my headquarters staff slept all around me, I pondered. I was of course aware that mine had been only a small part of a much larger whole. Our task had been essentially to free my commanders to focus on their larger and graver responsibilities. The 30,000 soldiers and civilians at Victory needed and deserved a safe place to sleep and to rest inside the wire. We had given them that. It had not been easy. After 365 days of ceaseless labor and stress I felt worn out. But I also felt a solemn pride. I had helped to build a first class team. We had accomplished our mission in preventing any major penetration of our huge footprint. No disaster had befallen us—and after a year in Iraq at the height of the war, that said a lot. I couldn't say we were winning the war. At best, we seemed to be holding our own. But we had done our part. I said a quiet prayer for those we had not been able to bring back, and for their families. Then I slept and dreamed of home.

CHAPTER 7

All the Way!

We travel not for trafficking alone;
By hotter winds our fiery hearts are fanned.
For lust of knowing what should not be known
We take the Golden Road to Samarkand.

JAMES ELROY FLECKER

Our return to home station was a blur of recovery operations, as our equipment containers arrived and we settled back into a garrison routine. In a private interview, General Vines congratulated me on our success and expressed his personal gratitude, an accolade worth more than any award. What came next was hard to swallow. The Army Staff had finally remembered that Dragon Brigade was a one-of-a-kind unit not found in the Army's other corps. We had been programmed for elimination as part of "Army Transformation." Our success would now be rewarded with deactivation. Having built the brigade into something it had never been before, my primary task now was to superintend its demise.

That gloomy news coincided with the pressures of readjustment and reintegration common to all soldiers returning from war. I found myself easily irritated at small things, like squabbling kids or bad weather. Beverly had been running things for a solid year without my help, and at times I felt unneeded, even superfluous. I had carried a weapon for 365 days and now felt naked without one. Behind the wheel, I experienced an instinctive startle reflex when traffic got too close, causing my wife to gently ban me from driving for weeks. After so many months of living in a heightened state, routine work at Fort Bragg seemed unimportant, even boring. Things improved as time went on, but for a while, I can't have seemed an ideal husband or father. All of this was the small change of returning from war. Like most I worked through it, helped greatly by a loving and understanding spouse. Not everyone was so lucky.

My final six months in command sped by as I waited for news of my next assignment. When I finally got the word, it wasn't good. I learned that I had been programmed for the Army G8, the budget and acquisition part of the Army Staff back in the Pentagon. When not with troops, I had previously served in policy/ strategy jobs and, given my prior history and civilian graduate education, that made sense. As I told my assignment officer, "I can't even spell G8!" Nevertheless, I was told the G8 himself, a senior general and former Sosh department alum, had insisted.

After some reflection, I reached out to former contacts and quietly let it be known that I'd much prefer to return to the National Security Council. The war in Iraq was at its height, it wasn't going well, and I was sure I could make a greater contribution there than toiling away in the Army budget office. A few weeks later I fielded a phone call from Meghan O'Sullivan, the brilliant young senior director for Iraq and Afghanistan at the NSC. After some sparring with the Army, orders materialized, and I found myself back in a suit at the White House.

Upon arrival, I was assigned as director for Iraq, with responsibilities for coordinating the military and security aspects of our policy and strategy there. Unlike my first tour at the NSC, I felt on familiar ground now. I was older, more experienced, with an intimate knowledge of Iraq and the Pentagon. With a network of contacts spanning the State Department, the Department of Defense, at CENTCOM in Tampa and the major headquarters in Iraq, I was able to keep a finger on the pulse of the war and, hopefully, give my bosses ground truth.

That truth was sobering. If our war aim was to enable an orderly transition to a capable Iraq government that could keep Iran out and the country together, we were losing. Shortly after my return to the States, in February of 2006, al Qaeda had attacked the famous mosque in Samarra, north of Baghdad and one of the holiest sites in all of Shia Islam. Hundreds had been killed in the factional fighting that ensued. A second attack in June had destroyed the mosque's famous minarets, causing another round of massive sectarian violence. Now, the Shia militias, led by Muqtada al Sadr's Jaysh al Mahdi and the Iranian-backed Badr Corps, came off the sidelines with a vengeance. Violence soared, and Sunni, Shia and Kurdish political leaders found themselves driven to their corners as the blood literally ran in the streets.

By now the Army was three years into the grinding conflict and the force was fraying. Though the Marine Corps and SOF troops were restricted to shorter tours (seven months for the Marines and six for SOF), the Army served 12-month tours with its brigades returning barely a year later. Even at home, field training kept soldiers away from their families for extended periods. This crushing "OPTEMPO" gravely concerned Army leaders, who faced not one, but two simultaneous conflicts in Iraq and Afghanistan.

Staring ruin in the face, the military chain of command and the State Department could think of no other option but to accelerate the transition to Iraqi control and back out. This approach was manifestly doomed to fail—we had not come close to building up capable new Iraqi security forces and the Iraqi government was both hopelessly corrupt and riven by sectarian feuds. In daily updates, NSC Iraq reported to President Bush: we are not winning.

The report card was grim across the board. Despite spending more than $16B on reconstruction since the invasion, our efforts lagged below Iraq pre-war levels in every major category. Violence had spiked more than 200 percent over the previous year. Several attempts to secure Baghdad had collapsed. The 2005 "National Strategy for Victory in Iraq" published by the White House was clearly failing.

All through the summer of 2006 our office pushed for a policy review that might lead to a different outcome. Steve Hadley, now the national security advisor, was supportive. But as they had since coming to power, Vice President Cheney and Secretary Rumsfeld held most of the cards. Secretary of State Colin Powell had departed in 2004, to be replaced by former National Security Advisor Condoleezza Rice, but despite a close relationship with the president, Rice was no match for the Cheney/Rumsfeld tag team. They remained invested in the strategy they had birthed.

All that changed with the mid-term elections in November 2006, which swept the Democrats into the majority in both the House and the Senate. President Bush realized at once the implications of this crippling defeat. The American people had spoken emphatically, rejecting his approach to the war and much else besides. Heretofore, he had been guided if not controlled by his vice president and secretary of defense. Overnight, that changed. On election day, I boarded a plane at Andrews Air Force Base with Deputy National Security Advisor J. D. Crouch, bound for Baghdad. By the time we landed, Rumsfeld was out.

The president moved swiftly to contain the damage and reverse course. Announcing Rumsfeld's departure the day after the election, he named former director of Central Intelligence Robert Gates as his replacement. Down in the NSC trenches, it seemed clear to us that the vice president had lost much of his influence; at last, a vigorous policy review was now in train, led by O'Sullivan and championed by Hadley. In the next few weeks, scores of experts would be consulted by the president and national security advisor. Some talked sheer nonsense, as when one well-known academic urged President Bush to "cut his losses" and reinstall a Sunni military strongman. Many were vague, arguing that we needed to "reconcile the warring factions," "build partner capacity" and "strengthen Iraqi governance," as though we had not been trying to do exactly that for three years.

One presentation, however, was compelling. Delivered by retired Army General Jack Keane and Fred Kagen from the American Enterprise Institute, the proposal called for a major troop surge of five additional Army combat brigades to the Greater Baghdad area, along with 4,000 additional Marines to Anbar province. Having traveled many times to Iraq, the authors were steeped in the details of the insurgency and could speak knowledgeably down to the district and neighborhood level. Their basic premise was that, until basic security was restored, economic and political progress would continue to fail. The plan was more sophisticated than merely a call for more troops. Now, they would move off the large Forward Operating Bases and actually live among the people, in smaller fortified combat outposts (COPs) as McMaster had done in Tal Afer.

Keane's session with the president excited strong resentment from the chairman of the Joint Chiefs, Marine General Peter Pace, and the other Joint Chiefs. Summoning Keane to the Pentagon, Pace scolded him harshly. Keane fired back. "I'm an old, retired guy. How come I know more about Iraq than you do?" In our cramped offices on the White House campus, we fielded the same complaints from irate generals and civilian officials from every direction. Our answer was always the same. "The president is free to get his advice anywhere he wants to. And right now, he isn't very impressed with yours."

Intrigued by Keane and Kagan, the president ordered the NSC into something like permanent session to explore the proposal. Where previously we had conducted separate meetings for deputies and principals once per week, both groups now met several times per week to discuss and assess the Keane/Kagen plan. This meant an enormous increase in an already crushing workload for the tiny NSC Iraq team, as each session required prep sessions, staffing papers and much besides. I recall getting text messages at one and two in the morning from Meghan as we labored far into the night. Still, we were fired up. We now had some momentum of our own.

Amid this churn, the much publicized "Iraq Study Group" issued its report. Chaired by former Secretary of State James Baker and former Congressman Lee Hamilton, the congressionally chartered, bipartisan group painted a bleak picture. Describing the situation in Iraq as "serious" and "deteriorating," the study called for a phased withdrawal from Iraq and negotiations with Iran and Syria to mediate an end to the civil strife consuming the country. The report was received courteously by the White House but rejected out of hand. There would be no disengagement. Not while there was one more hand to play.

It soon became clear that the uniformed military was not backing down in its opposition to troop increases. Understandably, the service chiefs were alarmed at the possible impact of a major surge on an already overstretched force—above all, in the Army. By now, Iraq and Afghanistan had consumed our ground forces, leaving little to respond to threats elsewhere. I, too, wondered if we could stand the strain.

But the president was determined, and it was hard to argue with his rejoinder: "You know what will break the force? Losing a war will break the force." After thorough discussion, the president made the tough decision to surge, announcing it to the nation on January 10, 2007.

Secretary Rumsfeld had already gone, but General Keane had foreseen that a new strategy would require fresh eyes and new leaders, and he urged POTUS to promote Lieutenant General Petraeus, then commanding the Army's doctrine center at Fort Leavenworth, and put him in charge of the war in Iraq. Petraeus had commanded the 101st during the invasion, and later the training command in Iraq.[1] He had done well but was not seen as standing out from his peers in those jobs. Theater command at the four-star level would be his true métier. He was duly elevated, while General Casey was named to be the new Army chief of staff. In the next few months General Abizaid, the CENTCOM commander in charge of the Middle East, would also retire. General Pace was asked to step down that spring after only two years, a rare occurrence. Petraeus would need the right kind of diplomatic counterpart and he was found, in the person of Ambassador Ryan Crocker. Crocker was deeply experienced in the Islamic world and a veteran Washington insider. The selection of Petraeus and Crocker would later be seen as inspired. They would form the ideal team to execute the president's high-risk strategy.

The selection of General Abizaid's replacement at Central Command was anything but. Apparently without much vetting, Admiral "Fox" Fallon was named as the new commander. Neither NSC Iraq nor NSC Defense was consulted. Both offices were stunned. Fallon, at the time the commander of U.S. Pacific Command, was vastly senior but not experienced in the Middle East. Pacific Command, a maritime theater, had always been commanded by an admiral. Central Command, primarily focused on land operations, had never been. Fallon was also known to be opinionated and abrasive, even haughty, and we felt sure that he and Petraeus would be oil and water. It did not take long for the sparks to fly.

Part of my job as an NSC director entailed meeting with allies and partners, as coalition backing for the Surge was important. Some offered nominal support, but our most important allies declined. I pressed my British counterpart hard, reminding him that if the UK refused to get on this train, many others would hide behind them and do the same. By now, the British had largely retreated from Basra city, their stronghold in the south, to the airport, leaving only a garrison of some 700 troops in the city center. It was known to us that British commanders had cut side deals with the radical Shia militias there, ceding control of the oil-rich south in exchange for being left alone. By now, Prime Minister Tony Blair had left the scene, leaving the colorless Gordon Brown in charge. We were informed that the British public had soured on the war, and as we surged the British accelerated their disengagement,

---

1   "Multinational Security and Training Command-Iraq" or MNSTC-I.

endangering our ground line of communication from Kuwait. The UK had been with us since the beginning and would be for years more in Afghanistan. But they were done with Iraq.

In late January, the first Surge brigade arrived in Iraq, and through the spring one arrived each month until all of the additional units were in place. Some Army brigades were required to extend their tours from 12 to 15 months, further inflaming relations with the Marine Corps, which stuck to its seven-month rotation policy throughout the war. I didn't begrudge the commandant of the Marine Corps for trying to ease the burden on his Marines. But the impact on the Army was profound, and the load was far from fairly apportioned. The Marine Corps would stay on short tours for the duration and would insist on operational independence from the theater commander all the way through 2012, when our troops were out of Iraq and only Afghanistan remained as an active theater of war. The special operations community enjoyed the same considerations. Eventually, Secretary Gates put an end to the bifurcated chains of command.

Late in the spring of 2007, I flew to Iraq and met with Petraeus and his staff. The Surge was in full career, but it would take some months for its effects to be felt and the general was already being accused of failure. His problems were complicated by the fact that from the beginning, his relations with Admiral Fallon were poor, something we knew well at the NSC. I did not fault Petraeus, who was unfailingly smooth and deferential. But under the civility was a burning determination to succeed, and it had become clear that Fallon was an obstacle, not an enabler. A small group of brilliant colonels staffed Petraeus' inner office. In private, their message to me was clear. "This isn't working."

The Petraeus-Fallon relationship was marred by two principal factors. The first was one of personalities. On his fourth four-star job, Fallon clearly considered the ambitious and newly promoted Petraeus a junior and an inferior. Possessed of a strong ego and imperious nature, Fallon was physically much larger and determined to impose his will on the slight, intellectual Army general. In an early meeting, Fallon reportedly called Petraeus an "ass-kissing chickenshit" to his face, an almost unbelievable breach of decorum between senior military officers, prompting one anonymous senior official to observe that reports of bad relations between the two "were the understatement of the century." For his own reasons, Fallon poisoned this crucial dialogue from the outset.

The other irritant was based on a difference of perspective. Fallon was instinctively opposed to the Surge, more concerned with Pakistan and Iran, and not well versed in the intricacies of counterinsurgency. Petraeus had literally written the book on the subject as the author of the Army's "COIN" manual at Leavenworth. Soon after taking command, Fallon described the Surge as likely to "wrap up" in October, a far shorter timeline that Petraeus'. An "independent assessment," led by a rear admiral from CENTCOM, confirmed Fallon's views. The system had failed to vet Fallon properly and it was now apparent that his policy views were out of synch with the president's.

As an active theater of war, and with defeat a live possibility, Iraq was the top priority and our commander in Iraq enjoyed real position power, whatever the organizational chart said. I was certain that, in the president's mind, Fallon was expected to mind the store across the rest of the CENTCOM area of responsibility and to support Petraeus, not fight him. I was just as certain that, as an experienced bureaucratic infighter, Petraeus would prevail. Eventually he let it be known he would resign if ordered to submit to Fallon's views. On my return I reported my findings and observations to Meghan. Privately, I put my money on Petraeus. A few short months later, Fallon's stark opposition to administration policy was publicly revealed in a famous *Vanity Fair* interview and he was summarily fired.

Halfway through my first year, Meghan assigned me to head a working group tasked to develop options for resettlement of a group of Iranian dissidents harboring in Iraq. These were the Mujahedin-e Khalk (MeK). The MeK had been founded in the mid-60s by leftist students opposed to the Shah. Prior to the Shah's fall, the MeK killed six American advisors and wounded several others, including a brigadier general. After the revolution, they were savagely suppressed by Khomeini and driven underground. In exile, they carried out violent attacks against the new regime in Iran, portraying themselves as leaders of the Iranian diaspora and of resistance to the mullahs. Attacks against Iranian embassies around the world were a hallmark, including one at the United Nations in 1992. Led by the charismatic Massoud Rajavi, avowedly Marxist and cultish, they became so violent they were listed as a terrorist organization both by the U.S. State Department and the European Union. Their marching song trumpeted "May America be annihilated."

During the Iran–Iraq war in the 1980s they sided with Saddam Hussein and fought as a unit in his army. Until his overthrow in 2003 they remained inside Iraq at Camp Ashraf, located about 50 miles from the Iranian border. Well organized and financed, they managed to convince Vice President Cheney and Secretary Rumsfeld of their potential as intelligence sources and as a future resistance organization. In a bewildering volte-face, U.S. forces in Iraq were now directed by the Department of Defense to treat them as "protected persons" at Ashraf even as they remained on the list of designated terrorist organizations. Much like Ahmed Chalabi and his "Iraqi National Congress," their claims were later shown to be fantasy. So far as I am aware, no meaningful or actionable information ever derived from the MeK, while they certainly posed no real threat to the regime in Tehran.

By 2008, with eventual transition to full Iraqi security control now in sight, a policy decision was urgently needed. Inside Iraq, the MeK were hated by all sides: by the Shia, for fighting with Saddam and his Sunni minority regime; by the Sunni, for being Iranian and Shia; and by the Kurds, for having aided Saddam in his brutal repression of the Kurdish minority following the Gulf War. Once U.S. troops left, the Iraqis were sure to go after the MeK with a vengeance. How to prevent the bloodbath?

Over the next 19 months, our group produced 26 iterations of a detailed policy paper, laying out options for consideration. Six times the paper went to the Deputies Committee. Six times it was returned for "further refinement." Every possible approach was examined: to relocate the MeK to the U.S., or to a third nation; to return them to Iran; to scatter them in small groups around the world; to turn them over to the Iraqi government in exchange for promises of fair treatment, and many others. All were discarded. Congress and state governments would not agree to allow them entry into the U.S.. Neither would any other foreign government. The Iraqis would make no guarantees, and Iran would make short work of any "repatriated" MeK members.

In the end, the U.S. interagency could not decide. Following the end of the Bush administration and "transition to Iraqi control," hundreds of MeK members were killed, wounded, or imprisoned by the Iraqi security forces and their Iranian supporters. Our efforts were seen by many as a classic failure, though the unwillingness of cabinet officers to reconcile their differences and the group's own terrible history were chiefly at fault. Today, aging survivors live in Albania where they were eventually relocated in 2012, when the Obama administration finally removed them from the terrorist watch list.

In early June of 2007, I watched with dismay as CNN ran a story about a Marine lance corporal handing out "John 3:16" coins on a street corner in Ramadi. I knew immediately this was big trouble. Within minutes Hadley's office called with an urgent message. The president would be briefed in an hour. I had that much time to confirm or deny the story. Here my past experience was helpful. Skipping multiple layers, I called down to trusted contacts in Anbar, who told me that CNN was on the mark. Later, I would be harshly scolded by an infuriated general in the Pentagon for "ignoring the chain of command." I understood his point of view. But in a 24/7 news cycle, the president's need for rapid and accurate information was overriding. An NSC director who lacked extensive networks and the will to use them was almost useless.

As the last Surge brigade closed in late June of 2007, we began to note promising signs in Anbar. In the preceding months, the tribal sheikhs there had increasingly come to realize that AQI, though Sunni and fanatically opposed to the Shia majority across Iraq, was not an ally but in fact a remorseless enemy. Many sheikhs had been murdered, along with their family members. From their perspective, the Sunni tribes could no longer oppose the Americans, Maliki's sectarian government in Baghdad, and AQI all at once. In an act of real courage, many switched sides, led prominently by Sheikh Abdul Sattar of the Abu Risha tribe. Sattar's father and two brothers had been murdered by AQI, and only months later he would be assassinated himself. But the Anbar Awakening was on, and it quickly began to take root.

A major part of the Awakening was the "Sons of Iraq" project, an effort to recruit Sunni tribesmen in Anbar to join the Iraqi police and army. Now encouraged by their tribal elders, these young men flocked to enlist. Our understanding of AQI networks also flourished, as no one had better insights on their locations, activities, and leaders than the sheikhs. A major player was Brigadier General John Allen, the Marine deputy commander in Anbar and a close friend. His sophisticated understanding of tribal dynamics, high intelligence and ability to bridge cultural gaps would prove decisive in making the Awakening the success it later became.

Back in Washington, the Surge came under bitter attack by the newly empowered Democrats now in charge on Capitol Hill. By now I was no political naif, yet some Democrats showed every sign of *wanting* the Surge to fail. Returning to Washington to testify in September, Petraeus reported signs of progress but was careful and measured in his responses, saying that success would be neither "quick nor easy." He was flanked by Ambassador Crocker, who testified that success was possible but could not be guaranteed. Both were assailed by Senator Hillary Clinton on national television, who opined that their testimony required a "willing suspension of disbelief." A full-page ad in the *New York Times*, paid for by a far-left political organization, accused Petraeus of "betrayal." The administration had lost the Congress. This was the price.

By now Meghan O'Sullivan, after almost five years in the White House, had moved on and accepted a chair and professorship at Harvard. I hated to see her go. Though she was years younger than me, I found her the ideal boss, tough, smart, and decisive but also compassionate and engaging. She was replaced by Army lieutenant general and Sosh alum Doug Lute, a career cavalry officer with extensive time as a troop commander and a graduate degree from Harvard. Formerly the director of operations on the Joint Staff, Lute was tall, square-jawed, and congenial. His easy manner and personality contrasted with a sharp, incisive mind. Meghan had played a key role in bringing the Surge into being. Lute would now manage an interagency process to make it succeed.

Soon after Lute took over, in September of 2007, NSC Iraq was engulfed in yet another major incident involving civilian casualties. Under disputed circumstances, private security contractors—in this case, my old nemesis, Blackwater—had fired on a crowd in Nisour Square in Baghdad, killing 17 civilians and wounding 20. Understandably, the Iraqi government and media were incensed. At issue, beyond the immediate questions of excessive force, were thornier legal and policy questions.

In the eyes of the international community, Blackwater was a mercenary organization, carrying out combat operations for profit. U.S. lawyers viewed the issue more narrowly, arguing that the security escort mission was "defensive" in nature and therefore, strictly speaking, not "combat." Although equipped with heavy weapons, armored vehicles and even armed helicopters, Blackwater and other private security contractors thus operated in a kind of legal gray zone, largely immune to prosecution by Iraqi or U.S. military authorities. Following an intensive FBI investigation, civilian charges were eventually filed and, years later, three Blackwater employees would serve light sentences while one, Nicholas Slatten, would be sentenced to life in prison. (He would later be pardoned by President Trump.) In 2009, a new Status of Forces agreement between Iraq and the U.S. allowed the Iraqi government jurisdiction over private security companies for the first time. Blackwater's license to operate in Iraq was pulled and the company sustained huge losses, though it survives under a different name.

The Nisour Square massacre resulted in legislation intended to bring private security companies more effectively under control, but the damage to U.S.–Iraqi relations and to the campaign was long lasting. At best, our efforts to gain the support of the Iraqi population were hamstrung by our image, in the eyes of many, as occupiers. American legitimacy, a precious commodity in any counterinsurgency campaign, would suffer badly in the aftermath.

During one meeting of the Deputies Committee on this topic, I noticed a new face representing the State Department. This senior figure, a well-known academic, had built a reputation arguing that our civilian leaders "had the right to be wrong," and to intrude deeply into operational matters to "ensure civilian control." I had first read his work in the late 1980s as a graduate student and remembered his admonition that "America should not be in the business of preparing expeditionary forces that will never sail"—published about six months before the Gulf War!

Our newcomer had been an ardent advocate of invasion, but he now found himself in the actual frying pan, where lofty suggestions to "restore stability" cratered against the realities of intractable, sectarian violence. Iraq interagency hands had now been hardened by years of immersion in the conflict, consuming dozens of cables and intelligence assessments daily to keep abreast. The official disappeared from our deliberations almost as quickly as he had arrived, another casualty of policy "tourism." Working Iraq was soul-crushing, painful, laborious, and unrewarding. Many couldn't stand the gaff.

As we approached year's end in 2007, we could see a significant reduction in violence in Iraq. By summer of 2008, the results were clear: the Surge had succeeded dramatically, with violence down by 90 percent and something like normalcy returning to the streets and markets. The Anbar Awakening with U.S. assistance had all but demolished AQI and the Shia militias, many supported directly by Iran, had essentially returned to the sidelines. Petraeus now turned his attention to "transfer to Iraqi control." In a carefully planned and measured way, U.S. and coalition forces would step back and "overwatch" Iraqi provinces deemed ready to transition.

Our principal problem now was Prime Minister Maliki. Elected to office in 2006, he was originally a compromise choice approved by the CIA and Zalmay Khalilzad, the U.S. ambassador, who praised him as free from Iranian influence. In fact, he was the preferred choice of Qassim Soleimani, the powerful head of the Iranian Quds Force, the external arm of Iran's Republican Guards. Over time he had shown himself to be a harshly sectarian politician, not a national leader who could bridge the confessional divide that gripped Iraq. In March of 2007, he launched "Charge of the Knights," a major operation to clear oil-rich Basra in the south of armed militias—principally his rival, al Sadr, and his Jaysh al Mahdi. Poorly planned and lacking logistical support, the operation teetered on the edge of failure until MNF-I poured advisors and support into Basra. (Later he turned his wrath on the Sunni, suppressing them ruthlessly and laying the seeds for the rise of ISIS on the ruins of AQI.) Throughout my time at NSC Iraq, I argued against supporting Maliki, on the grounds that we could not ultimately prevail in reconstituting a functioning Iraq with him in charge. Eventually I was told to desist. "Iraqi politics is not your lane. We've made a policy decision and it's final."

In later years, advocates and critics would argue fiercely about whether or not the Surge had been a success or failure. Many would try to take credit for its conception or execution—including some I knew had been staunch opponents at the time. My own view is that the Surge accomplished its intended purpose by setting conditions for a political settlement that unfortunately never materialized. Military action alone might bring about a reasonable level of security but could never reconcile Iraq's tortured politics and ethnic strife. That would require sustained diplomacy and statecraft, beginning with strong support for moderate Iraqi leaders able to bridge ethnic divides. The next administration, in its haste to disengage, would throw away the fruits of the Surge and depart, leaving Iran as the most influential player in Baghdad. With the State Department urging a hands-off approach, Maliki would win a contested election in 2010 and intensify his repression of the Sunni. The result was the Caliphate and the Islamic State.

By early 2008, I had become convinced that our approach to advising the Iraqi security forces was far from ideal. Since 2005, we had fielded Military Transition Teams (MiTT teams) composed of active and reserve officers and NCOs to advise Iraqi units. These were not cohesive units, but groups of individuals who received a few weeks of training in the States before shipping out for Iraq. Though placed under the operational control of nearby brigades and divisions, they were never seen as full equals—the Chickamauga Rule again—and their performance was uneven at best. Above all, they lacked credibility with Iraqi commanders, who were typically more senior in rank with far more combat experience.

At the working group level, I introduced an alternate proposal, to re-mission our combat brigades as "advise and assist" brigades, responsible for partnering with, training and advising Iraqi counterparts. As I saw it, this approach offered benefits across the board. Our very best and brightest commanded and staffed these formations. They were far better trained and far more cohesive than the MiTT teams, and able to bring fires and reinforcements more quickly when needed, as they owned these assets. As we handed over battlespace to the ISF and moved to "overwatch," this model seemed far more appropriate to the evolving mission.

For some weeks, my proposal was "cooked" in the interagency before it went to the Deputies Committee. There it was shot down by the Joint Staff, who opined that the three-star MNC-I commander, Lieutenant General Ray Odierno, was adamantly opposed. *Sub rosa*, the Army also expressed its displeasure about one of its own mucking about with "Army" matters at the NSC. The following year Odierno was promoted and, as the theater commander, reversed course and implemented the change. Apparently, from that perch the problem looked a bit different.

The focus of the latter part of my tour was the effort to stem the flow of foreign fighters through Syria into Iraq. General Petraeus had made this a priority and he was surely correct, as a steady influx of new recruits from across the Islamic world, and even from Western nations, fueled AQI and its offshoots. Suicide bombers in particular were almost never native Iraqis. Instead, they were recruited abroad, usually over the internet, and brought to Damascus on one-way flight tickets. From there, facilitators would guide them over smuggling routes and ratlines into Iraq. At the height of the war, they were flowing in faster than we could kill them—or to use the euphemism then in vogue, "remove them from the battlefield."

Stemming this flow required an interagency and multi-national approach cutting across many different departments and agencies. The State Department coordinator for counter-terrorism, retired Army Lieutenant General Dell Dailey, worked tirelessly to improve vetting and monitoring of terrorist suspects around the globe, a process that depended on better screening and tracking in their countries of origin. The Department of the Treasury intensified its threat finance activities; Transportation and Homeland Security helped host nations with airport security and screening; the intelligence community refocused on foreign fighter flows as one of its highest priorities; and allies and partners around the world stepped up intelligence sharing and consultation.

Our job at the NSC was to manage the process, resolving interagency disputes, preparing and circulating policy papers for review and discussion, scheduling high-level decision meetings, and framing the most important decisions for the president. The soldiers on the ground, and their commanders, rightfully deserved the credit for the dramatic reduction in violence that followed. But helping to solve the foreign fighter problem played a key role. We took great satisfaction in the results achieved.

In June of 2008, at the two-year mark, I asked permission to return to the Army. The campaign season was well under way and having lived through one presidential transition in the White House, I had no desire to experience a second. I was nearing exhaustion after four continuous years of 60–70-hour weeks and looked forward to a break. On my final day, President Bush graciously hosted me in the Oval Office, posing for pictures and chatting with Beverly and the kids. The Army obliged me with an assignment as chief of staff of the Army chair at the National War College, located in picturesque Fort McNair not far from the Navy Yard in Washington. After a short leave, I settled in for the start of the academic year. Now in my 28th year of commissioned service, after four combat tours, five years in the Pentagon, three years in the White House and more missed birthdays and holidays than I cared to count, I felt I had done my share and perhaps a bit more. I looked forward to a quiet spell of teaching before mandatory retirement.

It was not to be. Halfway through the fall semester my old commander, now-Major General Mike Scaparrotti, called me at home. Scap had recently taken command of the 82nd Airborne Division and was slated to take the All Americans to Afghanistan in the summer. He had a job in mind and needed a quality senior colonel with brigade command and 82nd experience. Did I have any suggestions? Reading between the lines, I asked for a day to think about it.

I had much to ponder. I had already asked more of Beverly than any reasonable spouse should have to endure. The family had not seen much of me in recent years. Another combat deployment would not be career enhancing, as further promotion so late in my career was not a realistic proposition. And I was no longer a young man. Now in my early 50s, I couldn't lie to myself. I had lost a step.

But there were other considerations. I remembered my father, in a similar situation, going to Beirut in his 29th year. I thought of Ladd Pattillo, well into retirement, volunteering to come back and deploy. My oldest son Chris had elected to defer college and, like me, had enlisted as an airborne infantryman. His unit, the 173rd Airborne Brigade (my old outfit from Vicenza), would deploy to Afghanistan the following fall as part of Combined Joint Task Force 82. The opportunity to soldier with my son in a foreign land was compelling. Nostalgically, I was tempted to return to the 82nd Airborne, where I had begun 33 years before, to end my career. I would have nine months to rest and spend with the family before going downrange. I thought of the wonderful younger officers I had served with—McFarlane, Fenzel, Burleson, and many others, now commanding battalions of their own and slated to go back into the box for their 2nd, 3rd, or even 4th combat deployments. I was a professional soldier. It did not seem right to shirk when others were continuing to sacrifice and serve. Finally, I was drawn to work once more for Scap, a great leader and valued friend.

As she always had, Beverly smiled bravely and offered her full support. I called Scap the next day and told him I thought I filled the bill and would be glad to go if he'd have me. The next six months flew by as I studied Afghanistan—its history, geography, politics, tribal dynamics and most importantly, the enemy. After the initial successful phase, Operation *Enduring Freedom* evolved into an "economy of force" mission as Iraq moved to center stage. The Taliban, badly damaged, hunkered down in the tribal areas just across the border in Pakistan to regroup and plot its return. For some four years, violence was relatively low, and U.S. and coalition troop strength were accordingly modest. In 2004, Hamid Karzai was elected president of Afghanistan following the drafting of a national constitution. Provincial Reconstruction Teams (PRTs) composed of both military and civilians were established in each province to plan and execute local reconstruction projects to benefit the local community.

On the surface, Iraq and Afghanistan seemed to have much in common. Both were Islamic states with long-standing conflict histories; both suffered from weak governance and ethnic strife; both faced dangerous local insurgencies; and both hosted large international coalitions on their soil. But there were major differences as well. Afghanistan was significantly larger in both land area and population. Its transportation network was far less developed than Iraq's and its terrain was far more challenging, above all the famous "Hindu Kush," the towering mountainous region that bisected the country from East to West. Unlike Iraq, there was little human capital in Afghanistan, as most technocrats and university graduates had been killed or run out during the years of Taliban rule. Much of the population lived in poverty in the countryside, unlike Iraq with its many cities. Warlordism, drug trafficking and corruption were rife and distrust of foreigners—all foreigners—was genetically imprinted in all Afghans. Not for nothing was Afghanistan called "the graveyard of empires."

In 2006, at the height of the war in Iraq, violence in Afghanistan began to spike. Suicide bombings and IEDs, at one point relatively rare, now became more common. Financed by foreign money and supported clandestinely by the ISI—Pakistan's notorious internal security service—the Taliban established "shadow" governments in many Afghan districts and provinces, murdered local officials and challenged the central government in the countryside. With Iraq in the spotlight, U.S. forces attempted to maintain control with only about 20,000 troops and a few smaller international contingents. The Afghan security forces, also hampered by lower priority, were plagued by low numbers, poor leadership, ramshackle logistics and lack of heavy weapons. By the spring of 2009, the U.S. commander, General David McKiernan, was forced to ask for a major troop increase and by May of that year his force had grown to just over 50,000.[2]

I had not anticipated any difficulties, but by the spring it became clear that the war college leadership did not support my detail to Afghanistan. Although I had secured the assignment of a well-qualified backfill, I had not considered the larger implications. Almost every military organization had been hit hard to provide officers to man our large headquarters in Iraq and Afghanistan, but somehow the war college had been overlooked. There was little interest on the campus in breaking that precedent. I was first asked, and then pressured, to withdraw from consideration. I persisted and the matter was eventually elevated to higher levels.

2   The coalition command in Afghanistan was styled the "International Security Assistance Force" or ISAF and headed by a U.S. four-star who doubled as commander U.S. Forces Afghanistan.

Marine Lieutenant General John Allen, one of the heroes of the Awakening, was now the deputy commander at U.S. Central Command. An old friend, he became personally involved and, quite late in the game, the decision came down in my favor.

In mid-June, I boarded a commercial flight via Ankara to Uzbekistan. From there I caught a C17 and flew into Bagram, the home of Regional Command or RC-East. (Afghanistan was divided into Regional Commands—South, North, West, East and Capital.) An old Soviet air base, Bagram was located about 30 minutes' flying time from Kabul, the capital, at 6,000 feet. In all directions, the mountains of the Hindu Kush towered above us. I was assigned a small one-man room, with a communal bathroom down the hall, that would be my home for the next year. The accommodations were spartan, but I considered myself lucky. As a full colonel I rated a private room. I stacked my gear and slept for 10 hours. Early the next morning, I began.

Just before I arrived, General McKiernan was abruptly relieved of command of ISAF, apparently because the new administration felt that a new commander with a stronger background in counterinsurgency was needed. He was replaced by General McChrystal. Overcoming the Tillman fiasco somehow, he had stayed in command of special operations units for some years before a short tour on the Joint Staff and was promoted into the ISAF job as the military's youngest four-star.

McChrystal was, I thought, a questionable choice. My dismay was based on more than our prior history. Most of his time as a general officer had been spent in the insular special operations community, far from the media glare, interagency wrangling, interaction with diplomats and fractious allies, and command of large organizations that were the necessary skill set for successful theater commanders. A more seasoned general with more diverse experiences was the ideal. He had also been tainted by the Tillman affair, and by allegations of torture conducted at "black" sites under his purview in Iraq. Nevertheless, we hoped for the best. After McKiernan's firing, we would need strong and sound leadership to succeed.

In the preceding months, I had worked hard to get up to speed on our mission, but I would have much to learn. General Scaparrotti, in a departure from earlier commanders, had elected to focus on the "information fight"—the struggle for the support of the Afghan population—as our top priority. For many years, influencing audiences in support of the Afghanistan enterprise had been poorly coordinated and synchronized. Recognizing the critical importance of information, his Combined Joint Task Force or CJTF-82 made it the centerpiece of the campaign plan. Traditionally, the different "messaging" entities found in the division headquarters—the public affairs (PA) and information operations (IO) sections as well as a newly created Key Leader Engagement (KLE) cell—reported to different heads, complicating coherent messaging. To fix this, Scaparrotti created the Communications Action Group (CAG), a small but powerful command and control node chartered to integrate and coordinate the information line of operation in support of the campaign plan. My assignment was to serve as its chief.

My background as a former brigade commander with multiple tours in the 82nd was helpful in bridging the gap between the Fort Bragg regulars who formed the permanent division staff, and the many reservists and augmentees who joined us to flesh out the CJTF staff. I set about trying to "build the airplane in flight." My immediate staff included a senior Department of the Army public affairs civilian, two Army Reserve lieutenant colonels (both former battalion commanders with Iraq experience and both future general officers) and a master sergeant (E-8) as my Noncommissioned Officer in Charge (NCOIC). This was none other than Nick Keane. Scap had somehow pried him loose from SOCOM. He had served extensively in Afghanistan since our last deployment together with Special Forces, seeing heavy combat in Uruzgan province. He knew as little about information operations as I did, but he knew the Army and he knew war. Once again, he would be my warhorse.

Now deep into the Global War on Terror, the Army still pressed on with its "modular brigade" concept, through Rumsfeld had long since departed. The practical effect was that none of the combat brigades task organized under the 82nd were "organic" to the division. Scaparrotti would command unfamiliar brigades with unfamiliar commanders—it would be "discovery" learning for all from the outset. The 4th Brigade (Airborne), 25th Infantry Division, commanded by Colonel (later Lieutenant General) Mike Howard came out of Alaska and was responsible for Khowst, Paktia, and Paktika provinces. The 4th Brigade, 4th Infantry Division, commanded by Colonel (later Lieutenant General) Randy George, was based in Colorado and held responsibility for Kunar, Laghman, Nangarhar, and Nuristan provinces. The 3rd Brigade, 10th Mountain Division, commanded by Colonel (later Major General) Dave Haight, covered Logar and Wardak provinces.[3] A National Guard headquarters with support troops from the 38th Division was responsible for the quieter Bamyan, Kapisa, Panjshir, and Parwan provinces, while a French regiment worked Kapisa province and a Polish battlegroup held down Ghazni province. In all, counting support units, CJTF-82 included some 24,000 troops and covered an area the size of New York state with 10 million inhabitants. With poor roads, towering mountains, and bad flying weather for much of the year, we would find ourselves stretched very thin indeed.

One of the causes of General McKiernan's relief had been his refusal to import a corps headquarters to handle the tactical and operational fighting, so that ISAF could focus on the politico-military, theater strategic and coalition aspects of the campaign (more than 30 nations were present and on the ground at the time).

---

3   The 173rd Airborne Brigade, commanded by Colonel Jim Johnson, replaced 3/10 in November 2009. Johnson was later court martialed and convicted on charges of fraud, adultery, bigamy, and conduct unbecoming an officer and reduced in rank to lieutenant colonel. Haight was also later accused of misconduct and demoted from major general to lieutenant colonel.

McChrystal moved quickly to establish a provisional corps headquarters, calling it "IJC" for "ISAF Joint Command." Later, trained standing corps headquarters would be provided, but for the coming year IJC would have to serve. Its commander was Lieutenant General Dave Rodriguez, another former 82nd commander. I knew him well; his daughter had babysat regularly for us on an earlier tour.[4] Rodriguez would make the most of his pickup team, but forming a trained battle staff out of a collection of individuals would take time.

Very quickly, I learned that Afghanistan was different from Iraq in at least two key ways. In Iraq, with its many all-weather, hard-surfaced roads, movement by vehicle was the norm. While IEDs were a major threat, they were usually not dug into the concrete/asphalt roadbed, an engineering task beyond the capabilities of most insurgents. Instead, they tended to be sited just off the roadway and triggered as the target vehicle moved past. Because we moved at speed, more often than not the IED blast was slightly early, or slightly late. Except for the EFP, the chances of survival were good.

In Afghanistan, with its sparse, unimproved roads, the IED would usually be buried in the roadway, triggered by a pressure plate and with its blast directed straight up. Thousands of culverts, used to divert mountain runoff, dotted the roads and provided ideal IED locations. These weapons tended to be much larger and, because they did not miss, very destructive. Accordingly, in Afghanistan helicopters were the preferred mode of transport.

But here, too, we faced difficulties. Dangerous mountain terrain and frequent bad flying weather degraded our ability to use our helos to best advantage. Our standard troop-carrying assault helicopter, the UH60L Black Hawk, had not been designed to carry heavy loads above 10,000 feet. Typically, only six fully loaded combat troops could be carried instead of the normal 12 in the Hindu Kush. To compensate, units often used the CH47D Chinook, a much larger and less agile helo not well suited for combat assaults. Occasionally, one would be downed with catastrophic results, as when a Chinook was shot down in Wardak province in 2011, killing all 38 aboard, including 25 Navy SEALs. (Eighteen ISAF Chinooks would crash or be shot down during our sojourn in Afghanistan.) In a long career, I had trained and fought all over the world. No place on earth was worse than Afghanistan. It was as if mother nature herself conspired against us.

In the months leading up to the deployment, I had studied the CAG concept thoroughly. It represented a novel approach, but one with real potential. The specified mission of the CAG was to "develop, synchronize and execute the RC-East communications strategy to gain and maintain the initiative against the enemy and maintain the public support necessary to achieve success in Afghanistan." Its work was principally carried out through weekly meetings with public affairs, information

4   Rodriguez would subsequently be promoted to full general and command U.S. Africa Command.

operations and key leader engagement chiefs (all lieutenant colonels), as well as the Psychological Operations (PSYOPS) company commander; weekly communications strategy working groups; and participation in all other major staff events.

To prepare for the mission we had studied *The Quranic Concept of War*, written by Pakistani General S. K. Malik. In his book, Malik identified the human heart and will as the primary object in warfare, inferring the primacy of the psychological domain. This view, which is foreign to traditional Western perspectives, is inherent in virtually all insurgent warfare. The enemy in Afghanistan rarely fought to take or hold ground; every operation was conducted with an information objective in mind. The object of the insurgent was to convince the population that the government could not provide security or basic services, an approach often used to highlight ethnic tensions and rivalries. For example, the insurgency in Afghanistan was (and is) a Pashtun-driven phenomenon, propelled by fears of domination by a minority, Tajik-controlled military or state structure and by historic Pashtun nationalist aspirations.

This did not mean that the Taliban were monolithic. In fact, though loosely controlled by the "Quetta Shura" (a group of senior Taliban leaders sequestered inside Pakistan and led by Mullah Omar), the Taliban was composed of many different groups, some—like the brutal Haqqani network—almost autonomous. Though not integrated with al Qaeda, they had never renounced their ties with our mortal enemy. Other Afghan warlords, like Gulbuddin Hekmatyar, wavered between attacking ISAF and seeking office inside the government. A particularly nasty case was Abdul Rashid Dostum, an Afghan Uzbek and Northern Alliance leader. In a checkered career he had fought with the Russians against the mujahidin, switched sides again and again, been tried for war crimes, and ultimately rose to become vice president of Afghanistan. (He was removed from office in 2017 amid charges of sexually assaulting an Afghan male.) In Afghanistan, the cast of characters was an inscrutable mosaic, hard to comprehend and wargame against. Many of the players had fought as mujahidin against the Russians in the 1980s. Though they lacked airpower and artillery, they were combat-hardened and knew the ground intimately. And they were ruthless, unencumbered by our rules of engagement and always ready to kill civilians to further their goals.

We communicated with the population in three primary ways. The most important was by radio or television broadcast. Some of the RC-East population (mostly in the more urban areas such as Jalalabad, Ghazni, Gardez, and Khowst) had access to television. The rest of the population relied on radio for much of their information and entertainment. Accordingly, we handed out hundreds of thousands of hand-cranked AM/FM radios, mostly in rural areas. Building on an existing network, CJTF-82 expanded to more than fifty 300-watt systems and added four 1,000-watt AM systems as well, greatly extending the reach of our messaging. These commercial systems, called RIABs (for "Radio in a Box"), employed locally recruited Afghan DJs and operated from NATO bases throughout RC-East. Using Afghan programming obtained through commercial contracts, the systems enabled coalition forces to reach into all but the most mountainous areas with local news, poetry, music and religious content, as well as with public service announcements crafted in accordance with our overall communications strategy. We also purchased airtime from commercial radio stations to augment their broadcasts. While ISAF headquarters conducted broadcast messaging nationwide, we focused on regional themes that were of more immediate interest to each specific local population. We supplemented broadcast messaging with print products such as posters, handbills, billboards, and leaflets, which were designed to communicate visually to a largely illiterate population.

As with radio and television spots, print products employed local Afghan staff to ensure coherent and culturally authentic messages. Our 40-man Afghan staff also promoted pre-testing, using focus groups throughout the local community. Prepared by the supporting PSYOP company, print products were vetted at our level during weekly boards (which included legal and cultural advisors as well as human terrain staff) and were then approved by me. In the weeks preceding the national elections in late summer of 2009, we disseminated a million "get-out-the-vote" print products every week—more than the Afghan government distributed across the entire country.

Civil-military cooperation had long been recognized as essential to success in COIN, a lesson going back to the massive COORDS program from Vietnam,[5] but execution on the ground had often been uneven and difficult. While agency cultures and doctrinal differences are always present, truly integrated civil-military operations seemed clearly the way ahead. Here Scaparrotti also broke new ground by embracing "unified action"—a first-ever attempt to genuinely fuse military and civilian organizations into one operational headquarters. At the transfer of authority from the 101st Airborne Division on June 4, 2009, there were three civilians posted to the headquarters. That began to change quickly. In July 2009, the U.S. Embassy in Kabul converted the political advisor position to that of senior civilian representative (SCR) of the ambassador. Empowered with "chief of Mission" authority to "coordinate and direct all U.S. Mission-related civilian personnel and programs in RC-East," Ambassador Dawn Liberi was directed to "serve as the U.S. civilian counterpart to the military commander in the Regional Command (RC), to senior coalition civilians and to senior local Afghan officials."[6] In this role, the SCR co-signed, with the commanding general, the CJTF-82 campaign plan (Operation *Champion Sahar*) on October 17, 2009. Except for purely kinetic combat operations, the ambassador would co-sign every order we published. This approach

5   For "Civil Operations and Revolutionary Development Support," headed by four-star civilian Robert Komer.
6   Liberi's authority did not extend to DoD civilians or civilian intelligence officers.

254 • THE GOOD CAPTAIN

bridged a deep divide: a military traditionally focused on conflict and combat, and a civilian process focused on diplomacy and development.

This unique organization, a true civilian/military hybrid unlike any seen before, included senior military Civil Affairs officers, as well as career experts from the Departments of State and Agriculture, the U.S. Agency for International Development (USAID), and other government agencies up to senior executive service rank. Drawing on the capabilities of the entire staff and tying in with parallel organizations above and below, it quickly energized development and governance. The civilian uplift began in earnest in early September with the arrival of eight USAID specialists in water, agriculture, governance, rule of law, program management, and economics—specialties with applications for both governance and development. The platform eventually grew to more than 175 personnel from the State and Agriculture Departments and USAID.

An interesting development was the "board of directors" concept, used at brigade level to coordinate and prioritize development projects. The brigade commander chaired regular working groups with his affiliated State, USAID, Agriculture, and PRT leaders to plan, coordinate, and prioritize funding and support for development projects. PRTs continued to play a critical role. Manned with both civilian and military experts, they provided a primary interface and capacity-building function with provincial governors and their staffs, serving as an execution arm for development and governance in the provinces. Most were led by U.S. Air Force or Navy O-5s (lieutenant colonels or commanders) with U.S. government civilian deputies, but RC-East also fielded Czech, Turkish, and New Zealand PRTs. Each included development and governance professionals and security elements to enable freedom of movement. All U.S. PRTs were placed under the operational control of nearby brigades to establish a clear link to nearby supporting headquarters and to ensure close integration with all stability actors across the brigade area.

Like everything in Afghanistan, stability operations were a hard and grinding business, fraught with setbacks and obstacles. Ingrained corruption, lack of trained bureaucrats and officials, widespread illiteracy, an active insurgency, and complex coordination challenges between U.S., NATO, UN, and nongovernmental organization bodies defined our operating environment. Still, unified action enabled us to achieve real progress. In one year, we built 47 schools, 206km of roads, 39 bridges, and numerous micro-hydro, generator, and solar power projects, as well as electrical systems projects that provided some 340,000 Afghans with access to reliable power. During our rotation, RC-East residents reported real improvements in education, medical care, roads, and the availability of jobs. Additionally, an accumulated backlog of more than 1,700 unfinished projects dating back to 2006 was reduced to just over 500 between July 2009 and April 2010, refocusing the program to primarily small-scale, sustainable projects that provided immediate results.

Unified action also enabled clear progress on rule of law, helping with evidence collection, removal of corrupt officials, and the establishment of sitting supreme court judges and mobile trial judges. As one example, five corrupt district governors were removed in Nangarhar province in the spring of 2010, and in early May a judicial commission from the Afghan supreme court charged five district line managers with corruption and opened investigations on another 13 in Paktika province. Across RC-East, 12 crooked Afghan Army and police commanders at the district and provincial levels were removed in one five-month period.

Gains on this front were halting but helped to combat the corrosive corruption that threatened progress in Afghanistan. Unified action had been considered theoretically for years, but it became an operational reality for the first time in RC-East in 2009. As a new construct, it experienced many of the birthing pains that always accompany new ideas and practices. In our view, the return was well worth the investment.

Since 9/11, U.S. and coalition forces had partnered in various ways with host nation security forces in Iraq and Afghanistan, both formally and informally. Here also, we committed to a new and different approach called "combined action." The previous model featured embedded training teams (ETTs) and police mentor teams, small organizations that accompanied Afghan National Security Forces (ANSF) units as trainers and advisors. In a sharp break with the past, CJTF-82 moved to fuse Afghan and U.S. formations into truly combined units. "Combined action" meant merging coalition and Afghan forces into single organizations to conduct counterinsurgency. We embedded our staff officers and units in Afghan units, in place of traditional advisors. Replacing small advisory teams with full-sized combat units encouraged the Afghans to fight, knowing that we were there in strength and ready to bring in fire support if needed. Previously, the ratio of coalition to Afghan soldiers or police was 1:43 in many areas. Through combined action, that ratio became 1:4.

In just 90 days, the percentage of Afghan-led operations increased 15 percent, the number of joint Afghan/coalition operations jumped 20 percent, and army and police recruiting showed strong improvement—a clear indication of growing confidence. All this placed heavy demands on logistics and engineer support. Many Afghan bases were derelict, which seriously affected morale. Co-locating headquarters and formations provided an opportunity to construct new facilities and expand others to improve Afghan quality of life and recruiting. In some cases, the Afghan Army moved to our sites. In others, we moved to theirs. In some cases, we built new bases.

The single most dramatic decision was to push out 35-man tactical command posts, each led by a U.S. brigadier general, to live, work, and fight with the Afghan 201st and 203rd Corps.[7] U.S. assets such as artillery fires, close air support, medical evacuation, intelligence, surveillance, and reconnaissance (ISR) platforms, and logistics could now be incorporated into Afghan operations to a far greater degree.

---

7   Afghan army "corps" consisted of a handful of brigades and were far smaller than U.S. or NATO corps.

In the same way, we benefited from Afghan cultural awareness, tactical experience, and local intelligence sources as never before. The result was a 70 percent increase in reporting and a striking 60 percent reduction in ANSF casualties after only 90 days.

By now, after years of war, we knew that Afghanistan was home to a dangerous insurgency characterized by highly organized networks made up of commanders, financiers, suppliers, intelligence operatives, propagandists, and foot soldiers. To smash them, General Scap directed a full-spectrum approach. Called "Joint Network Targeting" (JNT), it featured both lethal and nonlethal actions to attack systems, not just personalities, to disrupt and collapse insurgent cells. The previous rotation, with fewer troops, had delegated most targeting functions to the brigades. With more resources flowing into Afghanistan as we drew down in Iraq, the need to focus all of our capabilities—special operations forces and conventional units, ISR, fires, aviation, information—to find and kill the enemy became clear.

With each operation, the CJTF adapted its processes, learning from both success and failure. Our methods relied on painstaking intelligence work to establish "pattern of life" and to limit and prevent collateral damage during the operation. Insurgent networks in Afghanistan were highly adaptive and quickly replaced leaders and captured materials. JNT analyzed the entire network—to include recruitment, training, logistical support, financing, command and control systems, leadership, and negative influencers. We learned that "shredding" networks was possible by attacking not only key nodes in the enemy network, but also key functions, simultaneously. This often took the form of major operations that massed ISR and other resources for extended periods to maintain continuous pressure.

In Afghanistan, we faced an implacable and deadly enemy who had to be confronted when he could not be reconciled. An intercepted insurgent radio transmission put it succinctly: "They will kill us. They will kill us all."

Much of our planning and preparation had been done before we arrived, but the CAG, as a small part of the larger whole, accomplished much in the first weeks and months. Here my varied experience with the media, public affairs, and reservists stood me in good stead. As I had in many other assignments, I learned quickly to rely on the expertise of our subject matter experts and to confine myself to enterprise management: filling key slots, setting goals and objectives, finding money and building structure and process into our operations.

"Big Army" had allotted us a single Army Reserve Psychological Operations Company, though doctrine called for a battalion. Its commander, a major, was an experienced officer with prior service in Iraq, but his company deployed at only 60 percent strength and was not reinforced for the duration of the mission. Unfortunately, early in the deployment the company operations officer, a female captain, was found to be pregnant and was sent home without replacement. This unit performed miracles for the entire year and we owed them much, but CENTCOM and the Army Staff did us no favors in stinting these soldiers in such a way. They bore an unfairly heavy burden.

Early on, I was forced to replace my active duty Information Operations (IO) chief, an Army officer who lacked a sense of urgency or ability to make decisions and produce results. His deputy, Marine Lieutenant Colonel Steve Manber, was a reserve infantry officer with Iraq experience. A graduate of the 30-day Joint IO course, Manber had plenty of drive and persistence and would move mountains for me as the new IO chief. His first speech to his troops was memorable: "The colonel has put me in charge. You will perform, or I will choke you to death!" Later, he would command a light armored vehicle battalion and rise to full colonel. Fortunately, none of his soldiers were harmed in the process!

The rest of the IO team was colorful, to say the least. One ancient master sergeant, a reservist from Brooklyn, was a teamster in civilian life and clearly linked with the mob. When asked if he'd ever been arrested, he replied proudly, "Sir, I've never once been convicted of anything!" Another NCO came from the porn industry—"Production and distribution side, sir, I promise!" He proved invaluable in our effort to generate and disseminate CDs and video products. A reserve lieutenant worked in the medical supply business and was expert in supply chain management, which proved critical to our operation. Another reserve officer was an advertising executive, a priceless skill set. The CAG team, about 50 officers and NCOs, was thickly salted with reservists whose civilian backgrounds were a treasure trove.

Broadcast and print media proved to be powerful tools, but in an oral, narrative culture like Afghanistan's, nothing can replace traditional, face-to-face communications. Commanders and leaders at all levels routinely conducted "key leader engagements" or KLEs, indispensable opportunities to communicate effectively in real time with Afghan counterparts and local communities. While KLEs had been used for several years in Afghanistan, their deliberate use as a messaging tool in support of a coherent communications strategy—synchronized and in concert with other messaging—was an innovation.

Some of our operations were phased, long-duration efforts, like Operation *Jaeza* (meaning "reward"), an integrated campaign to establish tiplines. Commanders used their RIABs, face-to-face engagements and hundreds of thousands of print products to inform the population about the tiplines. Virtually every item handed out in villages and towns—school backpacks, flags, humanitarian supplies, even emergency food and water—was accompanied by counter-IED literature and tipline numbers. As awareness grew, increasing numbers of local Afghans began to call in the location of IEDs and caches, often receiving cash payments for making these calls under our rewards program. Many Afghans, though illiterate, possessed and used cell phones, but our units also handed out ISAF cell phones to trusted local leaders and personalities to facilitate call-ins. These calls soon increased by a factor of 10. By tracking the number and results of the incoming calls, the program could quickly present evidence pointing to the power of information in COIN.

My baptism of fire came only two weeks into my tour when, on June 30, Private Bowe Bergdahl left his combat outpost in Paktika province on foot, without his weapon or equipment, except for a compass. A troubled young man, Bergdahl had been rejected by the Coast Guard before enlisting in the Army, and he would later be diagnosed with behavioral disorders. His disappearance was quickly reported up the chain, and General Scap immediately called a DUSTWUN (for "Duty Status/Whereabouts Unknown") battle drill. We would later learn that Bergdahl was captured by local Taliban elements soon after his departure. For now, the war ground to a halt as we bent every effort to recovering our lost soldier.

One immediate response was to give RC-East priority for assets like the MQ-1 Predator, an unmanned aerial platform mounting different kinds of sensor packages. These were scarce and hotly contested resources, and they made a difference. Although we ultimately did not recover Bergdahl, these additional capabilities helped us to locate and attack enemy units and leaders we might otherwise have missed. CJTF-82 inflicted serious damage on the Taliban that summer as we "flooded the zone" with soldiers determined to find Bergdahl. Later, some would deny that any U.S. soldiers were killed in the search. I don't remember it that way, and Bergdahl's fellow soldiers don't either. They risked their lives to get him back. Some were killed in the attempt. Years later, Bergdahl would return home following a prisoner exchange to be dishonorably discharged, after pleading guilty to desertion and misbehavior before the enemy.

In the course of the search for Bergdahl, an intelligence officer approached me with a request for help. He had reason to believe that a wanted Taliban leader might have knowledge of Bergdahl's whereabouts. Our J2 intelligence section had narrowed down his possible locations to any one of 10 villages in RC-East. At this stage of the war, we had taught the enemy to be cautious about using radios and cell phones. How to flush him out?

Our PSYOPS company commander came up with a novel approach. Over the next 24 hours, his unit prepared one million leaflets featuring the enemy leader's name and picture, a heroic effort that literally saw some of his soldiers treated intravenously with IV fluids. On the reverse side of the leaflet, the locals were given a phone number and invited to call in with the target's whereabouts, encouraged by an offer of a hefty reward. The next morning at dawn, Master Sergeant Keane and I accompanied a tactical PSYOPS team in UH60 helicopters to drop the leaflets. A hundred thousand leaflets descended over each of the 10 villages like a paper blizzard.

Sure enough, our target was in one of them. Panicking, he came up on his hand-held radio to demand rescue. ISAF intelligence staffs intercepted the call and a response team, on strip alert at the airfield, was quickly flown in to grab him. Bergdahl was already in Pakistan, but the target turned out to be an intelligence gold mine. Like most "meat-eating" infantrymen, I had spent much of my career pooh-poohing "leaf-eating" psychological operations officers. Now, I gained new-found respect for their expertise and critical contributions.

Understandably, the media focus surrounding Bergdahl was intense, and we worked night and day to ensure that our many target audiences—U.S., local, international and NATO—received accurate and timely information, subject to operational security constraints. Here we worked closely with ISAF counterparts in Kabul to manage the media storm. Mostly, we were doing damage control. There is no way to "spin" a missing or captured soldier and barring his recovery—which seemed more and more unlikely as time went on—the best we could hope for was that the news cycle would eventually move on.

It did, on July 4, when a platoon-sized outpost in the Zarok district of Paktika province was attacked by a large number of insurgents belonging to the Haqqani network. Accurate enemy fires destroyed the defenders' mortar pit and crippled radio communications with a strike on the command post. A massive 800kg vehicle-borne IED, driven by a suicide bomber, attempted to breach the main gate but was defeated when small arms fire killed the driver. In the ensuing battle, two American soldiers were killed and 20 wounded, almost 50 percent of the defending force becoming casualties. Despite their losses, the U.S. unit repelled the heavy assault, holding their ground and killing more than 30 insurgents.

An attack of this magnitude was a big story and, understandably, news coverage was immediate and widespread. Across the board, major news organizations reported the event accurately based on information provided by our public affairs section, but blaring headlines trumpeted the high number of U.S. casualties. As soon as the story broke, I was called by an infuriated brigade commander. In his view we had "failed to shape the story." The real story was not friendly casualties but his unit's successful defense and high body count. What good was "this CAG thing" if we couldn't generate favorable press? I explained patiently that the best we could hope for was accurate reporting; the journalists in-country were not responsible for headlines contrived back in New York or Washington by editors hungry for market share.

A few weeks later, we had better luck. On August 26, in the Sar Hawza district of western Paktika province, an infantry battalion from 4th Brigade, 25th Infantry Division (the same brigade which owned Zarok), received word from local Afghan sources that a wounded Taliban commander had taken refuge in a local clinic and was seeking treatment for serious wounds. The battalion immediately notified its higher headquarters and launched a platoon to the scene.

Upon arrival, the platoon leader coordinated with the local Afghan Army, Afghan police leaders and the clinic director. The battalion had also contacted the local sub-district governor and chief of police. CJTF-82 units recorded each of these engagements to document the concurrence of Afghan officials, using audio and video gear provided by the CAG and pushed down to platoon level. Once informed that all civilians had been removed from the clinic grounds, and accompanied by Afghan security forces, the lieutenant conducted a cordon and search of the clinic.

Unfortunately, the lead squad leader was shot and killed as he attempted to storm the building, one of 47 U.S. soldiers killed that month in Afghanistan.

In the ensuing firefight, AH64 Apache attack helicopters launched several Hellfire missiles, resulting in the death or capture of all insurgents inside. Unit leaders met at the scene to inform village elders of the circumstances. Civilian development experts quickly arrived to assure local citizens that the clinic would be repaired. At the unit's request, local provincial and sub-district governors made public statements in support of the coalition; the statements were broadcast on local television and radio stations. Public affairs officers quickly informed local and international media of the facts.

The next day, instead of highlighting a coalition attack on a hospital, the *New York Times* published a front-page story with the headline "Afghan Commander Captured in Raid." This situation could easily have ended in disaster, handing a major information victory to the enemy. Instead, close cooperation with local authorities, good tactical decision-making, prompt and truthful messaging and rapid sharing of information with the media and higher headquarters resulted in a good news story, with Afghans taking the lead in communicating the news to the population. Like most success stories in COIN, it incorporated actions across all lines of operation, not just one. Actions on the ground, not "spin," guided the public's reception of the story. Among many, this event stands out as a best practice—a dramatic illustration of "what right looks like."

Like the other regional commands, RC-East found itself absorbed in the upcoming national elections through the month of August. Our role was to assist the Afghan police and army in providing a safe and secure environment for the election. This would stretch us, as the Afghan government had designated hundreds of polling sites that needed to be secured. Many locations had been concocted to discourage voting by populations not likely to support Hamid Karzai—for instance, in remote, mountainous areas inaccessible except by foot and mule.

With our units fully committed, the elections took place on August 20, and as expected, Karzai finished in front amid a swirl of charges of corruption and ballot stuffing. These allegations were almost certainly true; the ISAF senior intelligence officer later told me on a helicopter that Karzai had "stolen the election fair and square." Under intense international pressure, a special run-off election was scheduled for November, but it was canceled after the runner up, Abdullah Abdullah, backed out. Throughout our presence in Afghanistan, down to the present day, government corruption and lack of capacity has undermined our effort in fundamental ways.

By early fall, General McChrystal had been in command of ISAF for three months, but already found himself in trouble. In early July, he had issued his famous "tactical directive," enjoining commanders to "carefully scrutinize" use of fires in order to avoid civilian casualties. His logic in theory was sound, as alienating the population was clearly not the path to victory. In practice, however, he aggressively went after local commanders for real or perceived "violations," repeatedly calling for investigations and arraigning his commanders in daily video teleconferences. In the interest of professional survival, some tactical commanders felt pressured to avoid contact altogether rather than risk McChrystal's ire. In one almost comical episode, ISAF began to push for a medal to reward "courageous restraint," an idea roundly mocked and ultimately shelved.

The problem of course was that the enemy wore civilian clothes and mixed with the civilian population, routinely using them as human shields. When a small unit was fired on from an Afghan compound (or qalat), there was no way to know if civilians were inside. Long habituated to warfare, Afghan villagers understood this. The indiscriminate use of artillery or airpower for no clear reason enraged them. But returning fire when fired upon was well within the rules of the game. Another consideration was that, unlike the superbly trained special mission units McChrystal had commanded for years, conventional units simply could not be as precise. As the saying went, they were blunt instruments, a "chain saw" and not a "scalpel." In life-or-death situations they would usually respond with volume of fire. Inevitably, if in the line of fire, civilians would be hit.

Fairly quickly, McChrystal came under fire from the media and even members of Congress, often sparked by bereaved family members of soldiers who had been killed in action. His problems began to mount when, in late September, his confidential assessment of his mission and requirements was leaked to the *Washington Post*. In it McChrystal warned of "dire" consequences if he was not reinforced with an additional 40,000 troops (on top of the 17,000 reinforcements that had arrived near the end of McKiernan's tenure). Days later, in a presentation to a London think tank, McChrystal doubled down by describing the situation in Afghanistan as "serious and deteriorating." His meaning was clear. Without massive reinforcements we could not succeed.

These two events combined to infuriate the White House and President Obama. McChrystal was certainly within his rights to provide his views to the president. But the leak (attributed by Secretary Gates to a member of McChrystal's staff) and the London presentation convinced Obama that McChrystal was maneuvering to "box" him in by trying the case in public. Soon after, in a short, private session in Copenhagen aboard Air Force One, the president sternly reprimanded McChrystal for straying out of his lane. The damage to their relationship would turn out to be permanent.

On September 4, we assembled in the conference room for the morning Commander's Update, chaired by General McChrystal and including all the regional commands. As the briefing commenced, we were stunned to hear that an errant air strike up north, in Konduz, had probably killed dozens of Afghan civilians. This was every commander's nightmare. What had gone wrong?

The incident apparently began when two fuel tankers were stolen by the local Taliban and became stuck in a riverbank about 8km from the headquarters of the

German PRT in Konduz. A relatively quiet sector, Konduz was home to the German contingent for just this reason. Unable to free the tankers, the Taliban encouraged the villagers in the area to siphon the fuel for their own use. Many arrived at the scene. An American B-1 bomber in the vicinity observed the activity, prompting the German commander, *Oberst* (Colonel) George Klein, to request the air strike. Klein would later testify that a single local informant at the scene told him the villagers were Taliban. Shortly thereafter, two U.S. F-15 Strike Eagles dropped 500lb bombs on the target, killing more than 100 civilians.

To his credit, General McChrystal immediately commissioned an investigation and went to the scene, admitting to reporters that an accidental event had likely resulted in mass civilian casualties. For its part, the German government in Berlin continued to deny for many weeks that any civilians had perished. Nothing like this had happened in Germany since the end of World War II. Ultimately, the German defense minister's career was ended over the cover-up, though Klein himself was subsequently promoted.

The incident underscored the challenges of coalition warfare to an unusual degree. More experienced American commanders might have scrutinized the target more carefully before ordering the strike. ISAF's ability to message about the event was compromised by Berlin's insistence on running with a version known to be false. We resolved to learn from Konduz and do all we could to avoid a repeat. (Tragically, in 2015 yet another air strike, again in Konduz, killed scores when a *Médicins Sans Frontières* medical clinic was attacked by SOCOM AC130 gunships.)

As ISAF struggled with the fallout from Konduz, we faced yet another political crisis involving our coalition allies. In August, a Polish Army officer, Captain Daniel Ambrozinski, had been killed by a roadside bomb in Ghazni. At the captain's funeral, the Polish Army chief of staff, General Waldemar Skrzypczak, bitterly criticized the Polish government for failing to properly equip his soldiers. The Ministry of Defense struck back hard, forcing the general's resignation and igniting a furious debate about Poland's role in Afghanistan. In the end the Poles would stay, but our Polish battlegroup would labor under intense media and political scrutiny from Warsaw that made a difficult mission almost intolerable. Like the Germans, and many other contingents, the Poles were forced to limit their operations to reduce casualties to an absolute minimum.

In Bagram we had our own problems. On September 8 in the Ganjgal Valley in Kunar province, a 13-man U.S. Marine Corps ETT accompanying Afghan forces was ambushed by an estimated 100 insurgents, firing from high ground and surrounding the friendly force on three sides. Two U.S. Army Afghan Border Police advisors were also present. In a desperate four-hour battle, which saw the U.S./ Afghan force pinned down without effective artillery, mortar or close air support, the handful of American troops fought heroically to enable the larger Afghan force to disengage. Ganjgal was thus no victory, but rather a fighting withdrawal. Five

Americans were killed along with eight Afghans. Almost every American and many Afghan soldiers were also wounded.

Within 24 hours the story had gone international, not least because a reporter for McClatchy News, Jonathan Landay, had accompanied the unit and survived the battle. His reporting, and the account of Army Captain Will Swenson (the U.S. advisor to the Afghan Border Police there that day), harshly criticized the lack of support from a nearby Army battalion, the 1st Battalion, 32nd Infantry, an element of the 4th Brigade, 4th Infantry Division—one of our subordinate units. An added complication was that, to outside observers, the story appeared to suggest that Army troops may have failed to support Marines engaged in a desperate, life-or-death struggle. Three Marines and an accompanying Navy medical corpsman, moving at the front of the formation, had been cut off and subsequently killed. The families wanted answers. The Marines wanted answers. Congress wanted answers. And so did we.

A few days after the fight, General Scaparrotti called me in and asked me to conduct an investigation, standard procedure in matters like this. At first, I demurred. While I appreciated his trust and confidence, I worried that assigning his senior communications staff officer to investigate such an explosive incident might not play well in the press when the investigation was leaked, as it surely would be. The implication might be that his personal, in-house "spin doctor" had been assigned to ensure "the right result." I also warned Scap that if given the mission, I would go wherever the facts led me, without fear or favor. To his great credit his response was "that's exactly what I want." Orders were orders, and I started in.

Much to my relief, I was assigned two military attorneys, one Marine and one Army, as well as Marine Colonel James Werth, who would serve as my co-lead. An infantry officer, Werth was an Afghanistan veteran flown in from Okinawa, and he would prove an invaluable partner. We left immediately and flew north to Kunar to interview the survivors and key personalities. Our first stop was Forward Operating Base Joyce, home to 1/32 Infantry. Our first interview was with Captain Swenson.

At the appointed time Swenson shambled into the room and sat down heavily in the cracked, plastic lawn chair provided. Of medium height, lean and worn out, the young captain eyed us warily. I'd never seen an Army officer with longer, more unkempt hair. His uniform looked like it hadn't been washed in a month, and he wore civilian sneakers instead of Army boots. There was no salute, no handshake, and Swenson was clearly unawed by the presence of two full colonels. Wearily, he crossed his arms, and said, "So I guess you're the guys sent here to cover this thing up."

My immediate reaction was one of compassion. Here was a man who had lived through a searing tragedy and had been changed by it. Slowly, we pulled his story out from him. A veteran of Iraq, and on his second tour in Afghanistan, Swenson had requested an extension on this tour to stay with his Afghans. Along with the

Marine major commanding the ETT, he had coordinated for support with staff officers from 1/32. On the battlefield, he had effectively assumed command of the battle when the major went down with a gunshot wound. He had begged for support again and again as soldiers, Marines and Afghans fell all around him. His right-hand man, Army Sergeant First Class Kenneth Westbrook, was shot in the neck and mortally wounded. Assisted by Marine Corporal Dakota Meyer, Swenson roamed the battlefield under intense fire to rescue Afghan and American wounded.

Over the next 10 days, we toured the battlefield from the air and interviewed another 48 witnesses. The real story began to emerge. The 1/32 battalion commander was on leave in the States, leaving the executive officer, a senior major, in acting command. The battalion's S3 operations officer, with one rifle company, had been detached for a mission farther north in a place called Barge Matal. The operations sergeant major billet in the command post was unfilled. The fire support officer, an artillery captain, had been assigned other duties along with his senior NCO, leaving both key positions vacant. The battle captain in the operations center, recently fired from another job, had been given no training and was brand new. This was not a high performing unit.

The operation had begun before first light and by 0530 the formation was in a fight. A large ridgeline lay between the 1/32 headquarters and the valley nearby, obstructing line-of-sight radio calls. Throughout the battle, Swenson was forced to relay his calls for fire through the 1/32 scouts, positioned along the ridgeline and overwatching with their snipers. In the operations center, an artillery staff sergeant and an Air Force enlisted controller monitored the traffic and did all they could to help. At every turn they were blocked by commissioned officers who could not be bothered to take an interest in the battle, which they dismissed as a "routine contact." The acting battalion commander bore most of the blame. Though an experienced field grade officer and staff college graduate, he repeatedly denied calls for mortar and artillery fires and failed to alert his higher headquarters, delaying urgently needed helicopter support for almost two hours. During most of the battle, he remained in his office. By the time the brigade and CJTF staffs became aware of the fight and how critical it had become, the battle was over.

During our investigation two names surfaced again and again: Captain Swenson and Corporal Meyer. Several veterans of the battle stopped in mid-sentence, at a loss for words to continue as they struggled to describe their heroic actions that day. Our final report came down hard on the officers who had failed to support them, and they were duly cashiered, their careers ruined. But we also called out Swenson and Meyer for their exalted heroism, describing their actions as "worthy of the highest recognition." Both would later be awarded the Medal of Honor, while Marine Lieutenant Ademola Fabayo and Marine Staff Sergeant Juan Rodriguez-Chavez were awarded the Navy Cross. Disillusioned, Swenson left the Army.[8] I could understand his decision. Despite our technology and training, when it mattered most, his local chain of command had failed to come through for him and his men.

There were no excuses for these failures, but our overall approach to the war in Afghanistan played a role. With the success of the Surge in Iraq, the conflict there was winding down, but Afghanistan had not (and never would) see the kind of resources we had eventually committed to Iraq, though it was larger both in population and in territory. Artillery was especially in short supply and often farmed out in two- or even one-gun sections on isolated COPs, under junior leaders and lacking proper fire direction centers. General Scap pushed hard for more artillery but was rebuffed by the Pentagon.

We were also hamstrung by the requirement to man small, isolated outposts scattered across Regional Command-East, many located in terrain that made them all but indefensible. Early in the deployment, Scaparrotti had requested that many of the most remote and indefensible COPs be closed. Beyond supporting distance and lightly manned, they were vulnerable to an attack by insurgent forces, who could mass at will in almost overwhelming numbers. Just such an attack had happened the year before, at Combat Outpost Wanat in Nuristan province. Though its soldiers had held their ground and fought doggedly, nine soldiers were killed and 27 wounded of the 48 present. Subsequent investigations had tarnished the battalion, brigade and division commanders, effectively ending their careers. Bowing to pressure from President Karzai, General McChrystal denied most of these requests.

Our turn came on October 3, when, under similar circumstances, COP Keating (also in Nuristan) was attacked at first light by some 300–400 Taliban fighters. Defended by 53 American soldiers from the 3rd Squadron, 61st Cavalry, along with two Latvian advisors and 20 Afghan soldiers, Keating was surrounded by high ground. Observation Post (OP) Fritsche, with another 19 cavalrymen, stood on a nearby hilltop about 2km away and 2,100 feet higher. In previous weeks the COP had been hit many times, but never on this scale. Moving into position under cover of darkness from staging areas just across the Pakistani border, the assault force managed to infiltrate the perimeter and cut the firing wires of some of the claymore mines positioned there. At the outset, the Afghan soldiers holding one part of the perimeter fled, creating an opening quickly exploited by the enemy. Heavy machine guns posted on the mountainsides killed or drove out soldiers manning the observation towers. Accurate mortar and RPG fires suppressed the mortar pit and damaged several vehicles mounting heavy weapons.

Early in the fight the enemy gained entry to the COP, driving the defenders into a small foothold on one end called "the Alamo." In the CJTF-82 operations

---

8   After a break in service, Swenson rejoined the Army and is today a lieutenant colonel.

center, Lieutenant Andrew Bunderman's voice from Keating could be heard over the TACSAT channel.[9] Calmly, the young officer reported, "We are in our final defensive positions. We are being overrun."

Minutes later, an "aerial weapons team" (two Apache attack helicopters launched from Jalalabad) finally arrived on station. As the COP came into view, the pilots were horrified to see it on fire, with flames and smoke rising high into the air. As hundreds of enemy fighters streamed down the mountainsides, Bunderman spoke directly to the gunships. "We are barely hanging on. Shoot any enemy you see moving inside the COP." Incredulous, the senior aviator refused. Bunderman persisted. The Apaches opened up with Hellfire missiles and their 30mm chain guns, assisted by Air Force F-15s pounding the high ground. 155mm howitzers from Forward Operating Base Bostick, some 30km away, fired in support but with minimal effect given the extreme range. Braving intense fire from insurgent DShK 12.7mm heavy machine guns, the Apaches killed scores of Taliban until, low on fuel and ammunition and suffering heavy battle damage, they were forced to return to base. Others replaced them.

All day long the defenders fought, supported by small numbers of available helicopters and by Air Force aircraft, which unfortunately could not drop ordnance close to friendly troops. Foot by foot the defenders pushed the attackers back, finally ejecting them from the COP. Ground reinforcements were unable to reach Keating until nightfall. As at Wanat, the price of such heroism was high. Eight Americans were killed and 23 wounded. Although more than 150 attackers were killed, with many more wounded, we had come close to seeing an entire American unit wiped out. Only the courage of the defenders and aircrews had prevented catastrophe. Sixty-six soldiers were later decorated for valor, including nine Silver Stars and one Distinguished Service Cross. Two staff sergeants, Clinton Romesha and Ty Carter, were later awarded the Medal of Honor. Six Apache pilots and one F-15 pilot were awarded the Distinguished Flying Cross.

In Kabul, the decision was made to extract the unit and destroy the COP with air strikes. While a tactical victory, the fight at COP Keating (later dubbed "the battle of Kamdesh" for a nearby village) carried strategic consequences. McChrystal's tactical directive and unwillingness to close down isolated outposts were criticized again, while opponents of our involvement in Afghanistan trumpeted our losses as proof that we could not prevail. Back at Bagram, the view in the CAG was that the kinetic fight was over, but the battle of narratives was about to begin.

There were two stories in play. One focused on our losses and was sharply critical of the commanders at every level. The other celebrated the heroism of the defenders of COP Keating and their ultimate victory against overwhelming odds. One or the other would win out. My advice to General Scap was to find the most prominent

---

9   Bunderman would later be awarded the Distinguished Service Cross.

American journalist in country and go "open kimono" to show and explain what had happened in detail, holding nothing back. I urged him to grant quick access to the soldiers themselves, trusting that their innate honesty and authenticity would bring out the real story. Our outstanding public affairs officer, Lieutenant Colonel Clarence Counts, concurred. It was easy for us to proffer advice. As the commanding general, Scap had to decide.

As it happened, prominent NBC broadcast journalist Jim Miklashevsky was in Kabul and the next day he flew to Bagram at General Scap's invitation. Miklashevsky was a seasoned professional and he would in any case sniff out misdirection or "spin." His reporting lauded the grit and valor of the soldiers who fought at COP Keating, while highlighting the difficulties in supporting dozens of small outposts across Afghanistan's vast distances and daunting terrain. Subsequent investigations identified areas for improvement but largely mirrored press reporting. Any battle with loss of life invites criticism, a fact that all commanders must expect. Here, it could have been much worse.

In early autumn, my son Chris, a private fresh out of the Infantry School and airborne training, arrived in Afghanistan. His unit, the 2nd Battalion, 503rd Parachute Infantry, passed through Bagram on its way to its new AOR in Wardak province. (The battalion was commanded by Lieutenant Colonel Matt McFarlane, my old A Company commander in 2 Panther.) I was glad to see him, and we spent a couple of golden hours together before he boarded a Chinook and flew out to his new home.

Early on, I caught a bird to go visit him. His world was a small combat outpost in the Hindu Kush, called "Blackhawk," at 8,000 feet. His COP was surrounded by high ground on all sides, he washed his uniform in a bucket, and he slept in a timber hooch he and his buddies had made themselves, surrounded by sandbags piled high. The food was the worst I'd ever seen in more than 30 years in the Army. During the day he patrolled the mountains and villages. At night he took his turn in the towers. They gave me an hour alone and at first, I almost didn't recognize my own child. A strong, good-sized kid, they made him a machine gunner right off the bat. He was proud of that. But the unit was understrength, and there was no assistant gunner. So, he carried the gun, and 700 rounds, and the spare barrel bag, along with all his other kit. His equipment weighed out at well over 100lbs, which he "humped" at 10,000 feet and above, sometimes for hours each day. He had lost 30 pounds in 30 days. He looked at me and said softly, almost in a whisper, "Dad, I'm not sure I can do this." I hugged him and said, "Don't worry, it's the altitude. You'll get used to it soon. You'll be fine."

Over the next weeks and months, I found myself, more and more, stopping by the operations center. When Chris's unit got into a TIC (a "troops in contact"), I couldn't help it—a cold shudder ran up my spine. I did my best not to show emotion. When there were casualties, it was worse. I knew someone would call or come see me with bad news, so I never asked. I'd go through the next 12 hours in an agony of suspense. And now I began to see. I thought I understood the anguish of a soldier's parent. But I didn't. Not really. Now, I had my own skin in the game.

It was the hardest experience of my life. Occasionally—not too often—I'd check up on Chris. "He's a good soldier," his officer said. "He's tough, doesn't complain. We had a big fight the other day. He didn't hesitate. We're lucky to have him." On my next visit, he looked better. He'd put on a few pounds, he smiled more, and he was tight with his squad. They were great young Americans—hard, tough, committed, and fiercely caring about each other. The platoon sergeant, on his fourth combat tour, was a quiet, competent professional. The lieutenant, the son of a general, was doing fine. I knew there were no guarantees. But I felt Chris was in good hands.

One night, they came and got me up at 0100. "Sir," the runner said, "it's your son's captain. He says it's urgent." It took me a few minutes to get to the secure phone, and I died a little bit with each step. The young captain came on the line. "Sir, I wanted to tell you right away. Your son was involved in a vehicle rollover up in the mountains. He's a little banged up, but he's okay. I thought you'd want to know." At first, I wanted to scream over the phone. But then I realized he was young, trying to command in combat, with the weight of the world on his shoulders. I said, "Thanks son, I sure appreciate the heads up." Later, when the captain was gravely wounded and flown out of theater, I said a prayer, and asked myself, "Where do we get such men?"

As the year wound on, I'd hear bits and pieces. Chris's squad went out for 24 hours, but the winter weather moved in and the helos couldn't fly. Trapped up high, they were out for days, the squad leader went down with frostbite, and they ran out of food. They were lucky not to freeze to death. (That winter, an ISAF patrol working above 10,000 feet found a Taliban unit of 12 men in a cave—all frozen to death. In Afghanistan, even nature was an implacable enemy.) On another operation, Chris was knocked off his feet by a ricochet. His body armor stopped the round, and as he lay there stunned, an NCO grabbed him by the scruff of the neck and ran him out of danger. He held on to his weapon, though. He was proud of that. And I thanked God for that sergeant.

All of this he kept from his mother, and I did too. But she had been doing this for years, and without knowing the details, she knew. She knew her baby boy was fighting for his life, and for his friends. She knew he was in danger. She knew that call could come any day. On Skype, Beverly was invariably upbeat and supportive. At night when she was alone, it was sometimes too much, and the tears would come. And I thanked God for her, too, and for all like her. Chris would serve his year in combat and come home safely, after more narrow escapes. Today, he is an infantry captain, living his own history. I will be forever grateful for the time we served together, and for the great gift of his survival.[10]

---

10 Chris Hooker is now an infantry captain serving with the 3rd Infantry Division, after an initial

Far more than in Iraq, I conducted "battlefield circulation" via aircraft, sometimes accompanying General Scap but often on my own. This usually involved flying in a Black Hawk, escorted by Apaches. Though I had accumulated many hundreds of hours flying in both Army helicopters and Air Force fixed-wing aircraft, the weather and mountainous terrain in Afghanistan, combined with an active enemy, made flying more hazardous than I'd ever experienced in my career. Just how dangerous was brought home on October 13, 2009, when one of my officers, an Army aviator himself, burst into my office.

"Sir, one of our RC-12s is overdue and missing."

I knew this meant that a "Guardrail," an electronic warfare aircraft, had likely crashed or been shot down. For sure, we'd have to figure out how to manage the story. But first, we needed to find the crew and aircraft, with its classified and highly sensitive equipment. Aviation "flight following" had lost the aircraft's track somewhere in north-eastern Afghanistan, but the precise location was unknown.

Days went by as the search continued, with rapidly diminishing hope that any aircrew had survived. Finally, on October 19, the wreckage was discovered at 17,000 feet in Nuristan province—one of the most inhospitable places on earth. Almost certainly the plane had flown into the mountain. The mission now was recovery, not rescue.

The first attempt involved a Black Hawk with four soldiers plus aircrew, who flew to the site to recover the bodies and sensitive items. Hovering on the steep mountainside at 17,000 feet (dangerously high for a Black Hawk with troops), the pilot experienced a sudden loss of power and the bird went down. No one was killed, but the helo was now unflyable. Now we had two aircraft down, three bodies, and seven live soldiers stranded in Indian country, at altitudes so high that flying required oxygen. So far, we had kept the incident under wraps. But at any moment, the story might break, and the Taliban would be sure to both claim credit for the loss of two coalition aircraft—and begin hunting for the survivors. Now, time was the enemy, along with everything else.

Our aviators hastily scrambled a second attempt, this time with the much larger and more powerful Chinook and another rescue party. This effort successfully recovered all personnel, living and dead, along with the classified equipment from the RC-12. On subsequent flights, as we zipped through mountain passes in the dead of night, buffeted by high winds which threatened to slam our helo against the mountainside, I pondered the fate of these soldiers. There, but for the grace of God, we too might end up.

---

tour as a lieutenant in the 82nd Airborne Division. His younger brother David also served as an enlisted paratrooper, in Iraq, and is today an infantry officer and first lieutenant in the 82nd Airborne Division.

Later that autumn, I took a call from one of our brigade information operations officers. "What is it with you guys up there?" said the young major. "You're going about this all wrong." He was one of those bright young officers that old colonels usually find vaguely annoying—irreverent, bright, full of ideas, and always pressing the envelope. "Slow down," I said, "and tell me what's on your mind."

I was quite proud of what we had accomplished in a short period of time. We had gone to no end of trouble to train our Afghans, provide culturally appropriate program content, ensure full coverage of our vast area of operations, and come up with innovative "public service" messages that communicated our key themes and messages. More than 50 officers and NCOs worked for me, and I thought they were breaking new ground. Now, here was this young upstart who thought he knew better.

I had to admit the kid was unusually gifted. He had left the Army after five years, worked in the private sector, and ended up as a junior White House speechwriter. After 9/11 he came back in, made major and found himself assigned to the new IO career field. His assistant was similarly eccentric. A master sergeant, he had been born and raised in Pakistan, spoke fluent Urdu and Pashto, and wore a flowing beard and local Afghan dress. No one quite knew what to do with these two. Still, they seemed to know what they were about.

The major continued. "You keep sending us this recorded programming. It's all great, except for one thing. It's all meant for the men. And Afghan men aren't sitting around in the home all day listening to our broadcasts. They're out farming or working or fighting. Our listeners are the women. They have a lot of influence over their young men. And we don't have a damned thing to say to them."

I felt foolish. Because we never saw or interacted with Afghan women, we never realized they were there, playing key roles in Afghan tribal society from behind the scenes. The major's insight was blindingly obvious. How had we missed it?

I knew we had a big problem that we had to fix. "What do you suggest?" He came right back at me. "I spoke with a female engagement team (these were teams composed of female soldiers and officers employed to reach out to Afghan women). The Afghan women want to know about health care. They won't go to male doctors, and all the female ones have been killed or run off. We need to get a female Afghan physician on the air ASAP, and she needs to talk about pre-natal care. We're losing a lot of babies and mothers in childbirth. We do that, we're in business."

Sometimes—most of the time—you have to get out of the way and let the talent run. "Right," I said. "You're in charge. Move out and tell me what you need. We'll get it for you." Within a week, the major had female doctors broadcasting for two hours a day, not just in his brigade area but across all of eastern Afghanistan. We found the money, worked the contracts, coordinated with higher, and ran interference.

The results were spectacular. In only six months, the incidence of infant mortality and death in childbirth declined by 50 percent across RC-East. Units became aware that half of Afghan society was out there, unseen, and that it mattered. Local politicians picked up on it. Afghan attitudes changed measurably. Tipline calls to our radio stations shot up. Most important by far was that lives were saved. Lots of lives.

My young major had given me a lot to ponder. Somehow, after all our pre-deployment training, hours of cultural awareness briefings, mission analysis and pre-mission rehearsals, we had missed something vital and important. We'd been wearing blinders without knowing it. Years of experience in Afghanistan hadn't exposed it, nor had our doctrine, lessons learned systems or transitions with outgoing units. Our commanders at all levels were tough and hardnosed and knew how to fight. But this was a game we had to go back to school on.

On December 1, 2009, President Obama traveled to West Point to speak to the nation. There he announced his decision, after months of internal review, to send another 30,000 troops to Afghanistan—to be withdrawn in only 18 months. I watched the speech from a conference room at Bagram, accompanied by a number of Afghan generals. They were not encouraged. On the contrary, from their perspective the president had just put a date certain on our presence in Afghanistan. All the Taliban had to do now was wait us out.

The speech illuminated the central problem for us. It contained no roadmap, no specific change in strategy beyond more troops. They would certainly be useful, and once on the ground our ability to secure broader areas and kill more enemy would in fact improve. But the Taliban would continue to enjoy sanctuary inside Pakistan, and weak and corrupt governance in Kabul would continue to hamstring our efforts to hand off to the Afghans. Years later, they would still be unable to stand on their own without massive U.S. and international assistance. We could hold our own. But a decisive victory remained out of reach.

The fighting season had now ended, as field operations in the cruel Afghan winter were largely suspended due to the weather. As we neared the middle of our year-long deployment, we began to rotate soldiers home, in staggered waves, for their two-week mid-tour leaves. We hoped for a quiet holiday season, but our relative calm was shattered on December 30. Late in the afternoon, a staff officer pulled me aside. "Hey, sir—Camp Chapman just got blown up. I mean, blown up!"

Chapman was a small CIA base in Khowst province, close to the border with Pakistan and adjacent to Forward Operating Base Salerno where the airborne brigade from Alaska was headquartered. Though located in our battlespace, as a CIA activity Chapman did not fall under CJTF-82. On that day, an Arab intelligence asset, Humam Khalil Abu-Mulal al-Balawi, was driven across the border to meet with agency intelligence officers at the CIA base. Supposedly vetted at higher levels, al-Bulawi was in fact a committed jihadist. Waved through three successive checkpoints without search, he was met on arrival by a crowd of U.S. intelligence officers. Upon exiting his vehicle, he detonated a suicide vest, killing Jennifer Lynn Matthews, the chief of base, and eight others. The deputy chief of Kabul Station was also present and was gravely wounded.

I thought back to my experiences in Iraq and wondered how such basic security precautions could be ignored. There, even Iraqi generals escorted by American officers were searched (we searched the U.S. escorts as well to save face for all concerned). Unusually, Matthews was a targeter, not an experienced field operations officer. Overruling the objections of her security chief, she ordered normal security protocols to be relaxed to "build trust." It was a fatal mistake. Even now, a decade into the Global War on Terror, we could still drop our guard. Chapman represented one of the worst losses of life in CIA history. We grieved with our agency comrades and redoubled our watchfulness.

As I had been on other combat deployments, I was uneasy about the activities of special operations units operating in our battlespace. As in Iraq, they continued to pursue a raiding strategy, conducting multiple operations most nights to capture or kill enemy "high value targets." These night raids infuriated the Afghan population and government at the same time we were trying to build trust and confidence, as accidental killings were commonplace. Coordination with conventional counterparts was often notional at best and our battalion and brigade commanders grew increasingly vocal and frustrated. Many of these operations were "dry holes."

On February 12, 2010, we awoke to news of a night raid gone bad in Gardez, in Paktia province. Initial reporting seemed garbled, but the gist was that a SOF unit had fired on and killed two Afghan males before entering a compound in search of their target. Inside, they had found the bodies of three women in a back room. According to the unit leader, they had been dead for some time and had already been "prepared for burial." The commander surmised that he had stumbled upon an "honor killing." At first light, they had departed, leaving the local U.S. battalion commander to cope with an enraged local population. The target of the raid, a named Taliban leader, was not present.

One of my Afghan cultural advisors was from Gardez and had been in touch with family members via cell phone. Pulling me aside, he insisted, "This is not the truth. The men were not Taliban, and the women were shot by your soldiers. Please do not put this false story out. You will regret it." Alerting General Scap that the first report might be wrong, I then called Rear Admiral Greg Smith, a career public affairs officer and ISAF's strategic communications chief. "We have a disconnect here," I reported. "Before we comment publicly, I think we need to sort this out."

At midday, I participated in a teleconference with representatives from ISAF, RC-East and the special operations task force. The raid commander was present and stuck to his story. "I've been doing this a while," he told us. "I know rigor mortis when I see it. Don't let the Taliban spin this against us." A team from ISAF was hurriedly flown to Gardez to conduct a cursory investigation, which quickly affirmed the SOF version of events. Our Afghan counterparts, on the other hand, told a very different story.

Their investigators, led by an Afghan general, interviewed many of the local Afghans present on the scene. The evening had begun with a party to celebrate the birth of a baby boy, hosted by two brothers—a government prosecutor and the local chief of police. Both had enjoyed long and close relationships with U.S. military and civilian officials and were well known to us. Hearing a disturbance and fearing a Taliban attack, the host ventured outside to see what was happening. He was immediately shot and killed. His brother then attempted to drag him inside the qalat and was also killed. During the firing, three women sheltering in the front of the structure—two of them pregnant—were also hit by gunfire and killed. Far from being "bound and gagged," as ISAF reported later, they were immediately prepared for burial *after* the shootings in accordance with Afghan tradition, which involves binding the legs and jaw of females with cloth wrappings. Most disturbing of all, many witnesses described the raiders as prying the bullets out of the women and from the walls to remove forensic evidence. The U.S. battalion commander responsible for the area, after consulting with local elders, expressed his confidence in the Afghan version of events.

I had learned long before that bad things happen in war, and that accidental and unintended civilian casualties cannot always be avoided. This seemed to go well beyond that. I urged Smith not to run with the sanitized version of the story, which was almost certainly fabricated. To do so would not only infuriate the very people we were striving to protect. It would endanger the American soldiers who must live and work in the area throughout their year-long tour. Though generous and hospitable to a fault, Afghan tribesmen are also remorseless when looking for revenge. Unless justice was seen to be done, they would seek retribution.

Despite our pleading, ISAF released a press statement soon after, repeating the "honor killing" story line, vividly describing the "firefight" and announcing that the raid force had made a "gruesome discovery" upon entering the compound. Despite mounting evidence to the contrary, ISAF persisted for some six weeks, hotly denying any cover-up. Major media outlets like CNN and the *New York Times* repeated the story uncritically. Finally, an exhaustive account of the Gardez shooting, incorporating statements from dozens of eyewitnesses, ran in the London *Sunday Times*. Only then did ISAF revise its narrative. Vice Admiral McRaven, the overall SOF commander, was dispatched to Gardez to publicly apologize. Years later, internal investigations would peter out with no disciplinary action taken against any of the participants.

Although perhaps the worst, the Gardez incident was not isolated. Mistaken targeting and collateral civilian damage would dog special operations throughout the campaign, working against our efforts to win over the population. So far as I could see, there was little accountability. In Gardez, the work of years was destroyed in a single night. Few Afghans there would ever trust ISAF again.

As our long year ground on, we tended to focus on these spectacular miscues, but every day our units worked ceaselessly to protect the population, support development, and enable effective governance at the sub-district, district and provincial level. Junior leaders shouldered immense responsibilities while company, battalion and brigade commanders helped to build roads, clinics, and schools even as they fought a tough and resourceful enemy. Media reports often described Taliban "shadow governments" in virtually every Afghan district and province, as though they had everywhere displaced existing governance structures. In fact, intensive polling showed that confidence in the Afghan security forces was strong and getting stronger. Compared to earlier wars our casualties were light, a tribute to our leaders, our technology and the experience garnered from years of counterinsurgency. Yet each week, and sometimes each day, we lost soldiers. Every fatality in that god-forsaken place struck home.

At least once per week, MSG Keane and I would fly out to visit our units to get out of the headquarters and see our leaders and soldiers where they lived and worked. Although routine, Keane never allowed complacency to set in. Now well over 50, he carried an enormous rucksack filled with medical supplies, claymore mines, hand grenades, smoke grenades, extra water and rations and extra magazines for his rifle and pistol. Somehow, he had even managed to obtain a PRC-90 survival radio, normally issued only to pilots.

On every flight, prior to boarding the aircraft, Nick would give me the same pre-mission briefing. A veteran of half a dozen combat tours, including three in Afghanistan, he wasn't kidding. "Boss, if our bird goes down, we'll stay with it. Running for the hills will only mean we'll die tired. We'll dismount the door guns and I'll put out my claymores. And then we'll fight like hell. ISAF will be along to recover us. We've just got to stay alive until they do." I once asked him why he was so confident we would survive a crash in the mountains. "Because the great spirit told me. I don't plan on leaving the earthplane until I'm at least a hundred!"

On one such junket we flew north to the Shuryak valley in Kunar province to visit the 2nd Battalion, 12th Infantry, commanded by Lieutenant Colonel Brian Pearl, a bright young officer I had known in the Pentagon. The 2/12 headquarters was located in a breathtaking setting on a green, terraced hillside, surrounded by spectacular, forested mountains, snow-capped year-round. Escorted by two Apache gunships, our Black Hawk set us down at 1300. We spent most of the afternoon with Pearl and his staff discussing the installation of a new AM radio station in his battlespace.

Soon after dark, we moved to the helicopter landing zone to be extracted. The night was so black I couldn't see my hand in front of my face. Our helos arrived and set down only yards away, with only the soft green light of the pilot's night vision goggles visible; all other flying lights were extinguished. Moments later, as we climbed out of the valley, intense ground fire arced across the sky, while a heavy salvo of mortar rounds struck the 2/12 COP, injuring several soldiers. For our flight crews, blacked out and flying under night vision goggles through treacherous mountain passes, this was almost routine. We owed them much. During our long years in Afghanistan, we would not lose a single jet to enemy fire, but we lost dozens of helicopters and aircrews. As in Vietnam, they would prove to be our lifeline.

Three weeks before the end of my tour, I was summoned to Kabul to confer with counterparts at ISAF headquarters. My team arranged for a helo flight and coordinated for ground travel from the airfield to the headquarters, a routine movement. Early that morning, matters at Bagram caused me to reschedule my flight and I missed the ground convoy. Shortly after, a suicide bomber rammed the formation and detonated his weapon, a massive car bomb packed with 1,600kg of high explosive. The attack destroyed five U.S. military vehicles and 13 civilian cars, killing 18 and wounding 52, mostly innocent civilians. Two colonels (one American and one Canadian), two lieutenant colonels and two NCOs died in the blast. It was one of the deadliest suicide attacks ever in Afghanistan. I thanked my guardian angel, and marveled—not for the first time—at how often trivial things can turn out to mean life and death in war.

The very next day it was our turn at Bagram. So far, we had been left largely alone. Except for a rocket strike soon after our arrival which had killed two and wounded six, we had been left unmolested. That changed on May 19, when we woke long before sunrise to the sounds of small arms fire crackling around the perimeter, punctuated by the steady, dull crump of mortar rounds. Bagram was under attack.

Moving in under cover of darkness, four assault groups managed to infiltrate into position just outside the wire. Many were fighters dressed in American battle dress uniforms, some wearing suicide vests. As was common, a large vehicle rigged with explosives attempted to breach the main gate. Alert security guards killed the driver before he could detonate the massive weapon. Before first light, the heavily armed attackers attempted to scale the "HESCO bastion" walls surrounding much of the Bagram perimeter (actually collapsible wire mesh containers filled with earth and rubble, about six feet tall and topped with concertina wire). The obstacles were stout and hard to negotiate, and most of the enemy fighters died in the wire.

By happenstance, two fully armed Apaches had just returned to base following a canceled mission, arriving only minutes after the attack began. Alerted by the base defense force, they turned their fury on the Taliban, wiping out much of the assault force. A few insurgents managed to infiltrate a trailer park inside the perimeter, but they were quickly located and killed. Desultory firing continued for several hours before the last survivors were located and exterminated. No prisoners were taken. In a tragic denouement, a National Guard platoon pursuing a withdrawing insurgent wandered into a minefield. One Guardsman lost a leg after stepping on a mine. In all, one American was killed with nine wounded. On balance, we came off well. Had the enemy managed to get inside the base undetected, the death toll would have been much higher.

By now we were on "short final" and busy preparing to hand over to the 101st, our replacements. I was chagrined to learn that our sophisticated communications organization would not be carried over, as the 101st would revert to a more traditional organization. Sadly, our many radio stations, trained DJs and pollsters, and cultural advisors would quickly wither away. This was a tangible example of "not fighting the war for 10 years but fighting for one year 10 times." Painfully learned lessons would have to be relearned over and over again as units rotated in and out. We took great pains to capture our experiences in writing and publish them in leading military journals, but to no avail. General Scaparrotti had broken new ground with his innovative approach to counterinsurgency, and we had accomplished much. Now, most of our work would be shunted aside.

As we approached our handover, a media storm erupted at ISAF that would threaten the entire war effort. Earlier in the year, *Rolling Stone* reporter Michael Hastings had asked to embed with some of our units. We advised General Scap against it. Hastings was young, a sensationalist with an agenda, and far from the sober, experienced journalists we normally worked with.[11] There was no upside that we could see. Scap agreed, and Hastings went to Kabul where he succeeded in worming his way into General McChrystal's inner circle.

There he was embedded with the ISAF commander's personal office, staffed almost exclusively with officers from the special operations community. Accompanying the general and his party to Paris for a meeting with NATO leaders, Hastings took notes as McChrystal and his inner circle—mostly young, exuberant SOF alumnae—relaxed their guard over copious off-duty drinks. The resulting article, "The Runaway General," contained insulting quotes about President Obama, Vice President Biden, Special Representative for Afghanistan and Pakistan Ambassador Richard Holbrook, Ambassador Karl Eikenberry (the chief of mission in Kabul) and National Security Advisor Jim Jones, a retired Marine four-star. It seemed almost no one escaped their ridicule. McChrystal was immediately summoned to Washington and, after a brief meeting with President Obama, relieved of his command and retired. He had worn his four stars for barely a year.

We had now seen two successive ISAF commanders fired in 12 months. McChrystal's dismissal and the resulting furor were at best a distraction and at worst damaging to the campaign we had all worked and sacrificed for. I felt pride in what we had accomplished in RC-East. But I could not say we were winning in Afghanistan. This debacle clearly set us back. The Petraeus-Crocker team was reassembled and sent to Afghanistan to salvage what it could. This was a self-inflicted wound that need not have been.

At the one-year mark we handed over to our replacements and boarded the planes to return home. The flight from Kabul to Washington seemed to take forever and I had plenty of time for reflection. Since 9/11, I had been at war for 10 years, in the Pentagon, in Iraq, at the White House, and in Afghanistan. What had we achieved?

It was true that there had been no repeat of 9/11, and that meant a lot. But in both wars, we faced two insurmountable problems. We had tied ourselves to host

---

11 Hastings, troubled by chronic drug use, would die in a car crash at 33 in 2013.

nation governments whose incapacity and corruption were themselves prime drivers of the conflict, and despite enormous efforts we could not fix them. And we faced an enemy who fought from sanctuary with the most powerful weapon of all—time. Eventually, the American public and our allies lost faith and began to waver. We had made the same mistakes in Vietnam. But we had not really learned. In time our sojourn in Afghanistan would end in failure and my younger son would lead his paratroopers in the evacuation from Kabul. But that is another story.

A few weeks later, I stood in front of a room full of family, friends, and classmates at the Army Navy Club. As they read out my retirement orders, I couldn't help but feel flooded with memories. Many were painful, but even more I felt grateful. I stood before the crowd, trying to say something memorable, but at a loss. For 36 years, I had worn a uniform, traveled the world, and attempted hard and difficult things, always in the company of wonderful men and women. I knew I would miss them deeply. We had not always succeeded, but we had done our best, to save lives, to keep the peace, to do the right thing, and to serve as faithfully as we could. It was enough. It was more than enough. That night, I was conscious of many successes, but also failures and defeats. I had come farther than I expected, and perhaps deserved, the consequences of both virtues and flaws bound up in the same man.

Beverly and I drove home that night in silence, holding hands. Then I took off my uniform and hung it in the closet forever.

I live in retirement now, in the deep South, near an Army post. Often, the sound of artillery firing or barking machine guns carries across the heavy summer air. If I listen hard, I tell myself I can hear the jaunty tones of reveille at first light, and the sad, sweet notes of taps, lulling young troopers to sleep. My task has now passed to my sons. But I think I'll always be a soldier.

Resume of Service Career

Years of commissioned service   Over 29
Total years of service   Over 31

Military Schools Attended

Infantry Officer Basic Course
Infantry Officer Advanced Course
Army Command and General Staff College
The National War College

Educational Degrees

United States Military Academy: B.S. Degree, General Engineering
The National War College: M.S. Degree, National Security Studies
University of Virginia: M.A. Degree, Foreign Affairs
University of Virginia: Ph.D. Degree, Foreign Affairs

Major Duty Assignments

Oct 75–July 77	Enlisted Service
Jul 81–Oct 81	Student Officer, Infantry Officer Basic Course
Oct 81–Nov 82	Rifle, then Antitank Platoon Leader, 1st Battalion, 504th Parachute Infantry Regiment, 82nd Airborne Division, Fort Bragg, North Carolina
Nov 82–Nov 83	Antitank Platoon Leader, Company E (Antiarmor), 504th Parachute Infantry Regiment, 82nd Airborne Division, Fort Bragg, North Carolina
Oct 83–Nov 83	Brigade Liaison Officer, 1st Brigade, 82nd Airborne Division, Operation *Urgent Fury*, Grenada

Nov 83–Oct 84	Executive Officer, Company E (Antiarmor), 504th Parachute Infantry Regiment, 82nd Airborne Division, Fort Bragg, North Carolina
Oct 84–May 85	Student Officer, Infantry Officer Advanced Course
May 85–Jan 86	Adjutant/S1, 1st Battalion, 1st Aviation Brigade (Air Assault), U.S. Army Aviation Center, Fort Rucker, Alabama
Jan 86–Mar 87	Commander, C Company (Pathfinder/Airborne), 509th Parachute Infantry Regiment, U.S. Army Aviation Center, Fort Rucker, Alabama
Mar 87–Jun 87	Student Officer, Combined Arms and Services Staff School, U.S. Army Command and General Staff College, Fort Leavenworth, Kansas
Jun 87–Jun 89	Graduate Student, University of Virginia, Charlottesville, Virginia
Jul 89–Aug 92	Assistant Professor, Department of Social Sciences, U.S. Military Academy, West Point, New York
Aug 92–Dec 92	White House Fellow, Office of National Service, The White House
Dec 92–Jan 93	Military Assistant to Ambassador Robert Oakley, U.S. Envoy to Somalia, Operation *Restore Hope*, Mogadishu, Somalia
Jan 93–Jul 93	White House Fellow, National Security Council, The White House
Jul 93–Jun 94	Student Officer, Command and General Staff Officer's Course, U.S. Army Command and General Staff College, Fort Leavenworth, Kansas
Jul 94–Sep 94	Chief, Humanitarian Operations Center and J5, Joint Task Force Alpha, Operation *Support Hope*, Goma, Zaire
Sep 94–Jan 96	Deputy Commander, 3rd Battalion (Airborne), 325th Airborne Battalion Combat Team, Southern European Task Force, Vicenza, Italy and Operation *Joint Endeavor*, Bosnia-Herzegovina
Jan 96–Aug 96	Brigade S3 Operations Officer, 173rd Airborne Brigade (Provisional), Southern European Task Force, Vicenza, Italy
Aug 96–Jun 99	Special Assistant to the Chairman of the Joint Chiefs of Staff, The Pentagon
Jul 99–Jun 01	Battalion Commander, 2nd Battalion, 505th Parachute Infantry Regiment, 82nd Airborne Division, Fort Bragg, North Carolina and Operation *Joint Guardian*, Kosovo
Jul 01–Aug 02	Senior Aide de Camp to the Secretary of the Army, Headquarters, Department of the Army, The Pentagon

Aug 02–Jun 03	Student, The National War College, Fort McNair, Washington DC
Jun 03–Jun 04	Special Assistant to the Chief of Staff of the Army/Army Planner, Headquarters, Department of the Army, The Pentagon
Jun 04–Jun 06	Commander, XVIII Airborne Corps Combat Support Brigade, Fort Bragg, North Carolina and Operation *Iraqi Freedom*, Baghdad, Iraq
Jun 06–Jul 08	Director for Iraq, National Security Council, The White House
Jul 08–Jun 09	Chief of Staff of the Army Chair, National War College
Jun 09–Jun 10	Director, Communications Action Group, Combined Joint Task Force-82, Operation *Enduring Freedom*, Bagram, Afghanistan

Promotions

Second Lieutenant	27 May 81
First Lieutenant	27 Nov 82
Captain	1 Dec 84
Major	1 Apr 93
Lieutenant Colonel	1 Jan 98
Colonel	1 Nov 03

Awards and Decorations

Distinguished Service Medal
Defense Superior Service Medal (3)
Legion of Merit (3)
Bronze Star Medal (3)
Defense Meritorious Service Medal (2)
Meritorious Service Medal (5)
Joint Service Commendation Medal (2)
Army Commendation Medal (3)
Joint Service Achievement Medal
Army Achievement Medal (2)
Air Force Achievement Medal
Army Good Conduct Medal
National Defense Service Medal w/Star
Armed Forces Expeditionary Medal (3)
Humanitarian Service Medal

Armed Forces Service Medal
NATO Medal (Bosnia)
NATO Medal (Kosovo)
NATO Medal (Afghanistan)
Kosovo Campaign Medal w/Star
Multi-National Force and Observers Medal
Global War on Terrorism Service Medal
Global War on Terrorism Expeditionary Medal
Iraq Campaign Medal w/Star
Afghanistan Campaign Medal
Overseas Ribbon (4)
Military Outstanding Volunteer Service Medal
Army Service Ribbon
Ranger Tab
Master Parachutist Badge
Israeli Parachutist Badge
Canadian Parachutist Badge
Combat Infantryman's Badge (2)
Expert Infantryman's Badge
Pathfinder Badge
Air Assault Badge
Joint Staff Identification Badge
Army Staff Identification Badge
Presidential Staff Badge
Combat Service Identification Badge, 82nd Airborne Division
Combat Service Identification Badge, XVIII Airborne Corps

Other

Knight's Cross of the Lithuanian Order of Merit
Polish Army Medal
Order of St. Maurice
Order of St. Barbara
Order of the Spur

Commander's Combat Load Iraq (2005)

As a brigade commander, Colonel Hooker carried this load during dismounted combat operations in Baghdad in 2005. Line infantrymen might carry up to 30lbs more.

Item	lbs
Desert camouflage uniform (shirt and trousers)	3.0
Kevlar ballistic helmet with NVG mount	4.0
Ballistic eye protection	.5
Hearing protection	.2
Body armor w/side plates and shoulder guards	33.0
First aid kit	1.0
Tourniquet	.5
M22 binoculars	2.7
GPS navigational device	1.5
Motorola hand-held radio w/pouch	2.5
"Iraqna" cell phone	.5
Night vision goggles	1.4
Knee pads	1.0
Elbow pads	1.0
T-shirt	.3
Underwear	.3
Utility belt	.3
Desert boots	3.0
Socks	.5

(Continued)

Item	lbs
Gloves	.5
"Camelback" hydration bag w/water	7.1
M4 rifle w/sling	6.3
M68 close combat optic w/mount	.8
5.56mm ammunition (7 magazines)	7.7
M9 pistol	2.1
9mm ammunition (3 magazines)	1.2
Pistol holster	1.0
Rifle and pistol ammunition pouches	1.3
Smoke grenade	1.2
Strobe light with case	.8
Orange marking panel	1.0
Utility knife w/case	.5
Total:	**88.5lbs**

Acronyms

ALO	Air Liaison Officer
ANSF	Afghan National Security Forces
AOR	Area of Responsibility
AQI	Al Qaeda in Iraq
ARP	Aero Rifle Platoon
BDOC	Base Defense Operations Center
BIAP	Baghdad International Airport
CAG	Communications Action Group
CENTCOM	Central Command
CID	Criminal Investigations Division
CJCS	Chairman of the Joint Chiefs of Staff
CJTF	Combined Joint Task Force
CO	Commanding Officer
CODEL	Congressional Delegation
COIN	Counterinsurgency
CONEX	Container, Expeditionary
COP	Combat Outpost
CP	Command Post
CPA	Coalition Provisional Authority
CPOF	Command Post of the Future
CSC	Combat Support Company
CSM	Command Sergeant Major
DCO	Deputy Commanding Officer
DZ	Drop Zone
DZSO	Drop Zone Safety Officer
ECP	Entry Control Point
EFP	Explosively Formed Projectile
EOD	Explosive Ordnance Disposal
ETA	Estimated Time of Arrival
ETT	Embedded Training Team
EUCOM	European Command

FAR	Army of Rwanda (French *Forces Armées Rwandaises*)
FARRP	Forward Area Rearm/Refuel Point
FPCON	Force Protection Condition
GPS	Global Positioning Satellite; satellite navigational device
HMMWV	High Mobility Multi-purpose Wheeled Vehicle
IDF	Israeli Defense Forces
IED	Improvised Explosive Device
IFOR	Implementation Force
INMARSAT	International Maritime Satellite
IO	Information Operations
IRC	Initial Ready Company
ISAF	International Security Force Afghanistan
ISB	Intermediate Staging Base
ISR	Intelligence, Surveillance and Reconnaissance
JMPI	Jump Master Pre-Inspection
JNT	Joint Network Targeting
JRTC	Joint Readiness Training Center
JSOTF	Joint Special Operations Task Force
KBR	Kellogg, Brown and Root
KLA	Kosovo Liberation Army
KLE	Key Leader Engagement
LZ	Landing Zone
MACV	Military Assistance Command Vietnam
MASCAL	Mass Casualty event
MEF	Marine Expeditionary Force
MeK	Mujahedin-e Khalk
MEU	Marine Expeditionary Unit
MFO	Multinational Force and Observers
MiTT	Military Transition Team
MNC-I	Multinational Corps Iraq
MNF-I	Multinational Force Iraq
MNSTC-I	Multinational Support and Training Command Iraq
MSG	Master Sergeant
MSR	Main Supply Route
NATO	North Atlantic Treaty Organization
NCOIC	Noncommissioned Officer in Charge
NEO	Non-combatant Evacuation Operation
NGO	Non-Governmental Organization; relief agency
NSC	National Security Council
OP	Observation Post
OPFOR	Opposing Force

OPTEMPO	Operational Tempo
POTUS	President of the United States
PRT	Provincial Reconstruction Team
PSYOPS	Psychological Operations
PT	Physical Training
QRF	Quick Reaction Force
RAOC	Rear Area Operations Center
RC	Regional Command
REFORGER	Return of Forces to Germany
RIAB	Radio in a Box
ROTC	Reserve Officers Training Corps
RPF	Rwandan Patriotic Front
RPG	Rocket-Propelled Grenade
SACEUR	Supreme Allied Commander Europe
SCR	Senior Civilian Representative
SEAL	Sea-Air-Land; naval commando
SECDEF	Secretary of Defense
SETAF	Southern European Task Force
SF	Special Forces
SFOR	Stabilization Force
SIGACTs	Significant Activities
SMU	Special Mission Unit
SOCOM	Special Operations Command
SOF	Special Operations Forces
SOG	Sergeant of the Guard
TAC	Tactical Command Post
TACSAT	Tactical Satellite Radio
TAG	"The Adjutant General"; senior National Guard officer at state level
TF	Task Force
TOC	Tactical Operations Center
TOW	Tube launched Optically tracked Wire guided antitank missile system
UNHCR	United Nations High Commissioner for Refugees
UNISOM	United Nations mission to Somalia
UNITAF	United Nations Task Force
UNPROFOR	United Nations Protection Force
USAREUR	United States Army Europe
USAID	U.S. Agency for International Development
USLO	U.S. Liaison Office
USMAPS	U.S. Military Academy Preparatory School

UXO	Unexploded Ordnance
VBC	Victory Base Complex
VBIED	Vehicle Borne Improvised Explosive Device
VC	Viet Cong
XO	Executive Officer